THE LEAST OF US

Dreamland: The True Tale of America's Opiate Epidemic

Dreamland: The True Tale of America's Opiate Epidemic
(A Young Adult Adaptation)

Antonio's Gun and Delfino's Dream:
True Tales of Mexican Migration

True Tales from Another Mexico: The Lynch Mob,
the Popsicle Kings, Chalino, and the Bronx

THE LEAST OF US

True Tales of America and Hope in
the Time of Fentanyl and Meth

SAM QUINONES

BLOOMSBURY PUBLISHING

NEW YORK · LONDON · OXFORD · NEW DELHI · SYDNEY

BLOOMSBURY PUBLISHING
Bloomsbury Publishing Inc.
1385 Broadway, New York, NY 10018, USA

BLOOMSBURY, BLOOMSBURY PUBLISHING, and
the Diana logo are trademarks of Bloomsbury Publishing Plc

First published in the United States 2021

ISBN: HB: 978-1-63557-435-7; EBOOK: 978-1-63557-437-1;
BARNES & NOBLE SIGNED HB: 978-1-63557-858-4

LIBRARY OF CONGRESS CATALOGING-IN-PUBLICATION DATA IS AVAILABLE

2 4 6 8 10 9 7 5 3 1

Typeset by Westchester Publishing Services
Printed and bound in the U.S.A.

To find out more about our authors and books visit www.bloomsbury.com
and sign up for our newsletters.

Bloomsbury books may be purchased for business or promotional use.
For information on bulk purchases please contact Macmillan Corporate and
Premium Sales Department at specialmarkets@macmillan.com.

To
Ricardo J. Quinones,
1935–2019
Father, Husband, Scholar, Poet
Thank you, Dad

Precisely the least, the softest, lightest, a lizard's rustling, a breath, a flash, a moment—a little makes the way of the best happiness.

—*FRIEDRICH NIETZSCHE*

In as much as ye have done it unto one of the least of these my brethren, you have done it unto me.

—*MATTHEW 25:40*, KING JAMES BIBLE

CONTENTS

Introduction

Not long after my last book, *Dreamland*, came out, I was speaking in the small town of Portsmouth, Ohio, where part of that book is set.

After my speech, an older couple—thin, short, and pale—came up to a table where I was signing books. We were alone. Quietly, so only I could hear, the man said that their daughter was in prison for many years for a crime related to her opioid addiction. He said they were raising her young daughter and didn't know what to do. They were exhausted. They were concerned they wouldn't live long enough to see the girl through to adulthood. He was a man of few words and no tears. He looked shell-shocked.

"It's so hard," he said.

I was new at this and didn't know how to respond. We each held the other's hand, frozen in mid-handshake, this man and I, and stared into each other's eyes as his wife stood by in silence. I squeezed his hand finally, and I think I said something about them not being alone. That I was sorry. They moved on, and I can still see the man looking back at me and nodding.

This book grew from that moment and others like it.

In *Dreamland*, I had endeavored to tell the complex tale of our nationwide epidemic of opioid addiction—pain pills and heroin at the time. Doctors were pushed and pressured into an idea that wasn't always true: that virtually every pain patient could be prescribed bottles of narcotics without risk of addiction. This, in turn, led to the idea that pills could be prescribed in large amounts for long periods to almost anyone. As a species, we have five thousand years of experience with the opium poppy. It contains a substance that is both the best pain-killer we know and the most intensely addictive. Yet beginning in the mid-1990s and for years after we decided that only one of those was true.

This was the Opioid Era in America, characterized, from what I could tell, by a search for convenience and comfort and thus easy answers to complicated problems—among them, one magical pill for all human pain. This era was also about our own isolation and destruction of community in areas both rich and poor. It was about an unqualified belief in the private sector.

Opioid pain relievers in unprecedented number year after year were prescribed from coast to coast. They were overlaid on American populations riven by trauma or generational poverty, or well-to-do areas with large houses and barren sidewalks. They spilled over a culture in which so many addictive legal substances and services were already finely tuned to attack our brains. Predictably, narcotic pain relievers turned out to be addictive for a lot of patients the longer they used them. The pills sloshed across the country and onto street black markets, where many others grew addicted. Some of these newly dependent users moved on to heroin. As years passed, that market grew large enough to awaken Mexican drug traffickers.

This crisis spread and intensified nationwide. Still, I found that few people wanted to talk about it. Families were ashamed of their loved ones' addictions. Believing they were alone, families made mistakes trying to help their addicted loved one. They depleted finances; trust dissolved and marriages ended. When these loved ones died, their obituaries' cause of death were fabrications. Families isolated to hide the truth. So the scourge continued to spread like a cancer, devouring people and places across the country, abetted by a national silence.

I assumed *Dreamland* too would be ignored when it came out in April 2015. Instead, I watched public awareness ignite. Obituaries began to tell the truth. Parents came out of the shadows. I was surprised to be invited to speak around the country, and the invitations multiplied to more than two hundred speeches in four years. I spoke to conferences of public health nurses and narcotics agents, by social workers and addiction counselors, by doctors, judges, and to at least two dozen colleges. Perhaps most fulfilling of all, though, were the dozens of small towns where I spoke: Bluffton, Indiana; Chillicothe, Ohio; Spartanburg, South Carolina; Worcester, Massachusetts; Peoria, Illinois, and many more.

From the road, I watched the story change. After years of escalating, doctors' pain-pill prescribing fell, though not before creating an enormous new population of opiate addicts who would use anything that kept withdrawal away. Now the drugs came mostly from the underworld, piggybacking on the consumer market that the epidemic created. Heroin took the place of pain pills—for a while.

As I traveled, I then watched the dawning of the era of illegal synthetic drugs. Traffickers discovered that making drugs in labs was far more profitable than growing them. Synthetic drugs had been made before, of course, but nothing on the scale of what was underway by 2016.

Fentanyl was the era's poster drug. A wonderful medical tool, the hyperpotent synthetic emerged as the underworld's hyperprofitable heroin substitute. Supplies of it came from China, then from Mexico, as well. Fentanyl upended the dope world the way tech disrupted business. No farmland needed—no pesticides, no harvesting, no seasons, no irrigation. It shrank the heroin supply chain—from dozens of people down to two or three, none of whom were likely to be scary cartel types.

Illicit fentanyl spread first through the midwestern and eastern states. By 2018 it was all over the West as well. Overdose deaths shot farther north; more Americans died yearly than in the entire Vietnam War. Cuyahoga County, where Cleveland is located, saw overdoses double from 2014 to 2017—from 353 to 727, with almost 500 deaths involving fentanyl. San Francisco saw a similar increase between 2018 and 2020, when three times as many people died of overdoses as of COVID-19. Philadelphia had long been a heroin town, but by 2019 90 percent of 1,150 fatal overdoses were due to fentanyl.

Traffickers, meanwhile, had discovered a way to make methamphetamine in harrowing new amounts. While I was on the road, their meth reached all corners of the country and became the fourth stage of the drug-addiction crisis. Opiate addicts began to switch to meth, or use both together. This made no sense in the traditional drug world. One was a depressant, the other a stimulant. But it was as if their brains were primed for any drug.

This stage did not involve mass deaths. Rather, the new meth gnawed at brains in frightening ways. Suddenly users displayed symptoms of schizophrenia—paranoia, hallucinations. The spread of this meth provoked homelessness across the country. Homeless encampments of meth users appeared in rural towns—"They're almost like villages," one Indiana counselor said. In the West, large tent encampments formed, populated by people made frantic by unseen demons in Skid Row in Los Angeles, Sunnyslope in Phoenix, the tunnels in Las Vegas. This methamphetamine, meanwhile, prompted strange obsessions—with bicycles, with flashlights, and with hoarding junk. In each of these places, it seemed mental illness was the problem. It was, but so much of it was induced by the new meth.

Fentanyl and this new meth were in the interest of traffickers, not their customers. Traffickers had unlimited access to world chemical markets, and the population of American drug users had expanded coast to coast. These drugs could be made year-round, in greater quantities, cheaper and more addictive than anything grown from the ground, and thus could create or shift demand.

Their meth and fentanyl ended the notion of recreational drug use. Now anything could kill or mentally maim. What started as an epidemic of opiate addiction became, as I traveled, simply an epidemic of addiction, broadened by staggering supplies of corrosive synthetic dope.

I began writing *Dreamland* believing it to be about economic devastation. But I soon saw this addiction wasn't confined to the Rust Belt or Appalachia or tribal reservations. It found its way into well-heeled suburbs of Orange County, suburban Charlotte and Indianapolis, Fort Lauderdale. Unlike every drug scourge of the past, this one was essentially uniracial. It touched Black and brown communities relatively lightly. Instead, it involved White people in the great majority, including those who had done best in the economic expansions of recent decades. They were getting addicted and dying from drugs used to numb pain. People with no criminal record—workers, star athletes, pastors, and cops, the kids of mayors and judges—all got addicted. Parents who'd imagined some glowing life script for their newborns were, as those kids reached young adulthood, confronted with lying, stealing, conniving children, their bodies occupied by some mutant beast. Then came a felony record. Suddenly parents were cosigning for apartments, driving their addicted beloveds, now thirty, to a GED class.

The story wasn't at heart only about economic devastation. It wasn't just about those at the bottom. Not just hotel maids or supermarket cashiers or single moms. It was all of us.

This made more sense as I read what neuroscience can now tell us: that every human brain has capacity for addiction. Isolation is part of why some people get addicted and some do not. So was trauma. Abuse, rape, neglect, PTSD, a parent's drug use were as unspoken in America as addiction and as prevalent. The epidemic was revealing this. I also connected the epidemic to consumer marketing of legal addictive stuffs: sugar, video games, social media, gambling.

Attorneys general and county commissioners filed suits against drug companies to recoup the costs of this addiction crisis. When I finished writing *Dreamland* in mid-2014, I knew of three such lawsuits; now there were 2,600. Their subpoenas dislodged company records, foremost among them from Purdue Pharma and the Sackler family, who owns Purdue. While I was writing *Dreamland*, both seemed so impenetrable. Now, through those subpoenaed records, a fuller story could be told of their role in all this.

I saw America through the people I met at these speaking events, and the stories they told. Among the first was the couple in Portsmouth, Ohio. Most of the encounters were similarly brief. But like haiku, they encapsulated so much—such pain, power, sadness, and resiliency. Mothers told of their addicted children who had died. Addicts said they were lucky to be sent to jail. One woman was raising her deceased nephew's son; another family was raising a child they called their grandson, though they didn't know if their deceased son was his father. A teacher regularly washed a student's dirty clothes because the girl's strung-out parents didn't have a washer, and she missed school because she was too ashamed to wear them. Some judges had almost become social workers, yet they rarely found addicts willing to, in the words of one, "get into treatment if they're not facing the threat of incarceration"—such was drugs' control over their brains. Chronic pain patients told me how pain mangled their lives, and doctors wouldn't now prescribe the pills they needed.

On every trip I also saw the capacity to rise up. Groups assembled in county after county to fight the problem. They comprised more than just police, prosecutors, and probation officers. They also included insurance agents, the Kiwanis Club, PTAs, hospital administrators, college presidents, coaches, chambers of commerce, recovering addicts, doctors, and clergy. "Three years ago, you never would have gotten this group together in the same room," said one man in Scottsburg, Indiana.

None had done a pilot project. There wasn't time. They just formed up and groped for answers. There were no silver bullets. So they worked together quietly, making small changes. That was healthy, I thought. We had created this catastrophe, after all, by demanding one big, easy solution for a complicated problem: one pill for all pain.

When I visited these counties, I was often asked: "What places have you seen that are doing the right thing?"

"Right here." That became my response. People everywhere were leveraging talents and energies, reminding themselves how to work together. They learned each other's names and cell phone numbers, went out for pizza. They formed an antidote to the community destruction that got us into this in the first place.

Those conversations convinced me that our opioid-addiction crisis, *because* of its devastation, was also a great force for change. No other issue brought together Americans who didn't agree on anything else.

Some of them may have wanted a magic bullet. I don't have one. I told them I thought maybe we just needed to have faith in daily work and small steps. That innovation comes through collaboration with others. By doing that, they were refuting the cynicism of our age. Watching them, it occurred to me that I needed to find stories that reflected that—the unnoticed tales of community repair. That, in part, also led to this book.

The addiction crisis pushed new thinking that crossed political boundaries. In red states, I came upon experiments in new ways of doing jail—as centers of recovery instead of as the centers of recidivism and addiction they always had been. I spent time in drug courts, which use prison terms as leverage to pry addicts away from the potent street drug that has imprisoned their minds.

I was winding up this book when COVID-19 arrived. The virus forced us apart and showed us how we needed each other. It also re-created the conditions that spawned the opioid epidemic: isolation, widespread job loss. Alone, addicts overdosed and died. "Sitting with somebody, looking at them eye to eye—'We're going to get through this'—that piece is missing," a drug counselor told me. A narcotics officer in southern Ohio told me of a young man sober for eight months. Then he lost his new job at an IHOP, had a criminal charge from his past refiled against him; alone, he started using heroin again and overdosed.

The twelve months ending September 2020 tallied the highest number of overdose deaths in the country's history—87,000, according to a preliminary estimate by the Centers for Disease Control and Prevention. Much of that was due to illicit street fentanyl. By the time this book is published, we will likely have learned that close to 100,000 Americans died of drug overdoses in 2020—dwarfing any annual tally the country previously produced.

Then the Black Lives Matter movement gained renewed urgency from protests over what a jury later decided was the murder of George Floyd by a Minneapolis police officer.

These seemed separate moments, yet I came to see all three as connected. The opioid epidemic was about the destruction of community and the agony we create as we seek to avoid pain. COVID-19 instructed us on the importance of community, now that we had suddenly lost it, and how essential were those who nursed us and picked our lettuce. BLM showed that a sense of community was not possible without recognizing pain long ignored. BLM's point was also to reveal privilege. Part of our privilege was to relegate to police the jobs that we preferred to forget or not pay for—like dealing with the mentally ill on our streets, whose numbers multiplied due to methamphetamine.

Each was about who in America could breathe and who could not. George Floyd's final words were those, too, of the addict dying under the overpass, and the trucker expiring from COVID-19. Each asked us to consider who was worth our attention. With the face mask, we—many of us, anyway—accepted individual limits to spare our frontline doctors and nurses, to keep safe essential workers like paramedics and farmworkers so all could breathe.

The addiction epidemic jolted us into reexamining customs, beliefs, and how we lived. It seemed that COVID-19 and Black Lives Matter did the same, in equally impolite fashion.

Each insisted that we *see* our fellow Americans. That we are only as defended as the restaurant cook, the hotel maid, the grandparent on Social Security, the prison inmate. "Asking for grace—we're all asking for grace with each other. It's going to be a little messy," said Dr. Amy Acton, then director of Ohio's Department of Health, who became my go-to public official and philosopher early in 2020. "Eighty percent of us will be fine. Everything we do is to protect the most vulnerable."

Perhaps these jolts had to happen in succession. Perhaps the path to national reassessment begins when things fall apart. The addiction epidemic was already doing that. Nationwide death from abuse of the most isolating of all drugs was pushing Americans to come together in county after county. People I met were breaking down silos, acting on the idea that it was through reliance on each other, through community—which we had done so much to destroy—that we would most likely find some way out of this. Whether that attitude would survive COVID-19, I didn't know. But if it did, we would be better for it, I thought.

I came to see that addicts, gripped by drug-induced self-centeredness and isolation, are just extreme examples of each of us and our time. Once freed, they discover what we all need. They discover grace, patience with others. A feeling of being part of something bigger than themselves. Optimism and gratitude. A recognition of themselves in others. If we're lucky, we'll come out on the other side of all that besets us as Americans as I write, with the insight recovering addicts receive, and with wisdom enough to glimpse ourselves in them. If so, we'll be better for it.

That is what fueled this book—two stories that I set out to tell here. One is the story of an ominous die-off amid a global economy producing catastrophic supplies of dope cheaper and more potent than ever. The other is of Americans' quiet attempts to recover community through simple acts, guided by the belief—the message of our addiction crisis to those who would notice—that the least of us lies within us all.

PART I

Angie and Starla I

Alone

In its prime, the USS *Cape Cod* was a destroyer in the US Navy, longer than two football fields and with space for 1,500 sailors.

Late one night in 1989, the ship's massive bulk cleaved the waters of the Pacific Ocean on its way to the Philippines.

At the back of the ship that night, alone, on guard duty, stood a young woman of nineteen. She was five foot four and had the rank of seaman. Over her uniform she wore an orange life vest so large it seemed to consume her. The back of her life vest was hooked to a rope, which in turn was tied to a pole to keep her from being swept overboard.

Destroyers have no lights at night; they aren't cruise ships, after all. So during the hours she stood watch, tethered to that pole, with the quiet power of the ship beneath her feet and a full heaven of stars splashed above, she looked out on the darkest, most silent night she had ever seen.

Angie Manning had joined the navy to escape her small town of Elizabethton in the northeast corner of Tennessee. She was short and pretty, and timid as if snakebit. She had grown up in the church, the daughter of a Baptist pastor and his wife, the middle child of three. They lived in a small wood-frame rental on the outskirts of town, and Angie spent much of her childhood outdoors. Every summer, her father would break out an old canvas army tent and pitch it in the back-yard. Those nights, the family would squeeze in and sleep all together.

There wasn't room in the tent for anyone to even roll over. Yet those glorious nights in that tent was how she recalled her early years.

Her father died of cancer when Angie was sixteen. Her mother remarried a nice man who built houses and swimming pools, and the family moved to a new, bigger house. Angie's life quickly changed, with many new people in her circle. One afternoon, a person in that circle raped Angie. She told a relative but was told to never bring it up again. No visit to the hospital. No police report. Angie told a teacher, who told a counselor, but she never heard back from either one. "I didn't reach out to other people because of the shame," she told me. Bitter, she gathered her clothes in a trash bag and left home. After graduating from high school, fleeing all she had lost, Angie joined the US Navy, which sent her to San Diego and the USS *Cape Cod* for her first assignment. About a year later, she shipped out on the destroyer.

On that quiet night at sea, beneath the stillness and profound expanse above her, she thought of all that had happened. Her anger and pain rose and almost spilled from her. She had accepted God as she grew up in the congregations her father led. After all that had happened, though, God seemed distant.

Now, under the heavens, she wanted to know from Him that her rage was righteous, her bitterness just. Instead, as the night wore on, she felt a warm embrace, a stillness on the dark water that soothed her wounds. A peace descended on her, assuaging her pain, unraveling the knots of hate and rage. Later on, she took this to mean that she was to love, to care for others with patience, regardless of their transgressions, and through that let the poisonous anger and the bitterness pass from her.

All that night she cried, and the tears poured onto that big orange life jacket.

Through the years and all that was to happen, she found her favorite passage from the Bible in Psalm 46, and it seemed to come directly from that night she spent alone on the Pacific, fastened to that pole.

"Be still, and know that I am God."

The Project I
Chicago

The first time Ryan Rapaszky heard the term "the Project" come over a wiretap out of Mexico, he couldn't make sense of it.

It was August 2005. Rapaszky, a native of Cleveland, had spent four years as a Baltimore cop, and he was now a little more than a year into his career at the Drug Enforcement Administration, stationed in Chicago. He was in the middle of a case involving cocaine traffickers out of the Mexican state of Sinaloa when he heard the wiretaps. Sinaloa is the birthplace of drug trafficking in Mexico and home to one of the world's most fearsome drug cartels. Sinaloan traffickers had long before claimed Chicago as a major hub for their drugs, and from there sent their products to nearby suburbs, as well as to the cities of Milwaukee, Indianapolis, and Detroit.

For years the most widespread drug in Chicago had been cocaine. Sinaloan traffickers sold it to street gangs, who sold it on the street. In the last few years, the Sinaloans had seen that Americans were getting addicted to opioids, prescription pain pills first, then heroin. So after years of ignoring the low-class heroin in favor of cocaine and marijuana, Sinaloan traffickers started pumping the streets of Chicago with it.

Rapaszky thought his case involved only cocaine. It concerned a hapless boxer and part-time drug broker named Lutgardo Chavez. Chavez was thirty-five and had been illegally in the States long enough to speak passable English. He had participated in Chicago's Golden

Gloves competition in his late twenties. Now he scraped together money as a janitor at a gym and trained a boxer here and there.

At the gym, he met and befriended a boxer who let him stay at his house when the boxer was traveling. Just keep the house clean, he was told; don't ask questions of the people who come through. Among the visitors were Sinaloan dealers. Lutgardo Chavez began to do small jobs for them, acting as a gofer or chauffeur. In time, these connections let him sell occasional kilos of cocaine and keep whatever profit he made in the sale. He parlayed what English he spoke and his knowledge of the city into brokering drug deals between Mexican sellers and Chicago buyers, particularly street gangs. All in all, he was a useful but disposable part of the Mexican drug world in the United States.

It was in this capacity that Chavez began turning up on the wiretaps in Rapaszky's cocaine case. In late summer of 2005, Lutgardo Chavez and his Mexican contacts began mentioning this thing they called "the Project." It sounded new, almost experimental, and clearly involved making drugs. Must have something to do with methamphetamine, Rapaszky figured. Whatever it was, they were sending up samples. The early reviews seemed mixed: the substance had a strange green color and wasn't easily diluted. Still, the wiretaps showed they kept at the Project.

Then one day in August of 2005, Rapaszky heard Lutgardo Chavez call 911 to report that he was with a man he called his uncle, just up from Mexico. The uncle, he said, had sniffed something in a bottle and suddenly collapsed. It was as if he'd overdosed on heroin. This made no sense to Rapaszky, who believed his case was about cocaine. Chavez drove to an emergency room where doctors revived the uncle with naloxone, the opioid-overdose antidote. The uncle walked out of the emergency room that night.

A day or so later, on wiretaps, came news that the two men had taken a sample to Detroit, where a dealer had mixed it with black-tar heroin. Chavez called back to Mexico, excited. "The Project is working!" he said. "They mixed it, and it's working."

*   *   *

ABOUT THIS TIME, as it happened, the Drug Enforcement Administration and Chicago police were deep into an investigation of a South Side gang called the Mickey Cobras, which controlled heroin dealing around a housing project known as Dearborn Homes. A month after Chavez's "uncle" overdosed, a rash of overdoses hit the housing project. On one afternoon a dozen people dropped as quickly as Chavez's uncle had, and died. The overdose hotspots multiplied. The city's health department printed flyers warning addicts of a highly potent heroin on the streets, hoping to frighten users off the drug. Instead, addicts rushed to the housing project, eager to try it. To grab the market, dealers sold it in packets stamped with brand names like "Lethal Injection" and "Drop Dead." The new stuff crowded out any lesser dope.

As the Mickey Cobra gang sold it through the rest of 2005 and into the new year, dozens of bodies fell. Each user's death became an investigated event. Chicago cops accompanied medics, looking for vials, packaging material, any clues to its origin. Turf battles among agencies receded; officers shared information across departments. "It was such a big deal," Rapaszky said, "this cell of death in Chicago."

Then the deaths spread, first to Detroit and by the spring of 2006 to Philadelphia and other eastern cities. About that time, Rapaszky got a call from a desk agent at the DEA office in San Diego. "I got this crazy thing," the agent said. A nervous Mexican man had walked in off the street with a story about a chemical lab near Mexico City. "He's telling us they're making this synthetic heroin, and it's going up to Chicago." This Mexican fellow knew of the deaths in Chicago, and he was sure the lab was to blame. He provided a phone number of an investor in the lab. That number turned up in the DEA's database as connected to Rapaszky's Chicago cocaine case—the same number as the wiretapped phone on which Rapaszky had overheard Lutgardo Chavez and traffickers in Mexico discussing the Project.

Rapaszky flew to San Diego. There, in a room at San Diego DEA, sat a Mexican who had fled the industrial city of Toluca, an hour northeast of Mexico City, fearing for his life. There, he said, he had worked at a chemical plant operated by Distribuidora Talios. The company had opened in an industrial park near Toluca, and it looked legitimate. It possessed the highest-quality glassware, tubes, and machines, he said, and its status as a legal laboratory allowed it to easily procure chemical ingredients. The operation, he said, was funded by Sinaloan drug cartel members. Talios manufactured a white powder that the man called "synthetic heroin." This "heroin" could be diluted as many as thirty times. Rapaszky couldn't believe it. He knew heroin from his years on patrol in Baltimore, and no heroin he had ever seen or heard of could be diluted that much and still sell. But the man stuck to his story.

He spoke also of the fellow who ran the lab. El Cerebro, he called him, "the Brain," a great and creative chemist. The Sinaloan investors had wanted the Brain to make ephedrine. Ephedrine is a chemical essential to the manufacture of methamphetamine. After a Mexican government crackdown on imported ephedrine, it was now scarce, and they badly needed more. However, the lab's first investor—a man named Oscar Montoya—saw the huge market that synthetic heroin could mine in the United States as the opioid epidemic spread. This was what the Brain wanted to produce as well.

The "synthetic heroin" the young man described was fentanyl. Rapaszky knew little about it. His work computer didn't even autocorrect for the word. He wrote it on a piece of paper near his desk so he wouldn't misspell it on a teletype. He learned that the drug was a painkiller, like heroin, but made from chemicals; no plant involved. Since its invention in 1960 in a Belgian lab, it was routinely used in heart surgery and had gained popularity since the late 1990s, when doctors turned to prescribing opioids for a much wider set of ailments. Fentanyl was, he discovered, far more powerful than morphine. It had been occasionally produced illegally by underground chemists for sale on the street. But no one at DEA had heard of Mexican traffickers selling it, much less making it from scratch.

To raise more money for the Toluca lab, Oscar Montoya had prodded trafficking groups in Chicago with connections to the Mickey

Cobras—including, by coincidence, the group Rapaszky had wire-tapped. Montoya promised them ephedrine because, Rapaszky told me years later, "the trafficking groups didn't know what fentanyl was. Oscar Montoya saw the promise in fentanyl, but to recruit money from investors you have to tell them what they're interested in hearing. To them, the Talios lab presented the opportunity to make precursor chemicals for methamphetamine production."

The Brain, however, had his own ideas and manufactured fentanyl instead, the Mexican informant said. By early 2006, the traffickers invested in the lab understood fentanyl's great profit potential. They showed up at the lab and, in a power play, killed Montoya, seized the kilos of fentanyl, and took control of the lab. Everybody wanted the Brain for themselves. Meanwhile, the informant fled for his life.

Talking to the informant in San Diego that day, Ryan Rapaszky, thirty years old and in his first major case, realized that this man was describing an epic shift in drug trafficking: the Sinaloa cartel had discovered fentanyl. Now they wanted more of it. No longer was fentanyl the exclusive domain of a few rogue underground chemists. The lab had enough ingredients on hand, the Mexican informant estimated, to produce another sixty kilos—many millions of street doses. This, Rapaszky realized, was why overdoses were exploding in Chicago and now also in Detroit. Why, too, the deaths would spread beyond those cities, to St. Louis, Philadelphia, and Camden, New Jersey, among others. "Doctors and Big Pharma prepared the battlefield," Rapaszky said, "creating a market for the cartels, who then jumped at the opportunity to own the supply and feed the demand."

They did that first with heroin. Soon, though, they came to see the immense profit in the Brain's fentanyl. They already had distribution networks nationwide, including the Mickey Cobras gang in Chicago. "They realize they don't have to grow poppies," Rapaszky told me. "They now have a guy in a lab, and they can use their distribution networks to smuggle in samples first, and then kilograms, of his fentanyl.

"That becomes the Project."

Neuroscience I

"A Critical Point"

Nicole Avena was an unlikely grad student. From blue-collar roots—her father was a furniture salesman, her mother, a nurse—she was the first in her family to graduate from college. Science had engrossed her since elementary school, and she was an excellent student. In 2000, fresh from her undergraduate years studying psychology at Rutgers, she entered a PhD program in neuroscience at Princeton University.

The brain and nutrition fascinated her. She wanted to study what in the brain motivated behavior; why people make decisions to eat, say, a doughnut instead of a stalk of celery. What, she wondered, did the brain have to do with certain diseases? These were the questions she was asking herself when, as an intimidated twenty-two-year-old, she entered the venerable four-story Green Hall, built in 1927, that housed the university's department of psychology, within which also labored an assortment of professors interested in the science of the brain.

Avena arrived at just the right moment. Neuroscience had been a stepchild for years in America, housed, as at Princeton, in university psychology departments. By 2000, however, new technologies were allowing the specialty to flex and expand the questions neuroscientists could ask and measure. This began to add enormously to what researchers knew or could suppose about the brain. The next twenty years would amount to a golden age of brain research.

Just after Avena arrived, Princeton was among the first schools in the United States to buy a functional magnetic resonance imaging (fMRI) machine, which allows scientists to measure and take images of brain activity. This early fMRI was primitive. Nevertheless, their first experience with the technology opened vistas of possibilities to Princeton staff and students. "It created this vibe: we're going to learn about the brain things we never thought we'd be able to ever test," Avena told me. With that, a "brain scene" began to develop at Princeton, attracting people like her who were excited about these opportunities.

Avena's five years at Princeton earning a PhD were spent in nonstop talking, thinking, experimenting, all about the brain. Research in other medical specialties was constrained by what had come before, but the brain's intricacies remained a mystery. The field was "wide open," Avena told me when I met her as she visited Los Angeles. "You could sit there and think what would be something cool to study. It allows you to be creative in a way that most scientific disciplines don't. Every day something new was happening, and the brain was right in the middle of it."

Nutritionists wanted to talk with her about the brain. So did economists, to understand how consumers made decisions. Social psychologists wanted to work with the new neuroscientists. A lot of this came through the lab in the basement of Green Hall, where neuroscience was then housed.

That first day at Princeton, Avena found herself under the mentorship of Bart Hoebel, a renowned psychologist. Hoebel was a man of many interests. These included hot-air ballooning, Christmas tree farming, and running a nonprofit, the Delaware River Steamboat Floating Classroom, on which students held river ecology classes on a replica of an 1880 steamboat that he restored himself. As a scientist, Hoebel had an equally rambunctious mind. He viewed his group as a team, and he allowed his grad students ample say in what the lab studied.

Discussion about the brain flowed freely in Hoebel's lab. Creative approaches to studying the organ were prized, and there was minimal bureaucracy to get in the way. Under Hoebel's tutelage, Avena developed the skills of a master electrician, building Skinner boxes, where rats were offered hits of sugar-laden water if they pressed a lever or crossed an electric field that shocked them when they stepped on it. The lab had no money to pay an electrician. "Bart taught me to do all this electrical stuff because we had to," she said. "Back then, we were having a hard time finding funding for all this. People were still laughing at it."

Together, they and others in the lab embarked on the study of the addictive potential of foods on the brain—carbohydrates mostly, and above all, sugar. Could it be, Avena wondered, that processed food in particular, which promoted high sugar intake and obesity, affected the brain in ways that made it more like a drug? Maybe products in grocery store aisles like Pop-Tarts, cereal, or soda "are like a drug—something people have a compulsion to use," she said. Women's magazines made this claim; there were hunches this was true. Dieters reported having trouble quitting sugar. However, no science existed to prove it at the time. The lab's early experiments on sugar-dependent rats groped to see what evidence might develop for this idea.

Avena and her colleagues began each experiment by separating two groups of ten rats. They fed one group food and plain water. They gave the other group the same food, then a choice of plain or sugar water from 10:00 a.m. to 10:00 p.m. Within days those rats never touched the plain water again; they hit the sugar water all day long. Most nights for her five years as a grad student, Avena went to the lab at 10:00 p.m. to remove the bottles of sugar water and weigh the latest group of rats under experiment.

Shortly after arriving, Avena participated in another experiment on rats that were overfed sugar. The idea was to compare their brain reward pathways with those of rats that were fed drugs of abuse—morphine, alcohol, or amphetamine. They found in those sugar-dependent rats, Avena said, "neurochemical behavioral changes that . . . you'd expect to see if an animal was dosed up with morphine. But these animals were just overeating sugar. It suggested to me that a food—with no limitations on how much you can consume—could do something that's like a drug."

From there, the lab moved to another question. They compared two groups of rats, one of which was fed sugar water until that group of rats was dependent. The other group was fed just straight water. Researchers injected both groups with minute doses of amphetamine. The rats not dependent on sugar showed no effect. The sugar-dependent rats, however, turned hyperactive. This suggested that when these animals grew dependent on sugar, it "primed" them to use another drug.

Dependence on one substance, in other words, prepared them for dependence on another.

"I thought that was," she said later, "a critical point."

Meth I

"Streets of Bakersfield"

In 1999 a young man from New Mexico named Eduardo Chavez applied for a job at the DEA, hoping for big things.

He had grown up in the border town of Deming, where his father was a district attorney's investigator who did lots of undercover work. His father would have a beard for a while, then shave it off, then change his appearance again. He investigated other types of crime—embezzlement, murder—but Deming was drenched in drug-trafficking culture. It was the early 1990s. Mexico's trafficking groups were emerging, brazen and competitive. The border was right there. Chavez went to school with kids up from Mexico whose fathers were said to have died in one shootout or another. Some of the kids were young when they got a new Dodge Ram truck with chrome rims and massive speakers blasting *narcocorridos*—drug ballads.

Chavez found all this fascinating. "I can remember," he told me, "my dad said, 'Are you sure you want to deal with dopers your entire career?'"

He was. Chavez attended Georgetown University. There he wrote a dissertation on the Tijuana and Juárez drug cartels, predicting that both would disintegrate (which they did). The Tijuana group—under the bloody Arellano-Felix brothers—fell apart because they were too violent. The Juárez cartel lost its legendary boss, Amado Carrillo Fuentes, known as the Lord of the Skies for the 737s he flew into the city, filled with cocaine. (Carrillo Fuentes underwent plastic surgery to change his looks and died on the operating table in 1997, likely because the anesthetic didn't agree with the cocaine he was using. The four operating doctors were found shot to death by a road south of Mexico City.)

When Chavez finished the DEA training academy, they asked for his three top choices for his first assignment. Looking for action, he listed Houston, Corpus Christi, and Los Angeles. The agency sent him instead to Bakersfield at the southern end of California's vast Central Valley. The office, he was told, needed Spanish speakers.

Chavez arrived uninspired, knowing little about the town but the Buck Owens and Dwight Yoakam song "Streets of Bakersfield," which made the place sound threadbare. An academy instructor told him to keep his head down, and he'd be out of there pronto. Instead, Chavez came alive. His borderland Spanish made him invaluable as an undercover agent. "Within weeks I'm neck-deep in undercover work," he said later. "It was one of the best offices I could have started my career in."

In Bakersfield, Chavez witnessed a historic change in drug trafficking. Mexico's first traffickers were untamed rancheros—peasant farmers and hill folk from the ranchos, rough settlements on the country's frontier. In these villages, absent the law, gunplay was common, and those who showed weakness were trampled underfoot. Men there understood, furthermore, that life derived from the land. They were conservative and traditional. Yet they abandoned their beans, corn, and chile to grow drugs rooted in the earth—marijuana and the opium poppy. In Mexico, these were the only crops that made farming a route to something other than a life of brutish, unforgiving labor. Drug trafficking didn't require education, and they had none. It did demand a lot of what the ranchos had bred for decades: machismo, an independence of mind, an unsentimental view of life and death, a desire to work for no one but oneself, and a willingness to be the *valiente*—the tough guy, backing down to no man.

Men from this world formed the first generations of Mexican traffickers—the guys that Chavez's father had busted. In the 1980s they earned great profits shuttling tons of cocaine into the United States for Colombian cartels, who weren't familiar with the US-Mexico border. Still, they were mostly transporters, or farmers of land-based drugs.

In Bakersfield, though, Chavez saw something different afoot. Every case involved rough-hewn Mexican rancheros. But these guys weren't dealing in pot or heroin. They were working in clandestine labs, with chemicals, cooking methamphetamine. That in itself was strange, for meth had always been a White guy's drug.

FOR MANY YEARS only Hells Angels and other biker gangs cooked methamphetamine. Their customers were working-class Whites.

The bikers' method of making meth gave off a smell so rank that it could only be cooked in rural or desert outposts. As years passed, though, another recipe for methamphetamine was rediscovered. Japanese researchers had invented it in 1919, synthesizing it from ephedrine, a natural substance from the ephedra plant—used for millennia as a stimulant and appetite suppressant that also clears the bronchial passages. During World War II methamphetamine was marketed in Japan as *hiropon*, a word that combines the Japanese terms for "fatigue" and "fly away." Hiropon was given to Japanese soldiers and kamikaze pilots to help them over their fear of death.

The substance Japanese researchers invented was branded as Pervitin by a German company—Temmler—during the Third Reich. Pervitin fueled Nazi Germany, helping women endure childbirth and depression, keeping workers on the job and German soldiers awake for days. German author Norman Ohler tells this story in his terrific book *Blitzed*, claiming that German soldiers' widespread use of Pervitin was crucial to their swift invasion of France through the Ardennes mountains in 1940. Meth-addled Nazi soldiers in tank columns raced across the mountain range. German bomber pilots high on Pervitin plunged from the sky, with the Nazi terror sirens known as the Horns of Jericho wailing, followed by bombs. "Meth unleashed charge after charge in German brains," Ohler wrote. "Neurotransmitters were released, exploded in the synaptic gaps, burst and dispersed their explosive cargo: neuronal paths twitched, gap junctions flared, everything whirred and roared. Down below the defenders cowered, their bunkers shaking."

In the postwar years, ephedrine was used legally as an antihistamine in the over-the-counter medicine Sudafed. The ephedrine method for meth, though, lay dormant for a long time. It was rediscovered by the underworld in the United States in the early 1980s. It democratized methamphetamine. One place this happened was in the San Diego area, largely due to a man by the name of Donald Stenger.

Stenger, unlike the scattered bikers that cops by then were associating with meth, was middle class, smart, deliberate, and well organized. "He was the anomaly. He was a criminal genius, and he did a tremendous amount of research," said Jim Clem, one of the now-retired San Diego police officers who pursued him. Up to that point, the method for cooking meth that bikers were using not only stank, but also complicated. Stenger saw that the ephedrine method was easier. All you had to do was tweak one molecule in ephedrine, and you had meth. It was just cooking, following a recipe—it didn't really qualify as chemistry. And ephedrine was legal. Stenger had no interest in popularizing the formula, but it couldn't be contained. By the mid-1980s, every meth lab that Clem and his colleagues busted was using ephedrine.

The pursuit of Donald Stenger lasted more than a year and ranged across the West, from California to Utah to Arizona, with Stenger eluding investigators in a high-speed chase by driving into Mexico, where he reportedly owned several gold mines. Along the way, agents seized cash, planes, and a helicopter that inaugurated the San Diego Police Department's air unit. Clem finally arrested Stenger in 1986 in Colorado. He died in 1988 at thirty-two, in custody in San Diego County, when a packet of meth he'd inserted in his rectum broke open.

Largely because of Stenger's innovation, though, San Diego emerged as the meth capital of America, with supplies heading out across the country. With ephedrine, many more people could now cook meth in many more places—a motel room, a storage shed, a bathroom. And, beginning in the mid-1980s, they did.

Stenger's importance to this story also lies in geography. Implanting a new, easy way to make meth at the US-Mexico border made it inevitable that it would be discovered by the robust Mexican trafficking world then developing. Mexican traffickers up to then had always been the errand boys for Colombians, navigating their cocaine across the line the Colombians didn't know in exchange for payment. In time, Mexicans saw they could do this for themselves. Meth allowed them to make their own drugs, not rely on criminals from other countries.

Two brothers pioneered the Mexican meth industry, Luis and Jesús Amezcua from the state of Colima, living then in San Diego. They had come to Los Angeles illegally as young teens, stayed, and eventually ran an auto shop near San Diego, from which they smuggled illegal immigrants. The story goes that a local meth cooker dropped by the shop in about 1988, asking Jesus Amezcua if he could bring in ephedrine from Mexico. Amezcua at the time was smuggling Colombian cocaine. But he brought ephedrine in for the local cooker and, with that, discovered a market that began with Donald Stenger's innovation.

Ephedrine was an unregulated chemical in Mexico and the United States. Within a few years the Amezcuas were importing tons of ephedrine through the major Pacific Coast ports of Manzanillo, in Colima, and Lázaro Cárdenas in the state of Michoacán. They used the transport services established by traffickers who were sending their Colombian cocaine north. They had large warehouses in Mexicali, near a private cemetery they opened as a business, and in Tijuana, not far from the city's downtown. There they housed illegal immigrants and enormous quantities of ephedrine. Later they imported antihistamine pills, barrels of them, from which they extracted the ephedrine.

As they grew, traffickers gathered around them. Many of those who would emerge as the forces of the meth industry in northwest Mexico learned their trade during these years, using the Amezcua brothers' ephedrine. "They were working with all the big ones," said one man I met who had spent decades in the northwestern Mexico drug under-world. "They were importing and selling to everyone. There were various groups, and they all began setting up laboratories."

The Amezcuas' meth career lasted a bit more than a decade, until cases brought against them landed them in a Mexican prison, where they remain. By the early 2000s the meth trade had moved on, and new figures emerged who would change it.

But the brothers marked a new breed of Mexican trafficker. They were more interested in business deals, in alliances, than in the vengeance and endless shootouts so common to ranchero smugglers. They were the first Mexican traffickers to understand the profit poten-tial of a synthetic drug, and the first to tap the global economy for chemical connections. Jesus Amezcua traveled to India and Thailand, where he set up an office to handle his ephedrine exports. When an ephedrine factory in India burned down, he moved his focus to Europe—to Germany and the Czech Republic.

Some of this know-how went to California; some of it stayed in Mexico, where cooks were learning. In California, the Amezcuas saw that their only competition in meth production was undisciplined biker gangs. The brothers set up labs in rural parts of Riverside and San Bernardino Counties, and up in California's Central Valley.

In the Central Valley they tapped already existing networks of drug traffickers. Most of these were from the Mexican state of Michoacán, and from one town in particular: Apatzingán, pop. 110,000, the center of a humid, agricultural, and violent drug-drenched region known as Mexico's Tierra Caliente—the Hot Land. Cooking ephedrine-based methamphetamine was about as easy as learning to grow marijuana, and it produced more quantity, more quickly. Soon one cook was teaching another, and the knowledge spread.

California's Central Valley provided secluded areas on farms or orchards, sparsely covered by law enforcement. Apatzingán traffickers already had networks of Michoacán immigrants, farmworkers, farm foremen, and drivers that stretched from San Diego up through the valley.

Bakersfield's Kern County in particular, the first county north of Los Angeles, grew quickly into a center of meth production. Among the first Mexican meth operations ever busted in California were two in Kern County in 1989, each with 25-kilo boxes of ephedrine. At one bust, agents found a man in full hazmat suit and oxygen tank. He turned out to be a veterinarian from Michoacán who said he came up for four-month stints teaching the workers to cook. In 1990, a freeze devastated Central Valley agriculture. Meth cooks used the moment to recruit desperate farmworkers.

"In the early 1990s, the cooks were monkey see, monkey do. Like using a cookbook," said Larry Cho, who, as a federal prosecutor, took down a supply and stash house operation run by the Amezcuas out of the Orange County town of Placentia. "They weren't using anyone trained in chemistry. All these meth labs were exploding because they didn't know what they were doing."

But they learned, and with the Amezcua brothers' ephedrine, the new Mexican meth cooks scaled up their operations. Hells Angels cooks took three days to make five pounds of meth. Mexican crews soon learned to arrive at cook sites like NASCAR pit crews, with premeasured chemicals, large vats, and seasoned workers. They produced ten to twenty pounds in twenty-four hours in what came to be known as "superlabs." Soon the biker gangs were buying their meth from the Mexicans.

These operations involved an extensive division of labor: cooks, drivers, guards, and site brokers who searched for places to cook and bribed farm foremen to look the other way for a day or two. "They were upping the game to an industrial level," said Luis Li, a former Los

Angeles–area federal prosecutor who worked Amezcua-related cases during these years.

But that made them vulnerable. They had to move often to avoid law enforcement. With such large operations, their purchases of ingredients caught attention. Law enforcement targeted California chemical and supply companies that sold the traffickers precursor chemicals and glassware. Legislators enacted regulations on the sale of ephedrine, then regulated other chemicals essential to the ephedrine method: red phosphorus, hydriodic acid, iodine, and others. This happened first in California, then nationwide, in a series of laws spanning a decade.

EDUARDO CHAVEZ'S DEA assignment in Bakersfield ran from 2000 to 2004, and he can't remember a case involving pot or heroin in those years. He spent all his time chasing meth labs around the Central Valley, cultivating informants, buying undercover, and busting cooks from Apatzingán.

Toward the end of his Bakersfield assignment, he perceived a shift. The cooks and workers from Apatzingán began to vanish. His informants told him that they were heading home. In California, law enforcement had made things hard; the job was getting too risky, chemicals too hard to come by. The meth-cook migration would accelerate after Chavez left the state in 2004. Meth-lab seizures in the United States withered—from 10,000 that year to 2,500 in 2008. Today in the United States, they are rare, and "superlabs" are nonexistent.

What Eduardo Chavez saw in Bakersfield, too, was that Mexican traffickers were moving beyond their ranchero forebears. Traffickers were now connected more to a port than the earth, seeing their trade as the movement of product made as cheaply as possible, in forms as easy to smuggle as could be devised. Why own and protect farmland? Or hire farmworkers to harvest anything? Why depend on the seasons?

Or on Colombians to make their cocaine? The future of illegal dope, they saw, was in chemistry labs.

Methamphetamine taught them that.

"With meth," Chavez told me, "what they eventually figured out was if we can get the chemicals, and the chemistry expertise, and the lab equipment, then we can control the production from raw materials to finished product to end user."

That realization created the modern Mexican meth trade. To be sure, those meth manufacturers would have to smuggle their product into the United States. But the risks from law enforcement in Mexico—where the authorities were compromised and outgunned—were minimal. Access to world chemical markets was unimpeded through Mexico's two Pacific Coast ports. Now they could scale meth production to heights no biker gang in California could have dreamed.

Meth opened Mexican traffickers to the world beyond the hills where they were raised and left them with another question. That question, as Chavez put it, was this: "What else can we make ourselves without having to rely on farmland, or on a criminal organization in another country?"

Janssen

Among the most fertile scientific minds of the twentieth century belonged to a Belgian chemist named Dr. Paul Janssen.

Janssen was among the first to marry chemistry and pharmacology in search of new drugs. He combined them with a relentless intellect and an enormous capacity for work, becoming by the time he died in 2003, at the age of seventy-seven, the world's greatest drug inventor. His name was on 850 scientific papers; he presided over a hive of scientists in the Belgian village of Beerse, pop. 16,000, that was a world-class example of innovation through collaboration. Together they patented more than a hundred new medicines that have transformed our lives.

Janssen bore a passing resemblance to US president Lyndon Baines Johnson. The king of Belgium made him a baron. Janssen funded an early trip to the United States with money earned by playing chess. He was obsessed with chemistry; he could envision three-dimensional images of the molecules he was struggling to modify, and he doodled chemical compounds at meetings when bored.

At one point, eighteen of Janssen's innovations were on the World Health Organization's Model List of Essential Medicines. Janssen invented haloperidol—known commercially as Haldol—which calms the hallucinations of schizophrenics and allows them to be treated at home. The drug effectively ended the era of the insane asylum by convincing policymakers to release thousands of institutionalized mental patients who up to then could only be treated in a hospital. Janssen's Center for Molecular Design eventually came up with anti-HIV compounds. His antifungal ketoconazole has been a godsend for those, like me, with flare-ups from athlete's foot. Another drug, levamisole, kills hookworms and helps in the treatment of colon cancer.

Dr. Paul, as he was known, was born in 1926, the son of a doctor and a housewife. In Belgium during World War II he studied physics, biology, and chemistry while in hiding at a Jesuit university. A few years after the war, with money and office space provided by his father, he founded Janssen Pharmaceutica in Beerse.

Janssen abhorred hierarchies. Instead, he created an environment in which ideas seeped up from the people he hired. "Good scientists do not need to be supervised," he once said. He walked daily through the Beerse compound of Janssen Pharmaceutica, alighting in one lab after another to ask, "What's new?" He recruited heavily around the world, and his company opened labs worldwide. They were centers of innovation in dermatology and virology as well as in cardiovascular, allergic, gastrointestinal, and veterinary diseases. When revolution overturned the colonial government of what was then the Belgian Congo, he recruited many of the Belgian scientists who were expelled from the new Democratic Republic of Congo. Several were veterinarians. Janssen set them to work on topics they knew—animal parasites, for example. Their work made cold, tiny Beerse, near the border with Holland, a center for the study of tropical disease, parasites, and fungus. Janssen Pharmaceutica formed a plant protection department with a greenhouse, growing wheat, sugar beets, and fruit trees to study drugs that might protect them from fungus. (In 1961 Janssen sold his company to Johnson & Johnson, while retaining control over his research laboratory. For years he was Johnson & Johnson's largest shareholder.)

Janssen operated on the idea that drugs' effects on the human body are connected to their molecular structures. So the idea that fueled his company was this: find a molecule that had evolved to do a job in the human or animal body, then rejigger its structure in a way that allows it to do the job better than nature devised. Modifying that natural molecule, through laborious trial and error, would, he believed, result in better drugs.

It is this approach that makes Dr. Paul Janssen part of our story.

He was obsessed with finding new painkillers. This naturally led him to try to understand opiates, morphine above all. Nuclear magnetic resonance had been invented in the 1950s, and was just allowing scientists to see the structure of molecules. They theorized that our brains contain receptors—tiny way stations residing on each neuron in our brains. One of these way stations—the mμ receptor—controls pain, our bowels, and our breathing. Mμ receptors were later called "opioid receptors" because drugs derived from the opium poppy seem to fit on them and produce extraordinary effects: constipation, slower breathing, sometimes euphoria, and reduced pain.

Nature's morphine molecule—found in the opium poppy—works because it penetrates the barrier of protective fat surrounding the brain, locks onto the receptor, and stifles feelings of pain. But it does this slowly and inefficiently. Half the morphine molecules don't make it through the fat barrier to the brain.

Studying the molecular structure of morphine and other opiates, Janssen learned that they had in common a six-sided section of their molecules known as the piperidine ring. This hexagon had a nitrogen atom attached. The combination, he surmised, must be essential to the molecule's ability to attach to the receptor. So he did what medicinal chemists do: he manipulated the structure over and over, adding atoms to it, deleting portions, in an arduous trial and error. Finally, in 1959, he came up with a molecule that, tests showed, made its way through the brain's protective barrier. His invention also fit on the receptor far more snugly and efficiently than did the morphine molecule.

"A substantial portion of morphine doesn't make it past that barrier in the brain," said Carlos Valdez, a chemist at Lawrence Livermore National Laboratory in California, with whom I spoke as I tried to understand what Janssen had invented. "Heroin crosses the barrier much more easily, but then it partially converts into morphine once inside the brain tissue, slowing its absorption. The new molecule that Janssen invented crossed the blood-brain barrier very effectively, and most importantly, it wasn't converted into anything else."

In other words, the new molecule did the same job as morphine, only quicker and more efficiently. Or, put another way, Janssen's lab found that fifty to a hundred times less of this new drug was required to achieve the same pain relief as morphine.

All this made the drug a powerful painkiller. It wore off sooner than morphine, too. A patient could be quickly sedated, then walk away with few aftereffects once the operation was over. The dopey effects of morphine lasted much longer. This new drug's potential benefits to surgery were obvious.

Janssen called his invention fentanyl.

Fentanyl changed surgical anesthesia. In coronary bypass surgeries up to then, anesthesiologists used flammable gas. They had to put people out—render them unconscious, which depressed their blood pressure to dangerously low levels—to allow surgeons to operate. But in the late 1960s medical students watched a film that stunned the world of anesthesia. It was of a man undergoing stomach surgery while being interviewed on camera. That was fentanyl. On fentanyl, patients could be conscious during surgery, with blood pressure normal. Fentanyl was short-acting and could be reversed quickly with naloxone. People were in and out of it, without lingering aftereffects. (As a side note, I had a heart attack in a hotel in Atlanta in 2017 and was saved by the doctors and staff at nearby Emory University Hospital, who gave me, among other things, fentanyl during the procedure in which they fit a stent into my blocked artery, freeing blood to flow.)

Like a jazz musician exploring new improvisations on a song's chord structure, Janssen riffed off the piperidine ring over the next two decades, finding new molecules to hit the opioid receptors no matter where they were in the body. One place they reside is our bowels, which is why opiates create constipation. (Thus diarrhea is a common symptom of opiate withdrawal, as the body rebalances without the drug.) Janssen surmised that the piperidine ring might also be the basis for an antidiarrheal medicine. Trial and error led him to discover loperamide (brand name: Imodium), an opiate that attaches to receptors in our bowels but cannot cross the blood barrier into the brain and thus does not produce euphoria.

Janssen knew fentanyl's potential for abuse. It created the same euphoria in users as heroin, the same tolerance, the same withdrawal. In surgery, minute doses of fentanyl—measured in micrograms (a microgram is one-millionth of a gram)—produced helpful drowsiness and killed pain. In only slightly larger doses, it was fatal.

This was a time when American medicine rarely employed opioid pain relievers, fearing that the drugs would addict patients. Their use was heavily scrutinized in hospitals. Never were these drugs sent home with the patient.

For years Janssen would allow fentanyl to be provided only to anesthesiologists, only in limited supply, and only as a liquid sealed in glass vials. Constrain supply, he believed, and fentanyl abuse was unlikely.

Problem was, those precautions quickly loosened in harried US operating rooms. Many ORs stocked vials of fentanyl with little oversight. Thus anesthesiologists proved to be among the first addicts to Janssen's invention. In Tennessee, I spoke with Jack Woodside, a former anesthesiologist, who grew addicted to fentanyl on the job in the late 1970s. Woodside struggled, kicked, but relapsed frequently until he retrained in family medicine to get away from fentanyl. "For anesthesiologists, the predominant opiate [of addiction] tended to be fentanyl," said Woodside, who is now semiretired. "Back then, you just didn't find fentanyl that much outside the operating room. It wasn't available on the illicit market that I knew of."

Fentanyl's potency is its promise and its threat—and makes it key to our story.

In the years that followed, Janssen synthesized fentanyl analogues, fentanyl's cousins. They were molecularly similar to fentanyl, but tweaked just enough to allow them to be considered a separate drug. Chemists could create them, Janssen realized, by just adding or subtracting elements from the original fentanyl molecule.

In 1968, in a remarkable thirty-five-page chapter published in an obscure anthology of studies called *Drugs Affecting the Central Nervous System*, Janssen listed all the analogues of the fentanyl molecule. There were dozens of them—molecules that he imagined possible now that he had invented fentanyl through such trial and error. The chapter was called "Chemical Anatomy of Potent Morphine-like Analgesics." Many of the molecules he listed in the chapter were far more potent than the original fentanyl. They were theoretically possible to produce but not economical to make legally on a large scale. Given their potency, they were too tricky to administer to have much medical use. On this list were molecules with strange names that reflected their structures, intelligible only to chemists: furanylfentanyl, acetylfentanyl, cyclopropylfentanyl, and so on.

For the next five decades, most of these analogues remained obscure discoveries. They were forgotten in the pages of that lone anthology, or tucked away in dense patent applications.

In 1974 Janssen scientists synthesized a molecule with an entirely new level of efficiency in reaching the brain. They called it carfentanil. Carfentanil was ten thousand times more potent than morphine. It had no valid use on humans, they believed, but they saw that it sedated elephants, rhinoceroses, and other large mammals. In the United States, later, carfentanil was made legal only for zoo veterinarians to possess. (UK scientists concluded that in 2002 the Russian government used carfentanil to attack Chechen rebels who had taken over a Moscow theater, dispersing it through the building's air duct. At least 170 people died, including 121 hostages. The UK scientists based their conclusions on tests of items of clothing and blood belonging to British citizens who were near an exit and thus among the hostages revived by a Russian assault team that day. The Russian government has never commented on what it pumped through the theater beyond to say that it was a "mixture based on derivatives of fentanyl.")

Paul Janssen proved that once fentanyl was invented, it wasn't difficult to replicate.

Making fentanyl got easier as years passed. An anonymous chemist, known today only as Siegfried, published a simpler method, in English, for making fentanyl—with five chemical steps compared to Janssen's seven. The method fits on a single sheet of paper and appears on a rudimentary website of the kind common to the internet's early days. No one seems to know who Siegfried is or was, or when the paper was written. The author writes as if he, or she, is not a native English speaker. Still, as word spread throughout the underworld of fentanyl's potency and similarity to heroin, underground chemists discovered they could make the stuff more economically with what is today known as the Siegfried method.

Fentanyl had immediate benefits to medicine. More slowly, the underworld came to understand its advantages as well: that with knowledge of chemistry, a drug of immense potency could be produced in a laboratory, replace heroin, and, with much less risk and only a modest investment, generate astounding profits.

Sacklers I

"Overworked and Unprepared Doctors"

One day in 2008, outside the office of Dr. Michael Rhodes, a pain doctor in the small town of Springfield in north-central Tennessee, two pain patients awaiting their pill prescriptions erupted in a knife fight, with one demanding the ID of the other who was ahead of him in line.

A sales rep for Purdue Pharma, the company that makes OxyContin, was calling on the doctor and witnessed the fight. She reported the fight to her supervisors. Rhodes had lines of patients outside his office. A pharmacist and a nurse practitioner in the area told her that Dr. Rhodes was a major prescriber of narcotic painkillers, and thus a major source of the pills that ended up for sale on the street. Later a woman approached a Purdue rep at a conference in Tennessee, claiming her son had died of an overdose from pills Rhodes prescribed. Purdue sales reps filed reports on Dr. Rhodes with supervisors. Purdue even investigated him and found he "was feeding addicts." One addict he prescribed ninety OxyContin later died of an overdose. State authorities reprimanded Dr. Rhodes for gross negligence.

Yet the company decided to allow its sales reps to keep calling on Rhodes. The reps pushed him to prescribe more OxyContin, which he did. He grew into one of Tennessee's leaders, prescribing 319,000 OxyContin pills between 2006 and 2015.

Rhodes himself pleaded with the reps that he did not think he was competent to prescribe for pain. Still they pushed him to do so. He moved offices; they tracked him down. He told them he'd left the pain business; they kept at him anyway. In 2013 Rhodes's license was put on probation by Tennessee medical authorities who suspected him of wanton prescribing. Even then, Purdue reps visited him another thirty-one times over two years. Finally they stopped, six weeks after state officials revoked his medical license in 2015.

AS THE FIRST decade of the twenty-first century wound down, the drug company known as Purdue Pharma, based in an inverted glass pyramid on a main drag in the town of Stamford, Connecticut, had reason to feel good.

In 2007 Purdue put behind it a federal criminal suit alleging it had misbranded its signature drug, OxyContin. The company pleaded guilty to a misdemeanor charge and paid a $634 million fine. Along with its conviction, Purdue also signed something called a "corporate integrity agreement," in which it undertook to monitor doctors for signs that their prescribing was out of control and report them to government officials. The company reformulated OxyContin's timed-release coating in 2010, making it harder to crush and liquefy and abuse. All this was evidence to those within the company that Purdue was attempting to live by the spirit and letter of its federal agreement.

Really, though, the company hadn't changed much. It was hardly a modern, diversified pharmaceutical company. It was privately owned by one wing of the wealthy Sackler family. By then, in fact, the Sackler family was actually two.

One side comprised the heirs of Arthur Sackler. The oldest of three brothers, Arthur Sackler was a complicated, brilliant man, with several successful careers. He was a trained psychiatrist, who ran New York's first integrated blood bank. He later invented modern pharmaceutical marketing. This he did through direct contact with doctors via office visits and direct-mail advertising, none of which were used back then. Beginning in the early 1960s, employing these techniques, he made Valium the industry's first billion-dollar drug. The industry adopted his marketing strategies. He bought an advertising firm and founded a medical newspaper for which he wrote a regular column, proselytizing these methods. Pharmaceutical marketing was one thing before Arthur Sackler and quite another after him. He was a founding inductee to the Medical Marketing Hall of Fame.

By the early 1980s Arthur Sackler also had established a reputation for charitable giving to universities and museums, and as one of the world's most astute collectors of Asian art. He donated money to Tufts University in Boston; Tufts responded by naming its medical school for him. The Smithsonian has an Asian art gallery in his name on the National Mall in Washington, D.C.

Arthur Sackler died in 1987 at the age of seventy-three. His heirs sold their holdings in Purdue Pharma to his brothers, Mortimer and Raymond, and their families, and from then on had nothing to do with the company. The Sackler family divided. On one side was the millionaires, Arthur's heirs. The other, the much larger group of billionaires, included Mortimer, who died in 2010, Raymond, who died in 2017, and their heirs. It is this side of the Sackler family, owners of Purdue Pharma, that our story is about.

Years before, in 1952, Arthur Sackler had financed the purchase of a small drug company—Purdue Frederick—and installed his brothers as its directors.

Mortimer and Raymond were accomplished men, doctors like their brother. They briefly flirted with the Communist Party in the 1930s. Along with Arthur, Mortimer and Raymond were trailblazing psychiatrists at Creedmoor Psychiatric Center in New York City, helping to move the discipline away from lobotomies and electroshock and toward therapy and pharmaceutical treatment for mental illness. Mortimer and Raymond were dismissed from the Atomic Energy Commission in 1953, during the height of the Red Scare, after they refused to sign loyalty oaths. Later in life, each established an impressive record of philanthropy, funding the arts, sciences, and biotech. Mortimer lived much of his adult life in Europe, where he went to attend medical school because he was denied entry into New York schools due to their quotas on Jewish students. He later renounced his US citizenship. Raymond Sackler was knighted in three countries—France, the Netherlands, and England, along with Mortimer, by Queen Elizabeth in 1995; a planet is named for Raymond Sackler and his wife, Beverly.

Through all this, their company, now named Purdue Pharma, expanded. In the 1980s it came out with MS Contin, a timed-release version of morphine sulphate for terminal cancer patients. They followed that with OxyContin in 1996, aimed at the much larger, more profitable market of American pain patients.

Mortimer, Raymond, and their heirs held eight of the twelve seats on Purdue's board, and made the company decisions. Among them was to put in place something that Arthur's heirs and associates claim he never would have approved: the aggressive marketing, using Arthur's strategies and Arthur's ad firm, of a narcotic painkiller not just to terminal cancer patients but to pain patients of all kinds, using frequent visits to doctors by sales reps making unproven claims about its nonaddictive nature for pain patients.

In the thirty years that followed, these marketing methods propelled OxyContin to revenue in the billions—comprising 90 percent of the company's sales; to increase profits, Purdue had only to increase sales of OxyContin. To do this, its data showed, it had to increase sales calls to doctors.

OxyContin made the Sacklers fabulously wealthy. Pain-pill addiction, meanwhile, raised little concern outside a few regions of the country. A year after Purdue's guilty plea, overdoses surpassed car fatalities as the country's leading cause of accidental death. Yet Americans considered it a minor problem, involving somebody else: junkies who flouted common sense and deserved what they got or, in Appalachia, hapless hillbillies who were to blame for their continued dysfunction.

Across America, families of addicts lived in shame, hiding the truth of their loved ones' addictions and the manner in which they died. Media coverage was haphazard. Politicians found other issues to focus on. A nationwide silence accompanied addiction and allowed it to spread. The Sackler family and Purdue were left undisturbed. The Sacklers resided in Manhattan, the Hamptons, and London, vacationed in Aspen and on the Côte d'Azur. Wherever they lived, the Sacklers seemed far in every way from the unpleasantness of middle America.

Purdue, meanwhile, beat back OxyContin lawsuits. Most of the US medical world, in fact, lined up behind the idea that narcotic painkillers were nonaddictive for virtually every pain patient. Medical schools now taught this reliance on narcotic painkillers in classes on pain management. This revolution in pain management, achieved within a little more than a decade, was due largely to the kind of aggressive marketing to doctors that Purdue had perfected.

In the years leading up to its 2007 conviction and corporate integrity agreement, Purdue reduced its promotion of OxyContin; its marketing staff fell, as did its OxyContin sales. But the next year, Purdue's sales promotion ramped up once again. Sales quickly reached $1 billion—surpassing those of Viagra—and from there rose to $3 billion by 2010.

The company's conviction notably did not mention the Sacklers; instead three Purdue executives pleaded guilty, leaving the family's name unscathed. It graced museums and universities in Beijing, London, New York, and Tel Aviv. Eight years later, in 2015, *Forbes* magazine, as if in coronation, named the Sacklers as one of America's wealthiest families, besting even the Rockefellers, with an estimated net worth of $14 billion—all from sales of OxyContin.

But that year, public awareness began to grow. Families emerged from the shadows. With them came the realization that the scourge was a classic case of private profits and socialized costs. Virtually all the profits went to drug companies or drug distributors—or the drug underworld. But courts and jails were clogged. Coroners' budgets buckled. Public health departments and county emergency rooms were besieged. Foster-children agencies now had to find homes for thousands of kids abandoned by addicted parents; grandparents stepped into the breach to raise their grandchildren. Librarians found needles in the hedges outside their buildings.

Now no politician could be seen as indifferent. Attorneys general in particular set their staffs to dig into how the cost of this epidemic might be recouped. Their investigators came with experience, budgets, and subpoenas through which they made public heaps of drug companies' internal records.

Attorneys across the country delved into this material. All that intellect and expertise focused on this issue produced new legal approaches. Their investigations often targeted several companies. But atop every list sat Purdue Pharma. By 2017 attorneys general offices were lining up to sue the company. I was amazed to watch them, one after another: Washington, Louisiana, Pennsylvania, Oklahoma, Washington, DC, South Carolina, then later, California and New York. On it went.

Among the most comprehensive was the complaint brought by Tennessee attorney general Herbert Slatery—278 pages based on sales rep calls, sales training, and company emails, narrating how Purdue allegedly went about urging Tennessee doctors to prescribe its product. In 2018, Massachusetts attorney general Maura Healey's complaint was the first to add Sackler board members by name to a lawsuit.

I read these two documents with special interest. Each disgorged remarkable new information, offering a courtside seat to the tale of this national crisis. Each told a mesmerizing story, marrying Purdue strategic decisions to their influence over the prescribing of local doctors in far-flung small towns. Healey's complaint—277 pages—added voluminous narrative about how the Sackler board members pushed those decisions.

Taken together, the complaints assembled from Purdue internal records portrayed a company run by the Sackler board members, who behaved like de facto CEOs and directed sales strategy. Long after that

2007 conviction, Purdue was still aggressively pushing physicians to prescribe OxyContin. Sales reps overlooked warning signs indicating out-of-control doctors. Purdue reps were ordered to pay special attention to overworked and unprepared doctors, urging them to prescribe ever more OxyContin at higher doses. In the worst cases, these were doctors who admittedly could not responsibly prescribe such drugs— physicians like Dr. Michael Rhodes out in Springfield, Tennessee.

Henderson

B elgian winters are cold and gray, and in 1975 the Janssen
compound at Beerse had little charm. The buildings were white,
unremarkable; inside, their concrete corridors were lit by fluorescent
tubes running along the ceiling.

Yet for a week that winter, a young pharmacology professor named
Gary Henderson from the University of California, Davis, walked
through the compound feeling as though he'd been transported to some
kind of chemistry Shangri-la. Laboratory after laboratory was
crammed with the most intelligent, unassuming scientists, paid what
an assistant professor in the United States might earn, yet every one of
them absorbed in creating new chemicals that might be used by medicine to treat mental illness, diarrhea, or tropical fungus infection. Even
the secretaries spoke four languages. "It was such a different world,"
Henderson remembered. "They were people doing world-class research
and living very modestly." It was as if the research was so intellectually
fulfilling that interest in material possessions wasn't important.

At UC Davis, Henderson had developed the first test to detect
fentanyl in humans. Hearing of this, Paul Janssen invited him to Beerse.
At home after dinner one night, Janssen showed home movies of himself
and his wife in Africa, demonstrating the use of a new drug they were
calling carfentanil. The film showed the drug stopping a rhinoceros.
Shot with a dart, the animal stopped moving—just stood there.

Fentanyl produced a sort of mental indifference in the animal, so much so that Janssen's wife walked up to it and petted its nose. "You could immobilize the animal," Henderson said, "then reverse it with naloxone. In a few seconds the animal is normal." It was a remarkable world Paul Janssen had opened, Henderson thought.

Henderson would visit Janssen Pharmaceutica three times during the 1970s. Janssen spoke of a deal to distribute fentanyl in China. Chinese officials, he said, wanted a joint venture through which they could learn how to make the drug. Eventually the sides agreed. Janssen got access to the huge Chinese market and the assurance that pharmaceutical fentanyl would be manufactured at high quality. That joint venture marks the moment when China learned to make fentanyl. In 1985 Janssen opened the first Western pharmaceutical factory in China. Since then, Henderson said, "China has had the technology for producing fentanyl at an industrial level."

By the late 1970s Henderson's fentanyl test was in wide use. He turned to research other drugs. Until one day in 1978, when the director of the California Horse Racing Board in Sacramento drove the twenty minutes to the University of California, Davis and walked into Henderson's office with a strange request.

Could the professor develop a test for the presence of fentanyl in a horse? Actually, the director used the term "elephant juice," as the drug was called in the racing world, since it reputedly could stop an elephant.

Hovering at the edges of the racing industry, the director explained, was a shady class of people constantly looking for chemicals that could "hop a horse or stop a horse"—make it run faster, or slower. Fentanyl, he said, did the former. The drug was a narcotic when administered to humans; it doped them, slowed them, sent them into a stupor. But it threw horses into a manic rage—cats, too, for that matter. Opioids, in fact, tend to produce strange effects in mammals other than humans. Fentanyl will turn a rat stiff, to the point where you can stand him on his head. A horse on fentanyl will tear up a stall. On the track, the drug pushed the horse to extremes.

Henderson thought he could develop a horse-urine test for fentanyl. It took a while, but with that began a second stage of his chemistry career connected to Paul Janssen's creation.

By then, Henderson was a member of the California Association of Toxicologists. In 1979 he received a phone call from the coroner in Orange County, who had what seemed clear cases of heroin overdose: people with the needles in their arms, lungs filled with fluid, and friends and family who told of histories of abuse of the drug. They were hearing that a very potent heroin-like drug called China White was circulating. But tests showed no heroin in the victims' systems.

Henderson tested the fluids and found fentanyl. Coroners from around California started sending him fluid samples. At first it was once every couple of months. Then once a week. The cases peaked in 1984, with 45, including 31 in the county of San Diego. In all, 112 cases were sent to Henderson's lab at UC Davis, mostly from Southern California suburbs. Henderson identified ten separate fentanyl analogues.

Then the fentanyls vanished from the street as quickly as they had appeared. No one ever discovered who had made the stuff that killed those people.

That was Henderson's last foray into fentanyl. Nevertheless, his encounter with underworld fentanyl left him full of foreboding. To describe what he saw forming in the distance, he coined the now-common term "designer drugs." These were drugs of abuse made in laboratories, not grown from the ground. Long before the rise of China as a capitalist power and the advent of the global economy and the internet, the California fentanyl cases convinced Gary Henderson that "the future drugs of abuse will be synthetics rather than plant products."

As years passed, Henderson became something of an oracle on the topic. He wrote scientific papers in journals, warning of a coming tsunami of synthetic drugs, led by fentanyl and its analogues, which he assumed could number in the hundreds.

In 1988 he published a paper in the *Journal of Forensic Sciences*. He ended the paper with this bit of prescience: "The 'Designer Drug' problem may become an international problem. A single gram of any very potent drug . . . could be synthesized at one location, transported to distribution sites worldwide, and then formulated into many thousand, perhaps a million, doses."

Preventing this would be difficult, he wrote, for these new drugs "will be synthesized from readily available chemicals, may be derivatives of pharmaceuticals, [and] will be very potent. . . . They will be marketed very cleverly. . . . Restricting certain chemicals has only stimulated clandestine chemists to assemble the drugs from more elementary precursors. Locating these laboratories will also be a difficult task.

"Use of the illicit fentanyls has been restricted almost exclusively to California, and at the present time, they do not appear to be widely available, even in California. However . . . fentanyls could reappear at any time and would probably not be restricted to California."

The Project II

Toluca, Mexico

The Reclusorio Norte prison at the northern tip of Mexico City has been overcrowded almost since the day it opened in 1974. It is a massive thing of gray concrete and barbed wire, sprawling over 1.6 million square feet.

In January 2007 four American law enforcement officers, accompanied by a Mexican prosecutor, arrived at the prison. They made their way past women and children waiting to enter with pots of food. Mexican prisons don't generally feed inmates, so without loved ones nearby, inmates don't eat anything but the most meager rations. Inside, the warden led the group down a dimly lit corridor. They had been told not to wear khaki, for it was the color of inmate clothing. An inmate hierarchy was clear from the quality of the khaki each man wore. Some guys, apparently with no one outside to care for them, wore faded khaki T-shirts turned inside out. But others had pressed button-down khaki dress shirts.

The Project that Ryan Rapaszky had overheard discussed on wiretaps in Chicago had led him here. He walked the prison corridors as people swirled around him. The prison was far less controlled than those in the United States. No one was behind bars, but also unlike US prisons, no one tried to dominate others with menacing looks. The prison awed Rapaszky, though he felt he was right where he wanted to be. Clusters of people had died of overdoses in Chicago, and he had the resources to help track it to the end and stop it. He joined the DEA to work on cases like this.

He was accompanied by Eduardo Chavez, also thirty, and now, after four years in Bakersfield, stationed at the DEA office in Mexico City. Rapaszky had called Chavez to ask for help investigating "that claim by that Mexican fellow" who walked into the San Diego DEA office telling of a company making fentanyl.

Chavez found Distribuidora Talios near Toluca. A prosecutor asked a Mexican judge for a search warrant for the company. But the judge didn't know what fentanyl was, and refused. They returned to court with a chemist who convinced the judge that illicit fentanyl was indeed dangerous. The judge gave them a search warrant good for forty-eight hours. That was on a Friday. Mexican authorities raided Talios on Sunday. As it happens, El Cerebro—the Brain—had come to feed the lab's Rottweiler guard dog, arriving at the same time as Mexican authorities who, amazed at their luck, arrested him.

Chavez toured the Talios site. It was the work, he thought, of someone who appreciated the art of chemistry. It was well lit, orderly, with fire blankets, masks, lab coats, labels—no fast-food wrappers, no junk, no cigarette butts. Glassware came custom-made from India. A rotary evaporator that removes solvents stood to one side. DEA chemists later examined the lab. It was likely, they said, the most expensive and sophisticated illicit chemical laboratory that traffickers had set up in Mexico to that point.

The fentanyl-death outbreak of 2006 ceased with the closure of Distribuidora Talios. When supply halted, deaths fell. By 2007, the worst US fentanyl crisis up to that point ended. It was an example of supply reduction as the best harm reduction.

At the prison that morning, the warden led the agents to a meeting room with a table and three chairs. A short while later, prison officials ushered into the room a mild-mannered man of average height—El Cerebro.

His name was Ricardo Valdez-Torres and he arrived clean-cut and dressed in a Members Only khaki jacket. He was polite and had just showered. He bore no tattoos. He exchanged pleasantries with the warden. He had a bookish way about him. Occasionally he pulled reading glasses from the breast pocket of his khaki dress shirt.

"I was waiting for you guys to come talk to me."

HE WAS MEXICAN born, Valdez-Torres said, but he had crossed into San Diego with his family when he was a child and grew up in San Diego County. His English was better than his Spanish. As a young man, he owned a swimming-pool supply business. He said he had a degree in business from a local community college. At some point, he had the idea of cooking fentanyl, proposing it to a friend he met at the college. He never said how he'd learned the complicated process, nor why he was so interested in chemistry, a subject he had not studied. But he told them that in the late 1980s he'd been making smallish amounts of the drug—ninety grams at a time—in a house in Bonita, a town in a then sparsely inhabited eastern part of San Diego County. After a few batches, he said, his business was raided and he spent the next decade in a US prison. The paperwork on that 1991 case tells a different story. An undercover officer reported that Valdez-Torres was offering to make a pound of fentanyl for $1 million.

Whatever the case, Valdez-Torres pleaded guilty, then spent his prison years writing court petitions alleging ineffective counsel and requesting his sentence be vacated. Meanwhile, he got to know as many chemists and distributors as he could find while in prison. He seems to have left prison with a notebook of criminal contacts and insights into manufacturing fentanyl. Valdez-Torres said he left US federal prison knowing that he wanted to make fentanyl again, feeling that his talents were not exploited as fully as they deserved to be. To Eduardo Chavez, he seemed a man who believed his intelligence could not be confined to a classroom.

After leaving prison in 2003, Valdez-Torres was deported to Mexico and living in the city of Hermosillo, Sonora, where, two years later, some men visited him. They were emissaries, they said, of Joaquín "El Chapo" Guzmán, one of the heads of the Sinaloa cartel. Would he like, they asked, to get back into the chemistry business? Valdez-Torres was known as a fentanyl cooker, and he assumed that was what they wanted him to make. What they really wanted him to do was figure out how to make pharmaceutical-grade ephedrine. They had money to set up not a meth lab but a lab to make its precursor, ephedrine.

In 2005 Mexican authorities had followed the Americans' lead and restricted the amount of ephedrine they allowed in. With ephedrine, anybody could make meth. So all these traffickers needed to manufacture large amounts of profitable methamphetamine was a steady supply of ephedrine. As he got his Toluca lab up and running, Valdez-Torres took notes on how he might produce ephedrine; agents later found these notes at the lab. Meanwhile, though, he set to work on the drug he knew how to make.

In Reclusorio Norte, Valdez-Torres admitted that the Toluca lab was his creation. He had made fentanyl, he said; a batch of ten kilos had left the lab a few days before his arrest. But he knew nothing about where it went after that.

One kilo of the fentanyl he brewed up, he said, had to be cut—diluted—into fifty kilos. At a fifty-to-one dilution, he said, it wouldn't kill anyone. He knew this, he said, because he'd tested his product on mice and found that, at fifty to one, the mice didn't die. He relayed this information to the people who took his powder, but whether these crucial instructions traveled to the streets he had no idea. Investigators in Chicago, in fact, found that street dealers, thinking they had heroin on their hands, were reluctant to dilute it. Weak heroin was a constant complaint among customers, who were now hearing that an especially potent batch was circulating. Nobody on Chicago streets believed that this stuff could be cut fifty to one. "They thought it was a sales tactic," Rapaszky said. "It was inconceivable that you could dilute it that much." Many dealers sold it into the street drug world without cutting it at all.

Valdez-Torres told Rapaszky and Chavez that he wanted to be transferred to an American prison. If he was going to have to do a lot more years in prison, he didn't want to do them in Mexico. (He was extradited to a US prison, from which he was released in 2015, at which point he was deported and then disappeared.)

When it was over, Valdez-Torres stood, shook hands with them all, and was led back to his cell. The Americans rose to leave. An inmate scurried in, asking if he could shine Chavez's shoes. Sure. The man spread polish over the agent's shoes, then pulled out a cigarette lighter and lit the polish. Flames rose from the shoes for a few seconds, and the inmate put them out and scoured the leather. It was a surreal end to a strange meeting and remains one of the better shoeshines of Chavez's life.

WHAT BEGAN MYSTERIOUSLY as the Project—one amateur chemist's vanity sideline, in a lab that traffickers funded to make a precursor to methamphetamine—instead opened to the Sinaloa cartel a vista of the bounty that awaited them by making synthetic "heroin" from chemicals. With it, they could capture the US opioid market, which was rising to heights of demand that they could not have dreamed of.

"And that's what played out," Rapaszky told me. "He shined a light on it. [Before that] the idea of making fentanyl just wasn't on the [cartels'] radar. Now they have as much as they can make in a lab, which, from the lessons they learned from methamphetamine, is right in their wheelhouse."

Rapaszky remembered that during the interview Valdez-Torres had mentioned a moment when he was with the Sinaloan investors in his lab, making them understand the power of fentanyl. One of them had suggested buying a pill press. "Why don't we mix the fentanyl into counterfeit pills?" he said. The pills could be made to resemble the opioid painkillers that doctors prescribed by the millions up in the United States; pills could be a perfect container for cheap, potent fentanyl. Valdez-Torres said he nixed the idea, believing it would be difficult for Talios to maintain its front as a legitimate chemical distributor if it purchased pill presses and looked like a manufacturer. Still, Rapaszky remembered, "it was this scary moment where you hear the bells sound among the traffickers: 'We need to put this in pill form.'"

In 2008 Ryan Rapaszky was reassigned to Washington, DC, then in 2011 to Copenhagen. But the case kept returning to him. During his years in Copenhagen, Estonia had a fierce struggle with illicit fentanyl, and many people died. He gave PowerPoints to Estonian officials on the case involving El Cerebro.

Back in the United States, meanwhile, overdoses were now the leading cause of accidental death. People addicted to prescription pain pills began switching to cheap, potent Mexican heroin. In 2016 Rapaszky took over the DEA office on Cape Cod in Massachusetts. He watched as street fentanyl became the opioid epidemic's third phase, crowding out heroin—just as it had briefly done in south Chicago in 2006. The national death toll consequently set new annual records. On Cape Cod, every addict had had a hockey injury, or was injured on a fishing boat; either way, the doctors prescribed them opioids for the pain, and years later they were addicted and buying off the street what they thought was heroin. It was fentanyl, and many died.

When they did, Ryan Rapaszky remembered the Project. It was, he saw, a precursor of its own, an early warning of so much that was to come.

Clarksburg I

Doc O

T he town of Clarksburg drapes over rolling land in a valley in a
northern section of West Virginia, halfway between Pittsburgh
and Charleston.

Clarksburg is the seat of the county of Harrison, and the town
amounts to a population of a little more than 16,000 and three exits on
Highway 50. Clarksburg's downtown is a collection of three- and four-
story brick office buildings, storefronts, small restaurants, a theater, a
courthouse, and a newspaper along the east-west streets of Pike and
Main.

The Clarksburg skyline is punctuated by tall spires of downtown
churches, whose brick and stained glass suggest permanence and
respectability. The flocks of Clarksburg Baptist and Christ Episcopal
organized before the Civil War. Central Christian's building dates to
the early 1900s. During the prosperity of the twentieth century, they
were the spiritual home of Clarksburg's teachers, accountants, doctors,
and city councilmen. These churches were at the center of Clarksburg
in many ways, and they naturally saw themselves as indivisible from
their town. They fostered a feeling of duty to the community. When
coal miners were fighting for better working conditions during the
Great Depression, Christ Episcopal took in their children.

The buildings downtown embodied the aspirations of small-
town twentieth-century Americans to a life of modest but steady

improvement. In Clarksburg, those aspirations were founded on glass. West Virginia's high-quality river sand and natural gas fields brought glass factories to the area just as innovations in glass took hold. The mass production of plate glass made skyscrapers possible. Picture windows and sliding glass doors made small homes look bigger, allowing working-class families to feel part of the American dream.

Pittsburgh Plate Glass opened its factory No. 12 in Clarksburg in 1916, and for years it was one of the world's leading producers of plate glass. The town had family-owned factories, too—Rolland Glass, Harvey Glass. Several factories made marbles; Akro Agate was the nation's largest marble manufacturer in its day. In the 1960s, kids still congregated at the fences of marble factories at lunchtime, asking workers to throw them their rejects. Anchor Hocking employed eight hundred people to make tumblers, bottles, fruit bowls, and glasses.

The rest of West Virginia pulled coal from the ground and shipped it off to create products and wealth elsewhere. Out-of-state coal interests dominated West Virginia land ownership and politics. Coal bred a political culture of dependency and a one-party state for a century—first Republican, then Democrat. This made it politically difficult for the state to develop economic alternatives. But Clarksburg and several other towns up in northern West Virginia were different. Glass did not often leave workers mangled or dead. Glass was real manufacturing, in tune with consumer tastes, rapidly changing to meet them, and thus requiring constant innovation and technological investment. Glasswork was union work, and that buoyed the town. Locally owned businesses jammed Main Street. Glass artisans from France and Belgium came to Clarksburg; French was commonly heard on its streets for years. Doctors lived in and near downtown to be close to St. Mary's Hospital.

Beyond downtown, a constellation of neighborhoods formed— North View, Stealey, Monticello, Adamston. Each was a self-contained world, with its own churches, grocery stores, a school, and often a swimming pool—and inhabited by French immigrants, Italians, Austrians, and German Irish, most of whom were glassworkers. High school sports rivalries grew fierce. Clarksburg's good times earned it a reputation as Little Chicago. Numbers and slot machines flourished, along with betting on high school football games, in the neighborhood bars and pool halls where factory workers unwound.

In 1978 a young resident out of University of Maryland Medical School named Lou Ortenzio arrived, recently married. "Small-town living seemed so much better than suburban life," he told me as we drove around town one afternoon many years later. "In Clarksburg, every block had something going; there were no vacant lots. Mom-and-pop grocery stores in every neighborhood. All these houses were occupied by teachers, business owners, and people who worked in glass factories."

Many of Clarksburg's older physicians were retiring by then. Lou Ortenzio and two other young doctors opened a practice and soon were overwhelmed. They did hospital intensive care, obstetrics; they made house calls. In no time, Ortenzio was seeing forty or fifty patients a day in his office.

His patients knew him as "Doc O," a family doctor who took the time to listen, and who cared so much that the hours he kept lasted well past those posted outside his practice. Most of the doctors in town sent their families to him. "To me, he wasn't like a doctor; he was more like a big brother, somebody I could talk to when I couldn't talk to anybody else," said Phyllis Mills, whose glassworker husband, Paul, as well as youngest son and daughter and several relatives, were among Ortenzio's first patients. When Mills's son was born disabled, Ortenzio called often to check on the infant. "I wondered how he had the energy to go the way he did, from six in the morning until sometimes two in the morning," she said.

Most of Doc O's patients were older; they'd lived through the Depression, many had served in World War II. They had the aches and pain to show for a lifetime of hard work in the glass factories or the gas company, but they had retired with something approaching financial security. They owned homes and cars, had pensions and good health insurance. They suffered from the ailments of the old and did so quietly. This was partly generational and partly an Appalachian inheritance. One man came to him wasted away from cancer.

"Why didn't you come in earlier?" Ortenzio asked.

"Well," the man said, "I wouldn't want you to think I was complainy." It was classic Appalachia, and Ortenzio grew used to this kind of stoicism.

Ortenzio worked to establish a free clinic where the town's uninsured could get medical care. The Chamber of Commerce declared him Citizen of the Year for that. He had been trained to be holistic in his care. His professors had taught him that most of what a doctor needs to know to make a diagnosis could be learned from taking time to listen to a patient. X-rays and lab tests were to confirm what you gleaned from asking questions and paying attention to the answers. Ortenzio had been trained to help his patients help themselves. Part of his job was to teach them how to take care of their bodies. Pills were a last resort.

Drug salesmen visited weekly. It was a stodgy profession back then. Ortenzio remembers these sales reps as older men, with backgrounds in medicine or pharmacy, cultivating long-term relationships with doctors that the salesmen valued because they were part of Clarksburg, too. He remembered a man named Don Molinari, who repped for Eli Lilly and Co. and was a deacon in a local Catholic church. Once a week, Molinari would come around his office in a blazer or a business suit, usually with information about the drugs Lilly produced. He brought free samples of his drugs, but rarely gave away more than that. Molinari was a collegial fellow who studied his topic. Ortenzio grew to rely on the salesman's advice when it came to pharmaceuticals. Their relationship deepened in a way that was common then among doctors and drug reps. Molinari even asked the doctor to counsel engaged couples in his church about sex and health. When the Federal Drug Administration removed a Lilly drug from the market, Molinari dropped by, embarrassed and apologetic.

Before long, Ortenzio and his wife saw Clarksburg as home. They found a two-story, three-bedroom, one-bath house in the Stealey neighborhood southwest of downtown and at the foot of a hill, atop which stood the neighborhood swimming pool.

They set off to the bank for a thirty-year loan—and were denied. "The house won't keep its value that long," the banker told them. "The best we can give you is a fifteen-year loan."

Ortenzio left mystified. Clarksburg bustled with unified, hard-working people, and he saw no reason why it would not remain so.

Yet about the time Lou Ortenzio moved to Clarksburg, attracted by the quiet prosperity of a small American town that made glass, the prospects of both began to fade. Newer glass technologies needed larger factories, requiring the kind of flat land that was rare in the rolling hills of West Virginia. Nationwide, plastic and aluminum were replacing glass for many uses; Mexico and Asia emerged as competition. Unions, meanwhile, kept asking for higher wages, unable to imagine a world competing with workers in Oklahoma, much less Asia.

Pittsburgh Plate Glass closed its Clarksburg plant in the 1970s. The marble factories left, too. Anchor Hocking departed in 1987. That was the last blow. When I visited Clarksburg for the first time, the plant's hulking concrete remains stood just off Highway 50, near the North View neighborhood.

Soon Ortenzio was finding the banker's words prescient. People ebbed from the neighborhoods. Clarksburg's population dropped from 22,000 in 1980 to 16,000 today. Those who stayed faced unsettling prospects, particularly with the modest education that sufficed when a glass job meant you were set for life. The jobs now were at Walmart or pizza restaurants or in telemarketing.

Locally owned stores downtown faded, then vanished altogether after the Meadowbrook Mall opened on reclaimed strip-mine land out on the interstate. Homeowners were replaced by renters on Section 8. Those houses now sagged. Row after row were missing stairs, patched with plywood. The city demolished dozens of abandoned houses around town, leaving streets with toothless gaps. Resident associations closed the swimming pools they could no longer maintain.

Neighborhood schools were the social centers of Clarksburg. They had now to be consolidated, and with them went their neighborhoods and those high school games that brought people out in public.

The downtown churches faded with them, as people left for other states or towns. Those who remained grew old and died. Young people rarely joined these churches. Repairing their aging buildings took time and money; bake sales could only do so much.

Brenda Smothers was a file clerk at the Veterans Administration in town. She joined Central Christian Church in 1993 and served on its board for many years. She liked that all the downtown churches met together on Easter for a sunrise service outside Christ Episcopal, then walked over to Clarksburg Baptist for a pancake breakfast. When that stopped, "we just kind of drifted away," Brenda remembered, "kind of like family members do." As downtown streets emptied, the established churches, too, lost some of the connection to Clarksburg and to each other. Everyone seemed to hunker indoors, lose contact, worry about their own precarious situation, fearing what the outside would bring.

People, meanwhile, collapsed like the houses. Lou Ortenzio saw them in his office. He made house calls to the elderly and to nursing homes. He saw patients late into the night, listening as they poured out the details of their lives. Everyone wanted to be Doc O's patient. He was unable to say no. "I wanted to help everybody," he told me. "I wanted to make everybody happy."

Then one night in 1988, about seven, after the nurses and office manager had gone home, Dr. Lou Ortenzio, then thirty-five, prepared to see the last of his patients and return some phone calls. He opened the cupboard where the drug samples were kept. He reached in for a box of low-dose Vicodin—a pill that combined 7.5 milligrams of hydrocodone, an opioid pain reliever, with 500 milligrams of acetaminophen. The box contained twenty pills, each in a foil wrapper. With his practice bursting, he was weary, had a tension headache, and needed something to keep him going. Other doctors found the relief he was looking for from a beer or a cocktail, but then they smelled of it. As he unwrapped a pill, Ortenzio was sure no one would ever know, and he popped it in his mouth.

"It was a feeling like I'd never felt before," he told me years later, "this well-being, this increase in energy, able to leap tall buildings with a single bound. I'm tense and nervous and that anxiety is crippling. [The pill] took the anxiety away." The buzz lasted for four hours, propelling him through the night's work. He'd found a friend.

A REVOLUTION IN pain management was beginning through these years, holding that the country was in an epidemic of pain and urging doctors to make far greater use of opiate painkillers.

Americans got used to medical miracles that allowed them to avoid the consequences of unhealthy behavior: treatments for diabetes, high cholesterol, hypertension, and heart disease. As the country aged, patients wanted relief from pain. Doctors would suggest long-term strategies: exercise, better diet, quitting smoking. Patients didn't want to hear that—they just wanted to be fixed. Doctors felt their insistence.

The growth of managed health care required doctors to see an ever-greater volume of patients. Insurance companies, seeing narcotics as cheap and quick, cut back on reimbursing for other pain therapies that did not involve pain pills. Doctors seeing more patients had fewer tools with which to treat their pain, a topic most of them weren't well trained in anyway.

Meanwhile, a new pharma business model emerged: find a blockbuster drug and hire a legion of young sales reps to convince doctors of the miracles being invented. Nationwide, the pharma sales force ballooned from 38,000 in 1995 to more than 102,000 in 2005.

Don Molinari retired, and his kind of drug rep passed from the scene. Docs like Lou Ortenzio were used to a dozen sales reps visiting a week. Now it was a dozen a *day*, all of them young and good-looking, a couple of jobs out of college, and many of them women. The more prescriptions a doc wrote, the more they visited.

Ortenzio's oldest child, Monica, worked in her father's clinic for four summers between 1998 and 2001, while home from college. In the industry, these years are still viewed as the glory days of US pharmaceutical sales. Drug reps alighted daily on the clinic. "I knew them all, but I could not tell you their names," she said. "There were so many of them." When they learned Monica liked cream-filled doughnuts, they sent her some three or four mornings a week.

The new reps had no background in medicine or pharmacy. They were athletes and cheerleaders, former computer salesmen, and ex-military. They were, above all, genial, easy to talk to. They were often the only people Lou Ortenzio saw all day who didn't have something that needed fixing.

Many of them didn't know what they were selling, but they did know how to sell it. They did this, mostly, by giving stuff away. In the literature of psychology, giving stuff away is a quick route to getting people to like you. These new reps came armed with pens, stress balls, calendars, notepads—all the tinsel of the new pharmaceutical sales world, each emblazoned with the pill's name and company's logo.

The reps relied most heavily on one giveaway above all else: food. Some mornings these reps brought breakfast on their doctor visits. But the one thing they never missed—none of them, ever—was lunch. "Each [sales rep] had their turn every three weeks to bring lunch for the office," Monica said, "that's how many reps there were." Each day, a different rep would call her and ask which restaurant the office wanted lunch from: Oliverio's, the Italian place, or China One, or any of the sandwich shops. The smarter reps brought enough food for employees to take home in the evening. At noon every day, the staff ate in the lunchroom, while Lou Ortenzio and that day's drug rep lunched together in the back.

These gifts were intentional, of course, but they were also stand-ins for the real relationships that their predecessors like Don Molinari once had nurtured for years with doctors. The new reps knew little about Clarksburg. They weren't seen at church or at football games. They were part of the anonymity that settled with decline over this small town and so many like it across America. To Monica, Clarksburg felt like one of their stops on a very large route—one that they might transfer out of in a year or so.

In the go-go world of drug sales in the 1990s, the reps selling opioid painkillers were especially aggressive. Among them, Purdue Pharma, pushing OxyContin, stood out. The company paid its reps the highest bonuses ever registered in the industry. One West Virginia doctor I spoke to remembers running away from the Purdue rep when he showed up at her hospital. He would run after her.

The pills were sold as time-saving solutions for harried doctors who had been told that there was an epidemic of pain afoot, but who had little time or training to address it. Drug companies also offered doctors honoraria to speak about their drugs at conferences. That got a lot of attention later. But really, sales reps were good at their jobs because they relentlessly sold one idea: that doctors could end patients' pain without addicting them. This message was potent. Medicine was growing more specialized. Physicians had less time than ever, and patients were demanding miracles.

Opioids provided physicians with what gave them their deepest sense of professional fulfillment: a pleased patient, the feeling of having helped someone. This feeling of service was why so many had entered the profession. Sending a patient home smiling and grateful felt good and right—almost a narcotic itself. Drug companies understood this.

Lou Ortenzio, working every night until 11:00 to keep his patients happy, was that physician. Pain pills fit with his mission to fix as many folks as possible. It was just so much easier to practice medicine by prescribing a pill. The more you did it, the more patients you had. They expected a prescription with each visit; Lou expected to give them one. It wasn't in his makeup to say no to people who loved him. By the end of the 1990s, he was a leading prescriber of pain pills in the region. Neither he nor many others in medicine thought there was anything wrong with that. He had no time for his kids. But it endeared him to patients, and their love kept him in his office until late.

Many used up a month's supply of pills before the month was out; they were insistent, wheedling, demanding more. They lied. Some would curse and scream when he told them he couldn't refill their pain-pill scrips before the month was up, or that he wanted to taper them down. One nurse, suffering from chronic pain and anxiety, would approach him in his office parking lot, bearing gifts of quilts or canned goods, insisting she needed her pills that morning, had run out and couldn't wait for the monthly appointment.

The pain-pill revolution arrived amid Clarksburg's decline and engulfed whole families. The family of Phyllis Mills, Ortenzio's long-time patient, was one. Her husband, Paul, worked for Louie Glass in Weston, a town south of Clarksburg, for thirty-three years. On his salary, they bought a house and raised four kids. He retired when the factory closed in 2003. Their children, by then, could find work only in fast food or telemarketing. Pain pills replaced pot at high school parties.

A woman named Patty was among the first to be prescribed OxyContin in Clarksburg—by Lou Ortenzio. To that, he added benzo-diazapines. She was on disability for many years due to an injured back. Disability insurance provided her a Medicaid insurance card, which in turn gave her access to all the pills a doctor prescribed for her, taxpayer funded, all for a nominal monthly copay. Before long, Patty was hooked and providing those pills to friends with migraines or back pain. They, too, grew addicted, then went to Lou Ortenzio.

"If you had pain, you go to him," said Patty's daughter, Kayla Toryak. "I honestly think he was trying to keep his patients happy. But for years I thought the worst of him. I blamed him for tearing apart my mother."

Her mother's addiction was a constant throughout Kayla's child-hood. Kayla, at age six, found her mother overdosed, foaming at the mouth. Patty slept with men for pills as Kayla waited in the car; she stole money from Kayla: "I had to put a padlock on my door when

I was eight." As a child, Kayla accompanied her mother to Ortenzio's office, waiting among throngs of patients for hours before this doctor could see her mother. Within ten minutes, her mother would be out again. Kayla remembers her father yelling over the phone at Ortenzio to stop prescribing his wife these pills. "I never had friends over," Kayla told me. "I found her overdosed many times. Her addiction always came before me. I went without food and toilet paper."

Despite it all, Kayla was a straight-A student and a star athlete. When her high school basketball team vied for the state championship, her mother showed up high and couldn't hold the sign bearing the family last name; the mother of a teammate held the sign for her.

For Doc O, meanwhile, that late-night encounter with Vicodin in 1988 began a slow slide. By the mid-1990s, as a new drug sales force visited him daily, he was using the free samples. When he ran out, he found a friend, a middle-aged patient he could trust.

"I'm in some trouble," Ortenzio told him. "If I write you this prescription, can I ask you to fill it and bring it back to me?"

"Sure thing," the man said. "You're the doc."

Soon a dozen or so trusted patients were helping out Doc O. He was gobbling twenty or thirty Vicodins a day, hiding them above the tiles in his ceiling. He knew the acetaminophen in those Vicodins was harming his liver, but the hydrocodone was impossible to do without. In about 1999 he began writing pain-pill prescriptions in his children's names. His decline was a long time in coming, "but that," he said much later, "was my demise."

SEVEN YEARS LATER, in 2006, Tom Dyer was at home one Friday night. With his unruly white hair and glasses often perched on his nose, Dyer is a well-known guy in northern West Virginia, one of the region's leading criminal defense attorneys. That night, he ordered a pizza.

A while later, the doorbell rang. Dyer opened the door, and there stood Lou Ortenzio with a pie. For a brief moment, Dyer was confused.

Then he understood: Doc O was now the pizza guy. Standing at the door, "I was just speechless," Dyer remembered years later.

Those seven years had been a long road down for Lou Ortenzio. He had divorced his wife and remarried a woman who was a nurse at a local hospital. Through the last stages of his pill addiction, Ortenzio, a long-lapsed Catholic, found Jesus Christ in his appointment room. A patient prayed over him as Ortenzio knelt on the linoleum. In September 2003, with his wife's help, he tapered off the drugs at home. A couple of months later, he was baptized in a section of nearby Elk Creek where baptisms have taken place since the early 1800s.

He knew firsthand the danger in the pills he once embraced. They had been marketed to doctors as a boon to their practices. But Lou Ortenzio now saw them as a curse. He had no idea how to get his patients off them. Cutting people off made them sick. Ortenzio had treated these patients for years, and he knew every member of their families. There weren't enough pain clinics or specialists to refer them to in the area. Insurance companies still didn't reimburse for a lot of pain treatment that didn't involve the pills. He had few other pain-treatment tools at his disposal; it's unclear whether his patients would have accepted, say, exercise and other changes in behavior that those treatments require. So even as he got off the pills, he kept prescribing. "I had a hard time saying no."

Then federal agents raided his office. They interrogated his staff and confiscated hundreds of records. Their investigation dragged on for two years. His children testified before a grand jury that they knew nothing of the prescriptions their father wrote in their names. In 2006, prosecutors charged Ortenzio with health-care fraud and fraudulent prescribing. That year, 371 West Virginians died from narcotic over-doses, double the national rate. Statewide, physicians were writing 130 opioid prescriptions for every hundred West Virginians.

Working so late every night, Ortenzio had never been close with his children. The federal case destroyed what little existed between them. Later, his daughter Monica Ortenzio would remember patients telling her that her father was the most wonderful person alive. Some called Doc O a saint. That did not describe the distant man she knew. It felt strange to her that they would believe they knew him that well. Or maybe, she thought later, those patients were all leaving with large pill prescriptions. "He was a workaholic," she said many years later. "We spent a lot of time not knowing my father. He much preferred spending time with his patients."

More than a hundred of those patients wrote to the judge on behalf of Doc O. He hired Tom Dyer to defend him. He received five years supervised release—though no prison time. He lost his medical license, and his case was reported in the newspaper. Ortenzio's arrest sent terror through his patients across Harrison County. Kayla Toryak's mother and her friends were hysterical: "There was this huge desperation in finding a doctor who would prescribe them all the things that Lou did." Her mother went to the street for pills, which were too expensive, and she eventually turned to heroin. One night, she left a note on the table in the family's trailer, saying she was going to Cleveland. It was several years before Kayla saw her mother again.

Lou Ortenzio was now fifty-two and unemployed, with a criminal record. Never once had he filled out a résumé or worked outdoors. When a temp agency offered him a landscaping job at a golf course where, as a doctor, he took his family for Sunday brunch, he jumped at it. It paid $6.50 an hour. He did that for a couple of months, digging ditches. He worked as the janitor at a local community center and then returned to the golf course as a full-time landscaper.

Meanwhile, he found night work delivering for a local pizzeria, learning the shortcuts through town from Phyllis Mills's twenty-five-year-old nephew, also a former patient, who managed the place. Word spread, and folks were pained to see Doc O, in his Subaru sedan, delivering pizza to the hospital where he'd once seen patients. Yet the way Lou Ortenzio told me the story, every pie he delivered liberated him. His pizza shifts ended, and he had no late-night patient phone calls to return. No need to remember in which ceiling tile he'd hidden his stash of pills. Pizza delivery offered him a more humbled view of his place in the world. He was no longer the center of the universe to whom everyone came with their problems. All he had to remember was to bring the salad with the pepperoni pizza.

"You can't go wrong with pizza delivery," he told me. "You make people happy; that was what I had liked about being a doctor. You drive up, hot food in the car. You can hear the kids screaming, 'The pizza guy's here!' I made pizza deliveries where I used to make house calls. I delivered pizzas to people who were former patients. They felt very uncomfortable, felt sorry for me. But I loved seeing them again. It didn't bother me. I was in a much better place."

In Clarksburg, Lou Ortenzio was the first doc prosecuted for charges connected to overprescribing of narcotic pain relievers; he was the first to show residents that this was a new kind of American plague, with the drug supply not flowing from street dealers but from doctors and drug company reps. He embodied the new addict: a respected professional with a plaque on the wall, not a toothless back-alley user. And he was the first to publicly work at his own recovery without shame. "Most people would crawl into a hole," said Tom Dyer. "Lou went just the other direction."

All that began when Doc O, this beloved now-former physician, began delivering pizza to the townsfolk he had treated for thirty years. Much later, it took him to the frontlines in the next stage of the epidemic.

PART II

Angie and Starla II

"Like Our Family Survived and Had a Baby"

One day, toward the end of July of 2012, orderlies wheeled a woman on a bed down a corridor beneath fluorescent lights and into the maternal medicine ward of Sacred Heart Hospital in Pensacola, on Florida's panhandle.

She had green eyes and raven hair. She was a drug addict and a prostitute. She was in a vegetative state caused by several hours without oxygen following an overdose in a motel from a combination of drugs. She was now blind, could neither speak nor hear, couldn't walk, and had to be fed intravenously. But she was restless, and she turned often, and that was among the few expressions of her personality.

Her name was Starla Hope Hoss. She was from eastern Tennessee and two months pregnant.

The director of the ward was Jim Thorp, a doctor who had worked with pregnant, drug-addicted women as the pain revolution in American medicine spread. For years now, the casualties of that revolution had streamed through his ward—women giving birth to drug-dependent infants. But the most serious case Jim Thorp ever saw was Starla Hoss.

SHE HAD GROWN up in the town of Elizabethton, Tennessee, pop. 13,000. Her mother, Maude Buchanan, had fled her family when she was young, having been molested. She met Bill Hoss, who was sixty-five years old, and moved in with him, living with him until his death thirteen years later. They had two children. Starla was eight when her father died.

Beginning at age eleven, Starla was in and out of youth group homes. When she was sober, Starla was quiet and cheerful. When high, she wanted to fight. She began cutting herself at age twelve. She would use any drug: meth, opiates, bath salts. Later, she often landed in Carter County Jail. She married another addict in jail. They had a son, but the marriage soon dissolved. In 2010 or so, Starla moved to nearby Mountain City, known on the street as Meth Mountain for its robust meth-cooking industry. She found work at a Burger King and kept using whatever drug came her way.

One day a narcotics detective busted Starla at home with a boyfriend using meth. That began her career as an informant for the detective. Her fees for informing earned her more than her Burger King job. "She was paying two hundred to three hundred dollars just for drugs, all coming from [the detective]," Maude said. "She was busting that many people. These people lost their kids, their homes." Before long, word was she was on a hit list.

Starla fled to Pensacola with a boyfriend, leaving her son with her mother, and not long after, someone shot up her house in Mountain City. Later, Maude could gather only a few details of her daughter's months in Pensacola. Starla and her boyfriend arrived with nothing but their drug habits. Soon they were in a homeless encampment. At some point she met another man, Patrick, a user with a long record of petty crimes who, Maude believes, had her working as a street prostitute. Maude called, but this man often kept her daughter off the phone. When Starla did talk, she kept it brief. Patrick didn't allow her to leave their motel. After he lost his truck, they were on foot.

"They wasn't eating nothing," Maude told me. "They'd steal work crews' coolers. Whatever was in the cooler when they stole them was what they had to eat. For clothes, they'd knock over Salvation Army bins. I talked to her one night. She was waiting on some restaurant to bring some food out to the dumpster. She said, 'It's not nasty or nothing. Actually it's pretty good food.' "

By then, Starla told her, she was pregnant again and trying to stop using drugs.

Two days later Maude called, and Patrick told her Starla was at work. Maude called the motel room again later, and a girl told her Starla was at the hospital. Maude called the hospital. "You have a very sick daughter," a nurse told Maude. "You need to get down there." Maude can't drive and had no money. She borrowed from a pawn shop and rented a car. It was the only way her half brother would agree to drive her to Pensacola.

"I get there and she's just laying there," unconscious, tubes in her mouth and arm, Maude said. "Her feet looked like she had walked them off her body. I said, 'What happened to my baby's feet?' I ain't never seen anybody's feet bad as hers was."

Patrick told her they'd lost his truck and were walking everywhere. Starla had lost her shoes somewhere and after that, Maude believed, she worked barefoot as a prostitute to support their habits. On July 23, she had overdosed on several drugs. Patrick waited for hours to call 911, fearing the consequences. During that time, doctors believe, Starla's brain was damaged. The day Maude saw Patrick at the hospital was the last she saw of him. Maude had no money for lodging, so she and her half brother drove back to Elizabethton.

It fell to Sacred Heart staff to care for Starla, this woman no one knew, as the baby grew inside her. No one visited her. Nurses were left to wonder how she came to be there. They put her in a room across from the nurse's station so they could better attend to her, and they added curtains, flowers, and a radio so she could listen to music. Nurses and doctors spoke to her every day. "Hi friend, what are you doing today? We're here to give you a bath." Her eyes would follow them as they moved across her room.

As her tummy grew, Starla gyrated more. The nurses took turns sitting by her all day. Ellen Stanley was the nursing supervisor. "We didn't know if she would spontaneously abort," she told me. "We had no clues how long the pregnancy would sustain itself. I've been a nurse forty-two years in maternity, and I had never taken care of a patient like this."

The Reverend Ellen Blaise was the hospital's chaplain at the time. She was given a small harp as exercise therapy for her left arm, which she had badly injured in an accident. Her husband helped her recover, pushing her arms dozens of times a day. After her husband died, playing the harp became more than just a way of repairing her arm. It pulled her from her grief. She began playing it for patients as therapy—theirs and hers. Mostly she plucked simple spirituals—"Jesus Loves Me," "Swing Low Sweet Chariot," and "Be Thou My Vision." Several times a week, she played for Starla Hoss, and the music calmed Starla's thrashing.

Maude returned again a few months later, and Rev. Blaise found her a place to stay. They spoke often, sitting in the room with curtains as Starla twisted and turned. Then Maude went home.

Starla needed medicine to prevent pneumonia and blood clots. As they gave her shots, or started an IV, they watched her every movement, her anxiety, her grimaces, aware that this might cause her pain but that she could not communicate it.

On January 18, 2013, Starla Hoss gave birth by C-section, several weeks prematurely, to a daughter who came into the world with her umbilical cord wrapped around her neck and affected by the drugs the staff gave her mother to prevent clotting. The nursing staff cried in awe of the child and the mother, who tossed and turned and could not speak. "It was like our family survived and had a baby," said Ellen Stanley.

But the work was unrelenting and didn't stop just because Starla Hoss had given birth. There were many addicted women, still more infants in withdrawal. Jim Thorp and the nurses at Sacred Heart were running to keep up. The baby remained in the hospital for weeks. Starla, though, was taken from the ward, and years later, Thorp could no longer recall the last time he saw her.

Fentanyl I

Magic Bullet

S tarting in about 2014, a fentanyl gold rush began.

Following the bust of Ricardo Valdez-Torres's lab in Toluca in 2006, fentanyl had vanished from US streets. The opioid epidemic continued to surge nationwide via prescription painkillers. By 2013, many pain-pill users had become addicts and were switching to heroin. To those familiar with the drug world, that seemed where things would stay. But fentanyl was too profitable, and the swelling new market was too enticing. Thus, by 2015, a drug unknown to all but surgeons and anesthesiologists emerged as the third stage in the national epidemic. Clusters of twenty or fifty overdoses bloomed around the country—of people using heroin into which fentanyl had been crudely mixed.

Droves of dealers flocked to it. Some were addicts, or dealers of other drugs—crack or heroin. Others were computer-savvy entrepreneurs with no experience dealing dope. Yet virtually none of them had any idea how to properly mix such a potent substance.

That became clear as narcotics agents busted fentanyl mixing sites. These were often dumpy places, kitchens or basements strewn with unwashed utensils and crumpled fast-food wrappers. As agents busted these sites in those first years of street fentanyl, they discovered one of the reasons for this surging mortality. The amateur fentanyl mixers' tool of choice, it turned out, was the most successful product in the history of infomercials: the Magic Bullet blender.

When a pharmaceutical company invents a new drug, it spends a lot of time and money on the form in which that drug will be consumed by the public—especially if it's a powder. Chemists perform mixing tests. They combine the new drug with other filler powders in an enclosed stainless-steel bin that gyrates head over heels at a steady rate. The chemists take a sample of this mixture after five minutes of blending, another after ten minutes, then a third at fifteen minutes, and so on. Each sample then is dissolved in water and put through what's known as high-performance liquid chromatography—a process that identifies the percentage of each compound in that mixture.

This testing aims to learn how long the new drug and the blending powders must be mixed to create what's known in the industry as "blend uniformity validation"—in other words, that the drug is evenly spread throughout the mixture. Blend uniformity is the essential step in creating "content uniformity"—which is defined as a 95 percent certainty that the same amount of the drug is in each pill or capsule the company sells to the public.

Carl Anderson, a professor in the School of Pharmacy at Duquesne University in Pittsburgh and concerned with methods of drug mixing and manufacture, explained this process to me. "If you don't have material blended well," he told me, "you can never have an equal apportionment in each dose." Nothing stalls a new drug's release to the market like what the industry calls "failure of content uniformity," and drug companies devote a great deal of money and expertise to prevent it.

You could say, then, that what was taking place in America by 2015 was, in pharmaceutical terms, a "failure of content uniformity" on a national scale.

At first supplies of fentanyl were coming mostly through the mail, sold by anonymous vendors through marketplaces on the darknet, a part of the internet that requires an encrypted connection. Much of it was produced by China's new, sophisticated chemical companies, who'd learned from the joint venture with Belgian chemist Paul Janssen.

Fentanyl's greatest advantage to dealers was its potency. Very little of the drug was enough to get people high. That, in turn, made it easy to smuggle. Fentanyl's potency was also its drawback. If minute amounts of the drug could get you high, even a tiny bit more could kill you—the equivalent of a few grains of salt. To be handled and sold to users, it had to be mixed with larger quantities of other powders, each white like fentanyl. Indeed, never before had the drug underworld seen its profit, and so much profit at that, tied to the delicate task of mixing powders, particularly one as potent as fentanyl. Use of the Magic Bullet was a sign of how little each dealer knew about drug mixing—or cared.

"At every fentanyl search warrant we do there's a Magic Bullet—every one," said Mike Schmidt, a veteran narcotics investigator in Akron, Ohio, a town plagued by overdoses in a state that saw among the country's first fentanyl outbreaks.

"We go into these [drug-mixing] houses and we see thirty Magic Bullet blenders," said Jon DeLena, the DEA chief for New England, which saw similar surges in fentanyl overdoses.

After fentanyl began to hit Vancouver, British Columbia, in 2014, "we saw Magic Bullet blenders all the time," along with similar brands of blenders, said John Hartnett, corporal in the Royal Canadian Mounted Police Clandestine Lab unit. "There didn't seem to be any concern [among mixers] about the impact that this might have. This was the easiest way to blend their product and good enough, in their opinion."

The precise role that underground misuse of the Magic Bullet played in the tens of thousands of American deaths due to fentanyl is impossible to know. What is true is that as narcotics agents busted more and more fentanyl mixing sites in 2014 and into 2015—in houses, kitchens, apartments—the Magic Bullet turned up again and again. So did coffee grinders. But it seemed amateur mixers held the Magic Bullet in special reverence.

The blender's patent is held by Lenny Sands, CEO of Alchemy Worldwide LLC out of Sherman Oaks, a neighborhood of Los Angeles, which released the appliance in 2003. Mr. Sands is a recognized master of the infomercial. In Sands's scripted shows, the lovable couple Mick and Mimi use the Magic Bullet to meet every request of demanding houseguests: smoothies, salsa, guacamole, ground coffee, sliced apples, "even hard cheeses." The infomercial roused Magic Bullet sales to hundreds of millions of dollars across some fifty countries and single-handedly created the easy-to-clean personal-blender market. (We have one in my house; we use it to make smoothies, and we swear by it.)

Nothing in the infomercial, of course, suggests that the Magic Bullet ought to be used to mix synthetic narcotics. Yet that's just what happened.

The tiny dynamo proved an especially poor blender of highly potent, synthetic narcotic powders. Blender blades spin; spinning blades create a vortex, and an effective mix, when the substance is a liquid, but none at all when the substances are dry powders. When both powders are white, it not only creates a notoriously bad mix, but also is impossible to tell how poor the mix actually is.

Still, fentanyl spread. It did so because it was the drug underworld's great democratizer, and the Magic Bullet was some part of that. A more complicated, expensive, hard-to-find mixing machine might have deterred many of these new fentanyl dealers. Instead, the Magic Bullet was cheap—$29.95 at any Target, Walmart, or Best Buy. Its very name seemed to promise a solution to all of one's problems. It enclosed the mixture in a plastic bulb; you didn't need to use an open bowl from which you might inhale the product's dust. Each dealer appeared to imagine that this tiny appliance was not only great for making smoothies and salsa, but also all he needed to rake in millions from a synthetic substitute for heroin.

The blender fit snugly with fentanyl's disruptive allure, which was this: that with a minuscule investment of learning and money, anyone—even someone in boxer shorts in his mother's basement, without education nor connection to mafias or traffickers—could now make a killing. And beginning in about 2015, they did.

Neuroscience II

"These Rats Weren't on Heroin.
They Were on Sugar"

One morning in 2002, the staff in the Hoebel Lab sat around the oblong table in the basement of Green Hall at Princeton University.

They occupied a large windowless room. At the table that day were Bart Hoebel, the Princeton psychologist who led the lab; Pedro Rada, a Venezuelan doctor who had been coming to the lab for several years to work on its experiments; and several graduate students, among them Nicole Avena.

Avena was twenty-four and two years into earning her neuroscience PhD. The lab's basement digs reflected neuroscience's status at the time. Still, it was all she had hoped—exciting, do-it-yourself science, surrounded by energetic colleagues and mentors, studying an area few had considered and for which there was still little scientific evidence: the addictive properties of sugar.

The lab had been testing these properties on lab rats, and researchers found that sugar provoked reactions similar to those from drugs of abuse. Sugar seemed to play upon the same reward pathways in the brain as opiates, alcohol, and amphetamine. With those results in hand, Hoebel's goal was now to test sugar-dependent rats for the reactions that the American Psychiatric Association said defined addiction to drugs. Among these reactions were tolerance, cravings, and willingness to endure hardship to obtain and use a drug. They also wanted to test whether the animals, when deprived of sugar, entered withdrawal.

With that in mind, Hoebel had a suggestion that morning. Why not, he said, give a sugar-dependent rat the drug naloxone?

Naloxone is better known today by the brand name Narcan. It stops overdoses to opioids like heroin, fentanyl, or oxycodone. Naloxone immediately revives a person who is overdosing. However, the large doses that paramedics must apply to those overdosing on the street often send the person into withdrawal, the symptoms of which are, among other things, shaking, shivering, and anxiety. Today, naloxone is widely available as a lifesaver for heroin and fentanyl overdoses. At the time, though, it was known mostly to scientists and paramedics.

Hoebel's theory was that if sugar is addictive because it affects the brain in the way that morphine and heroin do, then providing those rats naloxone ought to have an effect. Sitting at the table that morning, Nicole Avena was skeptical. "I didn't think we would see signs of withdrawal," she said. Despite several successful experiments showing rats behaving on sugar as if they were on an opiate, this one just seemed too far-fetched. Still, being a freewheeling kind of lab, the group went along with Hoebel's hunch.

They set aside two groups of ten rats—one group dependent on daily, unlimited doses of sugar water, the other dependent on nothing. Then they gave each group of rats naloxone.

One reason scientists use rats for experiments is that they can discern emotions from the rodents' facial expressions and body language: pleasure, for example, or disgust; another emotion they can detect is anxiety. Anxious rats groom excessively and have a tremor in their forepaws.

As the naloxone took effect on the sugar-dependent rats, those were the first responses the lab noticed—the grooming and the shaking forepaws. Then the rats' teeth began to chatter. Avena had been working with rats for some time. "I had never in my life heard a rodent's teeth click like that," she said. The rats that were not dependent on sugar, meanwhile, were calm and unaffected by the naloxone.

Finally, the sugar-dependent rats began the "wet-dog shake"—a fero-cious shaking similar to what a dog does to dry off. These were symp-toms of withdrawal from an opiate, like heroin. "I wasn't expecting to see that," Avena told me. "These rats weren't on heroin. They were on sugar."

They published a paper on the experiment in the journal *Obesity Research* in 2002 and began going to conferences to present the results. Avena had grown used to researchers attending her seminars with arms crossed in skepticism at the idea of addiction to food, of a food affecting the brain's reward system the same way dope does. This time, though, she felt a different body language. Researchers were intrigued, full of questions about the idea that administering naloxone to a sugar-dependent rat sent it into withdrawal, same as it would to a heroin addict. Arms uncrossed. Hoebel returned from conferences excited at similar reactions.

Through the next few years, the Princeton lab emerged as a leader in the country in studying the addictive properties of sugar. "People were really starting to be keen on this idea," Avena said.

It was the right time—quantities of both sugar and opioids were flooding America.

The amounts of sugar in processed foods were reaching levels never before sold commercially in America. The American Heart Association would set guidelines for how much daily sugar consumption was healthy (six teaspoons for women; nine for men). Still, the food and drink indus-tries urged Americans on to ever-greater consumption of sugar, made cheap by government subsidies. Within a decade, one Frappuccino would come larded with more than double the daily sugar intake recom-mended by those AHA guidelines. Processed food, designed in labora-tories, massed ever-greater amounts of sugar, sometimes bundling it unnaturally with fat (sugar and fat are not found together in nature). Companies sold it in the form of cereals, cookies, cakes, sodas, sweet teas, condiments, and more. It was a commercial assault of an addictive substance that was likely without equal—other than alcohol and nico-tine, of course.

Meanwhile, the massive quantities of pain pills prescribed by doctors spread across the United States. Unprecedented addiction and overdose death followed. The drug underworld jumped to meet the newly created demand. First with heroin, coming in cheap and potent, mostly from Mexico. Then with illicit fentanyl, often mixed badly with a Magic Bullet blender.

Fentanyl II

Tommy Rauh

Tommy Rauh loved being big. He stood at just over six feet tall, and he weighed well more than two hundred pounds.

He enjoyed his role as his younger siblings' protector, his sister Ursula believed, and she thought of him as heroic and strong. He was the family Santa Claus at Christmas, and arranged fireworks displays on land they owned in southern Ohio on July 4. As a kid, he led his younger siblings in games, and as an adult he read bedtime stories to his young niece. He loved spy novels, and he played piano, guitar, and harmonica. He took his younger brother, Ted, to parties, to ride dirt bikes, and to hang out with his friends. He was a proficient scuba diver, and he produced a few raves when that was something that daring, rebellious kids did. He could talk to almost anyone.

Among his peers, too, he was a leader—a magnetic personality, big, like a Viking, they remembered, handsome with blond hair that he grew into a long ponytail his freshman year in high school. But Tommy wasn't much on school. He enrolled at four high schools in four years, never quite fitting in. Like a lot of young nonconformists, he used drugs—mostly marijuana and mushrooms. He had beautiful girl-friends, including a dancer who was an older woman, and this awed his high school friends. "If he'd played football, he'd have been the quarter-back, with a cheerleader for a girlfriend," said his friend, Shawn Cook. "But he was nonconformist to a fault."

Akron was a center of rubber and tire manufacturing. The industry spawned an ecosystem of satellite businesses. Jim Rauh, Tommy's father, was part of that. A junkman at heart, Jim Rauh took scrap rubber and recycled it. In the 1970s the rubber business declined, and Akron's tire-making headed to Korea and China. Factories emptied and their brick shells reminded everyone of what had been. But chemical research remained, and in time rubber scientists came up with ways to meld plastics and rubber into better tires. Akron turned to plastics and to polymers. Jim Rauh sold his rubber recycling company and pivoted to the new opportunities. He recycled plastic and from that progressed to making casings to protect cables and high-temperature wire.

Jim Rauh was also in the first wave of US businessmen to go to China in the 1980s, as Deng Xiaoping opened the country to trade with the West. Jim Rauh brought over containers of scrap thermoplastics, videotape, and chemicals that he'd recycled from Akron companies— none of which the Chinese could produce. His Chinese buyers went through these containers by hand, pulling out what they thought they could figure out how to use. They made marine rope by weaving together the mountains of discarded videotape Rauh brought with him. He was there at the beginning of the Chinese retail-goods revolution and watched as they learned to make plastic plates, plastic trays, shoe soles, and traffic cones.

It was a frighteningly poor country then, with horrible roads and desperate people. Life revolved around family and reverence for ancestors—though as years passed, a reverence for money and social standing emerged as well. Rauh noticed, too, the power of the government. A Communist Party official was the center of civic life in every village. Nothing happened without his hand in it.

Still, Jim Rauh felt a kinship with the Chinese. Like him, they were consummate junkmen, finding value in what others discarded. His visits spanned a decade. He saw an industrial sophistication emerging, and the clearest sign of that, he noticed, was the chemical companies that began to form. Soon there were hundreds of them. By the mid-1990s, Chinese companies could generate computer models of any chemical molecule, complete with its atomic weight—all done in clean, well-lighted labs.

Tommy Rauh went to work for his father at the family's rubber manufacturing plant in Akron. He had a streak of the salesman in him. He took it as a challenge to find a buyer for the large used machines that occasionally ended up in the Rauh warehouse. He never went to college, but as his father had not either, this was not viewed as a problem. The work was often physical. This was before widespread automation made it rare for workers to lift anything. Tommy liked the job and working for this father. Along the way, though, from an injury at the shop, he developed tendinitis. And so, early in 2002, at twenty-three, he went to a doctor.

Today, the treatment for tendinitis includes rest, physical therapy, and anti-inflammatories like ibuprofen or aspirin; surgery in the worst cases. Nowhere is there a suggestion that the ailment requires opiates, which mask pain and thus most likely would only serve to aggravate the stress on the tendon. But the pain-pill revolution was then in full swing. The doctor gave Tommy Rauh a renewable prescription for OxyContin.

A while later, Tommy had his wisdom teeth removed. Dentists, too, were prescribing large bottles of narcotic painkillers—thirty days' worth of pills for pain that dentists knew would last two or three days. This was standard now. Every year, 48 million routine surgeries took place in America. Virtually every patient during those years left with renewable prescriptions for big bottles of thirty, sixty, or ninety pain pills of one brand or another. Thus a firehose of prescription narcotics blasted at the US public for close to two decades. Routine surgeries became a gateway to addiction. The removal of wisdom teeth from what the American Dental Association estimates as five million Americans every year was part of that. Dentists feared losing patients should anyone feel pain from the operation; parents feared their kids might suffer from the surgery. Most of those dental patients took home bottles of sixty pain pills at a time. Thus wisdom-tooth removal led many into addiction, particularly young people. In 2003, one of those was Tommy Rauh.

One night at their cousin's house, he was alone with Ursula. He was unable to stop taking these pills, he told his sister. He didn't know what to do. He choked up. He had done something that he feared had changed him. He was afraid that it was too late to come back, that he might never be the same. Years later, Ursula thought back on that moment and knew that for her big, strong older brother to confide this to her, and to admit his powerlessness—well, that was something significant. At the time, it seemed a manageable problem to her. She went against his wishes and told her parents. They were just pills, prescribed by doctors. We'll get through this, she thought; we'll fix this. This should be no problem for someone like Tommy.

IN THE LATE 1960s, to the alarm of their countrymen and elected officials, US soldiers fighting in Vietnam began returning home addicted to heroin. Yet the great majority of those soldiers kicked dope when they got home. They were no longer at war. They were distant from the drugs. They were back home in places where heroin, if there was any at all, was expensive and feeble. The Far East heroin of the 1970s crossed two continents and an ocean and went through New York before reaching the addict's arm, weak and expensive. Nothing like what they'd encountered in Southeast Asia.

By the late 1990s, that changed. The supply of prescription pain pills was massive and everywhere, because doctors prescribed them. Heroin followed; supplies skyrocketed, and prices fell. If the pills were potent, the heroin was more so, for it came now from relatively close by, in Colombia and Mexico. Unlike those soldiers returning from Vietnam, these new addicts could not escape it. The dope was at their high schools, in their locker rooms. Even small rural towns had pill and heroin dealers. The sellers popped up in states with no history of opioid abuse: Utah, Tennessee, West Virginia, Oklahoma, Maine, Indiana, North Carolina, and they were all over the state of Ohio.

It was into this gathering maelstrom that Tommy Rauh entered, with his OxyContin prescriptions for tendinitis and for his extracted wisdom teeth. Within the year, he was abusing it to deal with pain on the job and the occasional hangover. He had come from a middle-class White counterculture where drug use was a form of adventure, particularly for a young man who had intellect and a thrill-seeking soul. That culture, however, formed in a time when the drugs were more forgiving than the street offerings of the new millennium. Attitudes hadn't changed, but the dope had. The days of recreational drug use were over in America. The drugs came fanged now: highly potent marijuana, corrosive methamphetamine, and powerful narcotic pain pills in unprecedented supply.

The family isn't clear when Tom Rauh switched from pain pills to smoking, then injecting, heroin. Maybe 2003 or the next year. It was as if he'd fallen in love—like seeing God, he told his sister, and he wanted to do it all day long. Heroin's withdrawal, though, wreaked vengeance; it was worse than with OxyContin. Eventually he went into addiction treatment and detoxed. Well, that's over, Jim Rauh thought. "I didn't realize the depths of compulsion that addiction brings," he said. "I didn't know it would keep haunting you day after day, keep tugging at you."

What his parents did see was that their son was not the same ebullient, adventurous lad. The nonconformist grew obedient—to dope. His talent as a salesman he turned on his family, selling them on the idea that he was fine, or on his siblings when he needed a ride or some cash. He relinquished what once gave him joy. To his siblings, it seemed as if some of him just departed. They waited for it to return, and it didn't. Life without dope turned drab, as if without heroin Tommy could not be happy again. This, too, was something that his family did not at first understand and came to realize only at great cost—that without his drug, an addict was left "so unfilled, so hollow," as Jim Rauh said later. "You're half the person you were."

Like many people with loved ones addicted to opiates, Tommy's sister, Ursula, later came to view the drug as almost a living thing, an alien beast. "Heroin is like a parasite," she wrote later, "it wants to survive and needs a host." Tommy Rauh couldn't rid himself of it.

Within his family, his addiction created anger, disappointment, disgust. They hid it from the world, and he hid the details from them. Was he using again? Was he on methadone? Or not? The lying and conniving were constant. Where did the person they loved end, and the disease they hated begin? The line blurred to invisibility. His siblings longed for their fun-loving brother; he would appear, and that gave them hope. But most of Tom's days were about finding drugs, asking for favors, money, or rides. The brain reward circuitry was fully activated, and the me-first impulse was stronger than any other motivation. "Every once in a while, if he'd scored, you could hold a conversation with him," said Ted. Obedience to the dope's mastery kept Tom from a trip to Europe that his siblings took one summer. They organized an intervention and forced him into a car to take him to a rehab center. On the way he jumped from the moving vehicle.

At home, even when it was bad, it was good—and vice versa. There was a warmth to the family when he was around, even when they knew he was using. He was Tommy when he was the lovable big brother; Tom when he was high. If he couldn't escape the dope, neither could his family. It moved in and lived with the Rauhs, lurking, part of every family decision.

Tommy went through a dozen rehabs in a decade. But the signs his family learned to read would always return. Treatment, then relapse. The supply of dope he found on the streets was unrelenting. Valorie Rauh, his mother, ached through the years as she witnessed her boy's transformation. She came to believe that he felt submerged underwater, and that heroin had convinced him it was the oxygen he needed to live. It had that kind of power to grind him down, even as he hated it, hated himself for buckling before it, and at times strained to break its hold. "When you see them suffer for years, for a decade of fighting, trying . . . you're not sure what to do," she said. "We tried everything with Tom." They sequestered him for a year on the remote farm the family owned, with no car, no keys, no phone. They would see him every weekend and bring him food. He looked healthy and built a patio and painted the house. They had finally found a way to keep him and the dope separate. But when he came back, the conniving did, too.

He spent nine months in a Northern California rehab center run by Scientologists. He stayed in California for another couple of years, using heroin, then joining a methadone program. There were long periods when he was away and his family heard from him only by phone. He came home sober, but soon was using again. He went to rehab in Florida, then to Mexico for therapy with ibogaine, a treatment for heroin that is illegal in the United States; there he spent time in a sensory deprivation chamber. It was as if a little more of the true Tommy returned after that, but it didn't stay. "He wanted nothing more than to defeat his addiction, to be with his family, to be welcomed and wanted and whole," Ursula wrote. But the dope was everywhere. "He didn't have to seek it—it was always knocking on his door."

His addiction was a decade old when fentanyl arrived. By 2015, it had crowded out the heroin on Akron's streets, and more people than ever were dying.

Spring returned to Akron that March, and so did Tommy, back from California and using again. He spent an afternoon on Ursula's back stoop. His father had taken his cell phone. Every addict's cell phone quickly fills with drug contacts, making the SIM cards an invitation to relapse. Tommy was nonetheless upset at his father about the phone. He had survived, so there was, too, a feeling his family perceived that he knew more than others his age, that some precious qualities were still intact. Yet he spoke of feeling passed by. He'd known his hometown in its doldrums, which is when he had felt most at home in it—romantically grungy. But now Akron was moving ahead; it shimmered and ran from that tough past. He and his buddies for whom recreational drugs had turned into something far more serious were left behind, standing and watching. He'd spent years grinding out the dope life. At thirty-seven, so much had happened, and he couldn't remember where all the time went. He felt old and that somehow he could no longer compete in this new world.

Through it all, though, Tommy Rauh remained optimistic. For all that dope took from him—from OxyContin to heroin—it never took that away. He'd fail and get up and try again. Neither he nor his family imagined he might not have another chance, not have the time, his sister wrote years later, "to find his way back."

Fentanyl III

"Is This Really Happening?"

By the beginning of 2014, as Akron, Ohio, rebounded from industrial decline, deaths from heroin overdoses were rising steadily.

Akron had last seen the drug during the 1970s, a decade of inertia, acrimony, and negativity in which heroin felt right at home. Those were dreary years for American towns that made things. Countries around the world learned to make those things cheaper and compete in ways few US workers or factory managers ever envisioned. The decade ground down a lot of towns, leaving them with empty factories, blighted storefronts, and a feeling of something essential eroding. Heroin happened to come along at the same time, dimming their optimism.

Forty years later, the drug somehow accompanied the arrival of better times. Old brick factories were filled or filling with workers. Akron was innovative again, in plastics this time. The city's most famous son, basketball superstar LeBron James, announced his return to the Cavaliers in Cleveland, forty minutes north, after jilting the region four years earlier for the Miami Heat. The rekindled vibe made heroin as incongruous in the new Akron as it was unwelcome. Then fentanyl, coming out of nowhere, started dropping people like a sniper's bullets.

In the spring of 2014 the chief of the city's police department, James Nice, called in two veteran narcotics detectives—Mike Schmidt and Tim Harvey. They were sons of Akron, graduating from Archbishop

Hoban High School a year apart. Both were raised by fathers who worked in the rubber plants and were laid off as those jobs evaporated. The detectives had worked patrol together, then shifted to the street narcotics unit, where the action was. Eventually they set up in the Pit, the Akron police bullpen that housed dozens of officers—local, state, and federal—all working drug cases.

Back then, the public nature of street-corner crack sales was accompanied by unrelenting mayhem—shootings, carjackings, and beatings over drug debts. The unit's target was the dealers selling crack on the corners. Schmidt and Harvey would make a few buys, then take down a drug house. "Two buys and a door" was how the unit described it.

The opioid epidemic was very different. It came with no street violence to speak of. On the contrary, it spread because it was quiet, insidious. Crime rates fell across America as addiction and overdoses rose. Instead of violence, the dead were the barometers now.

Later, some people would claim that the opioid addiction epidemic was only getting attention because the great majority of its victims were middle-class White people. That was true. The other truth was that the plague hid for years *because* so many of its victims were middle-class Whites. Families seared by the loss also had to navigate the shame. They covered up, mortified at how their loved ones had died, afraid to stain their memories. Newspaper obituaries reported that a twenty-seven-year-old died of a "heart attack"; a middle-aged brother "died suddenly" at home. Amid this nationwide silence the plague festered, metastasized, and, like a virus, took on a life of its own.

Behind each body rose a chain of dealers who remained unknown because so much of their work was done quietly—via cell phone and not in street sales. In 2014 a record number of Ohioans died from drug overdoses: 2,531. Of those, 156 died in Summit County, where Akron is located. That put the county at third highest in Ohio, and among the worst in the country. Added to that, fentanyl was muscling out heroin as the deadliest opioid in Ohio, propelling the death rate to record levels. Other states hadn't seen fentanyl yet. But some five hundred Ohioans died from the drug that year, and the number more than doubled in 2015, to 1,155; then *that* number almost tripled again by 2017.

Police had always treated an addict's death with indifference. A patrolman stood by as a coroner's deputy bagged the body and carted it away. Case closed. But by 2015, the rising toll of death in Ohio and a few other states pushed families out of the shadows. Authorities opened to new ideas; law enforcement was at the vanguard of this innovation, particularly in Ohio, where the first fentanyl overdose outbreaks took place.

In Akron, police deployed Mike Schmidt and Tim Harvey to every overdose death. With DNA analysis, they could extract identities from objects as mundane as toothbrushes, or baggies of drugs. Smart phones provided the deceased's contacts, recent phone calls and texts, emails, access to Facebook and Instagram accounts, photographs—clues about a person's last hours. Just as Chicago police had done during the fentanyl-death outbreak of 2006, Akron police could use these deaths as investigative events, gathering evidence that might take dealers off the streets. Addicts' deaths might be respected, and their families could derive comfort from knowing that their loved ones had not died in vain. Police work might also answer the question, Where's all this fentanyl coming from?

The two detectives' job was to prove that one drug had killed a person by tracking the chain of custody of that specific drug: who had sold that dose to whom up a chain of distributors, as far as they could take it. Schmidt and Harvey worked their first overdose death case up the supply chain and arrested a midlevel dope supplier. "We were kind of doing it as a one-stop shop," Schmidt remembered. "We were the crime-scene unit. We were collecting evidence, taking photographs, interviewing witnesses."

But soon Schmidt and Harvey found the new job frustrating. Most users had several drugs in their systems. Proving which one had killed someone was impossible. Often, too, they found a body alone. The deceased's friends fled after wiping the scene clean of drugs, paraphernalia, phones, and the backpacks that every street addict seemed to carry. Either that, or they would dump their friend, dead or unconscious, outside a hospital emergency room. After the detectives' first success, the job became a slog through the detritus of street addiction that had settled over Akron. By the spring of 2015, a year into the assignment, Schmidt and Harvey found evidence to lead up a ladder of suppliers in only five or six cases. Overdose deaths, meanwhile, kept rising. The idea that any of this would yield answers to the origin of the fentanyl on Akron streets seemed fantasy.

ON SATURDAY, MARCH 21, 2015, Tim Harvey responded to the scene of an overdose death in a bathroom on the second floor of a wood-frame house on a quiet, tree-lined street a couple of miles north of downtown Akron.

There, the body of Tommy Rauh knelt, facedown, as if in prayer, against the bathtub across the hall from a $300-a-month room he'd found on Craigslist. It wasn't far from his childhood home, which he'd moved out of because it was never easy being around his family when he was using. He was thirty-seven and had spent close to half those years fighting the torment that began with that doctor's prescription of OxyContin for tendinitis. He had survived years on pills and heroin, struggling, failing, but hoping that all was not lost. With fentanyl on Ohio streets, he didn't last a month.

His roommates said he stole and conned money from friends. His mother bought him groceries, and his sister had given him a new cell phone. He pawned his laptop and begged his mother to get it out of hock, which she did. It was part of the Rauh family agony: How far to go? When to help? When to refuse? Addiction came without a TripTik to recovery the family could follow. What's more, addiction repaid his obedience by snatching its own piece of him—part of his thigh, infected from shooting up. In the end, the leader, the handsome Viking who had awed his friends with his charismatic nonconformity, possessed little beyond the love and patience of his family.

His roommates that afternoon had heard him go into the bathroom, then knocked hard when he did not emerge. They called his mother, who had taken her son to the hospital earlier that day for his thigh infection. She returned. Together, they broke down the door.

Mike Schmidt had that Saturday off, so Tim Harvey sifted the scene alone. He had seen enough to know what happened. Heroin allowed users time to get comfortable before they drifted into overdose. In death, they often lay reclining, perhaps with a burned cigarette still in their fingers. With fentanyl, Harvey said, "it's a matter of seconds; they just drop."

A medical examiner's report later attributed Rauh's death to a massive dose of acetylfentanyl, one of the fentanyl analogues Paul Janssen described in the paper he published in 1968.

In the spring of 2015 the Summit County medical examiner found people in Akron dying with as little as twelve or fifteen nanograms (a nanogram is one billionth of a gram) of fentanyl per milliliter of blood in their system. That was all it took to kill a person. Tom Rauh's level was 1800 nanograms of acetylfentanyl per milliliter of blood. That was the highest concentration the Summit County medical examiner's office saw that year—or the next two years. When the toxicology results came in, Summit County medical examiner Lisa Kohler called the Rauhs. "I've never seen anything like it," she told Jim Rauh. A mountainous quantity of fentanyl—the only drug in his system.

Harvey left the scene of Tommy Rauh's death without much to encourage him that this case would lead anywhere. He had no witnesses. On Rauh's cell phone, a number popped up with drug-related texts, but no name was attached. Harvey also found green wax-paper baggies, which struck Harvey as strange. In Akron, dealers preferred to wrap heroin in those lottery forms that people fill out at gas stations, which are free and made of strong paper.

The next day Harvey and Schmidt sent the wax-paper baggie to the state crime lab for DNA and finger-print testing. Then they turned to the cell phone and that anonymous phone number. Before they got very far, a detective called from the quiet suburb of Fairlawn. A forty-eight-year-old addict named Bryan Stalnaker had died. Near his corpse were the same green wax-paper baggies. Stalnaker, too, had a cell phone. When Harvey and Schmidt examined the phone, the same number appeared, only this time names were attached: Sean and Bree.

The partners knew an Akron drug dealer named Leroy Steele. Steele went by "Sean" on the street. He came from an extended family with a long history of dealing drugs in Akron. Leroy Steele sold crack and went to prison for that; he ran mortgage-fraud scams for a time, which returned him to prison. He had a turbulent relationship with his girl-friend, Sabrina Robinson, known to everyone as Bree.

The couple owned a beauty salon and houses throughout Akron. Stalnaker did odd jobs at those properties in exchange for dope. The work marked the end of a long way down for Stalnaker. A local guy and the father of six, he had once managed a roofing company and owned a home on four acres. "When times were good, so was he," read his obituary. Then he'd fallen into heroin, lost his wife, and never reas-sembled his life after that. He married again, to a woman already addicted to heroin who introduced him to Steele and Robinson. The detectives searched houses where Steele was known to live. He was gone, but at one house, they found protein powder, baby formula, and powdered sugar—all used to mix with fentanyl. They also found a tub containing three grimy, dust-covered Magic Bullet blenders, which they assumed Steele used to mix the drug.

They learned Stalnaker performed another job for the couple: that of "tester"—shooting up new batches of Steele's fentanyl mix. Steele "would have him try it and rate it," Schmidt said. "If it was a 10, Steele would cut it again, trying to get it down to an 8 so he could stretch the product out." In one of his last messages to Steele, Stalnaker proclaimed a batch "close to perfect." Stalnaker overdosed two days before he actually died; Steele and Robinson revived him in a bathtub full of ice. The night before he died, Robinson drove him to his grandmother's house, where he was staying, exchanging pleasantries and slipping Stalnaker drugs in payment for his handyman work. Stalnaker's mother found him dead the next morning in his basement bedroom.

The detectives searched a second house owned by Leroy Steele. There they found eight cell phones. In those phones were contacts with numbers belonging to Rauh and Stalnaker.

"And that's when we see these emails with China," Schmidt said.

The emails showed Steele corresponding with a Chinese chemical company selling fentanyl and other illegal drugs. His contact was a man using the unlikely name of Gordon Jin. Many fentanyl vendors were on the darknet, accessible only through secure connections. Jin, however, advertised on the open internet. His companies operated apparently free of molestation by Chinese authorities. "We are professional acetylfentanyl manufacturer in China," Jin wrote in response to Steele's inquiry. "Our products are all best quality, a lot of US and Europe customers purchase largely from us every month. Price of 1kg acetylfentanyl is $6,800 USD, pls be noted that the price we offer including shipping cost." The detectives found emails with tracking numbers of packages addressed to fictitious names and sent to houses all over Akron and the nearby city of Canton. The quantities alarmed the detectives. A few grains of fentanyl could kill a person. Steele's orders were for half a kilo at a time.

Reading those emails, Schmidt and Harvey reached a moment that not many local cops attain—the realization that a case was transporting them far from street work to something bigger and more complex than anything they'd known. The death of Tom Rauh, in an upstairs bathroom in Akron, now connected them to the global economy, to China, and to the chemistry of molecules they'd never heard of.

Using email addresses in Steele's phone, the partners contacted Jin and ordered ten grams of fentanyl and ten grams of acetylfentanyl for $150 each, just to prove this was how it was done. They wired money to China from a local supermarket and a Walmart. A week later, two packages arrived, a box and a manila envelope. Each carried a glassine bag, which in turn contained a Ziplock baggie of white powder. Fentanyl and acetylfentanyl, respectively—each 99.9 percent pure, a DEA lab later confirmed.

"We were like," Schmidt said later, "'Is this really happening?'"

A YEAR AFTER the deaths of Tommy Rauh and Bryan Stalnaker, Leroy Steele and Sabrina Robinson were arrested trying to enter Canada. Steele pleaded guilty to their deaths and was sentenced to twenty years; Robinson did the same and received eight.

With the case connected to China, Schmidt and Harvey turned it over to the DEA. In Akron, the overdoses continued. Yet years later, the Rauh case still stood out to the detectives. So often drug cases have big gaps that investigators never connect. That's the way the job is—messy, disjointed, nothing like the television shows where every-thing resolves every episode; some things are never known. In this case, though, starting with a cell phone and a number, everything linked— from Tommy Rauh to Leroy Steele to somebody in China using the name Gordon Jin. That was how a middle-class Akron family with a problem they thought was theirs alone found themselves connected to a global system of drug and chemical sales, stretching to China, where Jim Rauh years ago had gone to recycle rubber and videotape. In Ohio at least, the case answered the question: Where is all this fentanyl coming from? "I don't think anybody in Ohio at the time knew it was coming from China," Harvey said.

Tommy Rauh is buried at Mount Peace Cemetery in Akron, not far from the warm brick home where he grew up. His obituary mentioned "his joke-telling, cooking, writing, chess playing . . . and his brave and beautiful heart," but not the addiction that dominated a third of his life.

Of Tommy Rauh's friends and schoolmates, his siblings can count at least eighteen who've died of drug overdoses in the past few years.

Jim Rauh, who through the years visiting China had formed such kinship with the Chinese people, feels differently toward their government: "I see this as a chemical attack on the United States, with the Chinese government's complicity. They're pushing this material in what I consider to be the third Opium War, just this time by Chinese against us and other Western countries, and fentanyl is its weapon of mass destruction."

Tommy Rauh's story—one of so many thousands—ends here. It began in 2002, when a doctor saw fit to prescribe him OxyContin for tendinitis. The pills ignited an addiction that Rauh hadn't kicked thirteen years later when, 6,700 miles away, Chinese chemical vendors had leaped into hawking fentanyl analogues over the internet and one of them shipped some to Leroy Steele, who made the mistake, it appears, of mixing it in a Magic Bullet blender.

The tragedy, his sister Ursula felt, wasn't just the death of her brother; it was all the time, effort, love, and pain that the family traversed, the hoping and living for the smallest encouragement. "We were trying, all of us, so hard, and he just wanted to live," she said. "At the baptism [of a nephew], he was back. I was holding his hand in church, thinking 'My brother's back'—like he was back from the dead. We soaked up as much as we could, then he was gone again—and he didn't come back."

All that remained was digital residue—the ghostly online presence of a name in China behind a website, a shell company, and an email address—all ready to vanish at the touch of a key.

Fentanyl IV

Gordon Jin

I n the People's Republic of China, the principal law enforcement
agency is known as the Ministry of Public Security (MPS). It
employs two million people and is housed in central Beijing in an enormous rectangular building next to the National Museum of China,
which in turn overlooks Tiananmen Square.

On the ground floor is a conference room with ceilings three stories
high and windows to match. Below, filling much of the room, runs a
dark polished wooden table, where the most formal of the ministry's
meetings are held.

One smog-free morning in May 2018, twenty-five Chinese officials
sat at this table; on the wall behind them was a massive red and gold
national flag. Some officials wore black uniforms of the MPS, others
were in business suits. An equal number of Americans sat across the
table, many of them from Cleveland—three federal prosecutors, investigators from the DEA, IRS, and Homeland Security.

As women served tea, the meeting that day revolved around Gordon
Jin. In northern Ohio, the name had come up first in the case of Tommy
Rauh from Akron. Gordon Jin had sold acetylfentanyl to Leroy Steele,
an Akron drug dealer, who mixed it in a Magic Bullet blender, and Rauh
died as a result.

Among those who spoke was the man whose investigation was the
reason for this meeting. Matt Fitzpatrick, known to everyone as Fitz,

was from a large family of Irish cops out of Buffalo, New York, on Lake Erie. That morning, he presented evidence that Gordon Jin was the online moniker of a major international drug enterprise based in Shanghai, sending kilograms of fentanyl, its analogues, and other synthetic drugs—of its own manufacture—through the mail to two dozen countries and at least thirty-five American states. These drugs, he said, had killed Rauh and Bryan Stalnaker, but also people in Tampa, Sacramento, Minnesota, and Liverpool, England.

Matt Fitzpatrick had joined the DEA after law school and spent nine years in his hometown before transferring down the lake to the Cleveland office. During those years, he had worked undercover crack buys, drug-dealer wiretaps—the kinds of cases he imagined himself doing when he joined the agency. In that Beijing conference room, gazing at the line of Chinese officialdom lined before him that morning, he was a long way from Lake Erie.

He had volunteered for this case, having never heard the name Gordon Jin, nor knowing all the case would require. That was back in December 2015. The country was awakening to the epidemic of opiate addiction that had been spreading for twenty years and included heroin. Now, though, rashes of overdoses to illicit fentanyl were erupting across states where the scourge had begun. In northern Ohio, in clusters of overdoses, dozens of people had died.

Fitzpatrick knew little about China and only a little more about the nether reaches of the internet; nor did he know much about fentanyl, though, like everyone in northern Ohio, he was learning. He had other cases he was already working. But these fentanyl blooms seemed a challenge. So when supervisors asked around to agents in the Cleveland office if they could find out more about this fentanyl and where it was coming from, Fitz said he'd look into it.

He had no idea where to begin. Then a postal investigator alerted him to one man they were onto who, they suspected, was getting small shipments of drugs from China. Fitz enlisted the help of Matt Cronin, a federal prosecutor in Cleveland who had worked white-collar crime cases, to write a search warrant for the guy's house in case he was unco-operative. "I really was busy that day and wanted to say no," Cronin said. "But I said, 'Okay, we'll make it work.' I didn't think it'd go anywhere."

With the search warrant as leverage, Fitz found the man and took the rare tack of approaching him on the street. We know what you're doing, he said; would you like to tell us how? "I didn't need another arrest on the book," Fitzpatrick told me. "I needed someone to show me what's going on. I was pretty sure this individual knew."

Sure enough, one day the man dropped by the DEA's Cleveland office. "There's this whole world out there you guys know nothing about," he said. On the many trading websites for legitimate chemicals, he said, were vendors worldwide who sold any illegal drug you wanted. They did this on the public internet, openly, if you knew where to look. Illicit fentanyl and its analogues were in highest demand. Get an email address and post on the trading sites, asking for what you want, he said.

Fitz opened an email account under a fictitious name, found a hotspot also not connected to the DEA, and posted to a chemical trading site his source had recommended: "I'm looking for fentanyl" is all he wrote. He and Cronin watched as over the next twenty-four hours responses cluttered the email account—dozens of them, from Ukraine, India, China, using names like Jim or Helen: *I can sell you carfentanil, acetylfentanyl, furanylfentanyl*. Fitz had never heard of any of them.

As he worked other cases, he took moments to sift through these responses. Vendors were eager, some offering discounted deals. It shocked him, the volume of criminal vendors who appeared from his quick email. As he grabbed a few hours here and there, he tried to fasten onto the most promising investigative target. This went on for months.

Among vendors vying for his business as those months passed, one improbable name stood out—Gordon Jin. Fitzpatrick had heard that name somewhere other than a liquor bottle. He looked through DEA databases, and there it was—the name used by a Chinese distributor supplying Leroy Steele in Akron with acetylfentanyl. Steele was now in prison for the deaths of Tommy Rauh and Bryan Stalnaker.

Gordon Jin kept on, operating as the Shanghai Pharmaceutical Company. He had thirty-six websites in two dozen languages— Portuguese, Hindi, French, Arabic—all openly on the internet. He offered, he wrote, "every possible chemical to meet the needs of our customers." Sixteen tons of these chemicals a month, shipped world-wide, the websites claimed, guaranteeing delivery in Europe, Russia, and the United States.

His shell companies' names changed frequently, as did their email addresses. They used encrypted email and messaging services to communicate with customers, and were incorporated in the British Virgin Islands, where laws prevent identifying the owners of corporations. The Jin companies transferred money out of banks in Hong Kong to get around Chinese government requirements on money transfers. What's more, Fitz found the Gordon Jin moniker connected to drugs in death cases going back eight years.

Using his alias, Fitzpatrick wrote asking for acetylfentanyl. Jin responded that the Chinese government had just ruled it illegal, but he offered to make large amounts of carfentanil, the rhinoceros seda-tive. Fitz began ordering small amounts of drugs from Jin, who duti-fully shipped them. They had bewildering names, drugs forming the extended branches of the molecular tree that Paul Janssen imagined when he invented fentanyl: 4-fluoroisobutyrfentanyl, furanylfentanyl, methoxyacetylfentanyl. Many were opioids unrelated to fentanyl, with names like U-48800 or U-47700.

As the investigation grew more complex, Fitz and Cronin began to recruit others from across the federal government in northern Ohio. By the time they were done, there was a feel of *Mission Impossible* or *Ocean's Eleven* to the team they assembled. Gary Kenst, from the Department of Justice, was an expert in the financial side of organized crime. Tim Stark from Homeland Security was an expert in bulk smuggling of cash and drugs. Dan Groseclose, from the IRS, had years investigating foreign finance and money laundering. The FBI's Monica Hantz was a cyber specialist, and Bryon Green, a Postal Service inspector, an expert in the darknet. Cronin added two colleagues from his office. Adrienne Rose was a veteran prosecutor of narcotics cases; Steve Sola had spent years investigating how criminals move money abroad.

Gordon Jin routed his packages through a company near Boston owned by a Canadian citizen, born in China, named Bin Wang. Bin Wang had an unexpected story. He was a chemist trained at a prominent university in China. He'd moved to Canada, naturalized as a Canadian, and found work at a pharmaceutical company. Then he was laid off. When he showed up in the Gordon Jin case, he was renting space in a building near Boston—apparently acting as the US middleman for packages coming from the Shanghai Pharmaceutical Company that flowed through his Boston office weekly. Many contained legitimate chemicals, orders for research labs or legal industries; but within those packages were also hidden drugs ordered from Gordon Jin. Wang repackaged these orders to the intended customers and took them to a FedEx or UPS office.

The group arrested Wang in August 2017 as he and his son were about to board a plane to Toronto. He's now serving a six-year prison term.

That's where prior cases involving Gordon Jin had stopped—with the arrest of someone within the United States, shutting down a domestic drug network. Pursuing Gordon Jin, the source of the drugs, involved going to China, which meant dealing with the Chinese government. Given relations between the two countries, Gordon Jin would likely never be extradited to the United States.

The agents met in a windowless conference room near Cronin's office to confront these realities. They had disrupted Jin's US network. Should they now go after Jin, knowing how much work remained to indict him, and that it would likely not lead to his extradition? A lot of the evidence from Bin Wang's case was in Mandarin. The opioid epidemic didn't stop adding to their workload. But neither had Gordon Jin ceased. His websites now sent fentanyl packages through a forwarder in Tonga, a world freight hub in the Pacific Ocean. To the investigators in the room, with years of their careers invested in attacking organized crime, Gordon Jin offered a chance to understand the future of global drug trafficking. So, in a scene out of some Hollywood blockbuster, they went around the room and voted—and unanimously chose to continue.

Fitz now dug through DEA databases, finding Gordon Jin's name in death cases around the country. He opened a new undercover email account, contacted Gordon Jin again with the new name. "At one point we had a long phone call about shipping and he offered to ship ten kilos of U-48800," Fitz said. "We started sending him Bitcoin [to pay for packages]. When we did this, we found information where a father and son were directly connected to the accounts, each signing off on accounts as Gordon Jin."

Gordon Jin turned out to be a man named Fujing Zheng, thirty-five, and his father, Guanghua Zheng, sixty-two—both of Shanghai. They were nobody's Scarface—no diamond-encrusted pistols, no revenge feuds. Fujing, the son, had hopscotched from job to job before landing in a chemical company where he apparently discovered the bounty of selling synthetic drugs online. His father was listed as a warehouseman, and from his photo he seems a man of humble beginnings. They employed no gunmen, no bodyguards, no drivers. They relied on encrypted communications and currencies. Drug traffickers for the twenty-first century.

The case took over Fitzpatrick's life for three years. His wife works in medicine and is required to keep patients' medical records private. At night, after the kids were asleep, they would sit at the kitchen table, each on a laptop, facing each other, typing and muttering into their screens, occasionally exclaiming "Dang!" or "What the he . . . ?"—yet each not allowed to tell the other why.

Beijing is twelve hours ahead of Ohio. Fitz stayed up late to call Jin, posing as a drug buyer, calling from his garage so as to not bother his sleeping family. The man seemed young and spoke a manageable English, proficient in at least the names and potencies of a wide range of drugs. They kept their conversations to business. But it occurred to Matt Fitzpatrick that he was really talking to an omen.

Gordon Jin's business had become technologically possible just as America's opioid epidemic was creating a wide new population of drug customers. That put fentanyl at the vanguard of the virtual underworld, as well: it allowed folks like Gordon Jin easy access to the world's great drug market and, within it, this newly formed consumer base.

Fentanyl could even be ordered with Chemical Abstracts Service (CAS) numbers. Every chemical described in the scientific literature since 1957—tens of millions of substances, with thousands added daily—has a CAS number, provided by the American Chemical Society. A CAS number allows for trade in chemicals, regardless of language or a chemical's synonyms. Fentanyl and its analogues each have a CAS number, and Fitz listed these numbers in his orders when he bought them undercover. Jin also provided nuclear magnetic resonance (NMR) spectroscopy tests—used in industry to gauge a chemical's purity—for each shipment. No more guessing at what you're getting from the dealer on the street.

These were huge advances in drug-trafficking efficiencies. Now you no longer needed a cartel, which in turn controlled land, labor, routes of transportation. All you needed was a Gordon Jin, a laptop, and a way to pay for shipping.

With this information, Fitz, Cronin, and the team flew to Beijing in May 2018 and that meeting below the vaulted ceilings of the Chinese Ministry of Public Security.

The Chinese officials seemed uninformed on the case, or the problem their chemical companies posed. Fitz and Cronin spoke, and answered questions. In the end, though, the Chinese expressed not much more than concern. As the Chinese government made one drug illegal, the Zhengs were astute enough to change its molecular structure, rendering their new product technically legal to sell in China. If he's not selling anything illegal here, the officials said, we can't arrest him. The meeting lasted two hours. The Americans flew home empty-handed.

Three months later, in August 2018, federal prosecutors in Cleveland went public with the indictment against the Zhengs. US officials shut down their websites and froze their assets; the US Treasury designated the Zhengs as drug kingpins. Nine months later, the Chinese government banned all forms of fentanyl, except that produced by companies the government licenses to manufacture it. With that, China's role as a provider of illicit fentanyl faded.

But China and the United States have no extradition treaty, so the Zhengs remain, as of this writing, at large in their homeland, where, according to one security-company report, it appears they have expanded their operations beyond the internet and are exporting fentanyl precursors and those of methamphetamine to Mexico through that country's Pacific Coast ports.

Jim Rauh has filed a civil lawsuit against the Zhengs in the death of his son. "If the Zhengs sold these drugs to their countrymen, they would be publicly executed," he wrote me. "Their and their governments' actions should be considered crimes against humanity."

The team assembled to investigate the Zhengs went its separate ways. Matt Cronin moved to Washington, DC, to coordinate opioid prosecutions nationwide. Other cases awaited Matt Fitzpatrick, and he turned to them. Agents around the country called to ask his advice as they ventured into similar cases. The Chinese chemical industry is now vast, and many actors within it sell drugs over the internet.

Occasionally he recalls that early in the case he searched Google Earth for the addresses where Bin Wang's fentanyl packages were headed. Up sprung photos of apartments in Atlanta, a trailer park in Tennessee, a boarding house in Reading, Pennsylvania, occupied by people who, he imagined, nurtured dreams of jackpot profits untethered to any realistic idea of how to handle or mix what they'd ordered. In the past, buying large quantities of such potent dope required months, maybe years, of cultivating contacts within a drug gang or mafia.

But with fentanyl, he thought, anybody can be Pablo Escobar.

Sacklers II

"A Fresh Start"

A lways Be Closing."

That motto is gospel to salespeople. It comes from *Glengarry Glen Ross*, a 1992 movie starring Al Pacino, Jack Lemmon, Alec Baldwin, and Kevin Spacey. The movie is about a suburban office of hapless salesmen hawking shady real-estate investments. To keep their jobs, "Always Be Closing" is the mindset they must adopt with clients, a pitiless approach to an unfair world made up of winners and everyone else. In the office sweepstakes, "first prize is a Cadillac Eldorado," Baldwin, a boss in from downtown, tells the staff. "Second prize, a set of steak knives. Third prize is you're fired."

At the Purdue Pharma's national sales meeting in 2009, as the company emerged from the dog days of its federal conviction, sales reps were apparently urged to adopt that motto as they sold OxyContin. Purdue reps took notes during the training. In those notebooks, later subpoenaed by investigators from the Tennessee attorney general, were the notations "Always Be Closing," "ABC," "Glengarry Glen Ross."

That year, 2009, it seemed Purdue Pharma was back. It asked the worldwide consultant firm McKinsey & Company to develop strategies to improve brand loyalty to OxyContin. Purdue's four-day national sales meeting in Scottsdale, Arizona, that January was attended by some 800 people, including 110 new reps hired six months earlier. The meeting's message was that Purdue Pharma was starting anew. Problems with the federal government were in the past. The company had expanded OxyContin's dosage strengths, adding 15 mg, 30 mg, and 60 mg pills to its lineup of 10 mg, 20 mg, 40 mg, and 80 mg pills. It seemed, too, as if the company would begin diversifying, instead of relying on OxyContin for so much of its sales. "They told us that we were going to have other things to sell besides OxyContin—a couple products that were not opioid related," remembered Carol Panara, a former Purdue rep I spoke with as I was researching the Sacklers and their company. "This is a fresh start."

The company's focus had changed, too. No longer were its targets the relatively few pain doctors and anesthesiologists. The new targets were family doctors, general practitioners, nurses, and physicians' assistants who prescribe pills. Purdue had created fifty smaller sales territories, allowing reps to spend more time with these professionals, who were generally overworked and untrained in pain management. The smaller doses, 10 mg and 15 mg pills, allowed reluctant family doctors to begin prescribing OxyContin more cautiously—and would lead to higher-dose prescriptions in the future, the company hoped.

Indeed, it was a heady time for the company. Each year set a new US record for opioid prescriptions. The Centers for Disease Control reported 243 million opioid prescriptions dispensed in 2009—seventy-nine prescriptions for every hundred Americans—up from 228 million in 2007. Purdue was selling more OxyContin than ever—close to $3 billion worth annually.

Years later, in 2017, a young Tennessee state prosecutor named Maggie Rowland combed the company's emails and internal documents from those years. To Rowland, it all felt familiar. She had sold cars in Kentucky before she entered law school. The Purdue documents reminded her of car-sales hustle.

Fresh from law school, Rowland showed up the summer of 2017 for her first day at work at the Consumer Protection Unit of the Tennessee Attorney General's Office in Nashville. She was cheerful and eager to embark on her career. She possessed what her colleagues came to see was an intense curiosity, as well as an ability to see the larger story in small details. On that first day they sat her in front of three computer screens, and she set to work digging into acres of subpoenaed Purdue Pharma internal documents the office had received from the company.

Rowland was from Kentucky and had gone to law school in Nashville, so she was aware of the pain-pill addiction crisis, but knew few of its details. Tennessee was among those states that tallied more opioid prescriptions every year than it had people; that year 1,776 Tennesseans would die of drug overdoses. Rowland's job was to discover what the company's internal documents revealed about how it promoted OxyContin in Tennessee between 2006 and 2015. She had done nothing like this before, but she waded into the documents, using keywords to search: *addiction, euphoria, overdose,* and the names of towns.

They paired her with an attorney in the office named Brant Harrell. Harrell is from Dallas, an amateur painter and a thin, soft-spoken fellow who you must sometimes lean forward to hear. When you do, you perceive a lawyerly care to avoid inflammatory, adjective-laden language; to stick to the facts that documents reveal and, above all, not speak outside what he calls "the four corners of the complaint" against any company under investigation, particularly when talking to a journalist. Harrell joined the office in 2005 and seemed to find his voice in the health unit's probes into shady telemarketers and purveyors of hormone replacement therapy. In that work, Harrell earned a reputation around the office for thoroughness in presenting evidence in lawsuit complaints against companies that his colleagues described as "Brant sued."

For months beginning in the late summer of 2017, Rowland and Harrell sat at their screens in adjoining offices on the nineteenth floor of a building in downtown Nashville, sifting grains of information, piecing together a narrative of Purdue's sales tactics in Tennessee.

Rowland, often unsure of what she had, brought Harrell what she harvested from the documents. The work looked like tedious data processing, but within a few weeks Maggie Rowland would get to the office each morning eager to flip on her computer. At twenty-nine, she was one of a small coterie of people in America to whom was being revealed some of the opioid epidemic's deepest roots and most disturbing stories. Among them was the story of Dr. Michael Rhodes.

There were others. One pair of Nashville doctors saw a stream of patients up from Harlan, Kentucky, for OxyContin prescriptions. A load of out-of-state patients is usually a sign of an out-of-control doctor, yet Purdue reps kept calling on the couple, pushing them to prescribe more.

It was detective work of the most plodding type, in which tidbits of information could not be ignored because, combined with other pieces, they produced insights into the company's strategy to mine Tennessee for OxyContin prescriptions. In the end, the company strategy that Rowland and Harrell described in the criminal complaint prized short-term profits above all else. It could be distilled into a philosophy that was, it seemed to me, simple enough for any street dealer to understand. "Their whole push was to keep people on [OxyContin] and get them to a higher dose because then they were more likely to stay on it," Rowland said. "It seemed that everything was driven by the [Purdue] marketing team."

IF "ALWAYS BE CLOSING" was an attitude Purdue reps were urged to adopt, so was the classic salesman advice "Never give someone more information than they need to act." The company had lists of the top 10 percent of prescribers in each state. Ignore the oncologists and hospice-care doctors in that top tier, sales reps were told, according to records Rowland and Harrell reviewed. Focus instead on the many family doctors, nurse practitioners, and physicians' assistants in that tier. Consultants' data showed that these medical professionals were likely to welcome pharmaceutical reps and prescribe their drugs, then repeat their sales spiels to others.

Lubricating all this were cards the Tennessee attorneys also discovered, offering patients a $75 discount off the copay on their first five OxyContin prescriptions. Purdue sales reps took the cards to clinics for doctors and their staff, and to pharmacies, particularly independent pharmacies, where the cards helped boost essential traffic in the competition with chain pharmacies. A Purdue internal report showed that patients using these "opioid savings cards," as the company called them, tended to stay on the drug longer than those who did not. Every $1 million the company invested in the cards, according to a company report, returned $4.28 million in OxyContin sales. Medical studies have found that two-thirds of patients using opioid painkillers for more than ninety days were still using them five years later. The savings cards prodded thousands of Americans to keep using OxyContin well past those crucial ninety days. Purdue, meanwhile, added to its reps' incentives with a "Toppers Club" sales contest, through which reps earned bonuses by increasing OxyContin prescriptions among the doctors they visited.

The company seemed to prize doctors who were already high-volume prescribers and seen as open to prescribing even more. These physicians seemed crucial to the Purdue business model. One of them was Dr. James H. Pogue, in the Nashville suburb of Brentwood. The Tennessee prosecutors found that Pogue prescribed 562,000 eighty-milligram OxyContin pills between 2006 and 2013, making him one of the state's largest prescribers.

Pogue generated an estimated $655,000 in revenue for the company during one six-month period in 2009. Between 2006 and 2012, Purdue sales reps called on Pogue more than four dozen times, frequently finding his office swamped with patients. Half those visits came after the state reprimanded him in 2009. By 2012 Pogue's parking lot, according to a news report that spring, was filled with cash-paying patients waiting six to nine hours for an appointment. Two months after that report Purdue put Pogue on a cease-calling list. That fall, the Tennessee medical board suspended his medical license.

Farther east, south of Knoxville, in the town of Maryville, the Breakthrough Pain Therapy Center was another place Purdue reps expended time and energy. BPTC would later close after its owners, Randy and Sandy Kincaid, two of their children, and nine of their medical staff were convicted of drug dealing and sentenced to federal prison terms.

As an operating business, Breakthrough Pain Therapy had no diagnostic tools associated with pain clinics: no examination tables, gloves, urine screens, "or providers who performed independent pain diagnoses." It did have prewritten prescriptions, often dispensed without a physician present.

Tennessee investigators found that while placing some staff on no-call lists, Purdue continued to call on other staff members at Breakthrough Pain Therapy. This included Buffy Kirkland, a nurse practitioner who worked there for several years. Between 1998 and 2017, Kirkland prescribed 68,000 OxyContin tablets, of which two-thirds were of 40 mg or stronger, according to the complaint.

Purdue depended on OxyContin for its profits. To increase them, the company needed ever-greater numbers of sales visits to doctors pushing OxyContin at ever-higher doses.

Which is perhaps why something the company called Region Zero occupied a special place at Purdue. Region Zero did not refer to a geographic area. It was instead Purdue's term for a collection of some 1,800 doctors nationwide whose prescribing the company tracked. That data led Purdue staff to suspect these doctors of uncontrolled prescribing, diversion of the pills, and abuse. These were doctors who sales reps were not to call on. But neither did Purdue report them to the government, as its 2007 agreement required. One reason might have been that Region Zero doctors accounted at one point for 10 percent of company sales.

At one point a staffer emailed Russ Gasdia, Purdue's vice president of sales, urging the company to report Region Zero doctors at least to insurance companies: "At a basic level, it just seems like the right and ethical thing to do," the email's author wrote. "Doing so could help those companies identify those physicians that may be of a concern. . . . If it reduces abuse and diversion of opioids then it seems like something we should be doing." That suggestion was rejected.

As years passed and Region Zero doctors were left alone by Purdue reps, their prescribing dropped off, offering more proof of the company's dilemma: once sales reps stopped calling on a doctor to promote OxyContin, that doctor stopped prescribing as much. The calculation was simple: more sales calls on doctors equaled more OxyContin prescriptions; fewer calls meant fewer prescriptions and lower profit. It resembled the problem facing fast-food or soft-drink manufacturers, whose products are known worldwide yet whose sales depend on relentless advertising and product placement.

Following its 2007 conviction, Purdue could have pulled back from the hard sell and lowered its annual sales targets and profit expectations. Instead, the company continued to pursue growing numbers of OxyContin prescriptions. Bonuses of sales reps were based on the number of prescriptions written by doctors in their territories; district managers' bonuses were based on how many prescriptions their sales reps generated; regional managers' bonuses were based on prescriptions written in those districts. Meanwhile, executive bonuses depended on how many orders for OxyContin left Purdue's warehouse. Executives had no incentive therefore to question the excessive quantities being shipped to wholesalers, particularly in areas that would be hardest hit by pain-pill supply and addiction, such as Kentucky, West Virginia, and Southeast Florida. Everyone made money the more OxyContin prescriptions doctors wrote. Companies with large sales forces have similar bonus incentives. Purdue, though, was using these incentives to hawk not lipstick or copy machines but a narcotic.

"This is not a one-off sales rep that went rogue," Brant Harrell said, "this is an institutional thing. This is top down."

Meanwhile, up in Massachusetts, another team of investigators was digging through its own set of Purdue records. When it was done, the team believed that these records showed that the decision to aggressively sell OxyContin was not made by company executives. Rather, their complaint alleged, it came from the family who owned Purdue and sat on its board of directors, family members who feared that even in these heady days, the company presented "a dangerous concentration of risk," and its days might be numbered.

Muncie I

In the town of Muncie, Indiana, the auto industry in its grandest decades made the city the transmission capital of the world. Warner Gear opened on the town's south side in 1901 and invented the industry's first manual transmission. Chevrolet followed with a seventy-acre plant, also in the south part of town.

Together, these plants employed thousands of people to cut the gears for, and assemble, what became known as the T10 and the Muncie Transmission. These were high-performance, four-speed transmissions that evolved by the 1960s to find homes in the manual-shift muscle cars of the baby boom generation: Plymouth Road Runners, Chevy Chevelles, Corvettes, Novas, and Camaro Z28s. Muncie transmissions typified an era, built for cars with power and dominance, like the US auto industry.

Hovering near the plants were small machine workshops—tool-and-die shops that supplied components to the big plants. These shops were often family owned, or run by a former plant worker unsatisfied with the nine-to-five and wanting to be his own boss. One former Muncie firefighter told me, "We'd go down alleys to get to a fire and pass one tool-and-die shop after another. It was a tool-and-die town."

Transmission workers filled the modest single-family homes in neighborhoods like Avondale, across the street from the Chevy plant. The houses told a lot of the town's story. They were owned by workers, who made enough to buy them and raise a family. People cared for their homes, and from them poured forth scads of kids who filled the streets on sunny afternoons.

Among them was Wes Russell. Russell, now sixty-seven, is a gruff, husky, and plain-spoken fellow in spectacles and overalls, with a mop of gray hair and a bushy mustache. His workshop, a couple of doors down Eighth Street from where Chevy had its plant, is about all that's left of Muncie's car industry.

Russell was the kind of independent spirit the car industry forged. He was a "car guy"—one of the many young men in Muncie—and across America—obsessed with automobiles. They were hands-on innovators without college educations who believed tinkering under a hood was the best life imaginable. They worked to support their car habit, and all the money they could spare fed their obsession. Russell installed his first engine—in his grandfather's car—when he was twelve. When he attended a vocational school years later, the auto teacher told him he already knew everything the class could impart.

On Muncie's south side during those years, the level of automotive knowledge was deep, handed down from father to son, who learned as well from friends and neighbors. This knowledge was communicated through a vocabulary incomprehensible to anyone from outside. "When I was young," Wes told me, "I could not fathom how you could make a living as a car mechanic because everybody I knew fixed their own stuff. Everybody, without exception. Guy didn't know something, he'd come and ask you. When he knowed something you didn't, you'd barter. I'd work on his stuff, he'd work on my stuff."

On Saturday afternoons, Russell and his buddies assembled their cars outside his grandparents' house. "There'd be six, seven hoods up, and we're all just tinkering around," he said. They'd race them out on the newly paved four-lane county road near the old Westinghouse plant.

As they got older, a good many of those car guys took well-paid union jobs at Chevy or BorgWarner, doing the same work for eight hours a day for decades. Their tinkering stopped. They betrayed their calling, is how Wes sees it. "They wanted the big money so they could buy more expensive toys," he said. "Most of those guys ended up brain-dead—alcoholic and brain-dead. They were like college-educated people; they lost all their common sense. [Production-line work] just melted their skull."

Wes spent several years stuck in a factory, but then quit. He never stopped tinkering in the way he had with his Plymouth Road Runner when he was seventeen. He opened a racing workshop, working on cars for clients, inventing his own race car with his son. He kept racing, too. For a while, he was one of the best in the area. Realizing that speed on the turn was more important than speed on the straightaway, he got a slight advantage on every turn by loading his car's left side with lead plates. This forced the inside tires to dig in, gain traction, and pass others on the turn.

It was that kind of innovation—infinitesimal and growing from intimate daily work—carried out in the tool-and-die machine shops in towns like Muncie that helped create the country's automotive advantage for years. These advances were easy to overlook because they were hidden under the hoods of cars on Wes Russell's street, or in the machine shops that sprung up near the Chevy and BorgWarner transmission plants.

The car industry's original independent spirit found refuge in those tool-and-die shops—nimble hives of car guys, burdened neither by union rules nor by the dictates of corporate finance men. They survived by combining hard work with a fierce attention to keeping costs low and innovation on the smallest level. When the Big Three car makers demanded seemingly impossible improvements in small parts' cost and quality, the shops achieved them. In this world, ego had no place. That's what made it so nourishing. They were proud of what they did. They saw the beauty of competition and how it pushed people to achieve beyond what they'd dreamed possible. Their ingenuity helped camouflage the Big Three's growing dysfunction through the 1970s and '80s.

Tool-and-die shops came in many shapes. The best of them were places of enormous collaboration, where grease and grime hid creativity. The owner was usually never far from the floor and his workers, each of whose names he knew. The best workers were those who'd actually failed more than a time or two, but who loved the puzzle of figuring out better ways of making something.

The machine shops embodied the idea that progress was not a revolution. Instead, it was a daily accumulation of small steps, tiny victories. "There are no big licks," Russell told me at his shop one day. "You just keep working. You find a little something that works, and you're just that much better than the next guy. In the shops, if I can make this piece a tick better for the same money, they're going to buy it offa me. But you can't sit on your laurels. You gotta continually work, because somebody will catch up and go by you."

Call it the "tool-and-die" philosophy of life. Work leavened with an occasional small improvement reenergized your creativity and sense of fulfillment, and left you with the feeling that there wasn't a whole lot more to reasonably expect from the American dream.

For the first decades of the post–World War II years, America faced competition from a tiny fraction of the world. Auto industry management and unions grew complacent and deluded. Management turned away from car guys and toward financiers for direction. Unions protected incompetence and added to product costs. People in towns like Muncie, meanwhile, allowed themselves to believe that education wasn't that important, as any kid out of high school could find a job in the plants.

The end took many years. Chevy and BorgWarner began cutting jobs in the 1970s. The Chevy plant finally closed in 2006; BorgWarner in 2009. Chevy's plant was taken down; its paved acreage was left empty, cracked by weeds and surrounded by chain-link fences. BorgWarner's brick buildings remained but were just as empty.

The small machine shops at the heart of Muncie's economy vanished. They took with them the car knowledge and rambunctious energy that produced tinkerers like Wes Russell. Coincidentally or not, as those Muncie machine shops began to fold, it was the philosophy of those tool-and-die guys that the rest of the country seemed to lose as well.

In south Muncie, Avondale was among those neighborhoods that *withered* as people, jobs, and vitality departed. It was held together by one man. He was younger than Russell but he, too, had grown up in the area. Indeed, he knew no place in Muncie, much less the country, but the streets of Avondale and felt literally that he could not leave.

Muncie II

M ike Kissick, whom everyone in the Avondale neighborhood in south Muncie knew as Bird, was born in 1958 in the middle of the town's greatest transmission years.

Bird was from a family out of Tennessee. He was tall and talkative, speaking of "back home" as if he'd actually lived in Jamestown, the Appalachian town where so many Avondale workers came from.

He grew up in a small house on Tenth Street. He was about sixteen when the city opened the Ross Community Center, located between his house and the Chevy plant on Eighth Street. Ross Center had a basketball gym, meeting rooms, and bathrooms. It was bounded to the north by employee parking lots and to the south by houses filled with autoworkers and their families. The city of Muncie built three such centers. Ross belonged to the south side.

Bird was husky and tall, about six foot three. He cooked biscuits and gravy that he claimed were the best around. He built birdhouses and worked as a handyman.

When he was sixteen, his father bought him a '55 two-door Chevy. "Now you can get your license and learn to drive," his father said. Bird drove that thing around the block two or three times, got out, and never again, for the rest of his life, drove a car. Young men across Muncie's south side had fully formed fixations on automobiles, but Bird never rode anything more than his blue Schwinn ten-speed.

In his younger years, he rode up to the north side of Muncie, near Ball State University, where he did odd jobs. Then one day he just stopped doing that. Shannon McCormick grew up down the street from Bird. "He told me he was riding his bike to Eighth and Battavia, six or seven blocks down from here," Shannon said. "He got to Eighth and Battavia, and for some reason he couldn't cross that intersection. He rode his bike back. He went back the next day and could not cross the intersection. When I asked him about it, he said, 'I don't know what happened. I didn't want to go across the street.'"

Bird never did again. His world was confined to an eight-block radius around his house and the Ross Center. He'd ride over to the gas station or to Ricker's grocery store, which now occupied his old elementary school. A preference for walking or biking became an out-and-out fear of cars. Friends would offer him a ride. He turned them down every time. "No, I'll ride my bike," he'd say. In the neighborhood that made Muncie the transmission capital of the world, no one remembers Bird ever even getting into a car from his late twenties on. For the rest of his life, he didn't go anywhere he couldn't reach on a bike.

At some point, no one quite remembers the year, Bird became director of the Ross Center. A woman named Jackie Cooper, in between jobs, volunteered to help. In time, she was made the center's codirector, and within a few years, Bird and Jackie were a couple. When his parents passed, Bird and Jackie moved out of his parents' house and into a house two doors down, across from the center. That's where Bird spent the rest of his life.

No one seems sure where his nickname came from. Maybe it was the birdhouses. Shannon McCormick believes that he was once called Big Bird due to his size, then that was shortened to Bird. Whatever the case, everyone called him Bird. Everyone but Jackie Cooper, who called him Mike.

All the kids knew him, and he became a guiding figure. Through the gathering storm of south-side Muncie's decline, he was a steadying presence, calm and good-hearted.

In the 1990s, the streets of the Avondale neighborhood filled with kids. Everyone knew each other. Every house was occupied. "Around here, when we did what we weren't supposed to do, we drank," said one young south-side father. "That was it. Nobody had no coke, no crack, no heroin, no meth. We were scared to death to ever touch anything like that.

"Then it was pain pills, prescribed by a doctor. Doctor wasn't prescribing you crack, so it wasn't that big a deal. It's a *pain* pill. It was something that someone who's supposed to help you gives you. No one thought 'I'm on the corner trying to sell my clothes to get a high from these. I'm not shooting heroin.' They didn't know they were going to slowly end up doing that. And that's what happened. I have at least ten friends who died—guys that I went to school with or who lived near here."

These pain pills were something like the opposite of the tool-and-die philosophy. They promised to resolve all pain, no risk or consequences, and achieved without hard work. They arrived in Muncie as the car shops died.

Houses started to empty out, said the young father. "Older people were dying; landlords were from someplace else. The house wasn't in great shape, or somebody bought it and rented it to drug users. Then there was meth houses popping up in the neighborhood, where they rent the house and cook meth. Nobody in the neighborhood knew until it blew up on them. That happened two houses down from mine."

To recover any tax revenue it could, the city sold houses that people had abandoned. Those who stayed realized that nearby houses were now owned by investors in Arizona and New York and elsewhere. These landlords didn't seem to care who they rented to.

For a while, a drug folk-craft emerged known as "shake and bake." This was the term for extracting pseudoephedrine from cold-medicine tablets and cooking them with other chemicals to produce a rough version of methamphetamine. This method offered a homegrown source of drugs—no trafficker necessary. Before long, Muncie police estimated that folk-meth production had contaminated some 150 houses. Once the transmission capital of the world, the town for a few years reigned as the meth capital of Indiana.

It took about twenty years for the plant closures, the closing of the tool-and-die shops, the loss of homeowners, and the arrival of the pain pills, heroin, and then the amphetamine to cripple Muncie's south-side neighborhoods. Those folks who hung on, like Wes Russell, ended up battling the neglect of out-of-state landlords, and the renters who came and went, leaving sofas and old TVs on the street when they departed. South-siders seemed to go outdoors far less; they stayed at home, cowed by the threats around them.

The men tinkering under the car hoods of Wes Russell's youth were replaced by fellows with tattooed necks, lounging on sagging porch steps, baseball hats worn backward, or riding by on bicycles meant for their children. Many were fathers to babies with different women, receiving government disability payments. It was a human loss that the country could not afford but did little to prevent as jobs went overseas. Neighborhoods like Muncie's south side were viewed as free-trade losers, and therefore, like addicts, responsible for their own demise. Some of that was true, some of it wasn't. Yet those attitudes made places like Muncie's south side easy to ignore.

As all that was taking place, the Great Recession hit, and the city budget collapsed. The mayor cut funding for Muncie's three community centers. One center was razed; a nonprofit formed to run the second. On the south side, a neighborhood association ran the Ross Center, bungled the job, and the place closed.

Somehow, though, Mike "Bird" Kissick kept a key.

WITH THE KEY to the closed Ross Center, Bird became its unofficial and unpaid director, rec supervisor, and janitor. When neighborhood kids wanted to play basketball in the gym, they went to Bird's house, and he opened it for them. Bird was the one they answered to when they misbehaved at the center. A family who wanted to celebrate a birthday or a wedding at the center knew to find Bird. He opened for seniors so they could play euchre, and for the older guys and their weekly Sunday morning basketball game. He painted the Ross Center, replaced the toilet paper, fixed the small stuff, and bartered for services among those he knew in the neighborhood when repairs were beyond his ability. He mowed the enormous stretch of grass outside the center. Neighbors got used to seeing him riding that mower in the summer, sometimes until seven or eight at night.

Bird provided his neighborhood an essential place to assemble, a refuge from the storm, all without the city's knowledge or budget. He treated the center as if it were his, and to a great degree, it was. "He made sure nobody done without," said Jackie Cooper, his girlfriend, as we spoke one afternoon on the stoop to their house. "He set right here and he watched every day."

Older kids congregated outside the center, and some started dealing drugs. A few people called them a gang, but one fellow told me, "It was just a bunch of kids who had nothing else to do, or were hanging out just because it was the thing to do." Bird saw to it that inside, though, the Ross Center was a safe haven.

It helped that he knew everyone, and he had an uncanny knack for following what was happening in every family, aware of every drama, trauma, and bit of sweet news. He was Avondale's internet. A blind woman—Mrs. Charlesy is how everyone knew her—lived across from the center. She could fend for herself in most matters, but Bird made sure her sidewalk was shoveled free of snow so she could get out to check her mail. He kept up Mrs. Clark's yard, too, as she descended into dementia.

Bird also drank many cans a day of Pepsi and Mountain Dew. He ate mostly junk food—he loved Pizza King, which had a south-side restaurant and delivered—and his mother's own Appalachian recipes. He'd been rail thin in his youth, but "his diet caught up to him when his metabolism quit," and he got thick, said his friend Shannon McCormick.

As the economy recovered, the city had money for a center director and hired a woman named Jackie Hanoman, who gave Bird a paid job again. She learned the neighborhood from him, the story of each family. "He was my mentor," she said. Bird would tell her how things were done back home, referring to Tennessee, where his family was from, as if it were his home, too. "He had recipes for biscuits and gravy and was horrified when he heard I'd never tried it," Hanoman said. It pained her to watch him quaff soda after soda.

As the years passed, and in this small way he cared for his surroundings, friends noticed that Bird's world seemed to shrink even more. "It got to where he wasn't even leaving the neighborhood," said Shannon McCormick. "He wouldn't go past Sampson [Street], two blocks west of his house. He got to where he wasn't going anywhere, so there was no need to ride the bike."

He combined a sweet-natured dependability and willingness to share everything with people he knew well with a mighty self-destructiveness. He never went beyond the area that he could see from his front yard, and he never stopped drinking all that soda.

The other thing Bird also never did was see a doctor. No one knew why, because he didn't explain himself—just that he was as stubborn on the subject as he was about getting in a car. For one thing, the neighborhood had no doctors. Even when Shannon McCormick told him he'd found a doctor who would pay a house visit, Bird said, "Shannon, I won't even open the door for him."

For years Bird kept a bandage over a growth below his right eye, afraid it might scare children. He never got it looked at, though a nurse once told him it would be easy to remove. Instead, he wore a bandage over it every day. As time passed, it grew to almost the size of a second nose. Yet Bird wouldn't hear of letting a doctor check it out—not even when fluid occasionally seeped from it. Instead, he cobbled together two bandages, then three, to cover it every day.

By 2015, he was clearly sick. Those last years, he hobbled around the neighborhood with a cane. He covered a sore on his chest in a bandage. None of his sores were treated, and Bird got testy anytime anyone suggested he ought to. His body weakened, and Jackie and his sister pestered him to get medical attention. He would not.

With a regular city budget, the center prospered. And as it did, Bird's health began to fade. Toward the end, he spent a lot of time sitting in front of the house he shared with Jackie, surveying the three blocks of the neighborhood that he hadn't left in decades, waving to those who passed.

On October 9, 2017, Bird was so weak that Jackie Cooper called paramedics. But he would hear nothing of a trip to a hospital. He was going to live on, he said. He wasn't going to die. "Not today, boys," he told paramedics when they arrived. They left. A few minutes later, Bird collapsed, unconscious. Jackie called them back, and he died in their ambulance as they were leaving for the hospital. Of cancer, it turned out.

Mike Kissick, a community center unto himself, was fifty-nine.

Muncie III

A few days after Mike "Bird" Kissick died, mourners filled the gym at the Ross Center to remember the man who, quietly, bound their neighborhood as best he could as so many forces tore at it. His old neighborhood friends showed up. Shannon McCormick spoke. He wanted people to know Bird when he was younger and rail thin. How they'd played basketball at Lincoln School until nine or ten at night. As a kid, Bird owned the neighborhood record for the longest bicycle wheelie—one full block on his blue Schwinn ten-speed—until that record was broken by a fellow who went two full blocks on one wheel. Bird tried but never could get that record back.

"Thanks for caring for all of our children," wrote one woman on his online obituary. His own phobias helped care for the neighborhood as it lost a lot of the can-do, car-guy effervescence that believed in slow and small improvements achieved by showing up every day. But through Bird some of that idea had survived.

Jud Fisher saw the beauty of it. Fisher is a tall, spectacled fellow, and president of the Ball Brothers Foundation. Ball Brothers made glassware and for years was the town's largest employer. All that's left of the company in Muncie today is the family's philanthropic foundation. Fisher, whose mother was a Ball, is its president.

Fisher's focus was on community rejuvenation, and he wanted to start with Avondale on the south side. The seventy-acre lot where the

Chevrolet plant once stood was now a desert of cracked concrete. Three companies Fisher had heard of had passed on the area as a place to relocate. This, he felt, was because "the place looked like a nuclear bomb blast." A big factory salvation seemed unlikely. Even if such a factory came, Fisher thought, it was likely to employ more robots than people.

The idea that fired Fisher was to reignite the people in a small place with tiny improvements to one neighborhood—something like the tool-and-die approach to life, though Fisher might not have put it that way. It was, Fisher thought, a lot like encouraging recovery in an addict who sees no hope; it required small steps. "I believe in the beachhead," Fisher told me. "You get people energized. It helps spread the glow. You start to create that village thing—you get that energy and vitality."

Others began thinking the same way. Habitat for Humanity had been working in Muncie for several years as abandoned houses spread like a pestilence. In Muncie, the organization focused less on building new houses and more on remodeling those that could be saved, one house at a time. Each finished place was owned and occupied by a neighbor with a stake in the house. Habitat focused too on the Avondale neighborhood. With neighbors' sweat equity, Habitat for Humanity built a community garden and a pocket park. The Avondale Methodist Church began holding community dinners every Thursday night.

Craig Graybeal was also at work on the south side. Graybeal grew up in Indianapolis and spent ten years in the US Army. Following September 11, 2001, he was deployed for six months to Afghanistan. He left the army and returned to study architecture at Ball State University in Muncie.

He and one of his professors formed a nonprofit they called ecoREHAB, which, like Habitat for Humanity, set about rehabbing one house at a time, enlisting students to help do what the private sector would not. "These are neighborhood houses," he told me. "If we tear them down, it's going to look like Detroit, a block with two houses. You can only have so many pocket parks and community gardens."

One problem was the houses where methamphetamine had been cooked. Meth houses stayed vacant for years, blighting their streets. Near the Ross Center, Graybeal found a 900-square-foot bungalow whose owner was fighting a meth-cooking charge. Graybeal bought it for $1,000.

Turns out, decontaminating a meth house is not that hard. Much of the contamination is dust that settles on walls, which are easily washed, and on carpets, which are easily removed. Rebuilding the house took longer than the cleaning, but it was straightforward work that Graybeal and his crew had done before. Before long, the house was reborn.

"It needed to be shown that it could be done," Graybeal told me. "The house is not cursed forever; only while it's contaminated. Now it's an asset. It's getting another homeowner back in. You can't perform neighborhood revitalization without invested homeowners."

Norma Ruttan, a widow, grandmother, and retired second-grade Catholic schoolteacher, bought the place for $34,500 in January of 2017. She had lived for fourteen years in a trailer, and this was the first single-family home she'd owned. She decorated it with photos of her grandchildren and Muncie memorabilia from another era. "I wake up with a feeling of gratitude," she told me, "for another day that I have this home."

A couple of blocks east of the Chevy plant is Versatile Metal Works. VMW is a partnership formed in 2010 between a journeyman machinist named Jeremi Dobbs and Gordon Cox, who owns Muncie's oldest mortuary. "There was that free spirit in this town—the ability to go out and say, 'I can do this. Let me figure out how to put a machine shop in my garage,'" Dobbs told me when I visited VMW.

The company, he said, was trying to recapture that. With eighteen employees and million-dollar machines, VMW now makes pulleys for volleyball nets, parts for locomotives and NFL helmets, tubes for ambulance suspensions, housings for air-conditioning units, and police K-9 cages.

As the business was humming, Dobbs and Cox bought a nearby lot where two crumbling houses stood. They tore them down and planted grass. Then a strange thing happened. "After we spent money to clean it up, I had this twitch in my mind: abstract art," said Cox, who at seventy-six is a straitlaced fellow, as morticians tend to be, and admits to never before having had such a twitch. On a section of grass a few blocks from the abandoned Chevy plant now stand sculptures cut and welded from scrap sheet metal: two kids running hand in hand, a couple reading, a buck with large antlers, some geometric abstracts, and, out front, a truck bearing the VMW logo.

VMW's art park is as out of place as it can be amid the south side's rough houses, railroad tracks, and cracked asphalt, yet it adds a quiet green break on a once-blighted plot. Not many folks in the area know what it is, or why. But "next thing you know," Dobbs said, "we have people knocking on our door, asking me to build artwork."

All this was the kind of thing Jud Fisher hoped would happen as he planned a project to leverage the energy now emerging in Avondale. His idea took six years to become reality, a lot longer than anyone imagined. A road needed to be rerouted, and an underground electrical main belonging to the local utility needed attention.

But finally in the spring of 2018, six months after Bird died, two youth baseball diamonds opened a block from his house on what had been the Chevy employee parking lots. A Little League formed around it. Bird's friend, Shannon McCormick, was its president. Almost four hundred kids—three to thirteen years old—from all over Muncie came to the diamonds to play, so many that there was a question as to whether they'd have enough coaches. "When games are going," McCormick said, "there'll be four teams playing and 150 people watching the games, seeing we can coexist—you got Hispanic, Black, White. Kids want to stay indoors connected to their phones, but when they're out here, they have a blast." As Bird would have wanted.

The 2019 Little League practices got underway one May afternoon. Aluminum rainclouds that morning gave way to an assertive sun over south Muncie, as if to announce that spring had finally come.

To one side, a line of tiny kids, some with their gloves on the wrong hand, threw off the wrong foot in a game of toss with the line of mothers and fathers a few yards away. Grandparents, with dogs on leashes, watched from tiny metal bleachers.

The neighborhood still had folks who seemed to add little—young men in tattoos on sagging porches, with backpacks and baseball hats turned backward. But there was more than that now. Ross Center bustled with kids playing basketball. Two blocks east was VMW's abstract art park. A block to the west stood the meth house Craig Graybeal had rehabbed. Beyond that was the Habitat for Humanity community garden. Small steps, each conjuring the spirit of the tool-and-die guys, tinkerers like Wes Russell, whose energy once moved Muncie's south side, and of Mike "Bird" Kissick, who did what he could to hold the place together when everyone else was bailing out. It seemed to me, after traveling the country chronicling the opioid epidemic, that the Avondale neighborhood was finally getting what a lot of the country needed. No splashy, magic answer. Instead, just folks moving in their own quiet ways toward community rejuvenation.

I stood on the grass as shadows stretched across the diamond that afternoon. A chubby boy, a leftie, only a tad older than a toddler, whacked seriously at a ball on a T. His hands in the wrong order on the bat, he missed once, then swung and missed again. A breeze wandered through and calmed the afternoon heat. The boy glared at the thing sitting helplessly before him. Then he took another swing, and the white ball shot across the thick green grass and into the hands of his father.

PART III

Angie and Starla III

"Who Do You Belong To?"

On January 24, 2013, a young woman with black hair and green eyes arrived from Florida at a nursing home in the small north-central Tennessee town of Huntsville.

Her paperwork described her condition as a persistent, irreversible vegetative state. She twisted and rolled, and turned, and stroked her chin. She was blind and couldn't speak. She could not eat or drink and required a feeding tube. She did seem able to hear and feel. The staff put her in a room on a mat on the floor, fearing she would tumble off a bed.

The paperwork gave her name as Starla Hope Hoss. She was twenty-seven.

There she lay for about a month, turning incessantly, lurching, sometimes rolling off her mat and out into the hall. The staff fed her four times a day through the tube in her stomach. They knew nothing about her that wasn't on her paperwork, which stated that she had come from Florida, that her brain was damaged due to lack of oxygen caused by an overdose. The feeding tube in her stomach twisted and turned with her. Before long she was covered in feces. Her hair grew tangled, greasy; her lungs rattled. And no one called to inquire about her. And no one came to visit her.

Until, that is, one day, a lady called to ask, did the home have a patient named Starla Hoss? A couple days after that a short, pretty woman, no longer timid, showed up at that nursing home in Huntsville, Tennessee.

Angie Manning was forty-two; her married name was now Odom. Many years had passed since that night aboard the USS *Cape Cod* when she was nineteen, on watch and tied to the back of the destroyer, under the silent and mighty expanse of darkness.

A lot had happened since then. In the navy, she fell in love. She met Tracy Lee Crouch, from Bowling Green, Ohio. They began dating and were married before a justice of the peace in San Diego. But they were very young. While in the navy, he'd had a motorcycle accident, for which he was given painkillers—unending amounts of them. In the navy, the pills were easy to get, and before long he was dependent. As he was about to discharge, Tracy asked the navy for help and was told he'd have to seek therapy on the outside. Tracy left the navy, while Angie stayed on to finish her time. In phone calls to his family in Ohio, Angie learned he had taken up with a girlfriend. After her enlistment was finished, Angie moved to Ohio to salvage her marriage. By then Tracy was using meth, pain pills, and alcohol. "He needed professional help, and at that time there wasn't much offered," she said. He beat her, and this caused two miscarriages. Still, she stayed, enduring the bruises.

They moved to her hometown of Elizabethton, Tennessee. There Angie returned to the church she grew up in, where her father's funeral was held. She played the organ in its services. She felt a comfort in reconnecting to her hometown, even as her marriage deteriorated. In the fifth year of her marriage, Angie gave birth to a daughter, Bethany, and this gave her strength to leave as her husband spiraled down. High on meth one night, he stood outside the home where she was staying with her mother and stepfather and bellowed that he wanted her back. Eventually, though, Tracy moved back to Ohio, where he died many years later in a car accident.

During the worst of it, Angie hid out with her mother and stepfather, waiting for the divorce to become final. Her pastor called one day. He was sure she would agree, he said, that "it wouldn't be appropriate" for a single mother to have a prominent role as the organist in the church. He said nothing about God, nor help she might need in this difficult time.

Angie left that church and never went back. She remarried in 1994, to a good man named Earl Odom, a factory worker who adopted her daughter, and her life took on a calm she hadn't known for many years. By 2000, she was directing after-school programs at three Elizabethton elementary schools. For a teaching credential, she wrote a paper on alternatives to abortion and what services existed in town for pregnant women and newborns.

Elizabethton is in the hills of eastern Tennessee, the largest town in remote Carter County, part of which abuts North Carolina and is made up mostly of scattered hamlets and hollers. Carter County's challenge is its isolation. It has no bus service, no taxis; the distances are such that if you don't have a car, you can't get anywhere. What Angie also found was that there were no services for children and pregnant women in Carter County. A lot of churches, but no place helping kids and their parents.

With no one stepping up, a pastor suggested to Angie that maybe it was up to her to fill the void. With that, her life path changed. While working at the school district, she founded the TLC Clinic to provide crisis counseling and adoption services.

Angie took no government money so as to avoid the constraints that came with it, but relied instead on local donations, many from churches. She did a church census to see where she might solicit funds—360 churches in a county of 56,000 people. She was not surprised. In Carter County, community was created in church; there, children were raised, business connections were forged, romances begun. But an addict or unwed mother entered these churches with difficulty. Clothes drives, casseroles for families with a terminally ill child—churches knew how to do that. But addiction was different. It was something on the national news that allowed folks in Carter County to take comfort that they didn't live in a big city. Churches had no custom of coming together in support of an affliction that many in the congregation believed would give them a bad name, or seemed to reflect the member's weak faith, or was the choice and fault of the person affected.

Some churches hid from uncomfortable facts. Others didn't know what to do. Many felt their responsibilities extended only to their congregations and no further. Whatever the case, their silence hid how widely addiction had spread. "I was tired of being quiet," Angie told me. "Silence is what's killing people. We put on the pretty face that's the look of church: everybody's dressed, looking great—'How you doing?' 'Wonderful!' But if we can get people to start opening up, can you imagine what we would learn?"

When she named her new clinic TLC, people thought it stood for Tender Loving Care. Instead, she named it for her ex-husband, Tracy Lee Crouch. Explaining the name allowed her to talk about many things: being a single mom, domestic violence, and drug abuse. The name "allows me the opportunity to share my story," she said, "then usually when I do, they're not afraid to share. You start hearing these stories."

Not long after doors opened at the TLC Clinic, the opioid crisis took root in eastern Tennessee. Soon, through her clinic doors came more women who were not just pregnant but addicted—to pain pills, then heroin or meth, or all of that. Angie had to learn how to help them, or their infants born into withdrawal. The TLC became Carter County's backstop, taking care of the epidemic's wounded and ravaged women, occasionally finding couples to adopt their infants.

On Valentine's Day of 2013, a woman called Angie. She had an infant and needed help. "You might remember me," she told Angie.

It had been a rough two weeks for Maude Buchanan. The state of Florida had called her. Her daughter, Starla Hoss, had given birth. The infant, they said, would enter the state's foster-care system if Maude didn't come get her. So Maude drove down to Pensacola and the hospital where her little granddaughter spent the first days of life. By then, though, Starla was gone. Later, it wasn't clear if no one at the hospital knew where she'd been sent, or Maude didn't do much asking. Whatever the case, Maude returned to Tennessee with only the infant. She had no money, no way of caring for the child. She called Angie.

"Your parents drove the bus that took us to church," Maude told Angie. In the 1970s, Angie's parents ran a bus ministry. Most Carter County country people back then had no cars. The Mannings went through the hamlets and hollers each Saturday, asking who needed a ride to church the next day, and giving out bubblegum to the kids. On Sunday the couple would pull through in a big yellow bus, fill it with kids, then head into Elizabethton, leading the children in Christian songs.

"But we met another time," Maude continued. "You helped my daughter get married in jail. Her name is Starla Hoss."

Angie Odom certainly remembered Starla Hoss. They had met when Angie was teaching an abstinence class at a girls group home. They got to know each other in long talks. Starla was a quiet girl, wanting to please, wanting to be liked, who would open up one-on-one. She told Angie she was the fourth generation of drug users in her family; she had started at thirteen. She said she was pimped out for drugs at fourteen. She spoke to Angie of wanting to leave drugs and reset her life. The girl had nobody to depend on and ached for unconditional love. "I'll always be there to help you," Angie promised. If Angie thought at all about that promise later, she realized she meant help with the small stuff of life.

When Starla left the group home, she disappeared. A couple of years later, she showed up at Angie's TLC Clinic with a you're-gonna-kill-me grin on her face. She was pregnant with her first child. Angie got her in to see a doctor and signed her up for monthly mommy meetings, through which she could get diapers and infant clothes. Four months into the program, Starla disappeared again.

A few months after that Angie was working at the jail, ministering to women, when she came upon Starla in custody, now close to giving birth. Starla had been on the way to get married when she was arrested on a probation violation. She asked for help in getting married in the jail. Angie was skeptical, but she bought a cake and arranged for a pastor. Not long after her wedding, furloughed from jail, Starla gave birth to a baby boy she named Ezra.

Starla called Angie one last time a few years later, asking for clothes for her boy. She was living in the town of Mountain City, with its reputation for meth. Come by TLC, Angie told her, but Starla never did. And that was the last conversation Angie ever had with Starla Hoss. She would wonder from time to time what had become of the lost girl.

Until Maude Buchanan and her sister showed up that Valentine's Day in 2013 carrying a car seat covered in a pink blanket. Bustling in the door, Maude said, "We gotta go smoke," and handed Angie the car seat. As the women smoked outside, Angie opened the pink blanket and peered in at a newborn girl with big dark eyes.

"I wonder who you are," she said. "Who do you belong to?"

The women came in from their smoke.

"I need to find Starla," Maude said. "This is her baby."

Neuroscience III

"Built to Be Social"

In human brains, behind each ear and just above the brain stem, lies a blue spot that has helped guarantee our survival.

It's known as the locus coeruleus (Latin for "blue spot"), though those who study it just call it the LC. In humans, the LC evolved early, as it had to. The main job of the LC is to send a chemical—called noradrenaline—to other parts of the brain that ignite warnings of life-threatening menace. Noradrenaline helps sound the alarm, pushes the panic button, in a sense.. Without it, we would have died off long ago.

Opiates change a lot in our brains. One thing they do is stifle the LC. They shut it down. Under their influence, the LC can no longer send the chemical igniting panic. Smothered so completely, the LC, product of millennia of evolution, is muted, even as the drug sends the body into overdose.

In fact, like some menacing extraterrestrial, opiates convince the LC that doing *without* them would be the life-threatening event. With opiates removed, the now-unbound LC leaps into action. Studies of the brain of an addict entering withdrawals show that the LC gets agitated, releasing outsize amounts of noradrenaline that produce alarm, panic, anxiety, and insomnia. The result amounts to, in effect, a chemical shriek that the addict must have the drug immediately or all is lost.

I submit the bizarre case of the tiny locus coeruleus because, in the smallest of ways, it illustrates how drugs of abuse, and opiates in particular, change the chemistry of our brains. When this happens, organs we use to defend ourselves, which evolved to help us survive, are redirected to betray us and aid our demise. That's a stunning result. It's what prompted users in Chicago in 2005 and 2006 not to flee, but to flock to the deadly new drug—fentanyl—that dealers then branded as "Lethal Injection" and "Drop Dead." I wanted to understand what allows that betrayal.

Luckily, technology has allowed us to learn more about the brain in the last twenty years than we've ever before known. Our neuroscientists are able now to ask new questions: What brain activity does curiosity stimulate? How about prayer? Trust? Virtue signaling? Righteous indignation? What does hearing a poignant story do to our brain chemistry? A similar golden age of genetics research, too, is teaching us a lot about the brain. Volumes remain to be revealed; the brain and the universe are the most awesomely complex, maybe ultimately impenetrable, places humans have chosen to study. But we know a lot, and can surmise more. So as I traveled the country, trying to understand the depths of this crisis and aware of what I didn't know, I sought out neuroscientists.

Very quickly our talks centered around a chemical the brain produces called dopamine. Dopamine prods us into an activity that we have learned will produce reward, good feelings. Dopamine rushes to a key node in the brain's pleasure circuit known as the nucleus accumbens, where it creates feelings of motivation. Do this because it'll be good—that's dopamine's signal.

This is what neuroscientists call the brain's "reward pathway." It's actually more complicated, but that's its rough map. The reward pathway exists to house and promote our most basic impulses and survival instincts. Above all, it rewards us with feelings of pleasure from activities that keep us alive: sex, eating, exercise. Other living things have a reward function—even worms. Reward is about self-gratification and the me-first impulse, but it is essential to human life. Seeking reward pushes us to achieve, to build. "Reward is the predominant driving force since *Homo sapiens* inhabited the planet," wrote Dr. Robert Lustig, whose videotaped speeches and fantastic book *The Hacking of the American Mind* were part of my education. "If we didn't like sex and food, we would never eat anything or reproduce. Reward is how humans get things done; it's literally survival of the species." Without reward, we would be like so many lottery winners, who lose purpose in life, grow depressed, apathetic, isolated, and lonely, and sometimes commit suicide.

Crucial to all this are what neuroscientists call receptors—which Dr. Paul Janssen spent so much time studying. Receptors are molecules within the cells in our brain and body that govern important functions and feelings. Our brain contains receptors of all kinds. One class of receptors in the brain, for example, governs pleasure and pain. These same receptors also inhabit our lungs, where they control our breathing, and our gut, regulating our bowels. A second class of receptors governs memory. They allow us to forget things we need to forget, especially in fear and anxiety. They keep us from getting too excited; they spur our appetite, and reduce nausea and vomiting.

The chemicals that transmit messages between one part of the brain and the other have a name. They're called neurotransmitters. Dopamine and noradrenaline are among the brain's many neurotransmitters. They help transmit messages between different parts of the brain. The way these neurotransmitters do this is by locking onto these receptor molecules, an action that produces these feelings—alarm, desire, pain, pleasure, reward. The list goes on. But the brain, always seeking equilibrium, creates neurotransmitters in only limited quantities.

By some bizarre coincidence of nature, however, some plants produce molecules that when introduced to our bodies activate these receptors as well. Two of the most famous are the opium poppy and marijuana.

The poppy produces the morphine molecule, which attaches neatly to the first class of receptors I just described. These receptors were discovered in the 1970s, and as scientists saw they were especially affected by opioids—morphine, heroin, other opium derivatives, as well as those synthetically produced, like fentanyl—they called them "opioid receptors." The neurotransmitters that the brain produces naturally to attach to these receptors they termed "endorphins"—a combination of the words *endogenous* and *morphine*.

Marijuana, meanwhile, produces a chemical called THC that attaches to the second class of receptors (discovered in 1988). These receptors were then deemed "cannabinoid receptors," and the brain chemicals that attach to them were called endocannabinoids (for endogenous cannabinoids).

Because molecules in these plants attach to these receptors in our brain and elsewhere, they can, in small amounts, enhance our lives. Marijuana can calm the nausea in chemotherapy patients and improve the appetite of AIDS patients. Morphine and other opioids, of course, numb pain and allow for surgery to take place. In the bowels, opioids can control diarrhea—as Paul Janssen knew when he invented loperamide.

But in larger quantities, far beyond what the brain can produce, these molecules prod our brain receptors to excess. THC in marijuana overwhelms the cannabinoid receptors and produces ravenous hunger and faulty memory. The morphine molecule locks with the opioid receptors to produce euphoria and numb pain. Opioid receptors in our lungs govern breathing; too much morphine molecule shuts down breathing, which is how overdose victims die. The morphine molecule also produces constipation in addicts. In withdrawals, without the drug, addicts suffer diarrhea. (Naloxone, the overdose antidote, is occasionally used to treat constipation.)

(Interestingly, the natural substances that make humans high actually evolved in their plants as pesticides, to keep predator insects from feasting on their leaves. Nicotine is a pesticide that tobacco naturally produces. So is caffeine in coffee, cocaine in the coca leaf, morphine in the opium poppy, and perhaps THC in marijuana as well.)

In modern life, many things now generate the charge of reward, though of varying intensity. These include shopping, sex, gambling, food, pornography, drugs, seeing a puppy or a baby, helping an old lady across the street, consummating a business deal, a pickup basketball game with old friends.

I spoke with Bruce Armitage, a chemist at Carnegie Mellon University in Pittsburgh. "I see it as all about stimuli," he said, "things the world provides to us that we don't make inside our bodies or in our brains. As our brains evolved, we lived in places where so much was limited to us. We had limited access to sugar, fat. Life was a constant struggle—kill or be killed. But nowadays you can text your dealer, you can shop to your heart's content, eat as much sweet and fatty foods as you want. Pretty much any substance you want to engage in you can, and without limit. Our brains tightly regulate how much endorphins they produce. Endorphins don't last very long in the brain. But when these substances or stimuli are available from the outside, there's no regulation to keep things in moderation. Our brain is just not strong enough to offer sufficient resistance, and we become addicted to them."

That's what addictive substances and activities do: they overwhelm, turn our bodies against their own self-interest. All drugs of abuse have been found to activate dopamine in our brains. The blast of dopamine they create stimulates the nucleus accumbens far more than other daily activities that give us pleasure—say, seeing a cute infant. That dopamine locks onto receptors in the nucleus accumbens, and from that we experience a rush of euphoria.

Among the first to talk to me about dopamine in this regard was Nicole Avena. Dopamine is released, she said, when we do something that our brain has learned will produce a reward. But when the activity is a food that we've gotten used to, the dopamine drops off. Avena had seen this in her lab. Using a process called microdialysis, she and her colleagues measured the dopamine level in the brains of rats while they were eating. Give a rat a Cheeto, they found, and his dopamine surges until he gets used to the Cheeto; then the dopamine falls back to a normal level.

Dopamine levels, however, don't diminish when a person uses a drug of abuse. They stay and prod the person to consume more. When the drug is removed, the dopamine plummets far below normal levels, leaving us frantically wanting more. This is part of how cravings are created. Avena's lab tested this, and sure enough, microdialysis showed that the brains of sugar-dependent rats never registered a reduction in dopamine while they consumed sugar water. When the sugar water was removed, dopamine levels crashed far below normal, "similar to what you would see in drugs of abuse," Avena told me. The rats grew frantic for their sugar water.

The nucleus accumbens, meanwhile, responds to this onslaught of dopamine by reducing the receptors available for all pleasures. Then two things happen: we feel less pleasure at more common moments that once pleased us; and we gradually need more of the drug to produce that same rush. The result is tolerance—chasing a feeling that will never feel as powerful as the first time you felt it.

Many parts of the brain are involved in addiction, which is why it's such a complicated phenomenon. One area is the hippocampus. There, our brain forms memory associations.

Our brains evolved to be learning machines; to survive as a species, we had to learn from experience. During most of our evolution, pleasure was the rarest of occurrences, to be treasured and enjoyed because it wasn't coming again soon: a sweet berry, for example, with the tiniest dose of sugar. Thus our brains can't help but associate with pleasure the thing that happened right before we felt good. Our brains associate pleasure with memories of those events—cues that signal something pleasurable is about to occur: we see friends with whom we've enjoyed a glass of wine, the smell of barbecue.

I acknowledge a fuzzy feeling for the sign for In-N-Out, the western US burger chain. I get a charge when I discover a true story I can tell that stuns and awes me. I also love basketball, so I assume the smell of a gym's wood floor triggers dopamine in my brain. Anyway, it's hard not to shoot around when I'm in a gym, even if I'm not dressed for it. These cues are relatively weak and easy to resist, if need be, because the pleasure they release is not overwhelming.

Drugs of abuse, it seems, take advantage of our brain's remarkable power to learn. Their euphoria produces strong memory associations in the hippocampus: a drug-using buddy, a needle, a phone call to the dope dealer. Heroin dealers seem to understand that forcing addicts to wait for them enhances their customers' anticipation, spurring their continued patronage. The Velvet Underground sang about this in "I'm Waiting for the Man," on its first album: "He's never early, he's always late. First thing you learn is that you always gotta wait."

(The Velvet Underground's entire first album, from 1967, amounts to a love letter to heroin and a cue for shooting up. Apart from "I'm Waiting for the Man," "Heroin" is the best-known rock song in praise of the drug. Some writers find "Femme Fatale" to be plausibly about heroin. More than that, though, the drone and thrum of the album harmonizes with heroin's euphoria, according to many addicts.)

Cues provoke a massive release of dopamine, reminding us that pleasure is just around the corner. Over time, though, they torment the addict: they trigger the dopamine that produces the urge for the activity that it associates with pleasure, but the nucleus accumbens has protected itself against overstimulation by providing fewer receptors for the dopamine to lock onto. So though the brain intensely desires an activity, it can produce less of the pleasure associated with it. The result is wanting, craving, desperation. An addict enjoys a drug less and wants it more. Pleasure declines, cravings increase. The normal delights of life now seem dull, too minor to compete. Pleasure only comes from the drug.

In all this, again, memory is crucial. Memory forms our personality. Who we are is in large part what we remember. This is what makes Alzheimer's disease such a tragedy. Drugs of abuse control memory, giving us a selection of what we can remember that is biased in favor of our continuing to use them. In so doing, they may also control who we come to believe we are. With no chemical competition standing up to a drug's domination, we become less social, we isolate, moving away from all that has kept us alive. Opiate addicts avoid old friends who might provide care, love, and healthy ballast by reminding them who they once were. They are as socially out of balance as their brain chemistry, so they hang out with other drug users interested in one thing.

All this resembles a strange case from the annals of neuroscience. In 1953, a Connecticut doctor examined a man named Henry Molaison, a twenty-seven-year-old factory worker who suffered from epileptic fits due to a childhood bicycle accident. The seizures prevented Mr. Molaison from working. As a last resort, the physician performed an experimental surgery that removed a thumb-sized part of each side of Mr. Molaison's brain that seemed to have to do with his fits. His seizures stopped. But the function of the removed area only then became clear. His short-term memory was gone. For the rest of his life, Mr. Molaison couldn't learn new facts nor remember what happened the day before; he couldn't learn new songs or remember the current president of the United States. He could go nowhere unaccompanied. He could learn motor skills, but he was introduced to the same people every day and forgot them as soon as he turned away. Molaison had part of himself erased with that surgery. He could remember no story to tell about his life and remained a stranger to himself. He described life as "like waking from a dream . . . every day is alone in itself."

Molaison participated in extensive research on his brain at MIT, with access to him limited to a hundred scientists. One of them, Dr. Jenni Ogden, wrote in *Psychology Today* in 2012 that Mr. Molaison was "a very happy and friendly person and always a delight to be with and to assess. He never seemed to get tired of doing what most people would think of as tedious memory tests, because they were always new to him! When he was at MIT, between test sessions he would often sit doing crossword puzzles, and he could do the same ones again and again if the words were erased, as to him it was new each time." Yet though his brain was a blank slate when it came to recent memory, Mr. Molaison remembered childhood events, the names of friends from the second grade.

(Mr. Molaison died in 2008 at eighty-two. His brain was then cut into 2,401 slices and digitized. He remains the foundation for a lot that the world today knows about human memory, and the most famous patient in the history of neuroscience.)

Reading the story of Henry Molaison, it occurred to me that something similar takes place in the memory of those who abuse hard drugs. They cannot remember, say, that their addiction has them living in a tent under an overpass—or, at least, that memory recedes—while vividly recalling the pain of withdrawals and the ecstasy long ago when they first used the drug.

I spoke about all this with Tom Gould, a neuroscientist at Penn State University, who has studied the hippocampus. "Drugs impair some memories but enhance others," he told me. "They shift the balance so the drug memories are stronger, especially memories of rewarding effects and craving. So you have an individual with real strong memory of the rewards [of taking drugs]. They're more impulsive. Meanwhile, the area of the brain that tells them 'Hey, don't do this' is not communicating as well. Somebody will remember that first high, and will be chasing that, and [is] less likely, in that moment, to remember the negative consequences of addiction."

It's a remarkable thing: the drug enhances those memories that would lead us to our doom, while the brain, which evolved all the weapons to keep us alive, can barely muster a defense.

In all this, the continued supply of drugs, and particularly of potent drugs, is an indispensable part. The more change in brain chemistry that the steady use of a potent drug creates, the more powerful the memory association and the more potential for long-term influence over the brain. This is why the quantity and potency of drugs on the street matter so much. Our revolution in neuroscience research has shown that around 30 percent of people have a genetic disposition for addiction. But no matter what a person's genetic disposition, no one gets addicted to drugs she hasn't tried.

Once a person is addicted to one drug, trying another, and another after that, is easier. We are not so different, it turns out, from those sugar-dependent rats in Nicole Avena's lab at Princeton. One drug consumed long enough primes us for another.

All of this works against what the brain naturally seeks, which is equilibrium, a balance of competing chemicals. Part of the brain creates a neurotransmitter called serotonin. Serotonin binds with the opioid receptor, too. Its job, when it does that, is to promote satiation, contentment, happiness, patience—telling you you've had enough, you're fine. Our brains have evolved to naturally keep serotonin and dopamine in competitive balance. Dopamine tells us that something better awaits us; serotonin says we have enough.

Drugs and other addictive substances increase dopamine while reducing serotonin. Desire overwhelms moderation and contentment. This may be why addicts so often suffer from depression—they're producing less serotonin to promote contentment. It's why, Robert Lustig said in one lecture, "the more pleasure you seek, the more unhappy you get."

The reward pathway, finally, stands in opposition to another part of the brain that is also about moderating our me-first impulses: the prefrontal cortex. The prefrontal cortex is just behind the forehead. It is in charge of executive decisions: planning for the future, reining in impulses, delaying gratification, considering others, and learning from mistakes. It connects to the brain's system of emotion and pleasure, acting as a brake on impulsivity. (Its connection to our system of processing emotion is why, neuroscientists believe, we take pleasure from solving problems.) When the reward pathway demands actions that feel pleasurable, the prefrontal cortex assesses their consequences. It develops many years after the reward pathway, which is there from birth. Before the prefrontal cortex is fully formed—in a teenager, for example—the reward pathway dominates the brain and governs behavior. Hence the me-first immaturity associated with teens.

Our brains have evolved so that when our nucleus accumbens sends signals that our survival is at risk, the prefrontal cortex is muted. This allows us split-second action to avoid immediate danger, without any backtalk from the prefrontal cortex.

Drugs take over that function. They shut down the prefrontal cortex. Only now they overwhelm the brain with impulses that tell us that the danger is being without dope. An addicted brain is one where a raging primitive reward system has silenced the prefrontal cortex's wise counsel. The reward system, unbalancing the natural competition among brain chemicals, gains a monopoly on the brain. Adam Smith, in describing capitalism in *The Wealth of Nations*, called monopoly a "derangement" and "hurtful to the society in which it takes place." That sounds to me like what's going on in the addicted brain.

Thus we return to the tiny LC, which, under opiates' influence, betrays us with its silence as death approaches. That's what drugs do. They co-opt, reprogram parts of the brain that evolved to keep us alive—like the LC. Those parts of the brain that rebel against the new regime—like the prefrontal cortex—are smothered like dissidents in a police state. The dictatorship of the reward pathway on drugs pushes us away from the balance—the competitive equilibrium—that helps us survive. From a broad array of activities, our lives adopt a single directive: finding more dope. Our brains are wondrous, mystifying, complex organs. From them have sprung awesome creations, innovations, inventions. Drugs dim those gorgeous lights to a gray obedience. Our brain on drugs resembles the regime that imprisons its great writers, artists, and scientists. It resembles, too, any culture so numbed by the babble of marketing that it doesn't have to lock up its most creative spirits; it just drowns them out.

Drugs diminish community—the impulse to live with others. In prehistoric times, our survival required belonging to a group. Anyone who isolated was quickly eaten, or starved. We—our brains—descend from people whose existence depended on banding together. So important was this that warm brain rewards come from customs like music, storytelling, and, as pharmaceutical sales reps knew well, eating with others.

As I was trying to understand all this, I spoke with David Linden, a neuroscientist at Johns Hopkins University Medical School in Baltimore who has written several books on the brain.

"Our brains didn't evolve so we could get high on heroin or alcohol or cannabis," Linden told me as we sat in his lab on the fifth floor of a building near downtown Baltimore one humid afternoon. "These pleasure circuits are there so that we eat food, have sex, and do prosocial things so that we survive and get our genes to the next generation. That partly means having babies, having community, and letting genes of our relatives thrive.

"Humans are really built to be social. When you try to understand the human brain and what it evolved for, social behavior is a large part of it. We are extraordinarily good at what we need to live in groups of people, like picking up on social cues: posture, language, facial expression, vocal tone. You need the social overtones and emotional cast to make sense of human communication."

Years ago, Linden wrote a book called *Touch: The Science of the Hand, Heart, and Mind*. Turns out touch is the sense we cannot live without, far more than, say, sight or hearing. "There really is a need for interpersonal touch," Linden said. "Social touch is like social glue. It communicates you can trust me, we're on the same team, we're allies." Touch helped us survive as a group.

Drugs and other addictive products turn us away from that. Heroin addicts retreat into themselves. The addict alone in his hoodie seems an emblem of the Opioid Era. Gambling, first undertaken as a social activity, turns quickly into something one does alone. Same with alcohol. Social media, meanwhile, more resembles prehistoric communication. On social media, we are unable to perceive the differences in tone and meaning that we have learned as a species through eons of face-to-face interaction. We see no facial expressions on Facebook.

Nuance is hard to tweet. We mistake a playful phrase for menace or insult. A medium designed for connectivity instead inflames our righteous anger and indignation.

Likewise, an addict, with natural communal impulses muted, devolves into an antisocial state. Her sole focus is on self-gratification, obeying her me-first impulse, isolated and alone, even as she lives amid millions of others. Any relationship serves her only inasmuch as it can help her score. In her addicted brain, Me has won the battle over Us.

As a culture, it seemed to me, we did more or less what she did. Not, of course, that we were all on heroin. But like a drug addict, we came to believe that we were fine alone. Communing with others was messy, awkward, put us in contact with people who didn't look, think, or believe as we did. It meant collective effort, sharing. Sometimes it cost us more in taxes. It was hard work. Sometimes it meant limiting what we wanted in favor of the community good. But modern life and our prosperity allow us now to live in houses with empty sidewalks, knowing no one, a separate bedroom for every child. Or segregate into regions where everyone believes, looks, and talks as we do.

As I traveled and spoke with neuroscientists, it seemed that one way of thinking of America in the last four decades is that we gradually surrendered—collectively, as a culture—to the brain's reward pathway. Our prosperity allowed us this luxury. We could follow the nucleus accumbens and the pursuit of dopamine and pleasure. This was one way of understanding the Opioid Era in America. Our epidemic of opioid addiction was just an extreme expression of a culture in which, in so many ways, Me won the battle over Us.

Fentanyl V

Kingpins

In the city of Manchester, New Hampshire, the first big fentanyl case happened in 2015. It involved a woman named Jeannette Hardy.

Hardy, twenty-five, was an out-of-work stripper, a heroin addict, who one night was shot by intruders. Instead of calling 911 from her apartment, she ran to a 7-Eleven. The patrolman who responded to the store then walked Hardy back to her apartment. Inside in plain sight were two kilos of fentanyl and $100,000 in cash.

It turned out that Hardy—an unknown to law enforcement—was getting five kilos of fentanyl a week from dealers in Massachusetts. That quantity placed her atop the drug trade for many miles around. She lived alone and didn't know to keep the drug safe. Word spread, and someone tried to rob her of the dope and shot her in the attempt.

"That was a turning point in New England," remembered Jon DeLena, DEA chief for New Hampshire. "That Jeannette Hardy all of a sudden is moving five kilos a week—she went from low-level user with a habit to where they're fronting her all this dope. This isn't how it's supposed to work."

Fentanyl in enormous supplies was opening the drug trade to almost anyone, which is one reason why it created such damage nationwide.

Years before, during America's real-estate bubble in the mid-2000s, people with paltry income and shaky employment, with no steady way of paying for one house, now owned several. Into the industry rushed shyster closing attorneys, corrupt appraisers, banks, and other lenders with no connection to any community. They offered adjustable-rate mortgages to janitors and restaurant workers. For a brief, intoxicated time, lenders got rich and buyers saw a chance to have more than just a home. They bought themselves cars they didn't need and took dream vacations. It marked the liberation of the nucleus accumbens in its battle with the prefrontal cortex. In the words of one lawyer I spoke with, "There was so much available money and so few impediments to accessing it."

Fentanyl was something like that in the drug world. By 2015, supplies of fentanyl were flooding in from Chinese chemical companies selling on the internet and Mexican traffickers. Like the home-loan industry a decade before, fentanyl took barriers that had kept the unprepared out of the market and replaced them with incentives that enticed them in. It was about as easy for a nobody in the drug business to come by large amounts of the stuff as it had been to own multiple houses during the real-estate bubble. Like the real-estate bubble, illicit fentanyl fit snugly into a part of American culture, for the drug was an invitation to almost anyone in the drug world to ignore the warnings of the prefrontal cortex and follow the me-first impulse of the nucleus accumbens. Jon DeLena put it another way: "Fentanyl made people into big-time drug dealers who shouldn't be."

Investigators traced Jeannette Hardy's story south thirty miles to Lawrence, Massachusetts. Lawrence is a drug distribution hub to New Hampshire, run mostly by dealers from the Dominican Republic. By 2015 Dominican traffickers had discovered fentanyl and were getting so much of it from Mexico that they began to spread the risk. They began fronting it to addicts who drove down from all over New Hampshire. In the drug world, opioid addicts are notoriously bad risks with large amounts of dope. They tend to use all their product and not pay what they owe. "Who in their right mind would front dope to a heroin addict? Nobody," DeLena told me. "But [the Dominican dealers] have so much product, so they take that risk that they won't be paid.

They're making it easy for addicts to become dealers—and with that the product is spreading."

All this was part of how fentanyl disrupted the traditional drug world, just as Amazon and Uber upended retail and taxis. Kingpin quantities of drugs were being made or available to be sold by people with no control of geography, no labor force. Procuring large quantities of illegal drugs once required underworld connections, and dealing with scary people. Fentanyl allowed a dealer to go around all that.

Thus, fentanyl reached every corner of America and pushed the overdose-death toll far beyond anything we've seen as a country. This wasn't because users demanded it. Instead, fentanyl was a boon to traffickers and street dealers. It aligned perfectly with their interests: an immensely profitable drug easy to smuggle, cheap, and highly addictive. That was why its damage was so great. Anybody could be a fentanyl kingpin. Even Jeannette Hardy.

By 2016, fentanyl was coming laced into heroin. Within a year or so, customers could assume that what might be called "heroin" was just straight fetty, as fentanyl came to be known. Every day became a game of Russian roulette. "I don't know any longtime fentanyl users," one addict-turned-counselor told me. "They all die."

Why would addicts seek out fentanyl, knowing it would likely kill them? The answer: that's the nature of addiction; it reprograms our brains so that their mission is not to ensure our survival but to pursue the drug. In the world of opiate-addicted brains, an overdose is not a warning; it's an advertisement. Dealers broadcast the fact. Though fentanyl terrified users and they clearly knew the dangers, they, like smokers and their cigarettes, couldn't stay away.

Fentanyl was so cheap and easy to get that it became the go-to additive in the competitive world of street drug sales. It was a street dealer's magic dust as he tried to get big, a way to punch up a drug's wallop. Once one dealer started doing it, his competitors had to follow or lose customers. Fentanyl was added first to heroin. By 2016 it was also showing up in cocaine and meth. These drugs don't often kill people, unless fentanyl is also part of the mix. But between 2012 and 2019, the CDC reported, cocaine-related death rates tripled, and those involving methamphetamine rose sixfold. Fentanyl was the driver of all that.

The other question arose: Why would dealers want to sell a substance so powerful that it killed their customers?

Individually, they probably didn't. But the power of free-market competition took hold. Anybody could procure fentanyl as easily as one of those home loans a decade earlier. It was more potent than any street drug before it. Anybody selling drugs that didn't include the powerful boost of fentanyl wasn't going to have customers for long. Dealers didn't dare *not* mix it in. About the only way to introduce caution regarding fentanyl into the street drug world is for district attorneys to charge with murder those who sell anything containing fentanyl that ends up killing a user. Fearing they will "catch a body," dealers back off.

Soon, fentanyl became a market-expansion tool. Even a casual user of cocaine or meth, once those drugs were laced with fentanyl, would soon be a fentanyl addict—and thus a daily customer. "They don't want fentanyl," said Richard Mason, chief operations officer at House of Hope in Columbus, Ohio. "But they get their meth or cocaine cut with fentanyl without knowing it, and they love the high and they go back for more. I don't think our clients at first were seeking fentanyl. Now they're just straight-up fentanyl addicts."

In the 1980s, Latin American heroin came in stronger and cheaper and outcompeted the heroin that for decades had been coming from the Far East. By the early 1990s, no Far Eastern heroin was for sale in America. That's what fentanyl did to heroin. When addicts grew tolerant to fentanyl's towering potency, simple heroin was too weak to prevent withdrawal. By the time I was finishing this book, heroin had all but disappeared from many areas of the United States—replaced by fentanyl from Seattle to New England.

This devastated opium-poppy growing in Mexico, according to some remarkable fieldwork by three journalists—Romain Le Cour Grandmaison, Nathaniel Morris, and Benjamin Smith—in their 2019 study "No More Opium for the Masses" for Noria, a French research collective. Mexican poppy farmers had been enjoying a bounty supplying the US opiate addiction epidemic. As fentanyl arrived in America, raw opium prices, the authors found, fell by as much as 75 percent in the mountainous poppy-growing areas of western Mexico. Depression settled on regions where many farmers grew almost nothing else. "The gringos now have this new stuff," a farmer told the authors. "They don't like heroin anymore, that's why we don't sell."

Much of this fentanyl originated from chemical companies in China. A lot of it arrived direct, in the US mail, the way Gordon Jin sent it to Leroy Steele. But another significant amount went to traffickers in Mexico. In time, though, they learned to make it themselves.

By mid-2019, Chinese chemical companies stopped selling fentanyl under orders from their government. Instead, they switched to selling Mexican traffickers the chemical ingredients with which they could make the painkiller. Mexico emerged as the center of illicit fentanyl manufacturing.

At first, Mexican traffickers exported fentanyl powder to the United States by the kilo, just as they'd done with cocaine or heroin. Soon they figured out, as darknet traffickers had as well, the value-added profit to be made by putting tiny amounts of fentanyl into a form ready to be consumed: counterfeit pills.

PILLS HAVE EVOLVED into almost a cue to our collective American reward pathways. This dates to at least the early 1960s, when Valium was marketed by Arthur Sackler as the convenient solution to the anxiety of being female—the industry's first billion-dollar drug. Since then, pills have carried with them the memories of problems solved, the association with convenience, the cue of a quick fix to a complicated problem. That's what pharma marketers understood about us. Beginning in the late 1990s, they promoted opioid pain pills to us with those messages in mind.

Drug traffickers understood our love of pills as well, but had no way of profiting from it—until fentanyl. Now the underworld could replicate any pill the pharmaceutical industry invented to treat our pain, anxiety, depression, ADHD. Fentanyl pressed into phony pills opened the American pill market to anyone in the underworld.

Quality pill presses were cheap on the internet. No need for Magic Bullet blenders. As bogus pills caught on, the alarming clusters of fentanyl overdoses faded—and the alarming headlines with them. The pills, though, made it more likely that people would die who'd never used anything so potent as fentanyl, but simply obtained a pill from a friend and mistook it for the real thing. Across the country, young people started dying from pills they thought were legitimate.

In Arizona, counterfeit blue pills resembling generic 30 mg oxycodone tablets began showing up in early 2018, two or three at a time, in the pockets of overdose victims. "You'd see these cases in Scottsdale, Chandler, Mesa," said Todd Scott, a DEA agent who ran a unit that responded to drug overdose deaths. Then in October, he said, two passengers on a shuttle bus heading from the border to Phoenix were arrested with thirty thousand counterfeit blue pills containing fentanyl. That fall, San Diego authorities seized twelve thousand pills in one load—a record that lasted until a week later, when they took down eighteen thousand. After that, the trade just blew up in a product rollout made possible because fentanyl could be made cheaply all year round. In 2019 Arizona officers seized 1.4 million of these pills.

Among the first couriers to bring them into San Diego was a woman named April Kelly. April was a heroin addict whose addiction began in 2004 with Vicodin prescribed to her after a C-section during the birth of her son. By 2017, she was experienced in going to Tijuana to bring back small amounts of heroin for her and her boyfriend. At the proposition of a trafficker, she moved to Tijuana and began crossing the bright blue pills, pressed in Mexico and containing only fentanyl.

In Tijuana, April viewed a sprawling, robust illegal-drug ecosystem, where it seemed everybody had access to wholesale quantities—shop owners, taxi drivers, barbers. Her connection was a working-class guy who also ran an auto-repair shop. But even he, a minor player, routinely had tens of thousands of pills on hand.

April proved talented at the job. She took across thousands of counterfeit pills at a time hidden in her Spanx bodysuits along her legs and thighs, the small of her back, her tummy. "I came to think I was untouchable," she told me. She took them into San Diego, then later into Arizona, at times flying them to far-flung parts of the country at the behest of her Tijuana connection.

This went on weekly for eighteen months as she grew into one of San Diego's main suppliers of the new product out of Mexico. The pills' quality was good enough that it was months before she learned they were counterfeit. The volume seemed endless. It transformed April Kelly, only a heroin user up to then, into a huge importer.

In time, she expanded to cross pills for other groups, as well. She got greedy and, thinking herself a major player ("I was a piece in a game, a nobody," she says now), began crossing kilos of fentanyl, coke, and meth in cars. In November 2018, a search dog alerted its handler to the various drugs in her car. She pleaded guilty and is now serving ten years in prison.

When I spoke to her, April believed she was part of a move by traffickers to expand beyond simply selling fentanyl powder that could be mixed into heroin—which was often done badly by American street dealers. They saw a new market emerging: Pain-pill addicts, whose access to legitimate pain pills was dwindling as doctors grew more reluctant to prescribe them. They were now desperate. "These customers aren't going to ask about the [pills'] quality," she told me. "If it'll take their sickness away, they'll be fine."

The pills emerged just as social media apps became the way kids communicated—gaming platforms, Instagram, TikTok, and Snapchat. Early on, no one, perhaps not even these companies, understood how these apps might be used in the marketplace. But the newly booming apps tended not to allow parental-monitoring software. The appeal of Snapchat, in particular, was that it automatically deleted communications. These apps, of course, allowed for connections of all kinds. One of them, though, was to allow anonymous drug dealers to market to the apps' young consumers.

The dealers were likely addicted themselves, supporting their own habits. Pharmaceutical-grade opioids were hard to procure as prescriptions were curtailed across the country. So they sold what they could find, which increasingly were the counterfeit pills from Mexico. Some dealers offered menus of apparent pharmaceuticals: first, generic oxycodone, then Percocet, Xanax, and Adderall. All phony and containing fentanyl.

Youths who had no clue how to buy a bag of heroin from a street dealer could, without their parents' knowledge, score pills that they thought were legitimate from dealers they found on these apps. As dealer competition heated up, their business model included, even required, home delivery. Few kids wanted to meet a drug dealer away from the safety of their homes, some were too young to drive, and during the pandemic year they were cooped up in their houses.

As the pills spread, kids with no tolerance for fentanyl began dying across the country as Mexican traffickers' new wares dovetailed with these social media apps.

Early on, Craigslist Los Angeles became a center for the sale of fentanyl under the code words "china" or "china plates." Under the headline, "White China Christmas Edition—$100," one ad read: "Were you served fake stuff? Are you sick? Let me help you ease your pain." A Wilshire vendor's ad read: "Mention #painpaingoaway for the sale prices." Similarly coded ads hawked crystal meth and black-tar heroin.

By 2020, though, the trade had clearly migrated to social-media apps and a younger, less drug-experienced audience. The deaths of teens who bought from dealers on social media increased as the ballooning supply of these bogus pills met the depression and isolation created by pandemic restrictions and the enormous new amounts of time kids spent online. A Facebook group for parents who lost kids due to overdose now has 11,000 members, many of those deaths coming in 2020.

I attended a protest of dozens of bereaved parents in front of Snapchat's Santa Monica headquarters in June 2021 just before this book was published. The parents carried signs with pictures of their dead kids—most of them under 20 years of age—and the headline "Snapchat is an accomplice to my murder." Most of the youths had died during the pandemic year. One woman, into a megaphone, called Snapchat a "drug-dealer storefront!"

The half dozen parents I spoke with said their first knowledge of this new wrinkle in the drug world was when they found their children dead. Among them were Roy and Wendy Plunk, who had driven from Arizona. Their son, Zach, a star high school running back, died the previous summer from a fentanyl-laced bogus Percocet sold to him by a dealer he found on Snapchat. The dealer delivered the pill at 3 a.m. The family's Ring camera captured Zach sneaking from the house. He was in rehab and struggling with his drug use, the couple said, and they divided the day into twelve-hour shifts to watch him. His father found him dead on the front lawn at dawn.

The company responded to the protest with a statement: "At Snap we strictly prohibit drug-related activity on our platform, aggressively enforce against these violations, and support law enforcement in their investigations," it read in part.

"We wouldn't be standing here if the (company's) statement were true," one father told reporter Sam Blake of dot.LA, a tech news site.

That day a protestor carried a sign: "Fentanyl changes everything."

Indeed. Dealers selling on social media were symptoms of that. So were the unlikely kingpins who were now part of the new fentanyl distribution infrastructure forged by the drug's many benefits to dope dealers. I kept looking for their stories. Eventually I encountered a young man named Wyatt Pasek.

Wyatt grew up in Orange County, California and attended Newport Harbor High School, among the state's best public high schools. He began dealing heroin, got his GED at a juvenile labor camp, and in 2016, at nineteen, he was dealing counterfeit Xanax tablets that he purchased on the darknet. The darknet trade in counterfeit 30 mg oxycodone pills, he noticed, was enormous. If he could undercut those vendors, he could grab a nice slice of that, he was sure.

"We didn't have to introduce a new product," Wyatt told me. "People were already addicted [to pain pills] through the pharmaceutical companies. People were starving for it. Instead of paying thirty dollars a pill for the real thing, they could pay five or eight for counterfeit pills. Pills are a lot more acceptable in our younger crowd, and in music and entertainment, than other opiates like heroin. It's more convenient. You can take it to a party. It doesn't smell."

An online Chinese vendor sold him a quarter kilogram—250 grams—of fentanyl for $5,000. The first order came hidden in the box of a puzzle that a family might put together on its living-room table. He had it sent from China by the slowest rate, so it got lost among the millions of packages cascading into the United States every day. On the internet, he bought a high-quality pill press that churned out five thousand pills an hour. He added a scale, and powders to bind with the drug. He bought a high-quality powder mixer, avoiding the Magic Bullet blenders as he considered them too risky. He mixed a quarter milligram of fentanyl in each pill. They cost a nickel each to make, and he could sell them on the darknet to wholesalers for $2 apiece. Four thousand pills per gram—$8,000 gross from each gram that cost him $20. On a grander scale, $2 million in revenue from that $5,000-quarter-kilo of fentanyl.

Wyatt hired two friends. One mixed the fentanyl and pressed the pills. The other shipped them to customers. He paid them $100 an hour, 15 percent of sales, and bonuses. They operated four days a week, eight hours a day, churning out tens of thousands of pills. Wyatt was twenty years old.

His first customers were acquaintances in Orange County. They bought fifty thousand or one hundred thousand pills at a time. He opened a vendor account on the darknet, using the name "Oxygod." He had no idea where his pills ended up. Nor had he any idea if they killed anyone—though he thought not, because of the care he took in mixing. Either way, though, he had no interest in the product beyond the cash it generated. "It was money," he said. "If I could have made the same amount making Legos, I'd be doing that."

His fentanyl business became an empire. It brought in $25,000 a day. He let his employees run it. Now he was just receiving daily cash, rarely even going by the operation. He told his family he was into crypto-currency and owned an exotic car company.

Cash seemed to overwhelm his brain reward circuits the way any drug would. "I was addicted to the easy money," is the way he put it. And right about then Wyatt Pasek became Oxygod. He lived in a penthouse in Newport Beach, rented mansions where he threw parties, hobnobbed with celebrities he won't name, went to strip clubs he was too young to legally enter. He drove a white Rolls-Royce. He leased high-end sports cars. He developed a bad codeine habit.

Cash became something he wore almost like a cologne. On his Instagram account, @yung10X, he posted photos of himself bathing in a tub of cash, counting cash leaning against some rare sports car, bills spilling over the hood, then videos of more cash, jewel-encrusted watches, and women with hundred-dollar bills stuffed in their cleavage.

His success dealing counterfeit pills laced with fentanyl inspired him to impart self-help advice. "Always believe in yourself, even when all else feels like you shouldn't," he wrote on an Instagram post. "Because if I didn't, I probably wouldn't have the greatest gifts of all TIME and that is the freedom! Freedom for time, freedom of location and most importantly freedom of finances.

"Life will give you what you put in to it," he wrote.

He was clearing drug paraphernalia from his penthouse in April 2018, getting out of the game, he said, about to open a rental-car business, then blaze a new career as a social-media influencer, when federal agents arrested him. With that, his days as a fentanyl kingpin ended.

When I spoke with Wyatt Pasek over the phone, he was doing seventeen years in federal prison, repentant, and writing his memoirs. He was twenty-three.

Fentanyl VI

"The Intention Is Very Deliberate"

Michael Tanner Jr. grew up in Akron, Ohio, cheerful, smart, tall and athletic, a great cook. A guy who loved kids, his sisters remember, and was loved by them.

The baby of the family, Mikey, as he was known, may have used his bright smile and outgoing way to hide the worst of his on-and-off battle with cocaine. At thirty-one, he'd been in this struggle for ten years and it had stunted his life and its opportunities, but he kept trying to break from it.

In the spring of 2014 he entered a rehab clinic, stayed for four months, then left believing he was prepared for sobriety. His sisters were skeptical and urged him to stay. It was his third rehab. "We didn't think he was ready," said Megan Pitts.

Michael Tanner moved to a halfway house in north Akron, where ten days later, on the morning of June 17, a Tuesday, his roommate came home from work to find him dead in his bed. A medical examiner's report found cocaine and fentanyl in his system—the first African American in Akron to die of that drug combination.

Meia Christian, his oldest sister, said, "I was in Target with him on Sunday and Tuesday I got the call." His sisters read his autopsy report later. That was the first either had heard of fentanyl.

Fentanyl has changed a lot about drug use in America. Among those changes, I began to see as I traveled the country, was to pull the African

American community into the opioid epidemic. Up to then, the victims of the addiction crisis had been, in vast majority, White. Then cocaine dealers realized that fentanyl fit their needs perfectly.

Cocaine comes from Colombia. By the time it reaches the streets of the United States, the drug has often been "stepped on"—diluted. Fentanyl is far cheaper. For pennies almost, a dealer can boost his $100-gram of cocaine with fentanyl. People of all races use cocaine, but it is a prominent drug of choice among African American users. So as the mixture began to hit the streets, Black people—like Michael Tanner, who had survived years of cocaine use—suddenly began overdosing, as if on an opiate.

Fentanyl arrived first in states where the opiate crisis had already created legions of new addicts, nowhere sooner and with more devastating effect than Ohio. I spoke with Tom Gilson, the medical examiner of Cuyahoga County, where Cleveland is located. Gilson also runs the county lab that analyzed seized illegal drugs. In 2014, he said, his analysts began seeing fentanyl in the samples. Cocaine deaths in the county had numbered a little more than a hundred for years. Then "fentanyl was put into everything—but fentanyl and cocaine mixes definitely become the story," Gilson said. By 2017, cocaine deaths had almost tripled. Far more White people than Black people died from this mixture. Yet these years mark the first time in Cuyahoga County that African Americans died from a synthetic opioid. "They thought they were buying cocaine," Gilson said.

Fentanyl and its analogues accounted for 20 percent of the more than two thousand overdose deaths in Ohio the year Michael Tanner died. Three years later, in 2017, fentanyl was in 71 percent of 4,850 overdose deaths statewide. Cocaine-and-fentanyl deaths rose more than tenfold during those years: from one hundred to over one thousand. Nationwide, cocaine-related deaths tripled between 2014 and 2019, driven by fentanyl, which accounted for some two-thirds of those.

A study by Harm Reduction Ohio found that tests of seized bulk cocaine, coming up from Mexico, found no traces of fentanyl. But small quantities of the drug seized from street dealers—five grams or less—showed that fentanyl began to appear and was especially common in seized quantities of less than a gram. Harm Reduction Ohio attributed this to sloppy local dealers, who didn't sterilize their mixing spaces—and so combined two powder drugs unintentionally.

Marisa Darden disagreed. Darden is a former federal prosecutor in Cleveland who has handled many drug cases. By the time she and I spoke in 2018, more than half of Ohio's overdose deaths associated with cocaine also involved fentanyl.

Who's doing this is an open question; the answer likely changes as fast as the underworld. But to Darden, the combination of cocaine with fentanyl was not an accident. In many cases, she said, fentanyl in cocaine was a marketing ploy by street cocaine dealers, most of whom are Black, to addict African Americans to a far more enslaving drug—in other words, to create a market where there was none. "Mid-level to lower-level dealers are mixing it up," said Darden. "The intention behind it is very deliberate."

NO ONE KNOWS the origin of the fentanyl that killed Michael Tanner. He had no drug on him when he died. But among the first to sell fentanyl in Akron about that time was a man named John Penson III.

Penson, too, loved to cook and was a fan of Western movies. He had a series of small-time jobs, the kind that parolees find when they get out of prison, as he had done at least twice. But what John Penson mostly did was sell drugs, mainly crack, which was why he went to prison.

Sometime in late 2013 or early 2014, fentanyl came to Akron, and John Penson saw the profit in it. "It was fast money, just like crack," said Jessica Sundell, his live-in girlfriend.

He would mix the drugs with other powders at their apartment, where he and Jessica and her kids lived, though she said he was careful to always use a mask and gloves and not allow her in the house while he was working. He mixed it with powdered sugar and Dormin, a sleep aid, using a Magic Bullet blender. "You gotta have a blender," Sundell said. "The Magic Bullet is the best one. The blades never go dull." (Again, this is a street myth. Please see chapter 11 for why blenders are very bad at mixing powders of any kind, especially highly potent narcotics.)

Penson, never sold fentanyl as anything other than fentanyl, Sundell said, and she doesn't remember him selling to African Americans. His market was Asians in Akron's International District. He also drove down to West Virginia to towns hard hit by pain pills and heroin, where he knew fentanyl had a waiting market.

But Sundell told me that the dealers she knew quickly saw that with fentanyl they could create opioid addicts who would buy daily, instead of occasionally, as many cocaine users do. Once one dealer did it, they all did it. "They do it because fentanyl is so addictive," she said. "They do it just enough for you to be become addicted. You're not addicted to coke, you're addicted to the fentanyl—but you think it's coke. I don't think [the customers] knew that it was mixed."

In the summer of 2016, Akron's street drugs changed again. Over the Fourth of July weekend, a cluster of deaths broke out due to carfentanil—the rhinoceros anesthetic, many times more potent than fentanyl. It's hard to know its origin, as well. But in Akron, a long-time drug dealer named Donte Gibson began ordering fentanyl and carfentanil mailed to him from China. By May 2016, according to court records, Gibson was selling the synthetic drugs across Akron and other nearby towns. Over the next two years, Gibson made enough from dealing this new product that his wife tallied almost $700,000 in bills at Saks Fifth Avenue. The couple added an in-ground swimming pool to their south Akron home.

Carfentanil killed 130 Summit County residents that year. By that August it was showing up in cocaine, and African Americans began to die from it as well. Among them was John Penson III. Penson survived two decades of a cocaine habit, but didn't last four months once cocaine mixed with carfentanil hit the streets.

Out all night at a bar, then partying at a friend's house early one morning in September 2016, Penson ran out of cocaine. He bought something he believed was cocaine. He passed out at 8:30 a.m. on a couch. The apartment residents went to work, came home, and found him in the same position. The Summit County medical examiner found carfentanil and cocaine in his system. He was one of six Black residents of Akron to die from a mixture of cocaine and carfentanil in a four-week period.

Donte Gibson was arrested in February 2018. After that, carfentanil tapered off, then disappeared from Summit County. Gibson and his wife, Audrey, were sentenced to lengthy federal prison terms, while the federal government auctioned off their Saks Fifth Avenue trove.

ON JUNE 23, 2014, six days after Michael Tanner Jr. died, hundreds of people attended his funeral. They lamented his lost potential and remembered his big bright smile. A fellow from his rehab stood to talk about how Mikey had mentored him.

Mikey's sisters are grateful that their brother's drug use did not prevent him from being part of their family. They remember a man whose character was fresh and joyful and at odds with the fatalism of addiction. He loved cooking with his mother and caring for her when she was ill. Megan Pitts still cherishes the last picture of her wedding day, when she and her brother danced the last dance after everyone had left.

The suddenness of his death still affects them. In the weeks before he passed, he seemed more reflective. He spoke of things he wasn't proud to have done, but also of a new life. He wanted to travel more, as he imagined a future different from his past. His father and others in the family had dealt with addiction for years and emerged to lead productive lives. Why not Mikey? his sisters thought.

"It's going to be a rough road, we thought, but eventually something will break through. Third time's the charm," said Megan. "Then it was just over."

Sacklers III

"A Dangerous Concentration of Risk"

In late 2013, out in Massachusetts, a woman named Maura Healey announced she was running for attorney general. A Harvard grad and point guard on the school's basketball team, she'd gone to law school, worked as a corporate litigator, and been with the attorney general's office for six years, running its civil rights division.

Awareness of widespread opioid addiction was confined to certain professions and neighborhoods. But as she campaigned, Healey began to hear about it from families everywhere. These people were often ashamed, quiet, and timid as they took her aside, but intense as they told their stories. "You could feel it was just boiling over," she told me.

It seemed to her that the drug companies selling narcotic painkillers merited special attention from law enforcement. Foremost among them, Healey came to believe, was Connecticut-based Purdue Pharma and its owners, the Sackler family, which controlled its board of directors.

US case law forms a bastion of legal protections for board members, insulating them from responsibility for their company's illegal behavior. But Healey said that when she'd been a corporate litigator she saw how easy it was "for a company to pay a fine, move on, and reorganize. You have to name names—executives and board members."

Healey won the job. Almost four years after her campaign began, on June 11, 2018, her prosecutors met with lawyers representing Purdue Pharma and the Sacklers, with the intent of suing the family by name.

The lawyers representing the family and the company that morning had been famous longer than most of the state prosecutors had been attorneys. Mary Jo White, representing the Sackler family, was the first woman appointed as US attorney for the Southern District of New York, the most prestigious prosecuting position at the Department of Justice; under President Barack Obama, she ran the federal Securities and Exchange Commission. Patrick Fitzgerald, former US attorney in Chicago, represented Purdue. He had prosecuted Illinois governors George Ryan and Rod Blagojevich for corruption.

Their message that day was this: No one has successfully sued the Sackler family board members—for good reason. To win, the state would need to disassemble all those legal protections in case law. You will lose in humiliating fashion, they said.

Up to then, Massachusetts prosecutors had subpoenaed only the sales-call records of Purdue reps aggressively pushing physicians to prescribe their timed-release narcotic. The company had sold millions of OxyContin pills in Massachusetts; thousands of state residents had died of overdoses. "The question became," said Gillian Feiner, a staff prosecutor, "Who was directing all this?"

The younger state attorneys believed that a new cache of documents could answer that question. Hundreds of lawsuits against Purdue were now grouped in a federal courtroom in Cleveland. From those cases had grown a mountain of Purdue internal documents: minutes from Purdue board meetings, emails between board members and staff, internal staff reports. A Cleveland judge had ruled that all public entities suing the drug companies could see those documents.

The day after meeting with those lawyers—on June 12—Healey's office filed a seventy-nine-page complaint against Purdue, with a section naming the Sacklers. At the news conference, prosecutors covered the walls with the first names of the eleven thousand state residents who'd died from opioid overdoses in the last decade. "We felt we were doing something new and important," said Feiner, "and we weren't prepared to back down."

During the next weeks, a fusillade of hard drives containing those Purdue documents fired out of Ohio to Massachusetts, thousands of records in each one. Through the summer and fall, as Purdue and Sackler attorneys moved to dismiss the case, Healey's office mined the mountains of emails, minutes, and memos. The office hired two paralegals and expanded the team to include a dozen lawyers and investigators, all working overtime.

Over several months, the team assembled records to piece together a much larger story following Purdue Pharma's 2007 conviction and $634 million fine. The narrative told of Sackler board members allegedly lashing the company to ever greater numbers of doctor sales calls, more prescriptions for OxyContin at higher doses, and higher profit before another lawsuit came around. "They just decided they were going to suck as much out of this company as they could," Healey said, "using it as their own ATM."

AS THE TEAM dug through the records from Ohio, a paralegal came across a five-page Purdue internal memo sent by Richard Sackler to his relatives on the board. Richard Sackler is the oldest son of the late Raymond Sackler, and was Purdue CEO from 1999 to 2003 and a board member after that.

The memo appears to have been written by board member Peter Boer, with Richard Sackler's collaboration, or endorsement. The memo outlined the company's paths forward following the 2007 plea agreement with the government. Purdue sold only one product and could expect further lawsuits. Thus the company amounted to, according to the memo, a "dangerous concentration of risk." The family now had two options, Boer wrote. The first: sell Purdue. To attract buyers, the company would have to diversify beyond OxyContin, reducing the cash sent in annual payouts to the Sackler owners and using it to acquire companies and invest in research and development. The second option was for the Sacklers "to distribute more free cash flow to themselves"—take cash out of the company, in other words.

This latter option appeared to become Sackler philosophy as the years passed.

In 2009 Purdue hired McKinsey, the worldwide management consultant, to study how OxyContin sales might be rejuvenated. Purdue's relationship with McKinsey dated to 2004 and would last until 2019. Through the years, McKinsey seemed to originate the idea that pushing doctors to prescribe more OxyContin and at higher doses was essential to Purdue's profit.

On Purdue's board, Richard Sackler seemed the driving force behind this idea. He kept the pressure on, insisting that sales staff come up with tactics for "exceeding 2007 Rx numbers." He wanted to know how sales staff would get patients to take higher doses and stay on opioids longer. How many patients had insurance reimbursement for unlimited quantities of Purdue opioids? How many were limited to sixty tablets per month?

The records showed that limits on OxyContin's use seemed to rankle him. When staff offered a plan to get pharmacies to increase their stocks of OxyContin from two bottles to three, Richard Sackler wanted to know why they couldn't get four bottles or more. When Purdue staff noted reports of deaths due to OxyContin and a 2001 public meeting in which OxyContin was compared to heroin, Richard Sackler said that addicts and drug dealers were creating a problem, while "no one is speaking for the patients in pain." Then in a confidential email, "We have to hammer on the abusers in every way possible. They are the culprits and the problem. They are reckless criminals."

"What else more can we do to energize the sales and grow at a faster rate?" he wrote on another occasion. When sales reps visited "non-high potential prescribers," Sackler wrote, upset at the waste of time, "How can our managers have allowed this to happen?"

He once proposed that he accompany a sales rep on a call. It didn't happen, but the idea seemed to express the urgency he and other Sackler board members placed on enhancing sales.

This trickled down to sales reps, whom company executives pushed hard to make evermore calls on doctors, said Carol Panara, the former

Purdue saleswoman I spoke to, who had worked for the company from 2008 to 2013. "Managers were riding with sales reps two days a month to push us," she told me. "The problem was that access to doctors was becoming more difficult. Some doctors had limited time, or sold their practices to hospitals, which meant less time to see reps. Also, they were more limited in what they could prescribe. At Purdue, the executives made us feel like we were never good enough. They always wanted more, like we were not closing enough (sales). But really this was about their increasingly excessive demands to squeeze as much as they could out of OxyContin."

Records showed that Purdue staff complained at times of Richard Sackler's micromanaging sales. One executive wrote to the CEO asking if he could get Richard Sackler "to back off somewhat" in his demands on the sales staff. "He is pulling people in all directions . . . [and] is not realistic in his expectations."

US pharmaceutical companies typically spend between 15 and 25 percent of their total sales on research and developing new products. Purdue did not. As years passed, the Sacklers did not diversify Purdue, either through R&D or through acquisitions. Instead, they voted to have Purdue pay the family $4 billion between the 2007 conviction and 2018. This included more than $500 million in both 2009 and 2011, and more than $800 million in 2008 and in 2010. Another $6 billion was sent to Purdue affiliates. In all, investigators determined, some $10 billion was sent out of Purdue to the Sacklers or affiliated companies during these years.

Yet even in the best of times at Purdue, the sales numbers never seemed to satisfy the family. OxyContin tallied $3 billion in sales in 2010, and that year Purdue paid the Sackler family $889 million. Both figures were record highs. Even so, Purdue staff noted that sales of the highest doses of OxyContin weren't meeting the family's expectations—$120 million less than what the board expected from that December alone.

Purdue board minutes reflect that the Sacklers seemed almost tormented, as if quarterly sales of OxyContin would never meet their goal. They rankled at how sales seemed to drop every year around the holidays, when sales reps took time off, then attended the national sales meeting every January. They might go several weeks without seeing their doctors. "Wouldn't it be better to have the reps get back to work for January and back in front of doctors," wrote board member Mortimer Sackler, son of one of the three original Sackler brothers. Richard Sackler responded: "Maybe the thing to have done was not have the meeting at all."

BY THE END of 2016, the description of the company as a "dangerous concentration of risk" seemed prescient.

Sales of OxyContin were declining, as were prescriptions of the highest doses of the drug. Younger doctors prescribed it less than their older peers. More than half of all Americans knew someone addicted to narcotic pain relievers. States were limiting prescriptions of the drugs. "We know of no other medication that's routinely used for a nonfatal condition that kills patients so frequently," Tom Frieden, director of the Centers for Disease Control, said of opioids that year.

Annual payouts to the Sackler family began to fall along with OxyContin sales—to roughly $200 million in each of 2014 and 2016. "Our myopic focus on extended release opioids with abuse deterrent properties has not yielded the results people thought it would," wrote Russ Gasdia, Purdue's vice president of sales, in a 2014 email that Massachusetts investigators found.

Instead, company records showed that Purdue ratcheted up the pressure on sales reps, upped their daily sales-call goals, and pushed them to more aggressively court "high-value" targets—doctors who were already prescribing a lot.

In 2013 McKinsey came up with a report titled *Identifying Granular Growth Opportunities for OxyContin* in which they urged the Sacklers to "Turbocharge the Sales Engine," for at stake was "hundreds of millions, not tens of millions" of dollars. McKinsey partners went on ride-alongs with sales reps to help fine-tune the sales pitch to doctors. McKinsey urged the company to make an even greater priority of opioid savings cards to increase prescribing and the length of time patients spent using the drug.

McKinsey also estimated how many customers might develop addiction to, or die from, OxyContin. At one point the consultant suggested Purdue pay its drugstore distributors rebates of $14,000 for every addiction and fatal overdose OxyContin caused, to ensure that chains like CVS and others would keep distributing the pill. Under the plan, for example, CVS pharmacies would be paid $36 million in 2019 to offset the 2,400 of its customers that McKinsey estimated would become addicted to, or overdose and die on, OxyContin that year.

Purdue never adopted that McKinsey suggestion. But the company started Project Turbocharge—later renamed E2E, "Evolve to Excellence"—based on many other of the consultant's recommendations, aimed at urging doctors to prescribe the pill, and at higher doses. With McKinsey, Purdue developed FieldGuide, software that allowed the company to target high-prescribing doctors.

McKinsey was among the companies that state attorneys general sued as they sought to recoup costs for the opiate crisis. As I was finishing this book, McKinsey posted a statement on its website apologizing for its work with Purdue, saying it had ceased doing "opioid-specific business" around the world. McKinsey "did not adequately acknowledge the epidemic unfolding in our communities," the statement read. "We have a responsibility to take into account the broader context and implications of the work that we do. Our work for Purdue fell short of that standard." It struck me that their statement described the Opioid Era in America—our new Gilded Age, where companies dispensed with any moral or ethical concern in the pursuit of making money. A while later McKinsey settled with the states, promising to pay $573 million.

Despite Peter Boer's memo describing Purdue as a "dangerous concentration of risk," the only diversification the company ever seemed to entertain was into products that profited from the crisis. It was as if, like a brain addicted to its drug, the company could see no way forward that did not involve opioids. One of these was a plan to sell naloxone, the overdose antidote. Demand for naloxone was surging due to widespread addiction. There was also a proposal to market a form of Suboxone—a pill that kept opiate cravings in check—that might generate $24 million annually by 2025.

An internal memo noted: "There is an opportunity to expand our offering as an end-to-end pain provider" from pain treatment to addiction treatment. This was possible because—contrary to what Purdue had insisted publicly and in sales calls to doctors—opioids used to treat pain, the memo read, are "naturally linked" with addiction.

Meth II

P2P

In 2006, narcotics agents were dealing with the death toll in Chicago, Detroit, and other cities from the first appearance of fentanyl, which few of them had heard of up to then. That same year, with far less notoriety though with equally far-reaching consequences, a change occurred in a synthetic drug they knew a lot more about.

A law enforcement agency on the southwest border seized some methamphetamine. In due course, the five-gram sample of that seizure landed on the desk of a thirty-one-year-old chemist named Joe Bozenko, at the DEA lab outside Washington, DC.

Organic chemistry can be endlessly manipulated, with compounds that, like Lego bricks, can be used to build almost anything. The profession seems to breed folks like Paul Janssen—people for whom almost every waking minute is taken up puzzling over chemical reactions, or alternate routes to the same chemical destination. Joe Bozenko is one of these. He's a garrulous fellow with a big wide smile and grows especially animated when discussing chemistry. He worked in the DEA lab during the day, taught chemistry in a local university at night. "Chemist by day, chemist by night" reads his Twitter profile.

At the DEA, his job was to understand these anonymous underworld chemists, samples of whose work regularly plopped on his desk. He analyzed what they produced, and diagnosed how they did it. A well-trained organic chemist could find new uses for old chemicals and different paths to the same chemical result. Bozenko loved attempting to comprehend the thinking of a clandestine chemist. In time he traveled abroad to these labs once they were seized. His first foreign assignment was a clandestine lab that made the stimulant MDMA in Jakarta, Indonesia. After that, he saw the world through the protective goggles of a hazmat suit, sifting the remains of clandestine labs in three dozen countries. He brought back commemorative law enforcement hats and patches from Bangkok to Tyler, Texas.

As it happened, he joined the agency as the global underworld, and Mexican traffickers in particular, were veering toward synthetic drugs, and away from their plant-based cousins.

Meth was the drug Joe Bozenko analyzed most as he settled into his job. It was made with the ephedrine method developed by the Japanese and sold during the Third Reich. Ephedrine could be transformed into meth with remarkable efficiency. It was almost one to one. As much ephedrine as you could get your hands on, that was about how much meth you could make from it. But you had to have ephedrine.

There was, however, another way to make methamphetamine. In fact, in the United States this method was the first to be widely used, mostly by the California biker gangs who dominated the meth trade into the 1980s. Its essential chemical was a clear, sweet-smelling liquid called phenyl-2-propanone—P2P. Many combinations of chemicals could be used to make P2P. Most of these chemicals were legal, cheap, and toxic: cyanide, lye, mercury, sulfuric acid, hydrochloric acid, nitrostyrene. This process of making meth was volatile, and though P2P had a pleasant aroma, when it was combined with toxic chemicals, the concoction stank, which is why California biker cooks hid their labs out in the desert or up in the pines.

Ephedrine was easier to make and smelled hardly at all. Bozenko hadn't seen seized methamphetamine from Mexico made any other way.

But the sample that arrived on his desk that day in 2006 was different. He tinkered with it for two or three days. He realized it had been made with the P2P method, which Bozenko, then seven years on the job, knew about but had rarely seen employed by underground chemists. Still, that was not the most startling aspect of the sample on his desk. There was something else about those few grams that to Bozenko heralded a changed world.

Among the drawbacks of the P2P method is that it produces two kinds of methamphetamine. One is known as *d*-methamphetamine, which is the stuff that makes you high. The other is *l*-methamphetamine, which makes the heart race but does nothing to the human brain; it is waste product. Most cookers would likely want to get rid of the *l*-meth, if they knew what it was. But separating the two is tricky, beyond the skills of most clandestine chemists. No one in the drug underworld, as far as Bozenko and his colleagues knew, had ever figured out how to separate the *d*-meth from the *l*-meth—until that 2006 sample.

The sample contained mostly *d*-methamphetamine. Someone had removed most of the impotent *l*-meth. "I've taken down labs in several continents," Bozenko told me years later. "No one had attempted to do this [separation] until the Mexicans got into the P2P method."

In time, he realized they were separating the two kinds of methamphetamine using something known as tartaric acid, a substance that naturally occurs in grapes and other fruit and is a byproduct of wine production. They dumped the *l*-meth in rivers or streams or buried it, where it pocked the Mexican countryside like some kind of toxic acne and leached into the groundwater. They sent the *d*-meth across the border. A patent from the 1940s showed how to do this separation with tartaric acid—but that, too, was alarming, for it showed the access traffickers had to the opaque world of chemistry literature.

For all its limitations, the P2P method offered traffickers one huge advantage over the ephedrine method. The chemicals that could be used to make it, though highly toxic, were abundantly available and used in legitimate industries—among them racing fuel, tanning, gold mining, perfume, and photography. A country's law enforcement could not, therefore, clamp down on supplies of these chemicals the way it had with ephedrine, not without damaging legitimate sectors of the economy. What's more, a trained organic chemist could make P2P, the essential ingredient, in many ways. It was impossible to say how many methods of making P2P a creative chemist might come up with. Bozenko counted a dozen or so at first. He put them up on a large diagram on his office wall, but then kept adding Post-it notes with new ones as they appeared. An underground website reported an "astounding array of synthetic routes" to making P2P. World markets, meanwhile, provided all the chemicals a trafficker needed.

As he dissected that sample in 2006, its implications hit him like a tsunami gathering in the distance. Unconcerned with law enforcement or the environment, and with access to world chemical markets through shipping ports, Mexican traffickers could ramp up the P2P method to industrial scale and produce potent meth in quantities that were, in effect, limitless.

LATER THAT YEAR, on December 15, 2006, in a small town named Tlajomulco de Zúñiga in the central Mexican state of Jalisco, a methamphetamine lab exploded in flames.

Firefighters responded to the blaze at a warehouse. The warehouse had once housed a factory making plastic dinnerware—plates, utensils. No one was hurt in the fire, nor was anyone arrested. But a fire chief called the local office of the DEA.

Abe Perez supervised the DEA's Guadalajara office back then. The warehouse stood on a cul-de-sac, Perez, who is now retired, remembered years later. Along this street, near the warehouses, were homes as well. Neighbors told him that they saw men at these warehouses coming and going at night. The residents "knew something was going on; the smells were giving them headaches," Perez told me. But they were afraid to say anything, or object to the vinegary stench that they could smell for blocks, and which seemed now baked into the street. So they lived with it as best they could until it exploded in flames, most likely due to a worker's carelessness.

Perez and his agents that day urged Mexican police and prosecutors to obtain a search warrant for the place. The process slowed, and the day ended with no warrant. That night another fire erupted, at a warehouse across the street, which, the agents later learned, contained chemicals used at the first warehouse. "The traffickers came in the middle of the night with gasoline and burned it, burned all the evidence," Perez said, "but we were able to get photos of the place."

Eduardo Chavez flew in from Mexico City the next afternoon. Chavez had completed his Bakersfield assignment in 2004 and had been stationed in Mexico since then. He'd helped shut down the Distribuidora Talios fentanyl lab in the spring of 2006. El Cerebro, Ricardo Valdez-Torres, was in prison. But that case had been a departure for Chavez. Most of his time in Mexico he'd spent lobbying officials to understand the threat of meth labs to their neighborhoods, farmland, and waterways. Now he and Perez stood outside the second smoldering warehouse. Each man had spent the early part of his career busting clandestine labs in rural California—Chavez in Bakersfield, Perez in eastern San Diego County.

Now they were both in Mexico, where meth labs had grown into warehouses. These warehouses were monuments of a sort. They showed that traffickers could enforce their will. The traffickers were well armed, with guns mostly from the United States, and they felt unthreatened by Mexican law enforcement. There was thus little need to move constantly. These labs could contain expensive, sophisticated flasks, beakers, and condensers. They could store large inventories of chemicals awaiting processing, and carefully design their operations to resemble production lines. All that was in this lab. Notes found on the scene suggested the cooks were used to getting 110 kilos per batch.

Like Joe Bozenko back in Washington, DC, the agents standing at the edge of the smoke and the stench that afternoon peered into a new drug world. For what struck both agents was what they were *not* seeing.

No ephedrine. It was an entire meth lab based on the P2P method of making the drug.

What's more, this was not up in the mountains or on some rural ranch. Tlajomulco (pronounced Tla-Ho-MOOL-Koh) lies fourteen miles south of Guadalajara, Mexico's second largest city. The seat of a populous county with the same name, Tlajomulco also serves as home to the international airport for metro Guadalajara. Tlajomulco itself is a small town (pop. 30,000), partly rural, with a delightful central plaza and two colonial-era churches. But Guadalajara makes everything from computers and cars to textiles. So Tlajomulco became Guadalajara's southern gateway, with industrial parks pushing into farmland. Trucks rumbled through the area daily from the ports in Lázaro Cárdenas, in the state of Michoacán, and Manzanillo, in the state of Colima.

In an earlier time, nothing about such a busy, populated area would have recommended it as a hub for illicit drug production. But Tlajomulco had everything needed to be a center of meth manufacturing: warehouses, proximity to highways, ports, and chemists. Meth traffickers felt confident of immunity from law enforcement and certain of their ability to intimidate neighbors into silence.

Only now, this smoldering lab signaled that another change was afoot. In 2005 Mexico had followed the United States' lead and limited the amount of legally imported ephedrine, which in due course fell from 226 tons in 2004 to 43 tons in 2006. Traffickers turned to illegal shipments, procured from around the world. The ephedrine method was still in use, but an era was clearly coming to a close. A new way of making meth was emerging. When it came to P2P, "the traffickers didn't know what they were doing yet," Chavez said. The explosion showed that. Still, years later he thought back on that moment and realized that it was almost as if they were witnessing a shift right then, that week.

Knowledge of the P2P method would spread and combine with access to world chemical markets to transform the Mexican meth industry. What began with one smoldering lab in Tlajomulco became hundreds, expertly run, and from them the supplies heading north widened to a torrent.

Separately, Joe Bozenko and Eduardo Chavez would think back and remember what each had witnessed in 2006—when everything was about to change.

Meth III

Ephedrine's Last Gasp

O ne day in February of 2007, a woman called the US embassy in Mexico City. The duty officer who took the call said she spoke Spanish with a Chinese accent. A Chinese man, she said, owns a chemical company in the industrial city of Toluca, outside Mexico City, where he is producing ephedrine used to make methamphetamine. The Mexican government had been restricting sales of the chemical, and in 2005 it set limits on the amount of it that could be imported. This man has nine tons of it in a factory, she said, and he lived in a mansion in Lomas de Chapultepec, one of Mexico City's swankiest neighborhoods.

His name was Zhenli Ye Gon.

The duty officer wrote Ye Gon's name, company name, and address on a yellow Post-it note and passed it to Eduardo Chavez, who, among the staff at the Mexican embassy, knew most about methamphetamine. "You're the meth guy," the officer said.

It was not an expertise he could have predicted he would ever possess when he took that first assignment in Bakersfield. But studying meth had indeed consumed his career so far. He had watched the drug's production move from California to Mexico. Now he was nearing the end of his Mexico City tour.

Chavez had never heard of Zhenli Ye Gon. He consulted Mexican authorities, who in due course wrote a search warrant for Ye Gon's house and factory.

The night before Mexican police raided the house, Chavez was in Albuquerque, preparing to move back to the States. A Mexican investigator called. We're going to search this guy's house tomorrow, he said. Do you think we'll need a lab truck? Chavez wasn't sure Ye Gon was even making meth; if he was, Chavez was certain he would not be doing so at his mansion. "No, he might have some money there, but that's about it."

The next day, the investigator called again. "We're inside, and his wife is here, he's gone; she says he's in the United States but she doesn't know where. Their bedroom is locked."

"Okay, just keep me in the loop," Chavez said. An hour later, the investigator called again: "He has a secret room in which he has a lot of cash."

"Okay. Good. That's what we thought."

"No, you don't understand," the investigator said. "This is more money than any of us have ever seen."

"Well, how much is it?"

Two tons of hundred-dollar bills, that was the estimate later: $205 million in cash, plus another $2 million in other currencies. "My jaw hit the floor," Chavez said later. Newspapers ran photos the next day of scores of neat stacks of the bills, four feet high, filling the corner of a room. Once the cash was packaged as evidence, it took seven flights to safely get it all to the Bank of America in New York, the only bank large enough to handle it.

Later, Ye Gon was found to have been living in Las Vegas, in a suite comped him by the Venetian Las Vegas hotel and casino, a property of the Las Vegas Sands Corp., then owned by the late billionaire Sheldon Adelson. Ye Gon lived at the Venetian for four months, losing, at various casinos, more than $125 million. During that time, the Venetian allowed him use of a private jet and gave him a burgundy Rolls-Royce that US authorities later seized.

Chavez wrote a criminal complaint against Ye Gon, alleging he had made ephedrine, and laundered money, for the Sinaloa drug cartel.

Born in Shanghai, Ye Gon had opened a chemical company in Mexico in 1997, naturalizing as a Mexican citizen in 2002 and marrying a Chinese-Mexican woman. His company, Unimed Pharmchem, operated a laboratory in Toluca, where Ye Gon owned land on which he planned a large campus of presumably legal chemical and drug production. But Unimed also imported from Mongolia some eighty-six tons of a chemical called N-acetylpseudoephedrine, which is molecularly similar to ephedrine but exempt from Mexican restrictions. He allegedly transformed the chemical into ephedrine at his plant in Toluca.

The saga of Zhenli Ye Gon grew complicated, and well documented, as years passed. A few months after the raid on his house, he was arrested in Maryland, where he'd fled, he said, to apply for political asylum, fearing threats against him by Mexican drug traffickers and politicians. "Cooperate or your neck," he said they told him. (The Spanish phrase was later put on T-shirts and sold on Mexico streets.) He was linked to HSBC, the bank fined for laundering money for the Sinaloa cartel. Ye Gon is now in custody in Mexico. His case still marks the world's largest seizure of illicit cash.

For our story, though, he's important as a last-gasp spasm of traffickers desperate for ephedrine. Ephedrine-made meth had showed them the future. Ephedrine was their key, they believed, to a new world of synthetic dope manufacturing. The new profits were so tantalizing, and now that they had it in their grasp, the indispensable chemical was getting hard to find.

Ye Gon was the lone source of ephedrine, and they flocked to him. "He'd been operating with a daily production of five hundred kilos of ephedrine" Chavez said. "He couldn't produce it fast enough. He was paying people extra to not take days off and work longer hours. A lot of the money he amassed was deposits for future deliveries. He had a waiting list. He didn't want to tell anybody no."

Several months later Chavez was in Las Vegas meeting with the Nevada Gaming Commission and federal prosecutors when the group received a call from the Venetian. Would they like to tour the suite the hotel had comped Ye Gon, where he'd lived while gambling away his proceeds from Mexican traffickers? His penthouse sat atop the Venetian's tower. It included a private pool on the balcony, a barber chair, a private card table, a sauna. Only a few years before, Eduardo Chavez had been busting meth labs behind the chicken farms near Bakersfield, California. Now he was looking out over Las Vegas from the Venetian penthouse suite of a Chinese man who'd grown rich supplying traffickers in Mexico.

In the end, the political pressure created by the Ye Gon case transformed the Mexican methamphetamine industry. In 2008 the Mexican government banned ephedrine outright, like cocaine or heroin. With that, the ephedrine method faded. Ephedrine's scarcity forced traffickers to discover the P2P method, using widely available, highly toxic legal chemicals.

The transition happened fast. By 2012, five years after Ye Gon's arrest, DEA chemists tested no samples of seized meth made with ephedrine. It was all made with P2P, a method that allowed a capacity for production surpassing anything possible with ephedrine.

IN JUNE OF 2011, Mexican authorities discovered a massive meth lab in the city of Querétaro, two hours north of Mexico City. It was a warehouse that could have fit a 737, in an industrial park, with roads wide enough for eighteen-wheelers. DEA chemist Joe Bozenko and his colleague, Steve Toske, were called down from Washington, DC, to inspect it.

They wandered in awe through the warehouse, filled with bags of chemicals stacked thirty feet high. Working through all these chemicals, the lab could have produced nine hundred metric tons of methamphetamine. That's what Joe Bozenko estimated. Against a wall stood a thousand-liter reactor, two stories tall, which required a stairway and a platform to mount.

This marked a new day, one that Bozenko might have foreseen in 2006 when he analyzed that first sample of methamphetamine made with P2P. Nothing like this had been achieved with ephedrine, nor could have been; no one could have imagined the accumulation of nine hundred metric tons of the chemical. Later, Mexican investigators would report that of the sixteen workers arrested at the Querétaro lab, fourteen died over the next six months from liver failure—due, presumably, to exposure to the chemicals at the lab. It was another sign of the toxicity of the P2P method.

Yet the size of the place wasn't even what most startled Bozenko; it was the hundreds of bags, among the stacks of chemicals, of a substance neither he nor Toske had ever thought could be used to make P2P: something called 2-phenylacetamide. Bozenko and Toske often consulted a book that outlined potential substances that might be precursors to making methamphetamine, but 2-phenylacetamide wasn't in it. It was clear to Bozenko that traffickers employed trained organic chemists who had access to the chemistry literature and possessed the skills to improvise new ways to make the ingredients.

Bozenko remained tied into the clandestine lab world through colleagues and membership in the investigators' association and his work analyzing labs elsewhere in the world. He didn't see another lab of that size in Mexico for years, nor did he hear of one. Something like it could clearly be replicated, but after Querétaro the meth labs in Mexico were almost always more rudimentary, usually in the rural outback under tree canopy. There were reports of dozens of them, new ones starting up every month. Yet they were not the chicken-farm labs that Eduardo Chavez had seen in Bakersfield. It seemed more and more people were learning the trade and opening labs of their own. As funky as these labs looked, each was set up to produce tons of the drug.

Hardin County I

About sixty miles northwest of Columbus, Ohio, out where corn-fields stretch in endless perfect rows, is Hardin County, with a population of 32,000. The county's Amish residents make furniture and baked goods; traffic signs with profiles of a horse and buggy are placed strategically around the region. Ninety-six percent of Hardin County is White and concentrated mostly in two towns. One is Ada, home to Ohio Northern University. The other is Kenton, the county seat, with a population of 8,000, where this story takes place.

Planted in the middle of rural America, Kenton was once also an industrial center. Rockwell International had a truck-axle factory here, employing more than a thousand people in the best of times. Many Rockwell suppliers set up in Kenton as well. That made the town a world capital of truck-axle manufacturing.

As is common among small towns doing well, Kenton had its share of vice—gambling, and bars catering to factory workers, where men fought a lot. Bar fighting was almost a pastime.

In their younger years, the Burd brothers—born to a truck driver named Robert Burd, who had four sons with three women and named three of his sons Robert—were known as some of the most prolific of Kenton's bar fighters. They were big and had played high school football under the great Mike Mauk, the coach who turned Kenton High into a football powerhouse. One of the Roberts went by Rob.

Rob Burd and his brothers tended to fight as a unit so the faceoffs didn't last long. Cops would get the call on the radio and know to go slow to the bar; the Burd brothers were at it again, and it would soon be over. The Burds were rednecks, proud of it, football players and hard drinkers. They'd punch out anyone who even offered them any other kind of drug.

Rob Burd had a girlfriend named Laurel Rogers. Laurel Rogers is a pretty woman with freckles and red hair, born for small-town life and content in rural Ohio. Out on the weekend, Rob would occasionally use her as a pretext to start a fight: "Were you looking at my girlfriend?" When he graduated from Kenton High in 1994, Rob took the second shift at the Honda plant down in Marysville, making Accords and Civics. Then he went over to Bridgestone, making car parts. Meanwhile, he and friends let off steam in bars, drinking and fighting. His mother was a bartender for many years. "We were angry people," Rob said, "and bored."

After a while, Rob Burd began to fear the consequences of carousing. He'd spent no time away from Hardin County. So he went with a cousin and they enlisted in the US Air Force, aiming for Monday, March 17, 1997, as the date when they'd enter the service. The Friday night before his induction, Burd heard that a fellow he'd once had problems with was just out of prison. This guy had cold-cocked Burd with a whiskey bottle at a party two years before, which is what got him sent to prison. Aiming to get even, Rob and some friends piled into two cars and raced to see who could get across Kenton first to a party where they might find the fellow. Along the way, Burd's car flew out of control as he tried to avoid a slower car, and he hit a telephone pole. One guy lost his ear. Rob spent six months in a wheelchair. His cousin entered the air force that Monday. Rob learned to walk with a pronounced limp, but was never again able to run.

Still, he gained enough mobility to find welding work at Rockwell International. His injuries made the work difficult. A family doctor prescribed him Vicodin, lecturing him on how dangerous it could be.

For a while, Burd wasn't even taking one a day and didn't need all the pills he was prescribed.

Among the lesser-known aspects of life in many of the Rust Belt towns during their days of industrial glory was the role in the spread of drug abuse played by the large factories that then sustained these towns. Enormous numbers of people, bored with the tedious work and earning union wages, provided stable marketplaces for drugs, particularly in the 1970s as mores loosened. Cocaine was easily available. By the end of the 1990s, prescription pain pills were also part of the mix. At the Rockwell factory, Burd found he could sell his Vicodin tablets for a dollar apiece. Then his use increased; he asked his doctor for something stronger. His doctor prescribed him 10 mg OxyContins, telling him to be careful, and that in Appalachia the pills were known as "hillbilly heroin" for a reason.

Rob kept selling the pills. His doctor cut him off. Rob found a doctor in Columbus with fewer scruples, obtaining huge prescriptions of OxyContin and fentanyl patches, using them and selling some; in time he was tearing into the fentanyl patches, eating the contents. "I still didn't understand what I was getting ready to go through," he told me.

NOR DID THE town of Kenton. The town was a lot like the country in that regard. For a silence accompanied the spread of opioids. Newspaper obituaries reported people dying "suddenly" at home. Some were former high school wrestlers and power lifters, Kenton High School having had stellar teams in both sports. Both sports created chronic pain, which meant the athletes were treated with opioid painkillers, to which many grew dependent, then switched to heroin. Among them was Johnny Ferrell, a former high school wrestler, who died of a heroin overdose in 2006. His nephew, Michael Ferrell, overdosed in 2013 at twenty, in the same bedroom as his uncle had years earlier.

"I was calling around trying to get my son treatment," said Jawna Ferrell, Michael's mother and Johnny's sister, who supported herself and her kids cleaning houses. "I ended up quitting my job just so I could search for places for him. There was nothing."

Another Kenton mom who battled this early on was Tracy Morrison, an emergency-room nurse at the time. She began seeing people coming through the ER vomiting, sweating, shaking. It took a while to realize that these people were on heroin. "Then we thought it was just in Kenton. We had no idea it was popping up in southern Ohio and elsewhere," she said. "No one was talking about it."

Eventually, Tracy's two daughters got addicted. They were in and out of jail. "Back then when somebody got arrested, they put it on the front page. Everybody knew it when your kid got arrested. You went in your kitchen and curled into the fetal position. They were charging them with everything; everybody got felonies, many as they could give 'em," Morrison said. "They would come home [from prison] to nothing. No medically assisted treatment, no job; no one would hire them. Then they screwed up, relapsed and went back to prison, or they died. It was as ugly as it could get. These people were being decimated with criminal charges, their families were being bankrupted. There was no treatment. The attitude was 'Well, those kids were raised wrong. It's the parents' fault.' Then people everywhere started dying; it got bigger and bigger."

A generation of the town of Kenton, Ohio, fell into dope. Yet most people in Hardin County, among cornfields and county roads where traffic jams were caused by farm combines and Amish horse-drawn buggies, hadn't awakened to the plague gathering around them.

ROB BURD WAS twenty-six when he first felt the shivering, the leg pain, and the diarrhea of withdrawal. It was 2004, and he was using a half dozen pills a day, snorting them all day long. His first overdose came at the home of his mother and stepfather.

During these years, the Rockwell axle plant gradually laid off workers; then it was sold to another company, which in turn resold it.

For decades the streets around the courthouse had been clogged every Friday and Saturday nights with cruisers, with kids headed in both directions. It was part of an outdoor life that typified the town back then, where people saw each other, communed in some way, out of doors. Then the police department shut down weekend cruising, citing the intolerable congestion. The last of the bars, which decades before had numbered in the dozens, closed as the factory that used to be Rockwell shut for good. Now there were fewer places for people to be together, fewer things for young people to do Friday and Saturday.

Pills, then heroin, replaced cruising and drinking among many whom Rob Burd knew. Life retreated indoors. The opioids were a symbol of that isolation, and they helped it along. As Kenton's pill users moved to heroin, Rob Burd was among them.

He shot up first at a dealer's house in 2005. Soon he was couch surfing at one friend's house after another. Every day became a grim grind to get his daily dope, figuring out who he could scam, what he would steal, how long this couch would last before his welcome wore out. He fathered children with three women. His brothers were ashamed. Old friends avoided him. His mother barred him from her home.

He spent his time around people who, like him, were interested in dope and nothing else. One was an obese fellow up from Kentucky, a pill dealer on disability who always had a bevy of young female addicts around him as he drove about town in a purple Dodge Caravan. For a while, Burd got high on the proceeds of sales of possessions belonging to a middle-aged farmer who got involved with a young female addict. The farmer had a Harley, a new truck, furniture—all of it went for drugs, with Burd helping him sell the stuff and siphoning off some of the dope.

Years of using and conniving wore out any belief in his own utility or virtue. It crushed him to think, as he often did, that he was now one of the "druggies" he and his brothers once hated.

Rob Burd was arrested for possession of heroin, given probation, then arrested again for probation violations or missed court dates. On it went, the arrest record typical of a street addict. He lost his license in 1997. For years, he was stopped often, then fined, for driving without a license. He became a regular encounter for law enforcement. His name was in the paper, telling a cautionary tale to those who knew him. Finally, the charges accumulated, and a judge sent him to prison for two years. There wasn't much else Hardin County knew to do with an addict. "The bus I went [to prison] on, one guy had robbed a pizza place; everyone else was a strung-out user like me," he said. Prison took him off the streets and away from dope for a while, but when he got out, he was quickly chasing it every day.

Just before his addiction to pills began, Rob had broken up with Laurel Rogers. "I wanted the picket fence and little family, and he was still the wild child," she told me. A month later, Laurel told Rob she was pregnant. Their son Layton was born in 2000, just as Rob slid into his addiction.

Yet they maintained contact. Rob's drug use tormented them both. She never knew if he was sober or not. He'd go to jail, then return. As he grew, Layton lived for the times he spent with Rob, even as he came to understand his father was somehow damaged. So Laurel stayed in Rob's life, hoping he would become the kind of father her son yearned for. She would drive them to the movies, give Rob money for tickets, then pick them up later. She gave Rob money to buy Layton birthday presents so her son wouldn't think his father had forgotten.

Laurel let Rob live in her basement when Layton was in kindergarten. Her son would rumble down the stairs each morning and, like a puppy, jump on his dad, wanting to play. Rob was often too doped up. One day his friends drove Rob, unconscious, to her house. Laurel told Layton to get inside, threw water on Rob, and told his friends to get him to the hospital.

That was on Mother's Day, and that's how it went. Yet Layton never let Laurel say a bad thing about his father. He ran to Rob every time, hugged him, and forgave him. "It's a natural thing for a boy to want to be with his dad," Laurel said. With wisdom beyond his years, Layton seemed to understand that his father was, for now, joined to some unseen shrieking mistress who demanded that Rob love her first and more than anyone else, including his chipper little son. None of that seemed to bother Layton. His love endured, stronger and more patient than the dope.

Layton was eight when Rob went to prison. Laurel often urged her son to write to his father. On those nights, in something like a Norman Rockwell image updated to the twenty-first century, a little boy sat a kitchen table in rural Ohio and, with his mother looking on, scrawled words to the heroin-addicted daddy he rarely saw.

Hardin County II

In 2013, a local attorney named Scott Barrett was appointed to replace a retiring judge at Hardin County Court.

Barrett is a strong Republican and a devout Christian and was likely the last person anyone would have thought to chart a radical departure from court tradition. But Ohio had begun a pilot program, urging five counties to start something called a "drug court." Hardin County was one of them. The judge Barrett replaced had refused. New to the bench, Barrett didn't want to start off by saying no to state officials. Problem was, he'd only just heard the term "drug court" when a judge from a different county urged him to start one. "I didn't know what he was talking about," Barrett told me.

An immaculately dressed, unfailingly polite man and now in his late sixties, Barrett was Kenton born and bred. His father had been a personnel manager at Rockwell International. His mother was the receptionist at the *Kenton Times* until the day Barrett graduated law school. Barrett had delivered the paper as a boy. He was the organist and musical director at First Methodist Church, and for forty years he practiced law in Hardin County. His life revolved around the courthouse at the center of Kenton, built in 1915 of Indiana gray limestone, which at three stories remains the town's tallest building. All that bequeathed Scott Barrett a traditional view of the jurist's role.

But the true extent of dope's devastation was by then emerging from the shadows in his hometown. Barrett figured that his new position might give him a chance to do something about it. So he read about brain science and the books of Alcoholics Anonymous and Narcotics Anonymous, and he visited drug courts in other counties.

To these courts, he learned, came addicts looking to avoid prison sentences for low-level, drug-related felonies; these were usually preceded by probation fines and violations, missed court dates, suspended driver's licenses, and many misdemeanors. Drug court was their last chance before prison, and therein lay the key. With prison hanging over them, the court also had a chance to pry them from dope's mastery and toward recovery.

Court clients had to attend twelve-step meetings, find work, call in daily and submit to random urine samples, get their GED; then they had to show up each Monday to report on their lives. If they lied, missed court or group meetings, didn't call in, failed a urine test, or committed another felony, they could be thrown out of the program, perhaps sent to prison.

Drug courts were spreading across the country due to the opioid addiction crisis. This expansion happened most surprisingly in red areas of the country, where the philosophy of "lock 'em up and throw away the key" had been what amounted to addiction treatment for years. Drug courts were becoming a big deal in Georgia. They were multiplying in Texas. And they were coming to rural Ohio, including, beginning one Monday in October 2013, Hardin County.

Barrett opened his court for business, calling it Recovery Court because the title sounded more hopeful. Nine people showed up, one of them a woman so drunk she passed out in her seat.

What Barrett learned as months passed was that opioids demanded an addict's total obedience. Proof of this was the extent to which people on these drugs were willing to lie, cheat, connive, and live in the worst discomfort—all in pursuit of these drugs. Urging them on was the cheapest and deadliest supply of opioids to ever appear on American streets. Under such conditions, it defied reason that an addict alone would simply decide to seek treatment. I had been to several drug courts in my travels. The way I saw them, they were a tool to push people into treatment. The threat of prison or jail was often about the only leverage available before addicts overdosed on the most potent street drug stream the country had ever seen. "Many people think that if we have a multitude of [treatment] resources, everything's going to be better," Barrett said. "It's simply not true. A multitude of resources does not encourage people to want recovery. It just doesn't work that way. If they're not kind of pushed into it, or forced—if they don't know something worse can happen to them—many people would not have any interest, and it would have no staying power."

The popular image was of an addict suddenly seeing the light. Now "ready" for treatment, she found a path forward and all was good. Barrett found that was hardly ever the case; reality was a lot messier. Most had to be prodded; many rebelled or had no confidence that they could succeed after years of being shunned, stinking, hated, and now stained with tattoos that felt as permanent as their addictions. Life seemed impossible without dope. Amid all this, assuming that hardened street addicts would just suddenly be "ready" for treatment was dangerous folly. Instead, said Mimi Zarzar, Barrett's court administrator, "you slowly move people to a readiness. They go from, 'I'm not sure I want this,' to 'Maybe I might want this,' to 'Yes, I do want this.'"

Barrett's Recovery Court was therefore designed not to achieve miracles but rather, through constant tending, to nudge people along, step by slow step. Many returned to drugs, or slipped up and didn't follow court rules. They were adults, but drugs had stunted their maturity. Thus his job, Barrett soon understood, was like herding children, attempting to create for them some small part of the stability they needed to move forward in the world. This usually amounted to teaching the basics: showing up on time, avoiding bad friends and F-bombs in job interviews, earning a GED, paying child support. As his court took its first halting steps, Barrett often assigned tasks to those who messed up: trash removal along the highway or a written essay on, say, avoiding bad friends. When one ill-tempered court participant threw feces on the porch of a neighbor, Barrett assigned him to clean the courthouse toilets.

Barrett battled another popular view: that if a public policy failed, it amounted to "government waste" to keep funding it. In speeches around the county, Barrett likened drug addiction to smoking; smokers knew cigarettes were killing them, yet they kept smoking despite the consequences and repeated attempts to quit. Most smokers, he reminded his listeners, needed numerous tries—and failures—to quit. Failure, he said, was no reason to stop trying, and learning how.

In this he walked a careful line, for to say that failure was part of addiction also seemed to Barrett to excuse any kind of bad behavior. Yet he knew prison would do little for many of those before him. He had no rulebook, no regulations to follow. Every week he sifted through the lives of the people before him, balancing one fact with another. He wore a black robe, but he ventured far from the world of traditional judging. "I thought I was going to be doing all legal stuff," he said, "but this is treatment stuff."

From there, Barrett's court became a place where authorities and addicts could commune, talk to each other. A Friday arts and crafts group began, to which participants could bring their kids. The court sponsored a softball team made up of addict clients. It had sober movie-and-pizza nights. This was the kind of community thing that had happened organically for decades in towns like Kenton, before the dope, the plant closures, when families, too, were less damaged.

Perhaps the biggest departure from tradition came from Aaron McPherson, the county probation officer assigned to Barrett's court. McPherson is a Kenton native, and it would be understating the case to say that he is an avid hunter and fisherman; his Facebook account is a constant stream of photos of McPherson holding up enormous bass or a large-antlered buck. He was also a star running back for Kenton

High School, and the 2,453 yards he gained in 2000 stands as the school's single-season rushing record. Shortly after taking the job, and as the Recovery Court was getting underway, McPherson began meeting with employers, urging them to hire recovering addicts and those fresh from prison. He seemed to know everyone in town, and in time, he was said to be able to place anyone in a job with decent wages—at $15 to $20 an hour. He would explain to each probationer: "If they want you there at eight a.m., you need to be there at seven forty-five. On time is being there fifteen minutes early.'"

Most of his probationers had never left the county. McPherson began organizing outings for his charges. He first took them hiking in Hocking Hills, a six-mile loop that amounted to the first difficult thing many of them had completed in years. Next, he took them mushroom hunting in southern Michigan. He began organizing Lake Erie fishing trips, calling it Get Hooked on Fishing. He now maintains a Facebook page promoting his TeamHardinOutdoors365. Probation officers from other counties "look at me like I'm crazy," he told me. "It takes a lot more work, and it's not like I get paid extra for it. But it shows them a different way. There's more to see than just sitting in Hardin County." McPherson became the rare officer to whom his probationers would actually admit they had used, without a drug test first, then apologize for days.

Under the high ceiling on his third-floor courtroom, Barrett's Recovery Court grew into a forum where the community could, in a sense, lay hands on recovering addicts. A group of women from St. John's Evangelical Church attended. The "church ladies," as they were known, prayed for the participants, learned their stories, hugged them, and brought them cookies at Christmas.

The relationships between Barrett and the participants, meanwhile, grew personal. With them he was both caring and firm—a parent dealing with his children. Barrett quoted to them the poet Robert Frost ("The Road Not Taken"), Disney's *Winnie the Pooh* ("You are braver than you believe, stronger than you seem, and smarter than you think"), and verses from the Bible. He and his staff soon knew which participant was bipolar, who was dating whom, where this one went to high school, whose mother was sick, how many baby mamas this guy had, on which arm that woman had her child's name tattooed. When Barrett's mother died in 2019, his Recovery Court charges wrote him cards and sent flowers.

Drug court allowed for that kind of intimate knowledge, treating each case separately, which in turn allowed staff to see early warning signs. While judges in other courts might have seen a client's drug possession as something to be either ignored or cause for probation, Barrett came to see it as a symptom portending deeper problems to come, warranting decisive intervention—sometimes jail—but usually with an eye to encouraging that person's recovery.

As years passed, Barrett's court collected its participants' tiny yet sublime victories, maddening screwups, and cataclysmic defeats that kept everyone humble. Through it all, though, Scott Barrett managed to remain an optimist—naive sometimes, he realized, in the view of his staff. He teared up at times. "A lot of these people have the potential for coming out of it, and you protect the community best by getting them into sobriety," he told me. "It is so exciting when they gradually learn that it's going to take little steps. That they're going to have to prove themselves—and they do."

From this third-floor courtroom a kind of community first aid was practiced that in small ways attempted to suture what dope and deindustrialization had torn in Hardin County.

And this was how things were when, in September 2015, Rob Burd sat down for the first time in Barrett's Recovery Court, a second prison term hanging over his head. Those in the court that day remember him as pale, sickly, his teeth worn to nubs; he stank, couldn't urinate without a catheter, had trouble focusing, forgot basic things, and lapsed often into a thousand-yard stare. Not two people in Kenton trusted him. Only his son Layton was happy to see him coming. "He was so emaciated," one of the church ladies recalled.

Court administrator Mimi Zarzar saw that his appearance reflected an inner despair. "In conversations with him, there was a sense of hopelessness. 'Can I really change my life?'" she remembered. In court that day were people with whom he'd used; their drug days together were a movie that played over and over in his mind; he despised that world, yet could not leave it. He didn't want to return to prison. But he feared what Barrett's court would ask of him and was unsure he was worth the effort, after all the nastiness he had caused.

ABOUT SIX MONTHS later, one afternoon in the spring of 2016, Keith Everhart, the sheriff of Hardin County, met with a local steel-factory owner. Everhart had been urging local businesses to hire recovering addicts, and did the same now with this factory owner.

He talked on about how folks looking to get away from drugs needed a hand up. The community needed to come together on this, because in tiny, rural Hardin County, surrounded by cornfields and crisscrossed by railroads, the opioid addiction problem, as much as folks had tried to ignore it, was out of control. I met Everhart on one of my trips through Ohio.

In the middle of the conversation, he told me, the mill owner stopped him.

"You hired any of 'em at your department?" he asked.

Keith Everhart looks every bit the small-county sheriff. He began working for the department as a deputy in 1997, right out of high school. He wears his brown hair in a sharp crew cut, dips Kodiak tobacco, watches Fox News, and attends the same small, rural Methodist church in which his parents raised him.

There is, therefore, every reason to imagine Keith Everhart as immovable regarding ideas that in US law enforcement have been conventional wisdom for a long time. One of those is that addicts need to be in jail. Indeed, that is where Everhart put them for most of his career as a deputy, and then as the supervisor of Hardin County's drug task force. "After that it wasn't my problem anymore," he said.

But as this epidemic began calling on Americans to reexamine ideas, customs, and policies once thought settled, law enforcement showed itself to be among the most nimble and willing to innovate. Among that group is Hardin County sheriff Keith A. Everhart.

He was elected sheriff in 2009. His arrest rolls featured the same names every couple of months, usually for the same small-time property or possession crimes. Hardin County had always lived at a safe distance from problems townspeople read about in Toledo, or Dayton, or Columbus, or Los Angeles. Now those problems involved people from down the street. "I got into the position I'm in and realized I don't know it all," he told me. "You gotta open up your mind a little bit and take chances."

When Judge Barrett opened his Recovery Court in the Hardin County Courthouse, he asked Everhart to be part of the team that met every Monday morning before court to discuss each participant's progress. On the Recovery Court team, Everhart saw that the inability to find work hamstrung many recovering addicts. So he started drumming up support for hiring recovering addicts. This is what took him to the office of that steel-mill owner south of town.

Everhart responded to the owner's question that day by explaining how difficult it was for law enforcement to hire people with drug addiction and felony records. Officers go through rigorous vetting, including psychological testing and financial audits, not to mention lengthy tactical training—all to be prepared to handle problems on the street presented by, very often, people addicted to drugs or alcohol. Working next to these same folks has struck many in law enforcement as heresy.

But Everhart left the meeting that day thinking the mill owner had a point. Here he was sheriff, asking others to do what he had not done himself. So Everhart dug through his budget and found money for a half-time, $10-an-hour landscaper/janitor position. "This wasn't meant to be a career," he told me. "The goal was to help someone learn to be an employee and get them into some other job. A bridge. I can only do about one at a time."

The first fellow he hired was a young man in Recovery Court whose drug use began when he smoked marijuana with his father at age eight. The kid kept on being late to work. It amazed Everhart to see just how lost addicts could be in the real world. "It was basically like raising a five-year-old," Everhart remembered. Barrett would admonish the young man on what was expected of an employee.

Watching all this play out weekly at Barrett's court was Rob Burd. Rob had slowly steadied himself in recovery. His counselor got him a room in a sober-living home she ran in south Kenton. He messed up a few times drinking. But within the structure of Barrett's Recovery Court, he worked up some confidence. He gained weight, and color returned to his face.

All this gave him energy to keep going. So did fear of prison. "I couldn't go back," he told me. "These young kids in there, all they want to do is fight. I thought, 'This is my last chance.'" He spent a year in the sober-living house, as younger addicts came and left. They raged against any attempt to order their behavior, like making their beds or a curfew. They couldn't stop hustling, but their cons always led back to relapse. "Instead of a full-time job, they'd go out and sell their county food cards," he said. "They didn't know anything about working an eight-hour job."

That Rob had worked and wasn't afraid of it, he came to believe, provided him a bulwark as he fought his way out of addiction. Meanwhile, Recovery Court grew on him. He hadn't come to the court ready to make a change, but Barrett and his staff had firmly nudged him that way. His screwups were not due now to his lack of desire for sobriety but to his dope-corroded memory. He forgot to go to meetings; Judge Barrett made him get a weekly scheduler.

Burd had a daughter, and seeing her threw him into a panic because he had no idea what to do with her, how to talk to her, what she might like. He sent photos of dresses to his counselor. She advised him on which one to buy. He began to feel at home as a father.

For the first time, Rob was sober when he saw Layton, who was now in high school. The two spent more time together. Rob had a roof over his head and was grateful for that, too. "It was the little stuff—seeing my family come back, talking to me, believing in me again," Rob told me. "I was just grabbing on to little things" for encouragement.

Meanwhile, Keith Everhart came close to firing the young man he'd hired as a janitor. Watching this, Rob Burd one day summoned the courage to take the sheriff aside. "If this guy don't work out," he said, "I'd appreciate a chance."

A short time later, Everhart found the kid a job at a local factory. The next Monday, in the summer of 2016, Rob Burd, now forty-one, a longtime pill-and-heroin addict, the shame of his family, scarred and scared as he made his ninth attempt to stay sober, showed up for work at 8:00 a.m. at the squat brick building on South Main Street in his hometown of Kenton, Ohio, that houses the Hardin County Sheriff's Office, which he'd seen only from inside its holding tank.

"I have no clue why he hired me," Rob said later. Neither did Everhart's deputies.

Hardin County III

In the summer of 2016, Sergeant Scott Holbrook was standing in the back lot of the Hardin County sheriff's office when he saw the new guy walk out of the office. The fellow had been hired a few weeks before. Holbrook knew him from the streets, a toothless junkie hired part-time by the sheriff to wash patrol cars, weed the lawn, and clean up around the office. The sheriff's office, Holbrook felt, ought to be a sanctuary from guys like this for deputies. Sheriff Keith Everhart had to admonish his deputies, "You don't have to like him but you won't be mean to him." When Everhart announced the hire to the staff, Holbrook said, "I was concerned that he had lost his mind."

That day in the parking lot gave Holbrook no reason to change his opinion. The fellow lingered in the lot, looked around, seemed lost, bewildered, as if he'd walked outside but now could not remember why.

Rob Burd's first months as the janitor at the sheriff's office were like that. Few of the deputies had anything to say to him. Fear of prison kept him sober, yet the shards of his memory returned only slowly after the years of abusing pain pills and heroin. He would walk to the end of a hallway and not remember why, then return and walk the hallway again to see if it came back to him. Each chore had to be explained to him step by step; then he had to do it immediately, or he'd forget. Everhart remembers seeing a lawn mower out in front of the sheriff's office late one afternoon. He called Burd at home to ask why he hadn't put it away. Burd couldn't remember what he'd done with it, or whether he'd even finished mowing the lawn.

It took a year and a half. Deputies watched it happen, day by day, this strange fog lifting only slowly inside a man's mind. Along the way Rob Burd became the first addict many cops in the department got to know without handcuffs; they watched his struggle, saw that he didn't quit, and came to feel for his befuddlement. "It softened us up a bit," said Holbrook. "Once you see somebody, knowing them personally, you start looking at other people and you see them a little bit differently, too."

Being around Burd changed narcotics investigations, particularly when it came to confidential informants. CIs, as they're known, are essential to most drug investigations. They're usually drug addicts with connections to the dealers who are the probes' main focus. Police recruit them when they've been arrested, offering them the chance to work off a charge by buying drugs from the dealer, then testifying in court. Once the case is done, though, investigators typically forget about the CI; as addicts, CIs can also be maddening to deal with. After watching Rob struggle, "We've started taking a closer look to see if we can offer [CIs] some help," said Terry Sneary, the department's chief narcotics investigator. "In the past, they were working with us, helping us take down a dealer, but then we were walking away. We knew we would encounter them again before long."

This journey from judgment to empathy was one the addiction crisis had pushed the country into as well. It revealed stories that made clear to many Americans that addicts were all around them, and always had been.

A couple at the department with dental insurance drove Rob to Columbus and had him fitted for an upper set of dentures; Rob paid them off over the next months. He began going to twelve-step meetings in Columbus, away from the Kenton meetings attended by folks he'd known in addiction. But the department became his true recovery sanctuary. It was where he watched TV and lifted weights.

He became a father to Layton there, as well. Soon the boy was a fixture around the department. He helped Rob detail the patrol cars; Layton never was much good at it, but it allowed the two to be together. He didn't mind if Rob was sweeping up, running an errand, or mowing the grass. If it was after school, Layton was there. They watched TV at the department on Rob's off hours.

Rob was desperate that Layton never be mad at him. Laurel Rogers had to insist that he be a father, not a buddy, to their son. He gave Layton a bracelet reading "Heroin Sucks"; Layton never took it off. He used Rob's addiction as evidence to his friends that his father was tougher, had gone through more hard times, than theirs had. He relished the stories of Rob's fighting days. "He finally was getting the time with him that he always wanted," Laurel said.

One afternoon, after Rob had been on the job about a year, Layton texted Rob a selfie from class. Later that day, Layton was driving down a straight and lonesome county road through cornfields north of Kenton. He loved heavy metal music. His parents believe he was listening to it loud, and that this was why, as he went over a railroad crossing, he didn't hear the train coming. The crossing had no gates or warning lights. The impact of the train propelled Layton's car fifty yards into a cornfield.

Over the next few days, the department mobilized around helping Rob Burd through the death of his son. Scott Holbrook sped in a patrol car to Columbus, where Rob was at a clinic with his girlfriend, scooped him up, and took him back to a treatment center that had just opened in Kenton. "I don't care if I have to lock you in a cell block and violate every right you have," Everhart told Rob, "but you will not go back to using." Hundreds of mourners attended Layton's funeral—among them, the entire sheriff's department.

Not long after that, Everhart asked him whether there might be another job Rob would want at the department. Rob began sitting in with the dispatchers to learn what they did. The multitasking was daunting, but as his mind cleared and he gained confidence, he thought he might give it a try. They put him on handling simple calls, no emergencies.

A year later, Rob passed his 911 dispatcher certification and began working full-time. Three people died his first week on the job, testing his abilities and nerve to keep going. "A guy hung himself and his dad called and I said, 'Cut him down.' His dad said, 'My knees are bad. I can't.' Then one guy fell. Then we had a wreck. I had to call in Life Flight. I wasn't ready for that. You call them in, put them on standby, give them the longitude and latitude. It sounded like a lot for me at the time."

He mastered the job of dispatcher, and stayed sober despite the stress. So over the Hardin County emergency airwaves, directing life flights and responses to calls from postmen threatened by barking dogs, came the redneck accent of a reborn man who once couch-surfed and wore out his teeth doing dope.

IT TOOK ROB BURD nine rehabs to leave his dark hole, and he wasn't altogether clear what allowed him to do so. Might be his age, the fatigue in living as a small-town modern-day leper. Fear of returning to prison was certainly part of it. The forceful nudging of Barrett's Recovery Court was another.

Perhaps what also helped keep Rob going was seeing people around him wanting him to succeed, the encouraging words from deputies who had ignored him, the confident smile of a set of new teeth. Maybe it was the elation of watching his life's forward movement put distance, step by plodding step, between himself and dope.

He was still paying off his upper dentures. He owed the state for his many fines for driving without a license. Every few blocks in Kenton stood a house where he used, overdosed, or wore out trust. People he worked with at the Rockwell plant, people he once knew as solid working folks, he saw wandering the streets, strung out, some still wearing Rockwell jackets. He had seen so much of Kenton shredded in his lifetime: the departure of the factory jobs and the people, the arrival of plentiful pain pills, then heroin, all of it turning the town isolated and defenseless. He'd helped in that shredding. That, he felt, was the shame and the waste of it all.

Yet the small story of one addict was only part of the change in Kenton, Ohio. Parents no longer have to quit a job to search for help for their addicted children, as Jawna Ferrell did in 2013. The rural town now has AA and NA meetings, recovery mentors, employers willing to hire former addicts, two treatment centers, a judge who knows their stories, and a probation officer who organizes fishing trips. Maybe Hardin County just learned to do what it did more naturally in long-gone decades: marshal the local talent, leverage its energy and expertise, break down some of the silos that keep people apart, and find for itself how to make them work best together.

In town, perhaps a new realization was dawning: that a recovering addict is more than a person who no longer does dope. A recovering addict discovers new dynamism, excitement for future possibilities, and gratitude for a second chance. Like fossil fuel—energy growing from decay.

The epidemic also seemed to require a new approach to failure: that it is something to learn from. I thought this often as I traveled to places like Hardin County.

I find baseball illuminating on this subject. At its core, the sport is about responding to failure. Ted Williams, modern baseball's greatest hitter, failed two out of every three times he stepped to the plate. That didn't stop him from playing. On the contrary, failure was his great motivation. Yet when it comes to addiction, we ignore our national pastime's most important lesson. We give ourselves no mercy, though we are pummeled by substances and services fine-tuned to assault our brains from Facebook, fast-food restaurants, casinos, cigarette companies, or drug traffickers.

Moneyball by Michael Lewis describes how the small-budget Oakland A's acquired a competitive advantage by finding gems among players the rest of baseball rejected as worthless. Sometimes it required enormous effort—transforming a catcher into a first baseman, for example. Like the A's, I thought, American businesses could extract competitive advantage, help their bottom line and their towns by hiring recovering addicts—this new raw material, rejected by others.

But just like a catcher being made a first baseman, recovering addicts pose unexpected challenges as employees. The last time I saw Rob Burd, his sweet story of redemption had soured. Shortly before the holidays in 2019, he told me, he got drunk, drove to a nearby town, and was lit up by a police car. He sped off and pulled over after a short chase. Alcohol had always been his biggest problem, bigger than the dope, he told me when we met at a diner in the town of Ada a few weeks later. Part of it may have been the memories of his son. He had just been getting to know Layton. "The holidays get me every year," he said. "That's just the first time I got caught."

Keith Everhart fired him. He didn't see he had a choice. "I'd let him get away with a lot," he said. "I worry about him, but he's got to get his life straight." When I saw Rob, he was couch-surfing again. He was still esteemed by folks at the sheriff's department he'd once repelled. One deputy loaned him money, let him sleep on his couch. Everhart let him sleep on his couch, too.

Rob got back into car detailing, which he'd learned at the sheriff's office. He was on disability, cleaning a car now and then. His daughter studied to be a dental hygienist and graduated. A small police department might have a part-time dispatcher job for him, he thought. He was staying away from alcohol and dope; his liver wasn't in the best shape.

In Kenton, a community came together, worked together, and through that helped one addict move on. It was a lot of work to help just one person. A lot of work for one small step, yet I thought it was a good story, and why I'd come to town. But just because one shows compassion for another in need doesn't mean it'll work out. It's not a Hollywood movie. It's life and it's hard. Instead, maybe the story in

Kenton was more about how nothing is a full success or a total failure. It was the kind of thing going on across America, towns taking a chance on someone, seeing it fail, though not completely, coming to understand the mix that was necessary—of compassion from those trying to help, and accountability from those struggling.

One winter afternoon, as the sun was setting, Rob found himself driving the country roads that cut straight and long through the cornfields north of Kenton when he came upon the railroad crossing where Layton died.

As he approached the crossing that winter afternoon, a train came chugging down from the north. The crossing gates lowered. After Layton died, Laurel had lobbied to have them installed. Rob pulled up. He had been through here before, but never as a train passed. They came so infrequently. He was all alone under a gray sky. He sat in his car and wondered what his boy had been thinking that day. He looked to his left. What Laurel and Layton's friends had left was still there—a glass angel, a photograph, a cross, Layton's soccer jersey number 3 painted on a guardrail.

After the locomotive passed, he waited for a while in the silence. Then he took his foot off the brake and went up and over the crossing and down and west, through the brown fields and into the dying light.

PART IV

Angie and Starla IV

"We'll Figure Out a Way"

O ne cold, gray morning in February 2013, Angie Odom walked slowly down the corridors of a nursing home in the town of Huntsville, dreading what she might find.

Her visit was the culmination of two days of feverish phone calling trying to find what had become of Starla. Maude Buchanan, Starla's mother, had shown up at Angie's clinic carrying an infant in that car seat. Starla had had an overdose in Pensacola, Maude said, and the last she saw of her daughter she was bedridden and pregnant at a hospital. Later, the hospital had called Maude to say Starla had given birth. Yet by the time Maude arrived in Pensacola to claim the infant, Sacred Heart Hospital had transferred Starla. Maude didn't know where. She had not thought, or known how, to look for her daughter. She didn't know what to do with the infant, either. It was all a lot for Maude to bear—which brought her that cold day in February to Angie's TLC Clinic.

Angie spent a day on the phone and found that a month before, not long after giving birth, Starla Hoss had been transported from Pensacola to this nursing home in Huntsville, Tennessee.

Now, Angie and a friend walked its corridors. Angie imagined that soon she would be asking Starla about all that had happened that led to this. They would have some kind of conversation, she was certain. After all, Starla had given birth. She must be able to talk.

They turned a corner, and there on the floor, halfway out the door to a room, lay the shy girl Angie remembered from the group home and the jail wedding. Starla was now spotted in feces, her gown wrapped around her neck, her hair greasy, groaning but unable to speak, blank and unblinking. Her breathing rattled. She stroked her chin constantly. Outraged, Angie sent for the nursing home director, who quickly had Starla cleaned up.

In tears, Angie and her friend sat by Starla, talking to her, praying, trying to calm her. Starla was like an enormous infant, gyrating, urgently needing what she could not communicate. Angie put Starla's mother on the phone, hoping Maude's voice would have some effect. It did not.

"I'm so sorry, Starla," Angie said, still in tears after a couple of hours. "I have to go back so we can get you moved closer to home. We'll figure out a way."

It took two weeks. Congressman Phil Roe helped find a rehabilitation hospital where Starla might be examined and some treatment found.

Meanwhile, Children's Services called Angie to say Maude Buchanan had failed a drug test. The agency couldn't leave the infant with her grandmother, and no one else in the family could pass the agency's background check. At Maude's behest and with nowhere else to put the infant, a Children's Services counselor arrived at Angie's home late that night with Starla's infant daughter, a diaper bag, a bottle, and some formula. Just until we find her a placement, the counselor told Angie.

Angie had cared for babies before. But this girl cried constantly, couldn't sleep; she needed to be rocked back and forth to grow quiet. She arched her back and cried when she was being fed; she didn't just spit up, she vomited often. She had mild cerebral palsy and tightened muscles, meaning she couldn't bend her legs easily. She also needed to be swung in a way that would terrify any other baby. Only then would she fall asleep, then wake and scream as soon as the movement stopped. Angie spent hours doing deep knee bends and moving from side to side while holding the little girl. She wouldn't lie down without screaming and could only safely sleep propped up; Angie slept in the sitting position, with the infant on her lap.

Two days after the infant arrived, so did Starla. A paramedic crew volunteered to go get her at that Huntsville nursing home. On the way back, Starla began to flail; one of the paramedics sang to her, and this calmed her. Angie and the infant were waiting for them at the hospital. Mother and child had not been together since the C-section at Sacred Heart in Pensacola a month before. Now, in a clean hospital room, with the warmth of her child upon her, Starla began to softly cry. "Nuzzle your baby, Starla," Angie said. Starla rubbed her chin against her daughter. Her cry went on and on as they lay together. In the years to come, Starla never cried again. But after touching her daughter, she ceased rolling in the same frenetic way and seemed to have arrived at some kind of peace.

Two weeks later, the hospital's chief of neurology arranged for a meeting with state officials, Angie, and Starla's mother and relatives. None of Starla's family showed up. Angie stood and held the infant and gyrated to keep her quiet, as before her sat the heads of the hospital's major departments. Each went through the tests they had performed on Starla. It was a somber meeting, and some of those at the table seemed close to tears. Finally, the chief of neurology spoke. Starla's vegetative state could not be reversed, he said. No amount of rehabilitation would help. She would never talk or walk or see. She would never feed herself. She would lie in a nursing home for the rest of her life. They knew of a couple of good options; there was one, in fact, in Elizabethton.

Angie, baby in arms, felt the room close in around her. She'd assumed the place in Huntsville wouldn't be able to do anything for Starla, but this hospital, she thought, might return the woman to some kind of normalcy—enough function to care somewhat for her child. Driving home, Angie was overcome with grief. Then what does this mean? she thought. Where does she go?

The Department of Children Services held a similar meeting regarding the newborn a couple of days later. This time Maude attended. A nurse began by saying the infant, too, might never walk or talk. She faced a lifetime of complications that were hard to predict. DCS staff said Maude had to submit to a drug test before they'd let the baby return to her home. Maude didn't like that idea. "We're going to talk to Angie and her husband about adopting," she said.

That was the first Angie had heard of this. She had assumed their care for the newborn was temporary. But she knew that three generations of Starla's family preceding the infant had been caught up in drugs, and that their home life was chaotic. Angie tried to think of other families who could take the girl. "There was no way I was going to let that baby go to state custody," she said.

A week or two passed. Children's Services scheduled a meeting to decide where the infant would go. The baby spent the night before the meeting shrieking. It went on and on, an exhausting, agonizing scream. Angie remembered the promise she'd once given Starla. "I'll always be there to help you," she had said. It was the kind of thing so many people say, in courtesy, with compassion at heart, but limited in intent. It was said in a moment, not thinking of what it might entail, never imagining it would come to something like this. She and Earl were new empty-nesters, in their forties. They had just purchased a Honda Gold Wing motorcycle and had done their first 1,300-mile ride to the beach through Virginia and North Carolina. They were older and might not be around to deal with health issues the girl had later in life.

But Starla had no one. The baby, with all her problems, would probably be shifted from place to place for the rest of her childhood, until, when she was emancipated at 21, she would be left to fend for herself, alone in the world. Angie knew that story. She had walked lots of crying infants around the TLC Clinic. None ever cried like this child, and they always went to their forever homes. Struggling to quiet the tormented child that night, Angie, in tears of her own, looked down at the infant and felt a drenching warmth, acceptance, patience.

It felt so much like that night, years before at age nineteen, tied to the back of the USS *Cape Cod*; and as she had on the deck that night, she opened herself to it.

With some trepidation, she spoke to her husband the next evening after dinner. She was meeting in the morning with social workers. They wanted to talk about a home where the little girl might be placed, Angie said, as she stood at the kitchen sink, making a bottle. Their decision would be final, probably foster care. In a recliner, Earl Odom sat rocking the infant. He smiled.

"She's home," he said. "She's where she needs to be."

Neuroscience IV

"Modern Skulls House a Stone-Age Mind"

In 2014 neuroscientists accepted the idea that the addictive potential of a drug of abuse had a lot to do with the size of the dose, how often the drug was used, and the speed with which it hit the bloodstream.

No studies, however, tested that idea when it came to food. So that year, a team formed to try. They assembled at the University of Michigan, in the psychology department's FAST Food Lab. The lab was designed by a professor named Ashley Gearhardt to look like a fast-food restaurant: a kitchen, a cashier, tables. It was painted in splashy yellows, oranges, and reds.

Gearhardt is from the small farming town of Covington, north of Dayton, Ohio. She had grown up wanting to be a therapist. During a college year in Oxford, England, she fell under the mentorship of a professor who showed her what the new neuroscience was revealing about the brain. Enthralled, Gearhardt's focus shifted. She got a PhD in psychology at Yale, and she was hired as a professor at University of Michigan. She joined a vanguard of young psychologists and neuroscientists that had emerged as fast food and highly processed food became cheap and ubiquitous. The question that most occupied the researchers who met at University of Michigan in 2014 was this: Have we engineered foods to rush such a dose of sugar, fat, salt that they imbalance the brain's reward system, causing it to respond as it does to addictive drugs?

Gearhardt built the FAST Food Lab to test that idea. Test subjects, she discovered over the years, consumed three hundred more calories per sitting in the dressed-up lab than in more traditional labs of white tables and fluorescent lights. It was a lesson, she thought later, in the power of cues and environmental triggers.

For this study, she teamed with Nicole Avena. For Avena, the years in Princeton had been crammed with exhilarating work. She was part of hundreds of experiments on sugar-dependent rats under Bart Hoebel. Together, these experiments pioneered the evidence that sugar was addictive and hit the same brain receptors as did drugs such as heroin. With those findings, the lab established a biological basis for the compulsion to seek food similar to the compulsion to seek drugs.

Hoebel died of lung cancer in 2011. Avena kept on at the lab at Princeton, which saw fit to move it to the other end of campus and the new stand-alone Princeton Neuroscience Institute. Meanwhile, Avena took a job as a professor running a research clinic at Mt. Sinai Hospital in New York City. Her career shifted. Now she was translating what she'd learned in her experiments on rats to how that might apply to humans—namely, what foods humans should limit or avoid.

Avena went on the TV morning shows from time to time, and she spoke at conferences about sugar and nutrition. Neuroscience had come into its own. Nicole Avena had been there to see it. In particular, technology—of brain scans and so much more—allowed what others once laughed at to be now taken as fact. "When you can see a brain light up in response to someone eating a milkshake, and light up to someone injected with morphine," she told me, "that can tell a story that we weren't able to tell with the types of tools we had twenty years ago."

She and Ashley Gearhardt met at conferences and became friends. Each saw in the other a researcher pushing the limits of knowledge on the effects of the proliferation of processed foods.

The idea that these foods—pizza, ice cream, soda, cheeseburgers, and more—were addictive would seem a good bet. "We already know all that," Avena's mother told her daughter. Why study it? But hunches aren't science, and in 2014 there was no systematic research into which foods were the addictive culprits, and why.

In Gearhardt's lab they were joined by Erica Schulte, a graduate student. They recruited University of Michigan students as test subjects and fed them fast food. The students they interviewed reported cues to binge from fast-food ads or logos, which is one reason why the companies rarely change those logos. For some students, the omnipresence of fast-food restaurants *was* the problem. There was no escaping the supplies of fast food and the invitations to consume it. And like dope, these foods were harmful. The students reported obesity, diabetes, high blood pressure, often isolation and depression, as well as despair at being unable to stop eating or lose weight.

"Food addiction," the team decided, was incorrect. Many foods were not addictive at all. Highly processed foods were the problem—especially those that included combinations of refined carbohydrates, sugar mostly, with fat and sometimes salt. High calories, negligible nutrition.

The engineers of these foods were sharpshooters, aiming at the brain. They stripped the foods of the natural nutrients, fiber, and water that slow their absorption into the body. These foods hit the brain fast and hard, like coca leaf when it is processed into cocaine, and from there into crack. Similar to crack, which brings a ferocious and fleeting high, these foods deliver what's known as a 'high glycemic load'—meaning a blast to the body's blood sugar. This wallop prompts food cravings, bingeing, and withdrawals.

The team's study, published in 2015, stands as the first to conclude that high-potency doses of engineered food shared properties with drugs of abuse and spurred "addictive-like eating." Refined sugar and fat together lit up the brain's reward system. Hearing this, I was reminded of the pill-mill doctors who discovered that prescribing a combination of opioids and benzodiazepines (Xanax) got patients quickly dependent, making them reliable customers. Together, the two drugs were more powerful than each alone. Avena and Gearhardt reached a similar conclusion regarding the combination of sugar and fat in highly processed foods.

As I was learning of their research, I came upon a paper from two scholars at the University of California, Santa Barbara: Leda Cosmides and John Tooby, a married couple in charge of the school's Center for Evolutionary Psychology and the authors of "Evolutionary Psychology: A Primer."

Among their ideas was this: "Our modern skulls house a stone-age mind." Their point is that our brains evolved over millions of years to help our ancestors adapt to the dangers and demands of prehistoric life, not to the modern industrial world of the last 150 years, much less to mass marketing.

"Each of our ancestors was, in effect, on a camping trip that lasted an entire lifetime," the couple wrote. "This way of life endured for most of the last 10 million years. . . . [That experience] sculpted the human brain, favoring circuitry that was good at solving the day-to-day problems of our hunter-gatherer ancestors—problems like finding mates, hunting animals, gathering plant foods, negotiating with friends, defending ourselves against aggression, raising children, choosing a good habitat, and so on. Those whose circuits were better designed for solving these problems left more children, and we are descended from them."

Eating, exercise, sex, connecting with others—all that helped us stay alive. Our brains evolved to reward us with feelings of pleasure when we engaged in them. We evolved prodigious memory to remember where food and threat resided; slow learners died fast. Our brain evolved to be easily distracted because those who weren't got eaten. Our brain also required that we be physically touched by others—hugged, squeezed, kissed, patted on the back—as a way of reinforcing the group that kept us alive.

This cerebral evolution, the couple wrote, "is so slow it's hard to even imagine—it's like a stone being sculpted by wind-blown sand. [The brain's] circuits were not designed to solve the day-to-day problems of a modern American. There just haven't been enough generations for it to design circuits that are well-adapted to our post-industrial life."

I returned to this idea again and again as I tried to understand the roots and persistence of our epidemic of addiction. It wasn't just that drug companies and traffickers plied us with addictive narcotics. Life in a mass-marketing world also inundates us with legal and addictive-products and services. Casinos hire the brightest psychologists to design rooms that are more difficult to leave. Chicken nuggets were invented in a lab at Cornell University by combining the bird's byproducts into a "chicken clay" that is 60 percent salt and fat, two elements that over hardscrabble millennia our brains learned to treasure.

As a culture we are just more distracted, more easily narcotized, our brain receptors so easily overwhelmed. The designers of Facebook's Like button have renounced their brainchild for having turned social media addictive.

The social media giant's algorithms are programmed to keep us engaged, which is best achieved through provoking strong emotion—especially outrage. Outrage is intoxicating. Our brains evolved to feel outrage at the transgressions of someone in our group. It was essential to survival. Enforcing social norms, correcting the misbehavior of others also made us feel noble. "When people decide to punish somebody who has behaved unfairly, we see activation in brain areas associated with reward," Molly Crockett, a Yale University psychologist, told the podcast *Hidden Brain*. "There's a visceral satisfaction in doling out punishment."

Left unchecked, the brain's reward system for moral indignation leads to the Spanish Inquisition, to witch trials—and to what goes on daily on Facebook and Twitter. Outrage keeps us engaged better than almost anything. This engagement allows social media apps to sell more ads, fueling their bottom line. In priming our natural outrage, an impulse that evolved to keep us alive, social media apps have us tearing each other apart. Like dope dealers—just peddling outrage.

Social media, moreover, ignites feelings of social activism, as if with every Like and Retweet we're changing minds and the world. Instead, tweeting and Facebook likes are to social activism what heroin, meth, and other drugs are to happiness. Both are easily achieved with little lasting effect.

"Lies are more engaging online than truth," said Yaël Eisenstat, former diplomat and CIA analyst, in a TED talk. She had worked for Facebook for six months, hoping to change it. "As long as [Facebook] algorithms' goals are to keep us engaged, they will continue to feed us the poison that plays to our worst instincts and human weaknesses."

Maybe, then, our mass-marketing society primes us for addiction—like those sugar-dependent rats at Princeton. Marketers understand that all of us are, or can be, addicted to their products. The brain chemistry of every one of us can be manipulated to that end. Indeed, perhaps, for the first time in human history, we are all addicted, to one thing or another.

If so, then Mexican drug traffickers and drug companies today take their place alongside video-game and fast-food engineers, soft-drink companies, developers of Facebook and TikTok, tobacco and liquor companies, pornographers, cell-phone designers, and gambling moguls, alongside Fox News, CNN, and Russian hackers that prod us to outrage, QAnon conspiracies, cancel culture, virtue signaling, and the glow of belonging to one tribe or the other.

It occurred to me that the opioid crisis involves much more than just drug-company marketing and narcotics trafficking. Finally, it returns to the smallest corners of our brains, which are as unprepared for the frothy excesses of modern life and marketing as any rural Ohio town was for the flood of pain pills that hit it in the mid-1990s. Or for the huge quantities of P2P-based methamphetamine that began arriving two decades later.

Eric and Mundo I

"All of a Sudden You're Stuck"

I n 2009, out in Los Angeles, a man named Eric Barrera was a long-time user of crystal meth when one night he felt the dope change.

Eric is a stocky ex-marine who'd grown up in Oxnard, not far from Los Angeles. The meth he had been using for several years by then made him euphoric, made his scalp tingle; he grew talkative, wanting to party. But that night, in 2009, he was gripped with a fierce paranoia. His girlfriend, he was now sure, had a man in her apartment. No one was in the apartment, she insisted. Eric took a kitchen knife and began stabbing a sofa, certain the man was hiding there. Then he stabbed a mattress to tatters, and finally he began stabbing the walls, gripped by manic paranoia and looking for this man he imagined hiding inside. "That had never happened before," he said, when I met him years later.

Eric was hardly alone. The new meth that had just begun to circulate in 2009 was different. Something had changed. Gang-member friends from his old neighborhood took to calling the new stuff "weirdo dope." "Every bag of dope that I picked up after that," he told me, "I hoped it would be euphoric like it was before. But the euphoria never came back. Instead I'd be up for days paranoid, wondering, Are they gonna raid the house?"

Eric had graduated from high school in 1998 and joined the Marine Corps. He was sent to Camp Lejeune, in North Carolina, where he and an African American marine were among the few non-Whites in the unit. The racism, he felt, was threatening and brazen. He asked for a transfer to Camp Pendleton and was denied. Over the next year and a half, he said, it got worse. Two years into his service, he was honorably discharged in 2000.

After the September 11, 2001, terrorist attacks, Eric Barrera was filled with remorse that he hadn't stuck it out in the Corps. Maybe he should have had thicker skin. He was home now without the heroism he imagined for himself when he joined the marines. The way he tells it, he drank and used meth to relieve the depression.

This meth cheered him up, energized him; he felt on his game, eager to chat up anyone. He'd stay up on it for four or five days, and he had to make up excuses for missing work. But he held his life together. He worked as a loan officer, then for an insurance company. At the time, he had an apartment, a wife, a lot of friends. Later, he had a souped-up Acura Integra that he used to street-race.

Then came that new meth in 2009. "Those feelings of being chatty and wanting to talk go away," he told me. "All of a sudden you're stuck and you're in your head and you're there for hours."

Eric Barrera was there at the dawning of the new P2P-meth era. Paranoia and delusions filled his days. He said strange things to people. He couldn't hold a job. To make money, he sold the drug, driving from a dealer's house to his customers. This meth, though, made him anti-social and incapable of following rules. He watched porn for hours. No one tolerated him for long. His girlfriend, then his mother, then his father kicked him out, followed by a string of friends who had once welcomed him because he always had drugs. When he described his hallucinations, "my friends were like, 'I don't care how much dope you got, you can't stay here.'"

By 2012, massive quantities of this new meth were flowing through Southern California, and prices for it collapsed. That year, for the first time in more than a decade of meth use, Eric was homeless. He slept in his Acura and, for a while, in abandoned houses in Bakersfield. This new meth had him hearing voices. A VA psychologist diagnosed him with schizophrenia and depression.

In 2013, tangled and tormented, Eric found his way into a VA treatment center where he finally got help. He was sober for a while and his mind was returning. Then one night he relapsed. He bought the smallest amount of crystal meth available on the street, a quarter gram. The paranoia and hallucinations rushed back. On a bus that night, his brain imagined Mexican cartel gunmen at every stop, looking to kill him.

Eric weathered that relapse and returned to recovery. His symptoms of mental illness faded. Through the VA he found housing and, without meth, was able to keep it. The voices in his head departed. His VA clinicians decided he was not schizophrenic after all. Eric filled his time volunteering at a treatment clinic, which gave him a feeling of being needed. His therapist asked him along to seek out addicted vets in LA's homeless encampments, and Eric discovered that he was pretty good at telling his story and mentoring others. So the clinic hired him as an outreach worker, looking for vets in the encampments that grew larger every year.

In 2018, when the *Los Angeles Times* reported that "L.A.'s Homelessness Surged 75% in Six Years," this made a lot of sense to Eric Barrera. Those were exactly the years when supplies of Mexican "weirdo" meth really got out of hand. "It all began to change in 2009 and got worse after that," he told me as we walked through a homeless encampment in Echo Park, west of downtown Los Angeles. "The way I saw myself deteriorating, tripping out and ending up homeless, that's what I see out here. They're hallucinating, talking to themselves. Now, it's people on the street screaming. Terrified by paranoia. These are people who had normal lives."

He was caught up in it until he clawed his way out, but even then, sober years later, he never knew how it spread, or why. The new meth was just there, more and more and more of it.

Meth IV

"Just Escapes All Limits"

Years ago while I was a reporter for the *Los Angeles Times* I met Timmy, a White fellow, shortly after he left the Latino gang in the L.A. neighborhood where he grew up. Drug use was a big part of his gang life until he found long-term rehab that helped. Absent dope, he got married, started a business and a family.

During a period of stress years later, though, Timmy started using methamphetamine. Things spun out of control, and he lost all that he held dear. It was in this addled state of mind that, in 2013, Timmy came up with a plan to go buy some meth in Mexicali, the Mexican town bordering inland California, and sell it in Los Angeles. Later he realized he'd have made more by claiming the refund on his business taxes. But under meth's influence, he told me, "it made sense."

At a Mexicali tire shop, he bought a pound of crystal meth for $1,800 and brought it back to Los Angeles. He kept this up over three or four trips. But he was using meth and this made him a poor salesman. So he never made money selling it. Nevertheless, he had a car in his own name and US citizenship, which meant border officials paid him less attention. So his Mexicali tire-shop contacts kept at him to get their meth across the border. "One person I met turned into ten," he said, "and everybody was trying to get it across."

Needing cash, Timmy ferried a load and was paid $7,000. From then on, he occasionally dropped his car off at the Mexicali tire shop as they packed the driver's seat with twenty pounds of crystal methamphet-amine. One time they filled it with so much that he heard the crunch of breaking crystals when he sat at the wheel. This world, he felt, was far from how TV portrayed it. No cartels, no sinister gunmen. Just a hive of independent brokers, amiable guys even, not given to violence, who could get together twenty, thirty pounds of meth in a matter of minutes.

From that tire shop, Timmy was witness to the early stage in the post-ephedrine P2P renaissance of the Mexican meth industry. Zhenli Ye Gon was in a Mexican prison. Chemists knew many chemical paths to making P2P. No longer was the meth industry dependent on one ingredient. Meanwhile, the Pacific Coast shipping ports of Manzanillo and Lázaro Cárdenas provided access to world chemical markets, especially China's. The trafficking wars of the previous eight years hadn't ended, but the bloodiest conflicts were resolved or resolving. Two groups emerged dominant: the Sinaloa cartel, the confederation of traffickers that had grown from the first Mexican dope runners; and the newly formed Jalisco New Generation Cartel (CJNG in Spanish), aggressively carving out territory through Mexico and along the border. Meth was the profit center for both groups, which saw their markets extending well beyond Mexico and the United States.

By 2010, something like a Silicon Valley of meth innovation, knowl-edge, skill, and production had formed in the states along Mexico's northwest Pacific Coast. Industrial Guadalajara, with Tlajomulco to its south, was a major node, and this included swaths of its home state of Jalisco. Clandestine labs, and meth-making knowledge, also spread through much of Michoacán, the state of Nayarit, and of course, far into Sinaloa.

In 2010 a man named Ignacio "Nacho" Coronel was killed during a shootout with Mexican soldiers near Guadalajara. Coronel was the Sinaloa cartel's meth baron. His fiefdom included Guadalajara and Tlajomulco, but extended to the Pacific Coast ports. Coronel knew the pioneering Amezcua brothers—Jesus and Luis—who had brought in their ephedrine from India, Hong Kong, then Europe in the 1990s.

From them, he glimpsed the future. Working as chief of the Guadalajara arm of the Sinaloa cartel, Coronel organized large labs, using Tlajomulco as his base. The lab that exploded in Tlajomulco in December 2006 is believed to have been his. "As far as I know, he was the first one to cook with P2P," said Mike Vigil, a retired DEA agent, who worked Mexico for several years as Coronel was rising in the Sinaloan ranks. "That's how quick he was. Ephedrine gets scarce and its prices go up, and he comes up with an alternative method." Because of Coronel, the Guadalajara area emerged as a center of meth production.

With Coronel's death, the meth-producing elements of his organization spun off to form CJNG. But to this day, the meth-making capacity of CJNG and the Sinaloa cartel are rooted in the career of Nacho Coronel.

Two years after Coronel's death, in April 2012, Leopoldo "Polo" Ochoa was shot and killed, along with two bodyguards in Culiacán, Sinaloa. Ochoa had grown up on a small rancho north of Culiacán. He became an international financier, reputed to have real estate, investment firms, and money-laundering capabilities in Dubai and Cyprus. A corrido—or ballad—about Ochoa's life and death claims that "he flew private planes to the Middle East, closing deals with Arab princes." For our story, though, Ochoa's importance was as the Mexican meth world's last large-scale connection to global ephedrine supplies.

The end of ephedrine, the rise of the P2P method, and the deaths of Coronel and Ochoa freed the meth world from constraints that confined it. "We just started seeing more and more labs springing up everywhere," said a DEA supervisor who pursued Mexican trafficking organizations during these years. "When the control vanishes, all these regional fiefdoms spring up. It was almost like a get-rich-quick deal. These folks who did not have any chemical experience started springing up all over the place. They'd show up at hospitals with burns from labs they'd botched."

Free of sustained law enforcement scrutiny, with unlimited chemical precursors coming through the Pacific Coast ports, Mexican meth

236 THE LEAST OF US

production expanded geometrically. Beginning in about 2013 and continuing for the next several years, the labs "just escape all limits," said a Sinaloan drug-underworld source I spoke with. "In a five-square kilometer area outside Culiacán [Sinaloa's capital city], there were like twenty labs. No exaggeration. You go out to fifteen kilometers, there's more than a hundred."

This did *not* grow from dictates from some underworld board of directors. Something far more powerful was at work, particularly in the Sinaloa area: a massive, unregulated free market.

It's common to use the term "cartels" to describe Mexican trafficking groups. But cartels collude to raise the price of what they produce. The Organization of the Petroleum Exporting Countries (OPEC) is a cartel and proved it in the 1970s, when its members cut back on oil production and the price of gas skyrocketed across America. Frequently, Mexican trafficking organizations are instead loose confederations. "People think it's direct command-and-control, a top-down hierarchy," said one DEA agent I spoke to who investigated Mexican drug-trafficking rings, "but it's far more complicated than that."

Listening to traffickers on wiretaps, he said, made this clear. The wires, he found, revealed a pulsing ecosystem of independent brokers, truckers, packagers, pilots, shrimp-boat captains, mechanics, and tire shop owners. In the United States, the system included meat-plant workers, money-wiring services, restaurants, farm foremen, more drivers, safe houses, mechanics, and used-car lots. The ecosystem harnessed the self-interest of each link in the chain, who got paid only when deals got done.

"We'd waste hours listening on the wire," he told me, "to people wasting *their* time calling around doing the networking as brokers, trying to set up drug deals, because they wanted to make money. There's a huge layer of brokers who are the driving force [in Mexican drug trafficking]. Maybe they own a business or restaurant in Mexico or in the US—this is something they do to supplement income. A large percentage of drug deals at this level don't happen. But it's like salesmen—the more calls you make, the more people you know, the more sales you get. So four or five people will be involved in getting fifty kilos to some city in the United States. This guy knows a guy who knows a guy who has a cousin in Atlanta. Everyone takes a small percentage of proceeds of the sale of that dope: 5 percent for making the introduction, 5 percent for the transport. There was far less connection to any kind of corporate command from above than we had assumed. And with the independent transporters operating at the border, there's no cartel allegiance. They're all just making money."

Meth supplies increased in part because of two seemingly contradictory events. First, hundreds of labs were seized and tons of meth destroyed; and second, meth prices plummeted. Between 2015 and 2019, the Mexican military raided 333 meth labs in Sinaloa alone. But no one was ever arrested. Far from being a deterrent, the lab seizures showed that no one would pay a personal price. More people entered the trade as a result. At one point in 2019, DEA intelligence held that, despite the hundreds of lab seizures, in Sinaloa alone at least seventy meth labs were operating, each with the capacity to make ton-quantities of meth with every cooking operation. That didn't even count the surrounding states.

With labs popping up everywhere, a pound of meth fell below $1,000 for the first time on US streets—a 90 percent drop from a decade earlier in many areas. Yet traffickers' response to tumbling prices was to *increase* production. Producers were independent, so each started more labs, hoping to earn with, say, five labs what he had been making with two when prices were higher. The chemicals they needed were flowing abundantly through Mexico's Pacific Coast ports. Authorities raiding meth labs found tons of crystal meth stashed away by owners who, like brokers of any commodity, were presumably waiting for the price to rise. Meanwhile, the competition among producers drove meth purity to record highs.

Pot was also part of this story. Marijuana was the gateway drug for Mexican traffickers. They learned the drug business smuggling weed beginning in the 1960s and it lifted many of them from poverty. They could depend on it to sell, year in and year out, no matter what harder drug was in fashion. Yet as American states legalized marijuana, Mexican pot revenue faltered. Many switched to making meth and found it liberating. Marijuana took months to grow, and was bulky and could rot. These traffickers were rancheros who bridled at working for others, but had few connections to move their product to the border. Thus, traffickers higher up the chain dictated the prices they paid to farmers. Exploiting pot growers "is how [certain traffickers] got big and stayed big," said the Sinaloan drug-world source I spoke with. "But with crystal meth, it's easy for anyone to get big. In ten days you've made it. It's not as bulky as pot, so in two weeks you're crossing the border with it. Within two or three months, you're big. They're all independent. So they keep producing more, even though the price falls. They want money, even if it's through more and more volume of production."

In the Southwest, the massive quantities of meth made possible by the P2P method made the drug more prevalent than ever. These supplies kept flowing east, covering the country in meth, all the way to New England, which had none before that. Brian Sallee, now a retired Albuquerque police narcotics supervisor who trains police departments on meth labs, years ago did workshops for New England cops about small-scale local meth labs. They're coming, he told his students. In fact, meth labs never did come to New England, Sallee said. The largest meth bust in New Hampshire was in 2016 with the arrest of a Mexican restaurant owner who had twenty kilos that he couldn't find a buyer for—until he met undercover narcotics agents. "The use of meth didn't hit New England until these supplies of Mexican meth arrived [in 2019]," he told me. "'I have the supply; it creates the demand'—New England is an example of that."

But it was across the Midwest and South that P2P meth wreaked the greatest change. Mexican traffickers had never been able to get their hands on enough ephedrine to cover those regions. The market was left to neo-moonshiners who cooked it up a few grams or an ounce at a time "shake and bake" style—by extracting ephedrine from Sudafed antihistamine pills. P2P meth wiped out these local Sudafed cooks in a market disruption resembling what Walmart did to Main Street.

The new meth flooded region after region, largely because of independent traffickers with connections to the Mexican meth world. The Louisville, Kentucky, area was one of those.

For years, Louisville had a paltry meth market. Pounds of it sold for $14,000. Then two men met in prison. One of them was Wiley Greenhill, a minor drug dealer in Detroit who had come to Louisville in 1999, attracted by Kentucky's vibrant street market for pain pills, which were fetching five times what they sold for in Detroit. He and family members "saw this as virgin territory," said Milt Galanos, who is now retired from the DEA, but who investigated Greenhill in Louisville.

At one point Wiley Greenhill was sent to prison, ending up in the Roederer Correctional Complex north of Louisville. There he struck up a friendship with another inmate, Pedro Núñez, from California. Núñez's father, a man named Jose Prieto, had built up a business as a state-licensed marijuana farmer in Southern California and had gotten into debt with the wrong people from Sinaloa, Mexico. The Sinaloans told Prieto that to settle his debt he had to sell their meth. Núñez told Greenhill that his father could sell him large quantities.

By 2015 both Núñez and Greenhill were out of prison, and the meth began to flow. At first Jose Prieto sent smaller quantities through the mail to Louisville. By 2016 the loads reached fifty to a hundred pounds a month, driven east by women Greenhill hired. Greenhill began inviting friends and family down from Detroit to help with the meth trade.

Jose Prieto proved eager to get his product out. He fronted Greenhill hundreds of thousands of dollars' worth of meth on the promise that it would be repaid. DEA agent Tim Fritz also investigated the Prieto-Greenhill ring and told me, "Jose Prieto would say, 'Whatever you need, we got it. Whatever you buy, I'll double it. You want ten pounds, I'll give you twenty—pay me later.'"

As months passed, the Louisville meth market expanded beyond anything seen before. The trade spread to southern Indiana and nearby counties in Kentucky as the number of customers grew. Other traffickers began to import meth as well. "These other groups had to compete and had to bring their prices down to what the Greenhills were doing," said Galanos. The price of a pound of meth fell to $1,200.

Greenhill bought into a used car lot. Cars were used to store and transport the drugs coming in from California. On the days when Prieto's meth shipments came in, drug dealers from miles around would stream through the lot. "It was like a drive-through," Fritz said. "We would count the vehicles. He had everybody ready before [the shipment] even touched down."

At the MORE Center, a Louisville clinic set up to handle pain-pill and heroin addicts, patients started coming in on meth, too—a trickle in 2016, then, within a year, a torrent. Before the Prieto-Greenhill connection, only two of counselor Jennifer Grzesik's patients were using meth. Within three years, almost 90 percent of new patients coming to the opiate addiction clinic had meth in their drug screen, too. Twenty percent of her clients are now homeless. "I don't remember having any homeless people in my caseload before 2016," she told me.

Prieto, his son, Louis, and Greenhill were arrested in 2019 and are now serving lengthy federal prison terms. They left behind a transformed meth market. Primed by the new supply, meth demand has exploded, with more users and more dealers as well, some of whom began traveling to California to find their own connections. The price of a pound of meth remains low. To compete, Louisville meth dealers now offer free syringes and delivery; others offer syringes already loaded with liquified meth so users can immediately shoot up.

Similar partnerships and arrangements transformed regional drug markets across the United States, swamping them with the enormous quantities of meth that the P2P method yielded, leaving local social services and families bearing the burden.

I spoke with a fellow I'll call Dillon, who several years ago became a meth distributor in his town in the western United States. The price of meth was $800 an ounce, which he found to be too high. "I thought I could bring the price down and addicts could live more easily—the Robin Hood of meth," he said. "It would bring down the crime rate if they didn't have to steal to get their dope."

He bought consistently from a Mexican man from a Tijuana meth-making family. The man traveled the western United States like a regional salesman, looking for customers for his family's meth. But as he sold the man's product, Dillon noticed his customers, solid people, were suddenly babbling, out of their minds, certain that government drones were following them. He complained to his source. The meth had a fishy smell, which he suspected was due to industrial chemicals that didn't belong in the mix.

Dillon was a solid customer in a region the family wanted to break into. So to Dillon's surprise, the man invited him to see his family's operation to show him they were doing things right. He met his connection in San Diego. They drove into Tijuana, then southeast for an hour or more through small villages. Finally, in the middle of nowhere, they came to a building the size of a Costco warehouse—high cinder-block walls, concrete floor, a ventilator, a diesel generator, a metal roof.

Two dozen employees were busy making, in Dillon's words, "more methamphetamine than you can fucking imagine. They were doing it in big commercial quantities." They had four meth batches cooking in large vats, each likely capable of hundreds of pounds in thirty-six hours, he was told. An enormous bin held what he took to be a precursor chemical powder. "They told me they had so much [meth] and they couldn't get it across the border," he said. Vacuum-packed pounds of meth, each wrapped in duct tape, were stacked like split logs, hundreds of them, waiting to be sent to market.

From what Dillon could tell, the family was an independent producer, not tied to any cartel. They had meth storehouses in Los Angeles, Las Vegas, and other cities, from which they supplied markets in the surrounding areas. "They never came off like the cartels are depicted, like savages," he remembered. "They were businesspeople. Their business just happened to be the exporting of drugs." He was nevertheless stunned to see all this operating unmolested out in the open, an hour from the border. Back in Dillon's hometown, their meth dropped in price in Dillon's area to $275 an ounce, but it never stopped driving people to schizophrenia.

AMID ALL THIS, I read *Good Habits, Bad Habits: The Science of Making Positive Changes That Stick*, a fascinating book by Wendy Wood, a psychology professor at the University of Southern California, who argues that habits change when they're harder to practice. Addiction isn't about rational decisions, she wrote. If it were, Americans would have quit smoking soon after 1964, when the US Surgeon General issued his first report on its risks. American nicotine addicts kept smoking, knowing they were killing themselves, because nicotine had changed their brain chemistry, and cigarettes were everywhere. We stopped smoking, Wood argues, by making it harder to do—adding "friction" to the activity. In other words, we limited access to supply. We removed cigarette vending machines, banned smoking in airports, planes, parks, beaches, bars, restaurants, and offices. By adding friction to smoking, we also removed the brain cues that prompted us to smoke: bars where booze, friends, and cigarettes went together, for example.

Corporations, Wood argues, try to do the opposite—to *remove* friction to using their products. Fast-food chains open restaurants all over the country. Soda companies fight hard for supermarket shelf space. After we finish watching one episode, Netflix immediately begins the next one.

Something like that happened with P2P methamphetamine. Traffickers could make it all year round. The very volume of their supplies reduced the friction to finding and using their product—just as any soda or fast-food corporation aimed to do. This helped create cues to use it. "Meth reminds me of what alcoholics go through," said the director of a Los Angeles treatment center I spoke with. "There's alcohol everywhere. Meth is now so readily available. There's an availability to it that is not the case with heroin or crack. It's everywhere."

Yet something else was different about this new meth coming in. Ephedrine meth was a euphoric, social drug, a party drug—the kind Eric Barrera remembered from his first years of using. P2P meth, made with toxic chemicals, was more sinister. As unprecedented amounts of it found their way to every part of the United States, so, too, did the mental derangement Dillon had seen in his customers and the violent delusions Eric Barrera had felt. This meth quickly drove users to symptoms of schizophrenia—violent paranoia, agonizing hallucinations, and fantastical conspiracy theories—as well as horrible dental infections. "I don't know that I would even call it meth anymore," one director of a drug-rehab center told me.

"Meth was meant to keep you up," said one Kentucky truck driver, who saw the change as he used it for many years. "You was able to concentrate on one thing. This meth now, though, you're hallucinating. It got so bad with the new meth, I screwed my windows shut, my doors shut, because I didn't want nobody around me. I locked my family in the house with me."

All this was noticed only by users, paramedics, cops, and drug counselors. The rest of the country was focused on the opioid epidemic. The funding and the headlines were about pain-pill or heroin overdoses, then fentanyl overdoses. Deaths allowed for memorials, outpourings of condolences on social media, a chance to remember the deceased's better days. Meth didn't kill people at nearly the same rate. It presented, instead, the rawest face of living addiction. Meth users dragged themselves through the nighttime streets, howling, hysterical, starving. That part of addiction, one counselor told me, "people don't want to touch it."

Nevertheless, all that and more came to big cities and to small towns alike as P2P meth spread across the country.

Kenton County I

Will Pfefferman makes his bed every day.

He yanks the sheet drum-tight across his king-size mattress. He fluffs the pillows just right, throws the bedspread over them, and pulls it tight, too, leaving it wrinkle-free. Then he's ready for the day.

The importance of this exercise was made clear to him not long before I met him, after he'd seen his buddy Mike on the street. Mike was a recovering addict Will met when Will was rehabbing from heroin in a treatment center in the Northern Kentucky town of Covington, near where Pfefferman grew up. Mike had visited the center to talk about his own recovery from dope. Now, though, Mike was shooting up again.

What happened? Pfefferman asked him.

"I quit making my bed," Mike told him. With that, Mike said, his discipline frayed, and he began to slouch in other parts of his life as well, until he was back on the streets. "He quit answering his door and his phone and quit making his bed," Will told me. "He didn't want to be bothered. He died a few days ago. He was well known and well liked."

Pfefferman is six foot four, 280 pounds, with a gleaming shaved head, a southern baritone, and an amiable nature. He looks like a bronze, if slightly pudgy, Mr. Clean. Pfefferman came to view his own recovery in those terms, in minding small stuff like making his bed.

He grew up on the streets of wide-open Northern Kentucky, the knob of land at the top of the state, across the Ohio River from Cincinnati. Northern Kentucky comprises three counties—Kenton, Campbell, and Boone—and the old-brick towns of Covington and Newport along the river, and, south of there, a jigsaw of big-box suburbs that went up in the last twenty-five years on what used to be farmland.

Will's father was a Campbell County cop. The family lived in a cottage attached to the county jail, where his mother cooked for the inmates. The couple used jail trustees as babysitters when they wanted to go out. Dave Pfefferman was a hard-drinking man. When Will was eight, he shot at his father with his dad's service revolver during a fight between his father and mother. The couple divorced, and Will grew up in the Newport projects, then one of the poorest parts of America.

For much of the twentieth century, the town of Newport was a mob-run Sin City, Cincinnati's red-light district, where illegal gambling, strip joints, and prostitution lubricated life and commerce. Dave Pfefferman ran card tables at casinos in Newport at night. One night he shot a guy in the leg during a drunken brawl, resigned his cop job, and, in Will's words, "became a man of the night." He was a bounty hunter for a while, then went into the strip-club business along Newport's notorious Monmouth Street. That lasted until city leaders and a group of upper-crust reformers from neighboring Fort Thomas organized the Committee of 500, and the Monmouth clubs gave way to an aquarium for tourists.

But for years, the mob kept drugs out of Newport. It was a competing vice and bad for business. Newport was, Dave Pfefferman remembers, "totally nude back in them days." The worst thing cops had to deal with was a drunk stumbling out of an after-hours club.

Then the gambling mob faded, and drugs crept in. Will Pfefferman grew up in that Newport, and he was a truant in juvenile hall by four-teen. A friend's father, an enforcer for the Iron Horsemen biker gang, introduced Will to his first opiate—Dilaudid—at sixteen.

With fists the size of ham sandwiches, Will started a boxing career at twenty-three, and under the name Billy Walker he fought seventeen times over the next fifteen years, losing only once. But drugs and prison stunted any athletic career Pfefferman might have had. "I led the prison in home runs hit, touchdowns thrown, and dirty urines," he said. He smoked marijuana every day in prison, which he procured from guards and friends who visited. While free in the 1990s, he married a stripper from "one of the poles at my dad's club." She needed protection, and he needed money for what was now a heroin habit. She provided a home for him whenever he left prison. They ran massage parlors that served the Northern Kentucky businessman-and-politician crowd, and Will's drug habit lived from that.

Through the years, Will went to prison five times, three times for assault on a police officer. He was notorious in the fight game and in the Northern Kentucky underworld. The papers called him "King Kong." His brawls with cops grew legendary. Using heroin, cocaine, and alcohol all day long, he grew unpredictable, and local police departments had what amounted to a mutual-aid policy when a call involved Will Pfefferman. Officers in Covington remember one tangle with him. From the outskirts, the brawl looked like a cartoon: legs, arms, and fists flailing in a cloud of dust. One officer went flying from the scrum, then a bit later another followed, until enough of them arrived on scene to reach the critical mass necessary to bring down Will Pfefferman. He did another prison stint for burglary, framed for it, he claims, by a sergeant whose finger he bit off during a brawl.

When free, he robbed dope dealers in Cincinnati with pepper spray or fake guns, getting high, blacking out and not remembering any of it and returning to the neighborhood the next night. One night, a dealer he'd pepper-sprayed the night before put a gun to his forehead. He wonders how he lived through it all.

Will stopped using heroin a few times, but he couldn't stick with it. His dad called him weak. In 2009 Will procured a tenth of a gram for a woman he knew from the streets. She turned out to be an informant, and he went back to prison. Four years later, at forty-seven, he got out with nowhere to go. He stayed with his first ex-wife and their son. He began using again and sleeping until noon, until his fifteen-year-old son, disgusted, woke him up and threw him out.

Three decades of addiction had led him through endless incarceration, a blown boxing career, no schooling, and failed marriages. All that now bequeathed Will Pfefferman what in addiction recovery is called the "gift of desperation." He landed, worn out and beat down, in Covington's Grateful Life treatment center. His peers—recovering addicts like himself—held him accountable. He stopped using heroin and got serious about working the twelve steps of Alcoholics Anonymous. He became a center supervisor. He mentored addicts. On the street he was known as Willie. He changed that to Will.

He left the center, and for the first time as an adult he didn't live off of drug scams. He found construction work, rented his own apartment. He made his bed every day, which felt a lot like what he was trying to do with his life. He struggled to pay his bills, but he felt better.

He moved to Appalachia and to Hazard, Kentucky, the buckle on America's OxyContin belt, where for eight months, with the zeal of the reborn, he helped get a state addiction-treatment center up and running. He started AA meetings at the local homeless shelter, and at jails in two neighboring counties. Then, in June 2015, he returned to Kenton County, ready to begin anew.

About that time, a group of Republican Kenton County elected officials was pondering responses to the pain-pill and heroin overdoses sweeping the region. Constituents were dying. Few families weren't affected in some way. Jail had always been a cost—a place to "throw away the key," where inmates vegetated for months. But the epidemic of opioid addiction showed the problems with that kind of thinking. Addicts clogged the court system and were in and out of jail every few months. The pressure created by overdoses in Northern Kentucky opened folks to new ideas. One of those ideas was that jail might be an investment in recovery, where addicts, now sober and thinking more clearly, had a chance to step toward change.

It was a remarkable shift of mindset. I'll tell you in a minute the story of how it happened. But one result was that on a Tuesday in August 2015, two months after returning from Hazard, big Will Pfefferman, a parolee two years off heroin, with a felonious past and notorious reputation, reported to work as a full-time drug-treatment mentor at the Kenton County Detention Center, ready to help with an experiment in how jailing is done in America.

"Time to spread the message," he told me that day.

AMONG THE CURIOUS aspects of the nation's opioid crisis was that it was perhaps the most uniracial in the country's history. It was almost entirely White America—poor, middle-class, and upper-class Whites—getting addicted and dying. This forced empathy and new ideas on the nation's largest, most politically and economically powerful racial group. The change was especially startling to watch in red areas of White America, and one place it began to happen first was the three-county region known as Northern Kentucky.

Northern Kentucky combines a suburban Republicanism with strains of rural libertarianism. When the region considered smoking bans, protesters showed up in lab coats and stethoscopes, doctors of freedom denouncing scientific data that measured deaths due to second-hand smoke. The Northern Kentucky branch of the Tea Party took up against the socialism of taxes that fund public libraries. Sen. Rand Paul may be Kentucky's most famous libertarian, but Rep. Thomas Massie, whom Northern Kentucky voters first elected in 2008, is Congress's staunchest, known as Mr. No for his votes against what he views as government overreach. During Barack Obama's presidency, "Obama Didn't Build This" signs appeared in front of businesses and private homes.

"We sue our libraries and we like to smoke our cigarettes," said Michael Monks, editor of *The River City News*, Covington's local newspaper. "And everyone loves to be tough on crime."

Yet as addiction and overdoses spread through the area like a medieval plague, quietly picking off people one by one, it cast a pall over suburban brick homes with lawns sloping past driveway basketball stanchions. Youths who once had to do few chores were suddenly hollow-eyed and alone inside their hoodies with some beast that pushed them to walk for miles, endure any humiliation, to get dope.

Monks's office is on Madison Avenue, Covington's main street, where abandoned buildings are seeing new life as boutique hotels and upscale condos. On the streets, meanwhile, he said, "it's a lot like an episode of *The Walking Dead*. You can see these walkers. They're breaking into houses. We hear on the scanner these bank robberies by people who have no idea how to rob a bank. They're desperate. It's a conservative position to be tough on crime, but in this they're recognizing that it's not working."

Northern Kentucky, moreover, was largely settled by German Catholics with large extended families. Many of these families are prominent in local business and politics. People born here stay here. Families belong to churches for generations. So a single case of addiction touched far more people here than it might have elsewhere, and enough of those were families with access to political power. "Everybody, whether it be through work or family, has seen this," said Kris Knochelmann, Kenton County's judge-executive—what Kentucky calls the "county CEO." Knochelmann is from one of those families; one of his relatives is a recovering heroin addict. "It's now everyone's issue."

Meanwhile, technology was allowing neuroscience to tell a far more vivid story about what happens to brains on drugs than had been possible before.

The throw-away-the-key approach to addiction faded in favor of prayers and requests for the kind of Christian charity that was not so evident here when the drugs were different and Northern Kentucky kids were less affected. Families lived in terror of late-night phone calls. "This disease of loving someone who has an addiction," said one mother, "it brings you to your knees and sucks the life right out of you." They also discovered that the policies many of them once supported had left their addicted loved ones with few alternatives besides prison or the streets.

Charlotte Wethington learned this before most. Charlotte is a thin, retired elementary-school teacher, a life-long Democrat with a lilting southern drawl. In 2002 her son Casey was addicted to heroin. She spent days on the phone trying to get him treatment or committed to a hospital. He overdosed twice and survived. Still, she found no help. "I felt so alone and lost," Charlotte said. "The best I got was that he had to want to [quit] and had to hit bottom." Then Casey was arrested for pot possession. Charlotte begged the judge to hold him. Pot was only the tip of a larger problem, she said. Instead the judge released Casey, saying he would be summoned to court within ninety days. Casey overdosed a third time. His court summons arrived the day his parents buried him.

Others in Northern Kentucky had lost children to heroin, but Charlotte Wethington was the first who made noise. Parents needed the ability to lock up their addicted loved ones, she felt, even those who had committed no crime. Otherwise, they would die. She fought on alone for a long time, contacting reporters, writing opinion columns. As her fight went public, other families joined her.

They began to lobby state legislators. Charlotte went office to office in Frankfort, the state capital, armed only with Casey's story. Meanwhile, those legislators were hearing from constituents from across the state. In 2004, at the behest of folks from libertarian Northern Kentucky, state lawmakers granted government startlingly coercive powers. "Casey's Law" allowed any relative or friend of an addict to petition a court to order him to treatment, or, if he left treatment, to jail while avoiding a criminal record. The petitioner need only show that the addict was a danger to himself or others.

Casey's Law recognized that with the supply of opioids now on the street, an addict roaming free risked death with each use. The law was Kentucky's first statutory expression of addiction as a disease, the symptoms of which are a brainwashed slavery that deprives the user of free will and turns him toward self-harm in the search for dope.

Northern Kentucky has felt that change deeply. While Democrats still can't get elected here, and the region twice went overwhelmingly for Donald Trump, it has grown tough, too, for any Republican who opposed new ideas about the proper mix of incarceration and drug treatment. Politicians embraced needle exchange. Judges facing election grew more likely to sentence an addicted defendant to probation. The word *junkie* plummeted from favor. *Compassion* became the buzzword. Families learned how opioids dominate the brain's reward pathways. And in Kenton County, the epidemic forced elected officials to conclude that nothing would improve without reexamining the gathering place of many of the old notions regarding crime and addiction: county jail.

County jailhouses inmates awaiting trial or those serving sentences for misdemeanors or probation violations. Jail is usually a parking lot for inmates, many of whom are drug addicts. Jail is their first and most common interface with the criminal justice system. This happens long before they do anything that warrants a prison sentence. In jail, detoxed of the dope that controlled their decisions on the street, addicts often behold the wreckage of their lives. Yet at that moment of clarity, they are plunged into a world of tedium and isolation, relieved only by predatory violence and extortion. Anyone seeking a different way of life is viewed as weak, and therefore a target. So instead inmates watch *Cops* or *Judge Judy*, sleep, trade crime stories, gamble, scam, plot, fight, "always on guard, always tense," said one Kenton County inmate. "Imagine your most stressful day at work, multiply that by two or three, then imagine that every day." Once outside, another inmate told me, "you're going to run right to the dope boy's house."

No other institution in our national life—perhaps not even prison—has such a toxic impact on crime, addiction, and mental illness as does county jail the way it's been traditionally run. The epidemic revealed that clearly. It also created constituencies for new ideas. So as these Kenton County officials confronted the addiction scourge and wrestled with the design for a larger new jail, they imagined a different way of running it—one that envisioned drug-habit recovery in place of boredom. They discussed jailed addicts' need for GED classes and daily twelve-step meetings, for health care, for mentors to help them retrieve driver's licenses and find clothes and housing.

Kenton County judges were already there. Years before, they routinely released those arrested for minor drug offenses on their "own recognizance." The OR, as it's called, is a promise defendants make to show up in court weeks later, and judges use it across America to relieve jail overcrowding. But potent, plentiful, and cheap heroin ended that practice in Kenton County. Defendants were overdosing and dying on the street before they could be tried for that first offense. So Kenton County judges kept arrestees in jail to save their lives.

Jailing addicts is anathema to treatment advocates. Waiting for a street addict to reach rock bottom and choose to seek treatment sounds nice in theory. But it ignores the nature of the new drugs on the street. Now, rock bottom is often death. To those facing the epidemic's grim realities, jail came to be seen as a necessary lever, a tool to force an addict to seek treatment before it was too late. Problem was that each inmate did nothing productive while in jail, waiting three to nine months for his case to resolve—at a cost to taxpayers of $42.45 a day.

In this evolution in thinking among Kenton County officials, the most important appears to have taken place in the mind of Terry Carl. Carl is a mild-mannered grandfather, not overly talkative, a lifelong Catholic, a US Navy Seabee in the Vietnam War, and a Kentucky reservist for many years. He is not the type given to grand experiments in public policy. He is also Kenton County's jailer, which is important, because Kentucky is the lone state to elect its jailers. Kentucky jailers can obstruct policies they oppose, but they also tend to see jail as an independent system—not part of a larger sheriff's office, as jail is run in most

American counties. They're especially sensitive to the costs of running a jail.

This is part of what made Terry Carl change his mind. Perhaps it was also that he was a systems guy at heart—not from law enforcement. Carl ran operations at a Cincinnati utility before he won the jailer job in 1999. What to do with drug addicts hadn't crossed his mind; he figured they belonged behind bars. Then he took over a Kentucky county jail as the pain revolution in American medicine began and pain-pill addiction spread.

Carl watched inmates cycle in and out on charges of needle and drug possession, check forgery, possession of stolen property, and probation violations, all spurred on by their addictions. Their petty crimes rarely meant a lengthy prison sentence. That was the problem. They kept coming back to jail, and Carl's facility was collapsing under their weight. "I'm still learning a lot every day about it," Carl told me. "But I really felt we needed to do something and not just sit on our hands and talk about it. I can't let my community die like this. All these young people, you talk to them and it gets to you that they're losing their lives over this thing."

Very few left detention in shape for recovery. Most addicts, stressed and weary and lacking any support, got high immediately. Soon they were back. Many others died. Carl came to believe any attack on addiction in the community *had* to involve changing how jail was done. The drugs on the street were too dangerous to allow them to leave defenseless.

One morning in May of 2015, Carl was among a group of Kenton County leaders that met in the conference room atop the courts building in downtown Covington. Kris Knochelmann, the county judge-executive, was there. So were judges, prosecutors, and the public defender.

Another man at the table was not elected to any public office. Jason Merrick believed he'd been asked to attend to offer opinions about drug treatment within county jail. On the topic of drug addiction, he was well versed.

Merrick had come from Northern California several years before. He lived for a while in Mendocino County, where he grew marijuana. He used meth, as well as the hyperpotent pot then emerging. He used some heroin and drank. He lived with a woman and her daughters on ten acres of rural land on a hill until his drug abuse forced his partner and her daughters to flee. Hallucinating lizards and sheriff's helicopters, Merrick moved to a tree house with his drugs and a shotgun.

One day his partner appeared below. "Come down," she called up to him, "and get the help you deserve."

Those words struck Merrick as kind. He eventually wound up with an aunt in Kentucky, then entered the Grateful Life Center. He embraced his sobriety and emerged as a leader. He took a job at the center while he got a master's degree in social work at Northern Kentucky University nearby.

Merrick's life made him an authority on drug treatment, and for it he now possessed a missionary's zeal. He cofounded a group called People Advocating Recovery. He spoke often in public and let audiences know from the get-go that he was a recovering drug addict. He sounded like a neuroscientist at times when discussing his own recovery: "The neurotransmitters are firing when they're supposed to. My dopamine and serotonin are leveled out. Scientifically, chemically, I'm in recovery, and spiritually I'm part of this community." He urged businesses to make naloxone as common as fire extinguishers. People in Northern Kentucky weren't used to hearing this kind of thing. But as heroin replaced pain pills, and then fentanyl replaced them both, a good many folks in Kenton County felt lucky to have Merrick in their midst. Among them were the decision makers assembled that morning atop the courts building.

The new jail design they came up with had an eye toward addiction treatment and inmates taking classes in recovery and obtaining their GED. They designated Unit 104, a seventy-bed men's pod, as the place for their experiment to begin.

None of the officials who met that morning in 2015 had a clear idea of what the unit should provide. They thought it should resemble what a private treatment center on the outside would offer street addicts, *if* they could afford it, which most could not, and *if* a bed were available at the moment they showed up, which it often was not. First, though, someone was needed to organize and run the thing.

"Your name continues to be brought up," Kris Knochelmann told Jason Merrick that morning.

They offered him the job of running the experiment, and the freedom to create it from scratch, trusting his experience and passion. Merrick was stunned; he remembered his days hallucinating in a tree house. Just make sure the curriculum is evidence-based and caters to the population in jail, they told him. "I figured [hiring Merrick] was worth a chance," Carl told me later. "I'd never seen a person that passionate about this issue. I've been wrong in my life, but I don't think I'm wrong in this."

Merrick set out, energized by the possibilities. He visited Louisville, which had been doing jail differently for a while. He went to counties in Kentucky, Ohio, and Indiana that the opioid crisis was pushing toward change. In time, he envisioned a pod where inmates worked on their recovery from the moment they awoke and made their beds until lights-out at night. No more watching *Judge Judy* all day. Instead they took classes in criminal/addictive thinking and changing responses to life's stress. There were twelve-step meetings run by inmates, visits from speakers from outside.

One of the first calls Jason Merrick made was to Will Pfefferman. They had met at the Grateful Life Center, where Merrick was Pfefferman's mentor. He saw Pfefferman struggling with his me-first criminal thinking, his anger at being called out for, say, not waking up on time. But weeks passed and Pfefferman began to examine his own behavior. His confidence grew and he too mentored new arrivals. Merrick needed an assistant, and he figured that most of the felons and users he would have to connect to knew Will Pfefferman. To them, Big Will amounted to a billboard that recovery was possible. Pfefferman had just spent months on that mountain in Hazard in service to others. To Will, Merrick's job offer seemed a miracle, the kind of opportunity that came with getting sober.

They teamed up. And early one morning in August 2015, filled with optimism and trepidation, this unlikely pair of recovering addicts—both now full-time employees of Kenton County Detention Center, hired by Republican officials in a conservative county—walked down a concrete corridor and into a unit of twenty unshaven men, veterans of custody, to drum up inmate interest in their experiment in changing jail. Pfefferman strode in slowly. He was on parole yet a full-time jail employee, with the county jail's emblem on his shirt. His grin seemed stiff, as if he were entering a high school reunion where he was unsure of his reception. Across the room, a middle-aged man threw open his palms: *What are you doing here?* One young man's eyes opened wide. Will nodded.

As he stood before these men, his booming drawl filled the room, but he felt scattered and unsure. His insides quivered the way they never had during prison brawls. He started in. They knew his story, he told them. He'd spent years behind bars, thinking he could quit drugs on his own, "but I come up short every time." He urged them to opt into the recovery pod about to open. Then, after a few awkward moments, he left. The men in the pod watched him go in wonder and silence.

At the next unit, though, the confidence that comes with being the biggest guy in the room returned. "What's up, fellas?" Pfefferman began again. "I'm Will. This is Jason."

Jason Merrick and Will Pfefferman embodied the kind of change happening in red America as addiction blindsided families who then began to think, and vote, differently. Neuroscience was advancing knowledge of addiction. Moreover, this epidemic came without the street violence that accompanied previous scourges. All this meant that political space opened for new ideas, one of which was that the isolation of traditional jail harmed addicts; they needed communities of support, mentors who could teach them order, find them ways of paying probation fines, and show them why, after years of chaos, they had to make their beds.

It felt like such a good idea. Yet despite the new thinking and the optimism, the Kenton County jail experiment they embarked on that morning came, for a few months, just a hair short of full-blown disaster.

Meth V

"There's No Way Into That Person"

Kirsten, a mother now in her thirties, began using methamphetamine at fourteen in Vancouver, Washington. She knew it as a euphoric party drug and she used it for several years, interrupted by periods of sobriety. Her use grew more serious in 2009 when, in her twenties, she moved to a small town in rural Central Oregon.

A few years after that, in 2013, she got sober just before giving birth to a son. But as months passed, she started using again. Only now she realized that the meth she was using was different. She assumed the change had something to do with her pregnancy. It was no longer the sensual party drug she was used to that had kept her craving companionship and chattering endlessly. On it, she had trouble talking, unless it was to herself. She heard voices. She ate poorly and rarely left the house. Her once-pretty smile faded along with the enamel on her teeth, which turned black and abscessed. Her head jerked uncontrollably. She gave her son to her family to keep him safe.

By 2016 she was seeing angels and demons. God spoke to her through people on television, telling her, she told me years later, "that He understood the world was in crisis, that people felt lonely and unheard," and this made sense to her.

She began barking like a dog in public, in what amounted to a cry for help. With only a slight hold on reality, Kirsten made it to a residential treatment center in a nearby town.

Those who took her in recalled how she spoke in a jumble common to schizophrenics—"word salad" is the psychological term. She couldn't focus or remember simple things. "She knew that what was going on in her brain was not normal and not the truth, but she felt that it was so real," said her recovery mentor at the time.

Everyone thought Kirsten was schizophrenic. Instead, it was the P2P meth at work. As I was working on this book, I began to realize that the drug was creating Kirsten's symptoms in people across America. I came late to this understanding. I had started this book focused on how Mexico produced quantities of methamphetamine so vast that they could cover the country and still lower the price nationwide. Then I realized that the story was even bigger.

Eric Barrera, the burly once-homeless ex-marine in Los Angeles, was the first to explain it to me. His mental decline matched exactly the switch I'd chronicled in the Mexican meth world from ephedrine to P2P, which happened in 2009, and ramped up significantly by 2013. I wondered if what happened to Eric was happening nationwide. I certainly knew meth was bad for the brain. Yet I'd heard nothing about these symptoms of schizophrenia, despite spending a lot of time studying drug trafficking. But if this drug was now nationwide, I figured Eric's symptoms would be, too.

For several months, about all I did was talk to addicts, counselors, and cops around the country—over the phone because the pandemic restricted travel. Meth was overshadowed by the opioid epidemic. But the people I spoke to told me stories nearly identical to Eric's. This new meth itself was quickly, intensely damaging people's brains. The symptoms were always the same—violent paranoia, hallucinations, figures always lurking in the shadows, isolation, rotted and abscessed dental work, uncontrollable limbs, massive memory loss, jumbled speech, and, almost always, homelessness. It was creating a swath of people nationwide who, while on meth and for a good period afterward, were mentally ill and all but untreatable by usual methods of drug rehabilitation. Ephedrine-made meth wasn't good for the brain, but it was nothing like this. Schizophrenia and bipolar disorder are afflictions that begin in the young. Now people in their thirties and forties were going mad. The new meth was also deadly in a way ephedrine meth was not. It was killing young people with congestive heart failure, a disease common to people over sixty-five.

Portland, Oregon, began seeing the flood of this new meth about 2013. By January 2020 the city had to close its downtown sobering station. The station had opened in 1985 as a place for alcoholics to sober up for six to eight hours, but it was unequipped to handle the P2P meth addicts. "The degree of mental-health disturbance, the wave of psychosis, the profound, profound disorganization [is something] I've never seen before," said Dr. Rachel Solotaroff, director of Central City Concern, the social-service nonprofit that ran the station. Solotaroff was among the first people I spoke to. She sounded overwhelmed. "If they're not raging and agitated, they can be completely noncommunicative. Treating addiction [relies] on your ability to have a connection with someone. But I've never experienced something like this—where there's no way *in* to that person."

On Skid Row in Los Angeles, crack had been *the* drug for decades. Dislodging it took some time. But by 2014 the new meth was everywhere. When that happened, "it seemed that people were losing their minds faster," Los Angeles Police Department beat officer Deon Joseph told me. Joseph had worked Skid Row for twenty-two years. "They'd be okay when they were just using crack," he told me. "Then in 2014, with meth, all of a sudden they became mentally ill. They deteriorated into mental illness faster than I ever saw with crack cocaine."

Dr. Susan Partovi has been a physician for the homeless in Los Angeles since 2003. She noticed increasing mental illness at her Skid Row clinics around the city starting about 2012; schizophrenia and bipolar disorder, which typically afflict the young, were showing up in people in their forties and fifties, too. She also worked at the L.A. County women's jail, treating women in their thirties for meth-induced heart failure. On Skid Row by 2014, meth was everywhere.

"It was crazy how many severely mentally ill people were out there," Partovi told me. "Now almost everyone we see when we do homeless outreach [on the streets] is on meth. Meth may now be causing long-term psychosis, similar to schizophrenia, [that lasts] even after they're not using anymore."

The new meth devastated with equal measure—on the West Coast, where it replaced the ephedrine meth that had been prevalent for years, and in the Midwest, where meth once had been made locally.

I called Jim Mahoney, a neuropsychologist at West Virginia University, whom I'd met on a visit to the school. Mahoney had studied the effects of ephedrine meth on the brain in the early 2000s at UCLA. The psychosis he saw then was bad, but it was usually the result of extended sleep deprivation. In 2016 Mahoney took a WVU job as a meth researcher and specialist in the university's addiction clinic. Less than a year into the job, the P2P crystal meth from Mexico started showing up. Mahoney was inundated with meth patients who came in ranting, conversing with phantoms. "I can't even compare it to what I was seeing at UCLA," he told me. "Now we're seeing it instantaneously, within hours, in people who just used: psychotic symptoms, hallucinations, delusions."

Sarah Skoterro, in Albuquerque, a veteran of thirty years as a drug counselor, remembered the meth years ago was a party drug. Then, she said, "around 2009, 2010, there was a real shift—a new kind of product. I would do assessments with people struggling for five years with meth who would say 'This kind of meth is a very different thing.'" Skoterro watched people with families, houses, and good-paying jobs quickly lose everything. "They're out of their house, lost their relationship, their job, they're walking around at three in the morning, at a bus stop, blisters on their feet. They are a completely different person."

As I talked with people across the country, it occurred to me that P2P meth that created delusional, paranoid, erratic people living on the street must have some effect on police shootings. Police shootings were all over the news by then and a focus of national attention.

Albuquerque police, it turns out, had studied meth's connection to officer-involved fatal shootings, in which blood samples of the deceased could be taken.

For years, the city's meth supply was locally made, in houses, in small quantities. When P2P meth began to arrive in 2009, those meth houses faded. Since 2011, Mexican crystal meth has owned the market with quantities that drove the price from $14,000 per pound down to $2,200 at its lowest. City emergency rooms and the police Crisis Intervention Team, which handles mental illness calls, have been inundated ever since with people with symptoms of schizophrenia, often meth-induced, said Lt. Matt Dietzel, a CIT supervisor. "Meth is so much more common now," Dietzel told me. "We're seeing the worst outcomes more often."

In 2016, New Mexico prohibited bail in most cases. Addicts arrested on the street used to get a break from the drugs that tormented them—and some food and medical care in jail. "You go to jail, you get off the drug. If nothing else it's an interruption in your lifestyle, which is usually on a seriously downward slide," said Michael Cox, a local defense attorney and special prosecutor appointed to investigate Albuquerque police shootings. "Now you get right out [of jail] and there's no break in what you're doing."

Police-involved fatal shootings reflected all that. For years, fatal police shootings numbered about two or three annually in Albuquerque. That figure doubled as the P2P meth took over. Between 2011 and 2020, 60 percent of the people shot to death by Albuquerque police officers—thirty-six of sixty people—had meth in their bloodstream, up from zero in 2009, according to coroner reports. "We knew when the Mexican meth hit because people went crazier. Before that, police shootings were not common," Cox told me. "Now there's this new category of people starting shootouts with APD SWAT when they have one bullet and acting like they thought it would work."

Houston, Texas, was another town transformed. Once solely a cocaine town, it was now flooded with meth as well. Meth-related overdoses numbered twenty in 2012. In 2019, there were two hundred. People were showing up in ERs, said one psychiatrist I spoke with, "experiencing symptoms that warrant stabilization in a psych ward: hearing voices, hallucinations, paranoia."

In Louisville, after the Jose Prieto and Wiley Greenhill connection began funneling meth there in 2015, the market expanded and the price dropped. Jennifer Grzesik, the drug counselor at the MORE Center for opioid addicts, remembers a man she had known as a heroin addict but was now using meth. He was consumed with paranoia that police were hiding under her desk. "He wasn't like that when I first met him," she said. "He switched to meth, and it made him a different person."

Southwest Virginia hadn't seen meth for almost a decade when suddenly, in about 2017, "we started to see people go into the state mental hospital system who were just grossly psychotic," said Eric Greene, a drug counselor. "We wondered where all these people were coming from. Since then, it's caused a crisis in our state mental health hospitals. It's difficult for the truly mentally ill to get care because the facilities are full of people who are on meth."

Symptoms could fade once users purged the drug and did not relapse. But while they were on this new meth, they grew antisocial, all but mute. I spoke with two recovering meth addicts who said they had to relearn how to speak. "It took me a year and a half to recover from the brain damage it had done to me," one of them said. "I couldn't hardly form sentences. I couldn't laugh, smile. I couldn't think."

Giti Mayton is a drug counselor and recovering addict in Columbus, Ohio, who began to see the new meth mangling patients in late 2017. They spoke of government conspiracies. They were impossible to talk to, to connect with. "I asked one of them, 'How did you get here?' He looked at us and said, 'Eleven.' "

Those with a history of trauma descended far faster into the abyss. Many of Mayton's clients were the children of the opioid epidemic generation. Their parents were hooked first on Percocet, OxyContin, then heroin. These kids were now eighteen or twenty-three, strung out on meth. This was part of the meth story nationwide, I found. The new meth addicts were often—though not always—opioid users or their children. Yet Mayton saw that they looked so different from meth users of earlier years. "Their limbs move in strange ways. Something's affected their nervous system."

I spoke with Jennie Jobe, from rural Morgan County, in eastern Tennessee. Jobe had spent twenty years running state prisons when she took over a drug court in 2013. Her court was part of a network of courts in Tennessee begun by Seth Norman, a now-retired Nashville judge. The courts stand next to housing for recovering addicts. Jobe administers a residential center that houses sixty-five men.

For its first few years, Jobe's court handled a lot of meth addicts when "shake-and-bake" manufacturing was still used. They were gaunt, she remembers, and picked at their skin. But they were animated, lucid, with memories and personalities intact when they arrived at her facility, detoxed of the drug after months in jail.

By 2017, as the P2P meth from Mexico arrived, the men were coming to her stripped of human energy, even after several months in custody. "Their dopamine receptors don't work anymore; nothing is pleasurable for months," she said. "Normal recreational activities where guys talk trash and have fun, there's none of that. It's like their brain cannot fire. All the functions of the prefrontal cortex, the decision making and immediate response we have to stimuli, are extremely slow. They've been so overstimulated that normal brain chemistry doesn't stimulate them. We don't see a lot of anger at first. Not a lot of fury at all. It's zombie-esque.

"The tooth devastation is amazing—nothing but blackened stubs in the front of the mouth. We are seeing twentysomethings in need of full sets of dentures. The teeth simply cannot be saved."

Treating them was daunting. Unlike opioids, methamphetamine has no medical treatment. Despite years of research, science has found no meth equivalent of methadone or Suboxone to help subdue cravings and allow an addict a chance to break from the drug and begin life repair. So that was one problem.

Also, the new meth, Jobe found, damaged the mind to a degree that kept a user almost incapable of the human connection that drug treatment requires. "It takes longer for them to actually be here mentally," Jobe said. "Before, we didn't keep anybody more than nine months. Now we're running up to fourteen months, because it's not until six or nine months that we finally find out who we got." Some can't remember their lives before jail. They have to relearn personal hygiene. "It's not unusual for them to ask what they were found guilty of and sentenced to," she said.

P2P meth seemed to be creating a caste of people deprived of memory and personality—versions of Henry Molaison, neuroscience's most famous patient, who had lost all his short-term memory when that part of his brain was removed.

Only a few people I spoke to ventured a guess as to why this was happening. One was Ken Vick, who runs a treatment center in Kansas City, Missouri. Vick was once a proficient meth cook and did years in prison for manufacturing the drug. "This meth is dirty," he said. "My belief would be that it's not cleaned [of chemical residue]. If you clean it, you remove weight, and if you remove weight, you're losing profit."

That made sense, that idea that the abundant toxic chemicals—lye, sulfuric acid, benzine, and so many others—used to make P2P meth might leave lasting damage. But I don't know of any study comparing the behavior of users, or rats for that matter, on meth made with ephedrine versus meth made with P2P. That now seems a critical national question.

Still, my reporting found that P2P meth in massive quantities *is* damaging minds, perhaps irreparably, across the United States. The growing homeless encampments in many cities and rural towns are meth's deadening creation, I'm convinced. Though other drugs and alcohol are part of the mix, many encampments are simply meth colonies. They provide a community for users, creating the kinds of environmental cues that USC psychologist Wendy Wood found crucial in forming habits. Encampments are places where addicts flee from treatment, where they can find the warm embrace of approval for their meth use. "It took me twelve years of using before I was homeless," said Talie Wenick, a counselor in Bend, Oregon. "Now, within a year they're homeless. So many homeless camps have popped up around Central Oregon—huge camps on Bureau of Land Management land, with tents and campers and roads they've cleared themselves. And everyone's using. You're trying to help someone get clean, and they live in a camp where everyone is using."

P2P meth's intense paranoia, combined with days without sleep, produces bizarre obsessions. One of them is coloring books. Some I spoke to spent hours coloring. Another obsession is with flashlights and headlamps. Paranoia plus endless nighttime hours awake prod users to light up areas where someone might be lurking. Meth users develop flashlight fetishes, collecting a dozen or more. The new meth has also promoted hoarding, which is why so many homeless encampments are filled with seemingly purposeless junk. Many addicts, up all night, ride bicycles through the streets, with flashlights and headlamps to dig through the trash for things to keep, sell, or trade for dope.

The new meth hit rural areas hard. Many of these areas hadn't seen much beyond shake-and-bake meth, which was always limited by how many Sudafed pills cookers could find from which to extract ephedrine. Southern Indiana was one such place.

I spoke with judge Mary Ellen Diekhoff, who runs a drug court in the county where Bloomington is located, home to Indiana University. For a long time most of her meth cases were for manufacturing the drug shake-and-bake style. In 2017, she said, "we started asking, 'What happened to the manufacturers? Where'd they go?' That's when we started hearing about this different kind of meth."

When I spoke with Diekhoff, the local meth cookers had been run out of business. Many of her drug-court clients were now delusional, hallucinating. One girl walked off the roof of a parking garage. As this new meth showed up, Diekhoff said, so did tents and homeless encampments in Bloomington; smaller ones formed in rural towns across southern Indiana.

In one town, a recovering addict I spoke to remembered how the meth years ago energized her to clean the house all day and party all night. After some years of sobriety, she relapsed in 2019. The new meth "would just keep me awake, but I was like a zombie. I'd pick my cuticles all day. It made my brain foggy. I was numb. I stayed in my home and didn't leave. People brought me drugs."

I met a woman named Holly. She and her boyfriend were heroin addicts who switched to crystal meth. They found that the drug was everywhere. "Most I'd seen in my life was a few joints on a table," she told me. "Then I saw quantities that didn't look even like they could possibly be drugs. These big chunks of crystals. They almost looked like from a cave—a stalactite or a stalagmite."

Cortney Baudendistel, a drug counselor in southern Indiana, remembers a client addicted to heroin who switched to meth. He began dressing in women's clothing, which he'd never done before. One day she found him in a government office, having emptied his backpack, sitting among its contents, shredding paper into tiny pieces. People were after him, he said.

"He was the first that talked about a different [meth] formula," she told me. "I remember talking to him and saying these things aren't supposed to happen on meth. He said, 'This is different.'"

HISTORY WAS REPEATING. Unprecedented supplies of a drug were again unleashed coast to coast. Only this time they came not from doctors and drug companies, but from traffickers, virtually all from northwest Mexico. With compliant law enforcement and guns smuggled from the United States, they could dash off their dope year-round with impunity. Never had one illegal drug from one general source spread so completely across the country.

America, meanwhile, offered traffickers a base of consumers whose brain reward systems were conditioned by lengthy exposure to potent dope. A drug of toxic effect was overlaid on a population whose lives had already been upended by pain pills, then heroin, then fentanyl. By now, many were using any drug that was available—Xanax, cocaine, alcohol, and marijuana, as well—and in combination.

What's more, when P2P meth showed up, cheap and potent, something happened that had never happened before: large numbers of opiate users switched to meth. Meth and heroin users had been separate groups, different cultures; historically they never mixed. That was understandable; the drugs affect different parts of the brain's reward pathway. The supplies of P2P meth changed that. By 2019 I had met many folks in Kentucky, Ohio, Indiana, Tennessee, and West Virginia who were using meth to get high, and Suboxone to control their opiate cravings from long-standing addiction to pain pills and heroin.

Suboxone is the brand name for a combination of buprenorphine and naloxone. Buprenorphine is an addictive opioid, but it also blocks the worst cravings, dims the withdrawals, and lessens the chance of overdose. It is an essential tool in managing an opioid addict's recovery, giving her time to move away from the drug world, restore family relationships, find work and housing, recover driver's licenses, get health and dental care, pay traffic fines. "That continuum of care over an extended period of time—that's where you find success," said Mike Yow, director of Fellowship Hall, a treatment center in Greensboro, North Carolina. "It takes time. It's not quick." It's also costly and labor intensive.

As fentanyl arrived and the overdose death toll rose yearly, saving lives became the urgent priority. Suboxone was the only tool that could be quickly rolled out. In the rush, life repair didn't always come with it. In some areas Suboxone clinics ended up looking a lot like pill mills: a doctor prescribing a drug for cash, with patients seen in a matter of minutes and without much attention to addiction's complexities.

For many, buprenorphine in the form of Suboxone was a lifesaver. They used it daily the way a heart patient (like me) uses daily blood thinners and anticholesterol drugs to stay alive. But part of a heart patient's recovery is life repair: weight loss, better diet and exercise, no smoking. Such continuum of care was often absent when it came to addiction.

That's one reason meth found such acceptance across America. Opioid addicts on Suboxone, without that life repair, were still connected to the drug world and still wanted to get high on something. They provided a ready market for Mexican traffickers' cheap and plentiful P2P meth. It reminded me of Nicole Avena's experiments on sugar-dependent rats at Princeton—only now playing out on people nationwide. One drug primed them for almost anything else that was available.

In a remarkable switch, meth became a fentanyl substitute. You generally don't overdose and die on meth, you decay. Meth kept withdrawal at bay, thus many seemed to believe meth was some kind of shield from fentanyl. Many users picked up meth, hoping it would keep them high, but alive, instead of dying on fentanyl. And while opiates had them nodding off, one woman I spoke with said meth "gets me off my ass to figure out how to get money: day labor, asking people to mow their lawns."

Historians note that societies' consumption of illegal drugs moves in gradual waves over decades: demand shifts from depressants to stimulants, then back. That's true, but that's not what happened here. There was nothing gradual about what occurred to the country's drug stream. In fact, P2P meth resembled an opioid in that it was not the party drug that ephedrine meth had been; rather, like an opioid, it was isolating. It sent the user into a shell she alone occupied. And as with fentanyl, P2P meth was entirely a supply-side business decision, based on the needs and profits of traffickers.

So an unprecedented event occurred. Massive supplies of P2P meth out of Mexico created demand for a stimulant out of a market for a depressant. In the process, traffickers forged a new population of mentally ill Americans.

OUT IN CENTRAL Oregon, Kirsten slowly emerged from her meth haze enough to convince those around her that she was not schizophrenic. She no longer received messages from God through the television. Her speech gradually made more sense. She had many bad days, and doesn't remember a lot. She had severe mood swings, cried often, felt anxious and then stripped of feeling. She had trouble making phone calls and connecting with others. For a while it felt as if she had been surgically altered.

Then one night, six months off P2P meth and in a sober-living home, Kirsten sat with her roommate and watched *Maid in Manhattan*, starring Jennifer Lopez as a hotel maid in love with a senator. The movie was pure schmaltz, but it swept her away, and for the first time in a long while she felt genuine happiness and empathy for the characters. She laughed and cried. "I was like a kid on Christmas day," she told me. "I was so enthralled with the movie because I hadn't felt this for a long time. I could feel my brain healing. I could feel my brain making connections. It felt warm."

Kirsten still battles. She went to the dentist every month for her first two years sober. Her teeth are fixed, but her memory remains damaged. "I couldn't read words for the first year," she told me. "I cannot remember something that you just told me. I still have depression and anxiety. I've never been the same since."

Guided meditation has helped her focus, control her anxiety, and clear her mind of the meth-induced clutter.

In Central Oregon, treatment providers are now used to meth addicts who seem schizophrenic. Thirty days in a residential treatment is far from enough to allow damaged brains to repair from P2P meth, but in rural Oregon, that's all there is. Emergency rooms routinely see young people with heart failure.

When I spoke with her, Kirsten had been clean for more than four years—one of the few in her area with that long in recovery from P2P meth. She manages a small sober-living house and mentors other addicts. "I would love for more research to be done," she told me. "I would love to know if there's anything I can do besides meditation and deep breathing to heal my brain."

Kenton County II

Steve Fariello has a big smile and an easygoing way about him that you'd think unlikely given his story of family dysfunction, juvenile delinquency, and drug life on the streets of Northern Kentucky. By 2016, at thirty-two, he'd been in and out of custody half his life. He could say with conviction that he preferred prison over jail, where the boredom was oppressive and "the caliber of people ain't that good." He'd been to prison three times. There, he'd hung out "with some pretty good guys. The closest thing to a normal life I ever had was in prison. We lifted weights, ate good, laughed, played softball. But in jail, you had no reason to get up in the morning. Go play poker, that's it."

Sure enough, arrested for meth dealing in 2016, he arrived at Kenton County jail and was sent to a pod where a half dozen guys he knew from a life of addiction sat playing poker. They hailed him like old barflies. He sat with them as they caught up—what crimes they were in for, what happened to a buddy, who'd died, who was using again.

As they talked, Fariello asked, "What's that?" Across the hall was a pod of men in blue jumpsuits. No one was playing poker, or slouching, or sleeping. Unit 104, his friends told him, was a new recovery pod, where you volunteered for a program to get off drugs. They were known as "quitters" in other pods.

"I stood up and said, 'I'm going to sign up for that,'" Fariello told me several years later. "They didn't want me to leave. Me being around made their time easy. I said, 'I did more time than any of y'all. I gotta do what's best for me.'"

Just like that he went, and he regretted it pretty quickly. In Unit 104, inmates governed themselves. One way they did this was by calling out each other for not putting forth their best effort, for getting up late, sleeping during the day, for lying or not making their bed. This went against everything that drug addiction and custody taught them. Dissolving the criminal code, learning to postpone immediate gratification and combat addiction—it all required using criticism to fuel personal change. In neuroscience terms, it was part of strengthening the prefrontal cortex in its battle with the nucleus accumbens's me-first impulse. In 104, they called it "holding someone accountable." But to Fariello, with almost half a life behind bars, it sure looked like snitching.

About the only reason he stayed was Will Pfefferman.

In the eighteen months since the seventy-man Unit 104 opened, Will Pfefferman had grown into the job. It made him feel worthy, energized, unlike anything he'd done in his life. It seemed as close to a calling as anything he had imagined possible. He remembered that leaving jail or prison, with no help, is where he had fallen so often back into the criminal and addicted life. He now drove inmates leaving 104 into town in his personal car so they could avoid the seven-mile walk. Through his church he formed a nonprofit that provided each departing inmate a week's rent in a sober-living house. After months of jailhouse carbohydrates, many inmates no longer fit their emaciated street-addict clothes. Or they were arrested in shorts and a T-shirt in August and released in January. Will would hustle to St. Vincent de Paul and return with clothes that fit the body and the season. It was an informal re-entry program, and at the time it was about all Kenton County jail had.

Will would greet his charges in the morning with his booming baritone. "Wake up, guys! Feet on the floor. You signed up for this!" Fariello knew Will from prison. To see him in recovery and helping others with theirs made him a beacon of sorts to Fariello. Will had done more years behind bars than anyone. When he spoke, Fariello and others tended to listen and to hope. "He was living proof you could do something different." So Fariello hung on in the pod, despite what he saw as snitching.

Some guys entered Unit 104 to reduce their time, or to avoid drug debts in other parts of the jail. Others seemed sincere, and Will focused his efforts on them. He understood when Steve Fariello came with complaints about snitching. He'd heard it almost daily since Unit 104 opened.

He took Fariello aside. When you snitch on someone, Will said, it's for your benefit. That's not what's happening here. When someone holds you accountable, it's not for his benefit; it's for yours. So that you can change, feel the effect of your actions on others. You gotta understand the difference. "When you do," Will said, "you start to learn what integrity is."

Then came pizza night. Fariello had already been through the chow line for his slice. Before others were served, in a classic bit of me-first thinking, he got back in line, not imagining anyone would call him on it. But another inmate did. Fariello punched his accuser and spent that Christmas in solitary. "At the time I was pissed. I would never do nothing like that nowadays, cut in line. But I wanted some more pizza."

To Will Pfefferman, Fariello's pizza incident crystallized the difficulties of running a jail pod that helped drug addicts begin recovery. Each new arrival brought years of custody and the street in with him. Will had seen this right from the start.

In the fall of 2015, shortly after it opened, Unit 104 descended into chaos. Supervisors were reluctant to boot anyone, hoping a third or fourth chance would be the magic one. Fights brought no consequences. Noise was constant. Classes were disorganized. Gambling, extortion, bartering, the power plays common to jail—all that continued. Some walked about naked after showering; a few even sword-fought with their penises. New attitudes trying to take root struggled against ingrained criminal and addictive behavior.

"It demoralizes you. That's not how you live in a civilized society," said one man I spoke to who was in 104 during those months. "When I came in here, I'm like, 'What in the hell are grown men doing?' You had forty-year-old men acting like twelve-year-olds. So it was, 'Are we going to make a change in who we are, or are we going to become the savages that the outside society thinks we are?' "

As the jail's new director of addiction services, Jason Merrick saw the entire experiment at risk. He turned to two inmates committed to their recovery. They came up with what became known as the Cardinal Rules: No bartering, no fighting, no poker, no yelling, no nudity, no noise after 10:00 p.m., no sexual stuff. Beds made military style each morning. No sleeping during the day. A new inmate had one day to dispose of any drugs or weapons on, or in, his body. Wakeup and break-fast at 8:00 a.m. Classes begin at 9:00. Lights-out at 11:00 p.m. Inmates clean the pod, its showers, and its bathrooms. Only three hours of unscheduled time a day. A panel of inmates judged whether others were abiding by the rules, and punished those who were not.

A half dozen men were quickly booted for violating these rules. Others came to see this was serious. Before too long there was silence at 10:00 pm; at 11:00 the pod was dark. The distractions had tapered. In other pods, drama, drug selling, gambling, and noise were constant, a way of relieving boredom. Officers found Unit 104 the jail's cleanest pod in five years. No contraband, no weapons, no filth. A waiting list formed to get into 104. In the Kenton County jail, African Americans made up a tenth of the population and thus were easy targets in other units; but that, too, seemed to fade in 104.

A kind of nurturing unity took shape, a camaraderie, guys sharing their worst mistakes and weaknesses so that one might throw an arm around another—"C'mon, brother, we can do it"—and they might inch ahead together. At least, those wanting to change were no longer isolated and preyed upon.

One afternoon I sat in a room off 104 as a self-described Kentucky hillbilly brought to order a Narcotics Anonymous meeting of eight other inmates. His knuckles were tattooed with L-O-V-E and H-A-T-E. The men, all of them White and most with hair cropped short, bore the hieroglyphics of the criminal world inked on their necks and hands. They told raw stories of lives in addiction. One man had lost his construction company, ended up in a tent, and pimped out his girlfriend's daughter. Another left jail with $40 to his name and headed directly to his dealer's house. It went on from there, tales that ended invariably in misty eyes. I'd never before seen men cry in jail.

The NA group broke for a 104 general meeting. A Black man stood and said he had a poem to read, about the death of the pop star Prince from a fentanyl overdose. He read his poem and the room of White inmates applauded. I was shocked; inmates typically don't stand and read poetry in US jails unless they have a death wish. "In another pod, I never would have done it," the poet told me later.

It would be nice to say old jail habits vanished. Instead, they coexisted with this nurturing culture. New personalities arrived as others went home. But behavior learned from drugs and the street were hard to exorcise. Many inmates had the dreams of shooting up that are common to addicts in recovery. A few snorted coffee, mimicking their drug use on the street. The addictions of many inmates were rooted in the beatings and molestations they endured as boys. Bottled up, that trauma kept men from progressing. The nationwide layer of trauma that the opioid epidemic exposed underlay a lot of Unit 104. But discussing such a volatile topic in jail was about as taboo as snitching. What's more, as men stopped using, feelings returned; memories stirred of how they'd treated their children or spouses. Anguish, anger, and hope were equal parts of doing jail a radically new way, and produced what Will called a "therapeutic chaos" of good days and bad.

Steve Fariello was kicked out of 104 twice, and ordered back by a drug-court judge each time. Just give me my ten years, he told the judge, I gotta get out of this jail. But later he felt relieved that the judge had forced him back into 104. "If it was up to me," he said, "I wouldn't be here right now."

One day he found himself walking around the pod with a friend, plotting his next dope move on the outside. The friend could get crystal meth for $500 an ounce now. Dirt cheap. They'd make a killing. Then the absurdity of the moment hit him. "I said to him, 'I don't know why we do this shit. Is it for the money? Because we don't got none. Is it for the women? Because they ain't worth it. And here we are walking loops plotting our next crime. It's kinda dumb.'"

It took him eight months to complete 104's three-month program of classes in criminal/addictive thinking and behavioral change. Then he was shown the door, and just like that, he was out and on his own. His sister picked him up and took him to his mother's house, where he salvaged some clothes. This time out, instead of telling himself he'd sell dope until he got on his feet, Fariello called his AA sponsor.

"What do I gotta do to stay sober?"

There's an AA meeting tonight, his sponsor said. The meeting was large. People that night welcomed Fariello, smiled and shook his hand—all of which spooked him. "It was scarier than my first time to prison. I broke a sweat," he said. "I could not relate to anyone who wasn't a felon." He found temp work at a packing warehouse, where he was forced to further converse with nonfelons.

At four months out, a friend gave him sheets of LSD, which he tried to sell. One night, though, he found himself in the kitchen of a drug house, with needles on the table and people he kind of knew. It had been years of this. This time, he felt a connection to sobriety and nonfelonious life that he hadn't before. The ways of the penitentiary and the street seemed pointless. Is this worth $50? he asked himself. He left the house, chucked the LSD, and told me he hasn't relapsed since.

"When I got out [of jail], I didn't get perfect," he said when I met him, three years later. "My first year I was getting in fights in sober-living houses. I would steal shit sometimes from work. I spoke with my sponsor. He said, 'You can't be doing that.' So I just hung in there like hair on a biscuit. All I did was I went to a noon meeting, to the gym, then to work. Every day. I started caring about other people. Slowly I stopped doing criminal shit."

Last I saw Steve Fariello, he was working as a pipe fitter for the city of Cincinnati. He still hadn't missed that weekly AA meeting that so scared him on his first night out of the Kenton County jail; occasionally he stood to lead the meeting.

Meanwhile, the Unit 104's experiment was, like Steve Fariello, roiling and imperfect—and would probably remain so. "We're building the car as we travel down the road," Jason Merrick said.

Yet in time 104 had an effect beyond its walls. For it made clear that to give recovering addicts a fighting chance, changing jail was only half the job. The greatest obstacles to addiction recovery were not inside jail at all.

Sacklers IV

"The Incentives Were Tilted"

In October 2013, under the headline "Wild at Heart," *Vogue* magazine published a feature on Jacqueline Sackler, wife of Mortimer Sackler, the younger, who sat on the board of directors of Purdue Pharma.

Hamish Bowles wrote the piece. Mr. Bowles, the international editor at *Vogue* in America, is himself recognized "as one of the most respected authorities on the worlds of fashion, costume history, and interior design," according to one biography. Calling her a "fine-honed beauty with exquisitely attenuated hands," Mr. Bowles detailed how Ms. Sackler oversaw the remodeling of her family's country home in East Hampton, Long Island. Her husband's family had a vacation home on the Côte d'Azur in France, but that didn't quite work for Ms. Sackler. So, Bowles reported, the family purchased the East Hampton estate, and she set about remodeling it.

To that end, Ms. Sackler hired both a prominent New York architect who "worked with Warhol at the Factory" and, as her color consultant, the "legendary tastemaker" Jacques Grange. A landscape architect was brought in to design the Sacklers' backyard garden—which bordered the tennis court and the guest house/Pilates studio—to appear wild and rebellious. The result was that the East Hampton summer place, Bowles wrote, "tucked amid breathtakingly lush gardens, marries the riot of nature with her own carefully curated style." The magazine noted its contrast to the couple's Manhattan home, which is "a showcase for their serious collecting adventures in contemporary art and design furniture. Sackler wanted [the East Hampton] house to feel, as she put it, 'unfussed with.'"

AS I RESEARCHED and wrote *Dreamland* that same year, Purdue and the Sacklers seemed to me unassailable atop the American One Percent. When they appeared in the media, they were embraced by fragrant journalistic love letters like Hamish Bowles's piece in *Vogue*.

Victims of the emerging national opioid-addiction epidemic, meanwhile, led ashamed and voiceless lives far from the lush gardens of the Sacklers' East Hampton summer estate. American families kept quiet as their loved ones grew addicted to the pills that funded those art-collecting adventures. They said nothing as their loved ones were ground into degradation in a marathon of torment that extinguished family savings, hope, and trust, until they wound up dead in a manner and place that no relative dared disclose in an obituary.

These families began to emerge from the shadows in 2015. Drug overdose fatalities each year surpassed the total of American deaths during the Vietnam War. OxyContin sales fell, along with Purdue's annual payouts to the Sackler owners. Far from being chastened, the company doubled down. It increased the doctor visits that their sales reps had to meet to one million in 2018, almost twice the goal during the banner year of 2010.

Meanwhile, media coverage expanded and gradually shifted from Purdue to members of the Sackler family who owned the company. You couldn't pick a Sackler out of a lineup, yet their name earned a notoriety greater than anything their generous philanthropy in the arts, medicine, and biotech achieved. Critical news coverage of the Sacklers now appeared—in *Esquire* and the *New Yorker*. Social invitations dried up around Manhattan. "I wouldn't invite them to my house," a socialite told the *New York Post*. "I like to socialize with people who are not involved in trouble."

Then the Sacklers couldn't give their money away. In England, the small South London Gallery was the first to return a Sackler family donation of $125,000. The National Portrait Gallery, which has a Sackler Room, and the Tate galleries declined future Sackler donations. So did the Guggenheim Museum in New York City, followed by, a few blocks away, perhaps the most painful blow of all, the Metropolitan Museum of Art, which already had a Sackler wing.

A special case was Tufts University in Boston. The late Arthur Sackler had donated money to the Tufts medical school in the 1980s, and it bore his name. Since then Purdue and the Sacklers had expanded their giving to the university. Raymond Sackler was given an honorary Tufts degree. Baseball caps emblazoned with "The Sackler School" sold in the school's store.

As awareness of the addiction crisis grew, Tufts hired two Boston attorneys to investigate the extent of Sackler influence on the university. They found that the family's influence did not "materially affect" the school's academics. Instead, "an appearance of too close a relationship" between the company, the family, and the school continued "in the face of growing evidence and concern" over Purdue's marketing of OxyContin. Based on that investigation, and student pressure, Tufts removed the Sackler name from five of its schools and programs, including the Arthur M. Sackler Center for Medical Education, while holding on to $15 million in family donations destined for cancer research.

This outraged Arthur Sackler's heirs. He had donated to Tufts well before his death in 1987, which itself was nine years before OxyContin was released. His heirs had divested their holdings in Purdue and were estranged from their relatives who owned the company. "The man has been dead for thirty-two years," said Jillian Sackler, his widow, in a statement. "He did not profit from [OxyContin], and none of his

philanthropic gifts were in any way connected to opioids or to decep-
tive medical marketing—which he likewise had nothing to do with.
It deeply saddens me to witness Arthur being blamed for actions taken
by his brothers and other OxySacklers."

(Full disclosure: Tufts's lawyers also reported that in the 2015–16
school year, a medical school committee declined to assign *Dreamland*
as the book incoming students would read. This was not at the behest
of the Sackler family. Rather, the investigators found, the committee's
decision was due to "the existence of the donor relationship with the
Sacklers and Purdue and the desire [at Tufts] to avoid controversy
regarding that relationship.")

In a cutting irony for a family of arts patrons, artists targeted the
Sacklers. Photographer Nan Goldin, who had battled an OxyContin
addiction, organized the throwing of mock prescriptions from the tiers
of the Guggenheim, and held a die-in of protestors in the museum's
lobby. Sculptor Domenic Esposito, whose brother fought heroin addiction, fashioned an eight-hundred-pound stainless steel bent heroin
spoon and carted it over to Purdue headquarters. Esposito began taking
the giant bent spoon around the country to raise awareness.

In early 2014 Mark Timney took over as Purdue chief executive
officer. Timney had been a president at the drug giant Merck. He arrived
at Purdue charged with remaking the firm, said one former employee,
by veering away from opioids and toward drugs for other afflictions:
psoriasis, ADHD. Diversification had been a path outlined by Richard
Sackler and Peter Boer in the April 2008 memo as they discussed ways of
moving beyond the federal conviction and defusing the "dangerous
concentration of risk" Purdue faced. Timney "wanted to transform the
company," said the former employee. "He wanted revenue from opioids
way down, and revenue from other products way up."

It didn't happen. The family had considered purchasing an anti-
insomnia drug in 2010 but passed, apparently because, as Richard
Sackler wrote in an email, it would result in a "loss of focus" on sales

of OxyContin. The Sacklers on Purdue's board apparently balked at diversifying. Timney left after only three years "to pursue other business opportunities," according to the news release.

In the end, there was no diversifying of Purdue into a modern pharmaceutical company. Purdue and the Sacklers, it seemed to me, struggled to kick their dependence on OxyContin revenue. "It's a very profitable business, and tragically the prescriptions that were the most profitable were also the most dangerous," said one state prosecutor I spoke with. "A patient on higher doses earns them more money, a patient staying on the drugs longer earns them more money. All the incentives were tilted toward the business that was the most damaging and the most dangerous."

Illicit fentanyl had done the same—it changed the incentives in the drug underworld. Purdue's dependence on OxyContin sales might have been hard to break. Drugs are, too. Dope convinces us we can only function with it alone—that it equals life, even as it kills us. It convinces the tiny locus coeruleus to slumber while the body nears death. Maybe money does something like that. Whatever the case, the Purdue of 2018 wasn't much different from the Purdue of 2008, despite that memo, despite a new CEO. Only the times had changed.

By summer 2018, the world seemed to have closed in around the family. Lawsuits against the company ballooned from three plaintiffs in 2014 to more than twenty-six hundred.

I was stunned. I recalled wandering through southern Ohio in 2013, reporting on the devastation among the people I met. I wondered how folks in that area might ever succeed against Purdue. They were frail, disorganized. The company seemed so big and impenetrable. But now the state of Massachusetts actually named the Sackler board members in its lawsuit. Some two dozen states followed, sometimes taking their language verbatim from the Massachusetts complaint. By the end of 2019, in a stunning reversal of fortune, all the Sacklers had resigned from Purdue's board of directors.

* * *

ONE DAY IN the spring of 2019, attorneys and paralegals from the Massachusetts Attorney General's Office piled into a couple of government cars and drove a half hour up the coast from Boston to a brick building in the town of Beverly that houses Northshore Recovery High School.

Northshore opened in 2006 to take in kids who've had enough trouble with addiction to disrupt their education. For years, principal Michelle Lipinski watched kids get addicted to plentiful OxyContin and then move to (increasingly plentiful) heroin. That was life-mangling, but at least nobody died.

Then the underworld got wise to fentanyl. Heroin vanished. Many students, in Lipinski's words, "made the jump"—went directly to fentanyl from alcohol, pot, and Xanax. "When they find that drug, you cannot rip it out of their hands," she told me. "It's everywhere. They can get fentanyl faster than I can get a pizza. Dealers come to you. Even if you're grounded at home, they'll deliver it to your window." It became impossible to get those kids back. Since 2014, Northshore has graduated more than sixty kids. By 2019 twenty-three of them had died—a 30 percent death rate. "Every autopsy is fentanyl," Lipinski told me.

Among the visiting attorneys that day was a tall, thin prosecutor named Sandy Alexander. Alexander had left a large firm to join the Massachusetts Attorney General's Office as it prepared to sue the Sacklers. Alexander was assigned to write the complaint; he kept a draft of it in a brick-red folder and carried it with him for months, stopping outside the office or near the subway to jot ideas. Meanwhile, the office staged moot court sessions—play-acting the different testimony and questions that might arise.

Amid all that, Alexander and others needed a break, which is what brought them to Northshore that day. "You can't sustain a legal team in an intense fight for years based only on studying the bad guys' lies," he said later. "You need to go somewhere to get a handle on the truth. Our truth came from places like Northshore."

Sitting in a common room, Alexander and the others listened to a dozen students tell their stories. Alexander was struck by how much the kids looked like his own. No longer on drugs, they were all touching, as if to reacquaint themselves with that essential sense. They were holding hands, one braiding another's hair, on sofas and in chairs, each seeming to lean on the others.

They were coming up in a world very different from his—amid a toxic soup of addictive options, many legal. Vapes came with 90 percent THC. These kids seemed to assume that drugs were indivisible from life, an element in everything they saw, listened to, and did. They weren't wrong, Alexander thought. But that wasn't even the biggest difference. It was the potency of dope that was higher than ever—merciless. The supply of it seemed endless, sold by astute marketers.

For all the mistakes teenagers make, it seemed to Alexander that the drugs and how they were purveyed now ensured that they received no forgiveness.

BEFORE RESIGNING THE seats on their company's board of directors, the Sacklers appointed longtime employee Craig Landau, formerly the chief of Purdue Canada, as the company's new CEO.

Landau is a physician, formerly in the US Army Reserves, who served in Operation Enduring Freedom, the invasion of Afghanistan following the September 11 terrorist attacks. He had been Purdue's chief medical officer, in charge of the research division that was now drained in favor of payments to the Sacklers. He had a central role in reformulating OxyContin in 2010, which was intended to make it harder to abuse. "He tried to be as objective as possible and data driven," said one former employee.

Landau had worked for Purdue since 1999, as it rode OxyContin out of anonymity. He was there while the addiction crisis spread nationwide. In fact, Landau wrote in a 2013 report that keeping patients on opioids long-term, as the company reps were urging doctors to do, offered, finally, "negative outcomes." Still, he had also assigned sales reps to every research team, to ensure researchers kept sales always in mind.

Now, as CEO, it fell to Landau to sail the ship into the hurricane. On Sackler orders, Landau ended the promotion of opioids by sales reps and fired hundreds of them. His scarce media interviews focused on "challenges" the company faced.

The Sacklers on the board acted as the "de-facto CEO," Landau wrote in an analysis of the company in 2017 that turned up among the documents state prosecutors retrieved. The Sacklers had paid themselves instead of investing in research or acquiring new companies. "The planned and purposeful . . . deconstruction of R&D," Landau wrote, "has left the organization unable to innovate." The company's relationship with the US FDA had "deteriorated," and its US business was in decline. He predicted that the company "will soon no longer be able to fund investments to affiliated companies and distributions to the family."

All Purdue knew how to do, he seemed to say, was sell one product, the sales of which were collapsing.

One day, after only a few months as CEO, Landau took the time to compose a remarkable email. In it he laid out in spare language, as if from the pen of the late poet William Carlos Williams, himself also a physician, a plaintive lament, a summation of this time in America, that described the epidemic's origins and the world his employer had pushed to create. "There are," Landau wrote,

> Too many Rxs being written
> Too high a dose
> For too long
> For conditions that often don't require them
> By doctors who lack . . . training
> In how to use them.

Kenton County III

Jo Martin is a tall, thin woman with straight reddish hair reaching below her shoulders. She is a devout Catholic, attends mass every morning, the mother of five and grandmother of thirteen, and has voted straight Republican all her life.

In the part of Northern Kentucky in which Martin grew up, no one was raised by a single parent, much less Child Protective Services. She had never been in a fistfight, used drugs, known a baby mama, or, for that matter, known anyone who'd been to jail.

At sixty-one, she was comfortably retired from AT&T, a widow whose children were grown. A friend urged her to tutor inmates at the Kenton County jail who were getting their GED. It took some nudging, but Jo Martin showed up at the jail and in time came to see it as church. She got to know those men and women as she tutored them in reading and math. Many of the men were in the jail's new recovery pod—Unit 104. Their lives were full of torment and turbulence. She loved them, prayed for them, and found them often born into horrific setbacks, abused, then abusive, and through it all, relentlessly committed to bad choices.

Tattoos in particular bewildered her. Nearly every person she tutored had them. They were impediments, she saw, and not just to renting apartments or finding work (who, after all, would hire anyone with REVENGE on his neck?); it also mired them in street life. The outside world viewed the markings as a modern leprosy. Often, her charges reacted to that by further embracing their dysfunction. Tattoos allowed them to reject the outside world they repelled.

A friend one day told her about Homeboy Industries in Los Angeles, begun by a Catholic priest named Greg Boyle, which offered paths out of gang membership, one of which was tattoo removal. She wrote to him.

"Come to L.A.," Boyle wrote back.

So she did, and there, Jo Martin learned to remove tattoos. Back in Kentucky, she invested $55,000 of her husband's life insurance money in a tattoo-removal laser machine and formed a nonprofit. "To practice," she said, "we did a whole bunch of people who weren't incarcerated, charging them nothing." She asked several charitable agencies to house her service; each declined. No one had seen such an endeavor succeed. So she rented an office on her own and opened Tattoo Removal Ink.

She began removing visible tattoos—from the face, neck, and hands—of those leaving Kenton County jail, at no charge. From one youth's forehead she removed "13.5"—"Twelve jurors, one defendant, and a half-assed chance of winning," he told her. This is coming off, she told him, and all this will be behind you; he broke into tears. "I'm like the den mother," she said.

Along the way, she removed a branding: a pimp's name—Charley—from a woman's thigh. One man had a Hannibal Lecter mask tattooed across his lower face. She saw "Life's a Bitch," "God's Child," and "I'm a pornstar. I f— teenage sluts" etched on necks and foreheads. And when I met her, she was removing the spiderweb from the back of Will Pfefferman's left hand.

"We also take off a lot of swastikas," she said, "and teardrops."

Jo Martin's Tattoo Removal Ink is important to the story of Kenton County because by the time it opened, it fit naturally into an ecosystem of recovery support outside the jail, yet rooted in the Unit 104 experiment.

For all the work inmates might do in 104, once released, they were waylaid by old friends who picked them up or saw them on the bus. They were getting high again within hours. They had no health insurance, no jobs. Housing was a problem. The small stuff, the logistics of that return to life, kept them stumbling—like where to get clothes that fit the season, or a ride to court. If there was one thing I found that the opioid epidemic was teaching folks across America about addiction recovery, it was that this small, daily stuff mattered, all of it. Kenton County learned this sooner than most.

What started in the Kenton County jail's Unit 104 was soon spreading beyond its walls, and Tattoo Removal Ink became part of that.

One place that first declined to house Jo Martin was a large nonprofit known as the Life Learning Center. A local philanthropist named Bill Butler founded the LLC to teach life skills as a way of alleviating poverty. As addiction spread and Unit 104 formed, LLC brought in Alecia Webb-Edgington, a short and energetic woman in her fifties who was a retired state police major and narcotics investigator. She redirected the LLC toward what addicted felons needed to remain sober and free.

Kenton County began shuttling inmates from 104 directly to the LLC to avoid the perilous bus trip. The day before I met Webb-Edgington, eleven people from the jail arrived. LLC staff fed them, then got busy finding them beds in sober-living houses. They fitted a couple for eyeglasses. One man was wearing only shorts; outside, the temperature was 21 degrees. LLC staff dug him up a pair of pants.

Kenton County jailer Terry Carl hired a social worker to sign inmates up for Medicaid. They often asked her for dental care, too. Ravaged teeth were as public a sign of street addiction as visible tattoos. Improved smiles, on the other hand, helped their confidence; then they dressed better and they got their hair cut, too. Some of them got tattoos removed by Jo Martin, who in the winter of 2019, three years after being turned away, moved her lasers into an office at the LLC.

Jason Merrick imagined now what he called "recovery-ready communities"—towns geared to helping addicts recover. "This is what rehabilitation looks like," Merrick told me. "It's a full continuum of care, not just punishment."

Merrick had promised recovery in 90 percent of clients. But the definition of recovery, too, needed changing, he believed. The old definition—abstinence forever—wasn't realistic, given the battles in the human brain between the reward pathway and the prefrontal cortex, which were messy. Recovery "is different for everybody; it means any positive change," Merrick said as we sat in his office at the jail one day. People failed out of Unit 104 and the LLC all the time; some took several tries to get it right. The trick was to show that while all this was complicated to orchestrate, it was cheaper and produced better long-term effects on addiction and crime than how jail had been run. Having seen other traditional jails, I didn't think that standard would be hard to meet. Would it happen? I had no idea. But it seemed worth some attention.

Still, I wondered how recovering addicts would fare, leaving jail for a world where drug organizations could flood neighborhoods from Oregon to North Carolina with so much potent dope that the price dropped to historic lows. Did *any* drug treatment stand much of a chance? It seemed to me an open question for the country so long as Mexican traffickers could produce such damaging dope in such massive supplies.

A FEW YEARS after I met Will Pfefferman, we drove south to Breathitt County one Saturday morning as the last of 2019's fierce winter left Kentucky. Will had left Kenton County jail and now worked for the Life Learning Center. He also ran a couple of sober-living homes. On weekends he was employed by a federal grant bringing cases of naloxone, the opioid-overdose antidote, and training in how to use it, to places like Breathitt County.

Breathitt County was known for two things. The first was bluegrass music. The county produced musicians who created and defined the genre for years: Sam Wilson, Nelson Young, Sturgill Simpson. Roy Lee Centers sang for Ralph Stanley for a while, until in 1974 he was shot to death in front of his young son, the victim of clan violence and family feuds. And that's the other thing Breathitt is known for. "Bloody Breathitt," it was called. Neither the law nor much of the world reached into its hollers. Coal mining sustained the county but maimed the people and scarred the land. Men murdered each other over debts, women, or revenge. In prison, Pfefferman remembered, most men from Breathitt were locked up for murder.

Nowadays, though, drug abuse had replaced the violence in Breathitt. Which is why Will had come here—five years clean, grateful he wasn't dead, no longer on parole, still making his bed, still a billboard of sorts for what recovery can achieve. There, in a motel conference room in the small town of Jackson, he spoke to paramedics and firefighters. On one table lay a plastic dummy faceup; stacked on another were boxes of naloxone. Blocking fentanyl usually required several doses of naloxone, he told them. "Remember, with that amount of naloxone you put them in instant withdrawal. They could come up swinging." This was a remarkable insight into opioids: their control of the brain's reward pathways can be so complete that even when an overdose victim is revived from death, his response is often to fight the person who revived him.

We spent a couple of hours in Breathitt County, then headed north again.

Will had found a way to use his "gift of desperation"—and just in time. So few had that opportunity anymore. Fentanyl sped things up, depriving addicts of what Will thought was crucial: the precious time to get desperate enough to change. Pretty quickly, they died. Fentanyl was now in everything, so clearly profitable was it to the trafficking world. Meth was now everywhere too, easy to make in the scariest quantities. Pfefferman saw that it was almost given away for free. Often meth was mixed with fentanyl. Folks who switched to meth to avoid fentanyl got it anyway, though they never knew it. "Last week, I had six sober-living guys show up in my houses; they all said they was using meth," Will told me on the drive. "But every one of the six was positive for meth and positive for fentanyl."

It was the final result of the opioid crisis. Two drugs, made not from plants but from chemicals, were defining the new dope world and now formed an unmercifully addictive, mind-twisting, and deadly concoction that no one demanded. What it meant was that the old revolving-door approach to jail and addiction was a death sentence to anyone hooked on street drugs. In response, a county in conservative, libertarian Northern Kentucky had turned to government and to fairly radical change. This began with Unit 104. But it went far beyond jail now and was a sign of how the epidemic was, in turn, changing the country.

That afternoon, as Will Pfefferman pulled his car onto the highway heading north, he could count himself as the beneficiary of that change. At fifty-one, having survived so much that killed so many, he knew himself to be that rare thing in the time of fentanyl and meth, a lucky man.

PART V

Angie and Starla V

"The One to Make It Out"

S o in the end, Angie and Earl Odom, as they were about to enjoy
their newly empty nest, adopted the infant girl born to a vegetative mother who, brain-damaged from an overdose to multiple drugs,
existed now in a nursing home a few miles away, unable to speak or see
or stand.

They named their new daughter Bella. Attending to her was no less
difficult as the months passed. "The only way you could get her to calm
down is stand and balance her," Earl told me. That went on for more
than a year. She couldn't keep down baby food but would throw it up
constantly, often onto Earl. She was so sensitive to touch that they had
to remove the tags to all her clothing. Nor would she tolerate wool or
polyester, clothes with sewn-on patches, socks, shoes, or onesies. So
they had her in diapers and the softest blankets they could find.

Even as she reached kindergarten age, Bella still couldn't stand
patches or sequins on shirts that rub against the skin. She could wear
only leggings and sandals, and she wore them as long as weather
permitted. She couldn't tolerate the smell of vinegar, or sandwich meat,
or most vegetables. Angie kept oils in her purse to put under Bella's
nose to mask the smell of some stores. The sound of the rain on the
family's metal roof, so soothing to some, was too much for the child.

Meanwhile Angie and Earl quickly came to understand that they
had adopted Starla as well. Starla's family rarely visited her in the

nursing home. Decisions about her care fell to Angie, who wanted her new daughter to know and love her birth mother. Angie visited Starla three times a week, at first with Bella in a car seat, then, as years passed, holding her hand as they walked through the nursing home. They spoke to Starla as though she could respond. They placed on the walls of Starla's room photographs of her before her overdose, of her late father in army uniform, photos with her mother, Maude Buchanan, and snapshots with her son, Ezra. On a table Angie put a photo of Bella, an open Bible, and stuffed unicorns, which Starla seemed to like rubbed against her cheek. Starla responded to soothing music, so Angie placed an iPod in the room, playing Christian music.

"Starla always wanted somebody to love her unconditionally," Angie told me one day, as we visited the nursing home. "Everybody needs somebody. I feel everybody's life has a purpose. Right now, what is her purpose?" Angie wasn't sure she knew.

No one for four generations in Starla's family had emerged unscathed by drug dysfunction. "Our focus is to protect Bella," Angie said, "to be there to make sure this does not happen to her in her life—that she will be the one from that family to make it out."

As she grew and was able to speak, Bella seemed a different kind of child. Instead of the Appalachian accent of Angie and Earl, Bella spoke in ways that almost sounded British. Her vocabulary included words Angie never used. "Constellation of the stars," she said; she asked a waitress for "marmalade" and told Angie that a café had once been a men's clothing store and also sold "textiles." For a while, at home, she asked often for "hot peppermint tea." "I say jelly, I don't say marmalade," Angie said. "I don't say constellation of the stars and hot peppermint tea. I don't even drink hot tea."

Bella's sensitivity seemed to extend beyond the physical. It was as if she hadn't formed the emotional calluses that most of us develop as we get older. She was left to feel life at its most raw or basic, and sometimes as a cacophony of senses. She was gifted with extreme empathy. Once in church, members of the congregation were lighting candles for those who'd died in the past year. Bella was overcome and began sobbing big tears. "I really don't know what's wrong," she told Angie, "I just feel very sad."

Any room with many adults overwhelmed Bella. She and Angie had to develop hand signs for when they were in a store and Bella was overcome with apprehension. "Do you have Jesus in your heart?" Bella once asked a friend. When he said yes, she replied, "That's good. You just have something really bad sitting next to you." Bella warned me once that a woman I was about to meet had "bad company around her, so watch out."

The barrier between the mundane and the spiritual barely seemed to exist to Bella. Angie thought it similar to a police dog, who can smell cocaine but can also lick the faces of his handler's children. Bella smelled them both, the darkness and the light. "We're just on a journey," Angie said of life with her daughter, "and I have no idea what's going to happen."

Bella was a smart girl, but like many kids born affected by drugs, she had trouble with abstract concepts. She loved being read to but couldn't spell her name, or remember numbers or the words to songs. She could act out any animal, but when Angie asked her to "show me your surprised face, your sad face," she could not.

This seemed to extend to love as well. Bella expressed love through actions and caring gestures. Her face didn't offer the outward demonstration of love that people notice and the world was accustomed to, even as she acted in loving ways. "She can give mommy a hug," Angie said. "But if I say, 'How do you feel, Bella?' she wouldn't be able to use words." This put Angie in mind of people who acted on faith as opposed to those who valued the appearance of piety. Angie had seen the latter in the church, when she was asked to step down as Sunday organist because of how it would appear to others that she, a divorced mother, had a prominent role. One night with a preacher on television, Bella said, "Why does he have to scream? You don't have to scream at God for Him to hear you."

For Starla, she developed a love that asked for nothing in return—the kind of unconditional love, finally, that Starla had always wanted. On Starla's birthday, Bella came with cupcakes. Bella and Angie would light a candle on one cupcake and stand over Starla's bed and sing "Happy Birthday." Later, her face smeared with frosting, Bella shared the cupcakes with the nurses on duty. She brought Starla her puppy or a pet rabbit and put them to Starla's face and conversed with Starla and the animals. When Bella was six, she asked Angie if Starla could come to church for Mother's Day. So that Sunday, a paramedic wheeled Starla into the church on a stretcher, in a pink dress that Bella had chosen, sure that Starla would have picked it for herself. Bella was waiting for her at the church door with roses, and sang "Jesus Loves Me" for her birthmother.

Through Bella, Angie touched a simpler faith, one closer to the Gospel of Matthew. Matthew was the tax collector who dropped everything to follow Jesus. He left behind all worldly worth, not thinking how it appeared to others that he would accompany this ragged man. The message of Matthew, Angie believed, was that "we're not to be like the Pharisees. In church, it's 'Look at me, I got it together. I've been three times this week to church.' Appearance—that supposedly makes you acceptable to God. In the Book of Matthew, it says you have to come to God as a child. Bella has taught me that."

Perhaps, for Angie, those lessons began years ago latched to the back of that navy destroyer in the dark silence of the Pacific Ocean when she discarded bitterness and judgment to embrace forgiveness. Something like that happened, something like Matthew, when Angie and Earl adopted Bella with no plan, nor any thought of how it appeared to others that she was also caring for a brain-damaged drug-addicted prostitute. Everyone wanted to help a child born dependent on drugs, Angie noted; few people asked about Starla. "God showed me through loving them both," Angie said, "that one is as deserving as the other."

One day, Angie, Bella, and another child were driving in town when they saw Joyce Vinney walking on the road and picked her up and took her to eat.

Folks in Elizabethton knew Joyce Vinney by sight. She was in her eighties, gaunt and crinkled from the years. Her second husband, who'd brought her to Tennessee from Chicago, had died in 1993. She'd given children from an earlier marriage, to a husband who'd died young, to their grandparents in Wisconsin to care for them. As a widow a second time, she lived all alone with her cats and her dog Whitey in her old house packed floor to ceiling with stuff. Joyce always wore the same unwashed gray sweater, and her toes overlapped under old tennis shoes. Every day she walked into town with an umbrella and a large purse. On the way back, she stopped at Wendy's to get a hamburger for Whitey. Angie Odom had seen her for years and occasionally picked her up.

This time, as she got in the car, Joyce reeked of cat urine. The smell filled the car, and Angie thought she would throw up; certainly, she thought, the little girls in the back seat would. They parked and walked to a restaurant. Bella took the old lady's hand as they strolled along. It had likely been years since the old woman had held a child's hand. They sat together at the restaurant and ordered and ate, and Joyce Vinney's smell filled the table. They ordered her a glass of the first sweet tea she'd ever had. "That's good," Joyce said. As they spoke, Bella stood by the old woman and sniffed her arm and, to Angie's surprise, didn't gag.

Later they dropped Joyce off at home.

"That woman didn't smell good!" the other child said, as they pulled away.

Bella paused a moment.

"Yes, she did," she said. "She smelled like honey. I could smell her spirit and her soul."

Neuroscience V

"Craveable, Mind-Blowing Flavor"

We live in a time when drug traffickers behave like multinational corporations and corporations behave like traffickers.

Both seem to understand our brains the way our neuroscientists do and have resources to prod them.

Take Wendy's, the nation's number-two hamburger chain. Wendy's has a "Made to Crave" menu. Its burgers are displayed in almost pornographic close-up photos, which companies know are cues to binge. The ads' message: pure, orgiastic pleasure. Thick burgers sweat fat as they bulge from their buns; each ooze slatherings of cheese, or bacon, or barbecue sauce. (Marijuana growers long ago began to copy this technique, as well, with their well-lit "pot porn" shots of glistening, engorged buds.)

"Let's face it," reads a company press release, "foodies want maximum craveability and quickly get hooked on the Deliciously Different flavors Wendy's is known for." To this lineup Wendy's then added chicken sandwiches. Each sauce-dripping wonder, the company promised, is "packed with craveable, mind-blowing, unforgettable flavor."

Taco Bell jumped into promotion using the imagery of drug addiction with its Cravings campaign in 2020, showing a young man worn out, desperate, and wandering through the night—conjuring, to me, a meth user—jonesing for the corporation's nacho fries. The tag line: "He. Can't. Escape. The Craving."

Neither Wendy's nor Taco Bell originated the marketing of fast food as crave-worthy. That title appears to belong to McDonald's. In 1997, a McDonald's ad campaign exploited the understanding that its name alone was by now a brain cue to binge. "Customers will connect with the advertising because it presents situations that everyone has experienced, where the mere mention of McDonald's triggers cravings," a company vice president of marketing told CNN at the time.

It is a sign of where we are that Wendy's, Taco Bell, and McDonald's use the language of drug addiction—hooked, cravings, triggers—as evidence of their products' tastiness. Any addict, of course, knows the truth: cravings and triggers are torment, evidence of controlled brain chemistry. "Craveable, mind-blowing" is a product description the Sinaloa cartel might come up with.

A lot of this grew from the great competition of the twentieth century. Capitalism won the battle with communism, and happily so. It then lifted hundreds of millions of people from poverty. This stands as among the great achievements of justice and human realization in world history.

But capitalism lost something, too—the one thing it claimed was essential to human growth: competition. For most of its history, capitalism was like the gritty tool-and-die guy in his shop, battling to move ahead against loads of competitors. Adam Smith insisted that capitalism required a moral compass. But it didn't take long after the Berlin Wall fell before questioning any free-market result was deemed softhearted and wrongheaded. Today, for the first time since Smith described it in 1776 in *The Wealth of Nations*, capitalism has no competition anywhere in the world. Even China has KFC restaurants —5,200 of them.

In the United States, unions, one brake on capitalism, weakened. Another—our tax laws—favor the wealthy. We caved to corporate conglomeration and largely gave up the antitrust battles of previous generations that allowed smaller and newer companies a chance to compete. Competition, the essence of capitalism, was stifled. When industry after industry merged into a few participants with gigantic power, we viewed that as the natural law of the market, then wondered why wages weren't growing at the lower end of the economy. Along the way, we lauded the private sector and laughed at government. We viewed not paying taxes as some patriotic act. Around the globe, meanwhile, the rule of law in general—reining in various versions of capitalism—grew threadbare.

So, in a sense, capitalism today is a monopoly. Without competition, capitalism has bent toward the agglomeration of profit and power in the hands of relatively few families, corporations, industries, and governments. The coercion of twentieth-century dictatorships as methods of individual persuasion and control has been replaced by marketing, far more benign and effective. Meanwhile, vast rafts of people—entire regions even—sit becalmed in seas of poverty and resentment.

We live in a time of concentrated economic power. Big Tech. Big Oil. Big Pharma. Amazon. Facebook. Apple. Google. Walmart. In a remarkable book called *The Myth of Capitalism: Monopolies and the Death of Competition*, authors Jonathan Tepper and Denise Hearn insist that these concentrations of power behave like monopolies. They live to limit competition, to make markets, to rewrite rules, to increase prices and hold back wages, all in favor of the continued expansion of their economic power. "The average worker feels screwed," Tepper and Hearn write. "They are bargaining against monopolists and oligopolists when it comes to getting paid." Rural areas are where this is felt most acutely, they write, and this helps explain the urban-rural divide.

The effect of quasi-monopolies on our economy reminds me of what happens in our brains on drugs. Drugs limit or skew competition of natural chemicals within the brain to ensure their survival at the expense of our well-being.

Marketing deploys great energy to convince us of the pleasures of buying this or consuming that, no matter how unhealthy. Drugs do something similar to our brains. Both marketing and dope invite us to confuse pleasure with happiness or fulfillment. I came upon a YouTube video of a speech in which Dr. Robert Lustig contrasts pleasure and happiness. Pleasure, Lustig said, is fleeting; happiness is long-lived. Pleasure comes from taking or getting; happiness comes from giving. Pleasure is achieved alone; happiness with others. Pleasure comes from substances or things; happiness does not. Pleasure releases dopamine in our brains, the constant search for more; happiness releases serotonin, producing feelings of contentment, an end to consumption. All of which means, Lustig said, that pleasure can prod our reward pathways into addiction; happiness cannot.

"America has devolved," Lustig once wrote, "from the aspirational, achievement-oriented 'city on a hill' we once were, into the addicted and depressed society that we've now become. Because we abdicated happiness for pleasure. Because pleasure got cheap." The supply of it was everywhere. Like street dope.

Capitalism has been a titanic force for human advancement and innovation; opiates miraculously calm our pain. Yet unbound, both act to exterminate us. Opiates can train our brains to ignore our approaching demise. Capitalism markets products that poison us, and narcotizes us with such comfort and convenience that we scoff at signs of our approaching end.

When I met Nicole Avena, she told me this about sugar: "Potency is a big player. It's one reason why we're seeing these addictive responses. Products from thirty years ago didn't have concentrations of sugar like we see today. The [processed food and drink] people consume these days are dominated by sugar, and potency of sugar is so much greater than it was."

Unprecedented potency combined with unrelenting supply. That describes the illegal drug stream on American streets. Today, one drug primes a user for others.

In the United States, all this is etching and twisting our brain reward pathways in ways unknown even a few decades ago. The United States is the world's leading per capita consumer of both opioids and sugar.

As in a drug-controlled brain, what was intended to keep us alive now threatens us. Food is made addictive; animals sold for our consumption spawn new viruses; plastic, a boon to humanity when employed for long-term uses, turns nightmarish when immediately thrown away; social media designed to connect us has us at each other's throats; and fossil fuels disrupt the climate.

As I traveled the country, it occurred to me that our epidemic of addiction is an extreme expression of so much of this. We turned healthy self-reliance into a grim isolation. Then pain pills were marketed grotesquely and supplied beyond reason. They were overlaid on the mass marketing of legal, addictive substances. Beneath that lay reservoirs of childhood trauma, stress, depression, community destruction, and PTSD from fighting two wars using the same small minority of people while the rest of us got a tax cut.

So opioids that perform great miracles of pain relief now kill us. And from industrial chemicals indispensable to our modern prosperity, traffickers stir potions that send us out of our minds.

Meth VI

Pimps & Tents

O n the Sunday morning of Thanksgiving weekend of 2020, the sun breaks sharply across the cloudless blue sky over tent encampments dotting the areas around some of the best-known streets of Los Angeles—Hollywood, Sunset, and Santa Monica boulevards.

For all its beauty, its weather, and its wealth, Los Angeles is also the nation's homeless capital. It's been so for years. But homelessness is different now—more prolific, more stationary, less transient. Much of it now is rooted in the voluminous supplies of meth that Mexican traffickers' switch to the P2P method made possible. As that happened, another change was taking place that made the drug even more damaging, at least in Los Angeles.

Tents. They protect many homeless people from the elements. But they have another, far less benevolent role. Tents and the new meth seem made for each other. With a tent, the user could retreat not just mentally from the world but physically. Tents often became pods of exploitation where people used dope, sold dope, or performed acts that allowed them to procure it.

In Los Angeles, the city's unwillingness, or inability under judicial rulings, to remove the tents has allowed them to stay for weeks, sometimes months. Encampments resembled Third World shantytowns. The tents went from gifts of compassion to hives of crime, addiction, disease—and now pimping.

Just as Airbnb allows anyone with a house to run a hotel, anybody with a tent can start up a sidewalk bordello. No need for a motel room or an apartment. A pimp just needs a woman he can control. Plentiful methamphetamine achieves that goal. Its effects created a woman sufficiently numb and removed from reality to do tricks in a tent on the sidewalk.

In Los Angeles, transgender women proved particularly vulnerable. They came from other parts of the country looking for surgery, therapy, drugs, stardom. They came friendless, lost, pretty, and young, and often without family to return to. A meth-addicted transgender woman was thus easier than most to control.

And that was the story of Ariel, a woman who liked *The Little Mermaid* and whom I met while she was in rehab, two weeks off the street. "You're used as currency for the drugs," she told me.

Ariel had come from a small suburb of a midsize American city. She had arrived in Los Angeles hoping for sex-change surgery and saddled with a meth habit. She did some rehab, but eventually ended up alone on Hollywood streets.

"There's these camps in Hollywood, on Vine and other streets—distinct tent camps where this happens all the time," she said. "They're selling you to somebody for dope. A lot of people who aren't homeless have these tents. Come from out of the area to sell drugs, move guns, prostitute girls out of the tents. The last guy I was getting worked out by, he was charging people $25 a night to use his tents. He would give you girls, me and three other people. He'd take the money and we'd get paid in drugs."

One day early in her street life, standing at a bus stop on Santa Monica Boulevard, Ariel met a man lying on the sidewalk nearby. He had a tent. He was fifty-five. He was nice to her. She was badly bruised from the street, and he pretended to care. "I just wanted somebody to tell me I was pretty and give me some drugs. He lured me in." Ariel lived in his tent as he built around it a complex shanty that eventually consumed the entire bus stop. "The bus wouldn't even stop there anymore," she said.

Every couple of days a meth dealer would drop by. Her man would use with the dealer, then make some excuse and leave. "He'd leave for an hour or two to make sure I had enough time to do with this guy what I needed to do to secure more drugs."

All around her were tents where similar relationships were unfolding. Little communities of tent pimps, their girls, and meth.

The man told her he was a Crip gang member and had done twenty years in the pen. Ariel never knew what to believe. He did know how to manipulate. He was good at that. "Meth and pimps are connected," she told me. "Their whole life is manipulation and getting people to do what they want. They're just out of prison where they learn this as a way of life. They find the most vulnerable, fragile people and control them. Meth makes it so much easier."

Under the influence of this new meth on the streets, Ariel's addiction and hallucinations ramped up. One night she imagined lines of police officers outside a motel room. To escape, she jumped off its roof and realized when she hit the ground that no one was there at all. But the voices and images of people after her never let up. They screamed at her, threatening to rape and kill her, then they'd disappear—but never for long.

It was all part of the life of chaos she led, homeless and P2P-meth addicted. There were street husbands whose real names she never knew. She ate, then didn't for a while. She slept in tents, sometimes in a motel room, or behind bushes on the street.

After more than a year of that, she was taken in at a house run by some Crips. These were younger guys, more aggressive, always armed. They trafficked guns and girls in houses—never in tents.

In fact, later it occurred to her that all around her always through those two years on the street were Crip pimps: Shoreline Crips, Crenshaw Mafia Crips, Insane Crips in Long Beach. She also saw Piru Bloods, 18th Street, and MS-13. It was as if the gangsters making headlines in the 1990s went to prison and came out two decades later in their forties, alone and without family. For some of these older gang members, it seemed that pimping girls on P2P meth in fetid homeless tents was the only job decades of incarceration had prepared them for.

The younger ones, not seeing their future in those old guys in tents, were more violent. They were, Ariel saw, what Crippin' had become. The Crips—fragmented into dozens of large cliques—had mostly stopped their warring, part of Los Angeles's general retreat from gang violence for the last dozen years. They transferred those energies to crimes that make money—selling drugs and guns, credit-card fraud, smash-and-grab jewelry store robberies. And pimping.

Ariel spent about a year working in Crip houses in Hollywood and South Central Los Angeles. It was still chaotic, but there was a shower every day, and always there was meth. The supplies were unending. She calculated that in one twelve-month period, she spent only $40 on the drug, though she used it several times a day. It was always given to her.

The men who ran these houses used Ariel and other girls as testers for their methamphetamine. They gave her stuff that immediately felt different from the meth she used in tents. It was 2018, just as meth and fentanyl were being mixed and sold together. "Suddenly, I wasn't really hallucinating anymore," she told me. "I could distinguish the voices in my head; they weren't as vivid as before." Then, strangely, she began nodding out. That never happens on meth, which is a stimulant; yet here she was falling asleep.

She bought test strips, which indicate when a street drug contains fentanyl. She dipped the strips in the meth they were giving her. Each time the test strip came up positive for fentanyl. She realized this was why she was nodding out. They needed her as a guinea pig to ensure their meth/fentanyl mix wasn't going to kill customers. If she died, it was too strong.

Perhaps, too, she thought, they gave her these concoctions because working girls on P2P meth went out of control, babbling, screaming. This was tolerated in a tent on the street. But pimps working girls in houses couldn't make money with a woman in such a state of mind.

Fentanyl seemed to calm her meth-induced psychosis, her hallucinations. "I never had in-depth conversations with these people," Ariel said. "They're not deep individuals. They're telling me, 'Make me money or I'm going to hurt you.' But I one-hundred-percent believe that had to do with why they gave me that meth mixed with fentanyl. They knew what they were doing."

When she needed a break, she visited Cowboy, who had a spacious tent installation on Highland Avenue in Hollywood. Cowboy sold dope and pimped girls. "He was the kingpin for a little bit," she said. "I never worked for him. I only went there when things were crazy with other people. I used him as a hideout." He also accumulated what he called a "bike shop"—dozens of stolen bicycles, handlebars, frames, tires.

Ariel never rode a bike, but everywhere on the street were meth addicts on bikes. Nothing indicated meth-induced homelessness like a bicycle fixation. Stolen bikes went hand in hand with the drug. Bikes allowed for mobility for people without cars. P2P meth seems to provoke the hoarding of junk, which is why tent encampments are so often full of bizarre collections of seemingly useless stuff. Bikes allowed a user to travel greater distances looking for junk. In the homeless P2P meth world, bikes became currency, easily exchanged for dope. "Bike shops" popped up across Los Angeles as both tents and meth spread.

Later on, in the rehab facility where I met her, Ariel would wonder how she survived. She left the streets with the help of a Hollywood social worker, who yanked her from a tent and found her a drug-rehab bed. Detoxed from meth and away from street pimps, she said, "It's been a process of retraining my mind that [these men] are not who they say they are."

This retraining took time. In the tent encampments, the pimps and the other girls felt like family, with their constant bickering and melodrama, occasional violence, and togetherness. She felt like she was sinning against that, Ariel said, telling me all this. The whole experience resembled a cult that way, she thought later, a cult made possible by meth and tents.

HOW DID THIS new meth achieve that? How did it make a person want the drug, even as it kept her on the streets, pimped, hallucinating? Even as it destroyed her?

Some partial answer to this question occurred to me after a trip to Columbus, Ohio, where I visited the ER at Riverside Methodist Hospital one winter day. The night before, police found a forty-year-old man wandering, talking nonsense. In years past they might have taken him to the jail's drunk tank. But Columbus is one town that has taken seriously the addiction crisis's mantra: "We can't arrest our way out of this."

Like many American towns, though, Columbus has invested little in mental-health housing. So if jails won't do, police often take people in this man's condition to Riverside's emergency room. The next morning, as mood stabilizers calmed the patient, the ER staff learned more about him: he suffered from anxiety, and maybe he was bipolar, though it was too soon to tell; his mother was bipolar. Perhaps at the root of it all, staffers were not surprised to learn, he had been molested as a child. Overlaid on that traumatic past now was the new crystal methamphetamine.

"When I first came [in 2015] we never saw meth," said Dr. Megan Schabbing, a psychiatrist and director of the ER's psychiatric ward. The city then was grappling with opioid addiction. Riverside opened its ER psychiatric ward to deal with those patients as police stopped taking them to jail. But nothing quite prepared the hospital for P2P meth.

This began, if Megan Schabbing is any gauge, in May 2018, about the time she and the staff were getting used to treating patients on fentanyl. "Within a week, it was multiple people coming in on meth," she remembered. "Elaborate delusional sentiments, violent. I watched a guy run through a set of very hard doors. We call it supermeth.

They're brought in by police, bashing in car windows, walking into a stranger's house. They appear to be psychotic, look like they're schizophrenic. But when they're off the drug, they're not.

Riverside spent millions of dollars to retrofit its ER to become more like a jail. Sixteen of its 92 rooms now have televisions encased in metal. Video cameras in the rooms watch each patient. Beige metal garage doors slide down and seal off the monitors, cords, and wires that these patients have used to harm themselves or others. The ER for years showed football games on TV on Sundays, but it stopped because the waiting rooms were filled with folks beset by mental illness induced or magnified by the new meth.

Schabbing's job description was retrofitted as well. Her job now became digging into underlying causes of the drug use of men and women who ended up in Riverside's ER. Most often there was trauma: beatings, molestation, rape, war deployment, childhood chaos, or neglect. For many of these patients, she discovered, the delusions fueled by the new meth became the point—the drug's attraction. "Most would tell me, 'I can stay out of reality on the street with this super-meth. The meth is cheaper and can keep me high longer,'" she said. "When they come to us, it takes them days to figure out who and where they are. But that's not a bad thing if you're on the street."

If P2P meth made them homeless, it also helped them bear it.

Meth VII

Colt

By 2018, P2P meth was all over America. This was the result not of one mastermind but rather of a roiling, unbridled free market that produced colossal quantities of the drug then found ingenious ways for passing it through heavily guarded walls at the border. Meth thus made it to all corners of America, in something resembling how thoroughly prescription pain pills blanketed the country two decades before. Still, that was the production end in Mexico. I wanted to understand the retail, street level in the United States that was just as important in allowing this to happen. In that search, I met a man I'll call Colt, whose story helped.

Colt had grown up sheltered in a Baptist church in a small town in a southern state. His father was a church deacon; his mother taught Sunday school. Colt was twenty-three when one Friday night at a party, the way he tells it, friends pushed him to use cocaine. They insisted, and he relented. That was it. For years he couldn't get enough of it. Eventually he began to sell it, until a bust in Atlanta cut off his sources.

His coke addiction consumed the next several years. Then in 2013, an old cocaine connection called him from California. He was selling meth now. Did Colt want in? Colt did. One reason P2P crystal meth spread so completely across America, Colt told me, was because a distribution network was already in place. Traffickers used the dealers they were supplying with Colombian cocaine to sell the meth they made themselves. "Everybody just switched to meth," Colt told me. "That's exactly what I did. The guys I was getting it from did; the guys I was selling it to did."

His connection began sending him a pound of meth a week. "It was untouched, shards the size of your hand," he said. "Everybody was blown away by it."

Colt visited his connection in Los Angeles. "I was the man in our little bitty town," he said. "I wanted to see the stuff nobody else gets to see." He flew to L.A. and they drove through the town of South Gate, a suburb southeast of Los Angeles, to the place where his connection bought his dope. For three blocks before they arrived, his connection was pointing out guys on bikes, on foot, each with a cell phone, a network of look-outs watching for cops. They came to a one-story, three-bedroom house. "Don't say anything," the connection said. Inside, every room was filled with four-foot stacks of hundreds of Tupperware containers filled with meth, each duct-taped to be shipped across America. For a country boy like Colt, first time in L.A., face to face with what he was part of, it was a scary sight. They didn't stay long.

Back home, the meth supplies Colt was receiving pushed the price from $100 a gram down to $30. His connection was eager to sell him whatever he wanted.

A good chunk of what Colt sold, he said, was to people trading goods stolen from Walmart. Walmart was another reason meth spread quickly to small towns and rural parts of America.

This did not surprise me. I routinely encountered users and dealers who told me that a large though unmeasurable amount of the drug trade in their area was fueled by goods stolen from Walmart. I ran into this a lot writing *Dreamland*, and found more of it as I traveled the country after the book was published.

By the early 2000s the retail giant had consumed many locally owned businesses, leveling Main Streets in small towns, regurgitating the goods they sold onto the floors of Walmart stores. Children's shoes, steaks, electronics, tools, perfume—it was all there under one roof. All of it could be stolen and traded to dealers for dope.

Meanwhile, the chain cut back on a lot of what might have helped deter shoplifting. Lee Scott, Walmart's chairman from 2000 to 2009— the years when the opiate addiction crisis was gathering force—came in to boost profits by cutting costs. Workers already weren't paid a lot. Under Scott, Walmart stores cut staff on the floor and greeters at the entrances, all of which deterred crime. It seemed to me that their store design already encouraged shoplifting, with dimmer lights compared to other stores, no videos in restrooms or at blind corners. With automatic cashiers at the exits, shoppers could spend an entire outing at Walmart and not see an employee.

In a good many towns, Walmart was the only store. In others, it was one of the few, coexisting with a supermarket, maybe a Big Lots or a JCPenney. Either way, I found, no chain had a reputation among drug users for being easier to rip off than Walmart. I heard this over and over. They avoided Target because of its wider aisles and brighter lights. Whatever the dealers wanted in exchange for their dope was usually available at Walmart. The chain offered an easy shopping experience—and an easy shoplifting experience, as well.

"It was convenient," said Monica Tucker, who runs a drug rehab center in eastern Tennessee but was a meth addict for seven years, and supported her habit at Walmart. "Anything you were requested to get [by the dealer], you could find it there. We stole lots of food. We weren't eating because we were on meth, but everybody else was hungry at the dope dealer's house."

With opioids, then later with meth, plentiful drug supply was paired with this easy source of goods to barter. Had there been the same vibrant Main Streets, ecosystems of the locally owned stores that were the lifeblood of many owners who lived in town and returned their profits to it, both the opioid crisis and the meth problem might have spread less quickly in many parts of the country.

Walmart's focus was not on deterring shoplifting, but on catching suspects and calling the police. Thus the ways of ripping off Walmart grew legion. One woman Colt knew had a purse lined with what he took to be aluminum foil to blunt the store sensors. Police spent huge amounts of their time at their local Walmarts processing shoplifters that the chain hadn't invested money in deterring. Under Lee Scott, Walmart's profits increased 249 percent. But Walmart stores made theft easy in many towns just as the population of drug addicts was exploding.

The town of Paducah, Kentucky, was one place that studied the Walmart effect on crime and police time. Fifteen percent of the department's crime reports, the town discovered, came from two Walmart stores. Cops were always at the store processing suspects. Some officers spent their shifts at the store. "The [shoplifting] reduction strategy for the Walmart stores was for [Paducah police] to do more," a city report noted. At one point, police administrators met with store managers, asking them to help deter the crime. The managers bristled at the idea, insisting that it was officers' job to come when they detained a shoplifter. Finally, Paducah police decided not to send officers to the store for thefts under $500 in value, leaving it to Walmart employees to file reports online. Police weren't sure how much of what was stolen funded drug consumption. But "if you were to remove Walmart, you would see a very different picture of crime locally," Mike Zidar, a Paducah police crime analyst, told me.

(I contacted Walmart to see what they had to say. No one from the chain got back to me.)

With enormous properties and few staff to watch them, some Walmart parking lots also became prime spots for drug deals. The stores supplied drug-world matériel: scales to weigh drugs, the Magic Bullet blenders used to mix heroin and fentanyl. Dealers would deplete the supplies of baby formula, used to cut cocaine or heroin, and kerosene, needed to cook methamphetamine when the "shake and bake" method was in vogue.

I met Jason, who spent the Lee Scott years working at Walmarts in Kentucky and Ohio. The demands on managers of Scott's cost-cutting pitted one against the other, he said. Staff was scarce, he said, and store departments had a sloppy look. The feeling spread in many stores that no one cared. "It reminded me of the street world, inside a building."

"People get in certain situations and will do what they have to," said one veteran Walmart manager I interviewed. "About half the stuff stole from Walmart they sell to get their money for drugs. The other part is stealing for food to feed their families."

Colt's meth business owed a lot to Walmart. Many addicts stole merchandise then redeemed it for gift cards. Colt got a lot of these from his customers, back when the chain gave gift cards for exchanged new items even without a receipt. One of his customers obtained a key to the Walmart laptop cage from a friend who worked at the store. Colt took in several stolen laptops, as well as flat-screen TVs that weren't under lock and key at Walmart. Some of his customers piled the TVs into their cars so fast that the screens broke. Colt would give them next to nothing in dope. Then he'd buy the same TV from Walmart, return with the broken TV and his new receipt and get a refund.

Through all this, the meth supplies rolled in, Colt told me. "I was living the dream," he said. At the height of his meth dealing, Colt had nine Jet Skis, a camper, a Range Rover and a BMW M6, a safe full of guns, and loads of Christmas presents for his kids. Every three months he took a vacation cruise. "When I got my first BMW, people would stop and take pictures of me at the red light," he said. His celebrity status was intoxicating.

Meanwhile, his dope alighted on a hometown that had already been through the pain-pill epidemic that consumed much of his generation. This was the other reason meth met such a warm welcome across America: so many towns where it hit were reeling from opioids. In Colt's town, these were kids of parents who'd done well, had pensions, but the only work these young people could find in town were tedious factory jobs. Without much to do, a lot of his generation got hooked on pills, then moved to heroin. They bought meth believing it would ease their heroin withdrawals, and they ended up full-time meth users.

Colt was indicted in 2014. He bailed out and for the next two years was free, using and selling the meth from California. His addiction was ferocious, and nothing could take him away from it. Authorities made him an offer of many years in prison. Colt thought he'd fight it, took it to trial, and lost. He spent the next two years in jail waiting to be sentenced.

At first, locked up, he thought constantly about the drug and how to get it. Supplies in town were limited now that he was no longer selling. Now in jail and away from the drug, his head slowly cleared, his body rebalanced, and the desire faded. Nevertheless, he had changed the market. Now his town was full of meth users. He was still in jail a year after his trial when new sources began bringing meth to town in quantities even Colt hadn't seen. A few inmates in jail had shards of it. Colt surprised himself by refusing it.

At his sentencing, the local DA put on the stand officers who testified that Colt was about the biggest drug dealer in the area. His family begged the judge to show mercy. He was an addict who needed help and would respond to it. They hired a psychologist to testify to that. In the end, his addiction and lack of a prior conviction helped. The judge accumulated the time against him: fifteen years. But, she said, "I'm going to give you one more chance. You can prove me right or prove me wrong." So he was sentenced to a residential drug treatment program, with prison hanging over his head if he was caught again.

Colt completed the treatment and now lives in a bigger town far from where he grew up. He's a foreman, still sober, works as much overtime as he can, and paid $20,000 in taxes in 2020. All the toys he accumulated while selling meth are gone, seized or sold.

"I'm starting all over," he said the last time we spoke, as I continued my search to understand why P2P meth had spread coast to coast. "I'm still scared. I have nightmares two nights a week about being in jail."

Meth VIII

Rashad

As I traveled, I met another man who helped me understand how meth had spread in such unprecedented quantities across America.

As we spoke, he told me the story of one of the two most memorable nights of his life. It happened on a fall Friday in Columbus, Ohio, under in 2001. A football descended from the dark sky toward a young man, number 20, streaking down the field.

Rashad Martin was fourteen then, only a freshman at Walnut Ridge High School.

He was fast, with good hands, and played defense. It was midseason at cornerback and he already had a half dozen interceptions. He was one reason why the Walnut Ridge Scots dominated that year.

That night, against Eastmoor Academy, the older starting receiver was playing poorly. So the coach sent in Rashad. "You can catch anything," his coach told him. "Just run straight. Beat the man who plays your position—beat him and catch the ball."

Moments later, as he raced past his defender and that ball spun through the air to Rashad Martin, panting and arms outstretched, there seemed, for a brief second, nothing he might not do. The football came down into his hands. His team won, though years later he could no longer remember the score.

He was raised on Napoleon Avenue, a street in east Columbus where kids grew up unprotected. Napoleon cuts north-south through an African American neighborhood, abutting the tiny suburb of Whitehall. It exists isolated in many ways from the rest of Ohio's capital. The people on Napoleon were mostly women and children. Families had lived there for decades, but in the 1990s few of them were men over thirty. Many men were in prison for drug deals or shootings; others had been murdered. Rashad's father was shot to death by a youngster in a drug deal when his son was one year old. Rashad's mother raised three children alone and worked a city job. The street was a cloistered community, one young man told me, where "we took care of each other." The rest of Columbus didn't seem to matter, or enter.

As Rashad reached adolescence, it was part of street life that Napoleon's promising young men display their gumption by selling drugs—mostly crack, but also heroin and pot. They sold in search of something more—more money, more stuff, a claim to importance, respect. Asked how many of Napoleon's young men sold on the street, one of them, himself incarcerated, told me, "It'd be easier to say how many wasn't."

Rashad was of an entrepreneurial bent, keen to help his mother pay bills and possess the stuff that meant he was no longer poor. He never used drugs, but he saw older guys sell crack and saw the money was good. At fourteen, the year he caught that touchdown pass, they let him work, slinging small amounts to cars that drove up. After his first weekend working, he went to an indoor flea market with the hundred dollars he made and bought video games for the PlayStation his mother had given him for Christmas.

By sixteen, he and six or eight of his friends were fully involved. "We was all together every single day," he said. Rashad was making $800 a week. He'd get home from selling crack in time for his mother to arrive from work. His money helped the family pay bills. At night he was upstairs doing his homework. "I'd do my hours on the corner, but by the time she got home, I'd be in the room studying. I knew I had to stay in school for my mother not to know what's going on." By eighteen he was the man around the neighborhood, a leader of the guys his age who grew up on Napoleon.

He never missed school. He had new clothes and shoes, good grades, and talent in sports, which meant attention from girls. "Who wouldn't want to go to school with all that?" He went to high school by day, football practice in the afternoon, and after that he was selling crack on Napoleon to make his money. He transferred high schools twice, looking for the football recognition that would lead to a college scholarship. By his senior year at suburban Reynoldsburg High School, on a team that didn't do well, crack's quick money had taken the place of football in his life. Whatever promise America held for him was wrapped up in it.

He graduated in May 2005. He hadn't even had time to think about where his life was going before he changed it irrevocably. Two weeks after his graduation, he shot and wounded a man on Napoleon who he believed was about to rob his buddies. Turned out it was a police officer. Rashad went to prison for ten years.

His years in prison were spent fending off fights, taking every prison program he could find. There weren't many. He read a lot—self-help books mostly, on how to be a man, how to control emotions and postpone gratification.

He got out in 2015, a stocky, handsome, light-skinned Black man in long dreadlocks. Napoleon Avenue, he saw, was looking rough—boarded-up houses, youngsters robbing and shooting, police coming through. He looked for work. Walmart. Meijer supermarket. Construction jobs here and there. Nobody wanted a felon, much less one with a police-officer shooting on his record. Now twenty-eight, Rashad Martin found himself asking family for money to eat, for clothes.

Then he met a woman who sold Percocets, the prescription pain relievers containing acetaminophen and the opioid oxycodone. Rashad knew nothing about any opioid epidemic. No African American he knew used these pills. He had no idea how to sell them. "You don't gotta cut it. Everybody's doing them," the woman told him. "When people ask, tell them thirty dollars apiece."

He began selling Percocets to middle-class White kids in downtown Columbus bars. "I never understood it, never got into it," he told me. "I just was doing it because it was bringing money in." Before long he was selling five to six hundred pills every week, eventually buying them from the woman's brother.

One day, the brother was out of Percocets. "Maybe you can get rid of this," he said, and held up a baggie containing a chunky white substance. Rashad thought it was crack.

The dealer laughed. "Naw, that ain't crack. That's meth. That's ice."

Rashad had never seen methamphetamine. It was another thing White people did.

"It's the next thing," the dealer said.

Rashad didn't know where he might sell it, but a friend said he knew a woman, and she became a steady client. Through her, he met a young man who bought everything he had. Soon, Rashad Martin was selling pounds of a drug he'd never seen a month before to this kid.

Seeing this, another friend, a marijuana dealer, told him to come over one day. At the apartment was a tall man, up from Mexico. He spoke poor English. Rashad came to call him the Big Dude. "This guy don't believe that you can run through this stuff like you're telling me," the friend told Rashad. The Big Dude had five pounds of meth, asking $6,000 a pound. Rashad took it and came back three days later with a bag of money, having sold each pound for $12,500.

The Mexican took his cut of the money and flew back to wherever he was from. The next week, a package the size of a briefcase arrived at the dealer's house. In it was something that looked to Rashad like an air vent, made of metal. They wore goggles as they used an electric saw to cut open the cover. They peeled it back, and inside were ten pounds of methamphetamine.

Rashad sold this to the kid, who seemed to have endless connections in Fairfield County, just south of Columbus. After that, a metal air vent arrived every week. When they met again, the Mexican was thrilled. "My hunch was his circle of guys, his family or whatever, got all this dope and they don't know who can move it," Rashad told me. "When

I got to his attention, he was like 'Yes!' Anyway, that's when it got crazy." It was the spring of 2017.

Though addiction tends to cross all barriers and boundaries, drugs can divide along racial lines. From the days when California bikers made meth, it had been exclusively a working-class White drug. Years later Mexicans began to cook it, and in time Latinos began to use it. Yet no user, dealer, or narcotics officer I've spoken to can remember an African American who used or sold methamphetamine.

The new supplies of P2P meth changed that. As Mexican traffickers aggressively pushed the glut of new merchandise, more of the drug world migrated into meth. One reason meth spread so completely across the United States was that this included, for the first time, African American dealers in region after region. By making so much of the drug, Mexican traffickers, wittingly or not, opened a mid-level and street sales infrastructure to meth that the drug hadn't had access to before. America's history bequeathed the country a marginalized population of Black men made vulnerable by stunted life opportunities and an abiding sense of being left out or left behind. Now meth was more available nationwide and traffickers were eager to supply it. The supplies of meth coming from Mexico meant that money and connections to the drug were easy to make and both in quantities unimaginable before. For the first time, African American dealers gravitated toward it.

Leveraging this sales network happened gradually. By 2014, Skid Row's Crip gangs had switched from selling crack to meth. In the Midwest, by the end of 2016, African American dealers were taking up this new business opportunity, though knowing little about the drug they were selling. In Louisville, it was Wiley Greenhill's organization. In the Columbus area, the person first at the center of that change was Rashad Martin, with his new, unexpected connection to this Mexican, with whom he could barely communicate yet was eager to send him all the meth he wanted.

Rashad supplied all the friends he'd sold crack with on Napoleon. He gave them a special price of $2,500 a pound. One young man remembers Rashad at the house with what looked to him like "a bag full of broken glass." "Once 'Shad started making his money," he told me, "he made sure everybody around him was trying to make some money. He put a lot of people in position to do well."

Word spread among the African American drug world in Columbus about Rashad Martin and this new dope. "I'm telling my friend that this is producing some real money," Rashad said. "He telling everybody, 'You got to get into this.'"

While all his friends were buying chains and gold teeth with the money they made, Rashad was socking his cash away. One night friends were at his apartment, heading to a strip club. Rashad went upstairs to put money in his safe. The cash wouldn't fit. "I'll catch up with you later," he yelled down to them. That night he spent hours counting his money for the first time. More than $100,000.

He sat back, stunned. That packed safe fulfilled something of the promise he'd felt he had within him ever since he caught that ball running down the field in ninth grade. Later he would remember it as the second most memorable night of his life. With the money packed away, he quickly felt broke again, which is what he wanted. He prized his ability to postpone gratification, like an entrepreneur.

By now his phone was often clogged with calls from people on Napoleon asking for help. He bought diapers for pregnant women, paid rent for mothers. Meth made him the street's benefactor. "Knowing that I can help the ones I love around me," he told me, "that's what made me feel cool."

In September 2017 he rented a two-story house in a new subdivision built on farmland east of Columbus, far from where anyone he knew would look. He outfitted it with four 80-inch televisions and bought himself a Dodge Challenger.

He found more customers in Fairfield County, which is 90 percent White and largely rural. His customers, and their customers, the way he understood it, were heroin addicts switching to methamphetamine. Meth was said to help with heroin withdrawals.

One day in November 2017 he told the Big Dude: I'm selling the stuff you send me within two or three days. I can handle more.

The Mexican didn't speak much English, but Rashad understood what he said next clearly enough.

For the next three days, the Big Dude said, don't leave your house.

So he didn't. Rashad holed up at home, ordering pizza and playing *Call of Duty* on his 80-inch. On the third day a knock came at his door.

He opened it, and there stood a Mexican man he didn't know.

"Can you open your garage?" the man said. In the driveway stood a Jeep Wrangler. Rashad opened the garage and the man pulled his Wrangler in and shut the garage door. Over the next ten minutes Rashad stayed in the house and listened to noises from the garage. Then the man knocked again. The Wrangler was outside. "Close the garage," he said. The Mexican drove off, and Rashad never saw him again. In the garage sat a large truck tire around a rim.

A friend came over with a machine to remove the rim. Inside the tire, snug as sardines, were fifty tubular packages, sixteen inches long, three inches in diameter, each bundled in plastic wrap and covered in hot pepper and mustard. Inside each tube was a vacuum-packed baggie of methamphetamine, weighing a little more than a pound, in the form of clear shards of what looked like glass; when one shard hit another, they clinked. Sixty pounds of meth.

This had turned into something bigger than he'd ever imagined. The Big Dude could not be all that big in the drug world he occupied, or he wouldn't be making sales calls to Columbus, Ohio. Yet he seemed to have more meth than he could get rid of.

What's more, the Big Dude now wanted only $1,500 a pound—a fourth of what he'd been asking just two months before. Rashad sold the new stuff quickly. From then on, twice a week, the Mexican shipped more than fifty pounds of meth to a Columbus business, where Rashad would collect it, drive it to a safe location, and dispense it among his friends. Money just rolled in. A woman doing Rashad's laundry called to tell him that he'd forgotten $20,000 in his pockets. His photo showed up on posters for a party at a club, advertising the fact that he'd be attending. They asked him to make an appearance. He was a star. He spent twenty minutes walking through the crowd that night, then left.

Meanwhile, his neighborhood largesse increased. "I took care of my whole street. It was looking bad, and I wanted to bring it back to life." Because no one on the street used meth, the money went straight into people's lives.

He went on Facebook on Mother's Day and told a hundred women that he was thinking of a number between 1 and 100 and would give presents to the twenty who came closest. He spent the next day driving around meeting the women, giving them $500 in cash. He called families to get their kids together and paid for them to go to the Zoombezi Bay water park, north of town. He bought a car or two for families he knew.

He fronted meth to several youngsters on the block who were barely getting by selling crack, a business that was fading. The way he saw it, they could make money and not go around robbing others. One of his friends, with years into street dealing, told him one night that he'd never accumulated more than $20,000 at one time. Selling Rashad's new dope, he had $200,000.

Napoleon's desperation seemed to recede. "Everybody started doing well on their own," Rashad said. "It stopped the police from being up there all the time because people wasn't shooting and robbing. People stopped calling my phone so much needing me to do stuff because everybody started doing well on their own."

Rashad began to spend his money, too. He rented a mansion in Las Vegas for his birthday. He hired a party promoter, who put Rashad's photo on a Las Vegas billboard, standing on the balcony of the mansion in a black-and-red sweatshirt with "Richy Rich" in gold across his chest. The billboard's fine print claimed that half of the Pittsburgh Steelers football team would be there.

Rashad flew twenty friends to Las Vegas. More than sixty people showed up that night, including several Pittsburgh Steelers, his favorite football team. He hung out with famous rappers. He was far from

Napoleon now. "I'm around people who have hundreds of millions of dollars, and I know I'm not no little person no more."

For the next few months he partied in Charlotte, Detroit, Atlanta. Supplies kept coming up from Mexico twice a week. He'd fly into Columbus, take care of the load, then head out on another trip.

He marveled at how his life had changed. He actually never wanted drugs. The football that fell out of the night sky into his hands that Friday night his freshman year seemed to promise more than this. He had imagined himself a business owner one day, but if this was how it had to be, then a lot of easy meth money wasn't bad. He knew no one who used it and never saw the cratering faces, nor heard the howlings of those wandering the early-morning streets.

Then, in June 2018, it all came apart. He and nine others were arrested in what police called Operation Crystal Clear. Rashad Martin pleaded guilty. With the officer shooting on his record, and no record of addiction, he was sentenced to fourteen years in state prison, which is where I spoke to him.

As in Colt's small town, or Louisville following the Wiley Greenhill–Jose Prieto connection, the Columbus meth market was transformed. Supplies of meth now seemed endless, as other dealers found Mexican connections eager to supply them.

When I last spoke with him, Rashad talked of one day owning a legitimate business. He'd heard that a few of the friends he grew up with on Napoleon may have moved into legal endeavors—perhaps using the meth money as capital they'd likely never get a bank to loan them.

"I believe that anything I put my mind to, I can be good at, but other things take more time," he told me, the last time we spoke. "This happened overnight. I could have stopped doing it. I had enough. I just felt so many people needed me. It's hard to stop when your phone is buzzing. So many calls from people. They need me to help. It's hard to stop when you're helping out not just families, but neighborhoods."

"It's hard to say, 'Naw, I'm done.'" Money will do that.

Sacklers V

"We Feel Absolutely Terrible"

O ne night in April of 2019 in a gentrifying section of Queens, New York, a crowd assembles at a majestic three-story turn-of-the-twentieth-century factory that is now a space for weddings and photo shoots.

The crowd tonight is here for a performance-art piece. The piece centers around Joss Sackler. Ms. Sackler has a PhD in linguistics; she owns a clothing line; she employs an entire PR team; she is said to be very interested in "women's issues." She is, above all, the wife of David Sackler, who is the son of Richard Sackler. Both men had resigned from Purdue Pharma's board of directors a year earlier.

Tonight's event is billed as *Joss et Ses Amis.* That is French for "Joss and Her Friends." But the event also has a subtitle. It's in English: "Undeterred." *Joss et Ses Amis: Undeterred.* Tickets are $700. The event will feature "curated wines." Ms. Sackler greets arrivals in a flowing, floor-length gown—a blue Elizabeth Kennedy, *Town & Country* reports. Her guests mingle as waiters serve them those curated wines. Then the crowd is escorted into another part of the building.

The evening takes place as anger grows nationwide at the Sacklers for the role that Purdue and OxyContin played in igniting the nation's epidemic of opioid addiction. Apparently undeterred indeed, Ms. Sackler, her flowing gown rustling, climbs a platform and the performance begins. She stands before the crowd in the pose of a discus thrower, while an artist cuts off pieces of her very expensive designer gown, then blowtorches more of it. The platform rotates. The artist spray-paints both Ms. Sackler and what remains of her Elizabeth Kennedy. A woman off to the side whistles a German folk song. Rock photographer Lynn Goldsmith documents the scene. As the performance winds down, Ms. Sackler is apparently overcome by the paint fumes. She collapses, to the gasps of the guests, but then revives to their whoops and hollers.

Mingling at a table afterward, while speaking with the fashion-model daughters of Rolling Stones guitarist Keith Richards, Ms. Sackler suddenly pulls down part of what remains of her gown and reveals to the crowd her left breast. For this, she receives more cheers.

AS THE CRISIS of opioid addiction proceeded, you would search in vain for much from a Sackler that felt like a sincere expression of anguish for their countrymen and women. Instead their news clippings revolved around how unfair the media coverage was—that Americans sought a villain, were ganging up on them, ignoring their philanthropy, that OxyContin was only a small part of the painkiller market. (The family would later publish a website—judgeforyourselves.info—denying personal responsibility, insisting the narrative that OxyContin caused the epidemic was flawed.)

Indeed, it is folly to attribute this epidemic to one drug, one company, one family—like the bad guys in some soap opera. So much more went into it. We Americans, so many of us, demanded convenience, to be fixed, wanting miracles and unwilling to do the work of wellness, unwilling to change what we bought, ate, and drank. We insisted doctors cure all our pain. Pills seemed to fit the bill. Insurance companies stopped reimbursing for therapies that did not involve pills, leaving doctors with fewer tools to address pain.

What's more, OxyContin did provide, as the family said later in a statement, "life-changing relief" from pain for many Americans. It's unconscionable that a too-common result of the opioid epidemic is that doctors cut off patients from their pain medication when they have used them without problem for years. But then, if Purdue had marketed OxyContin in a more restrained way, we might be lining up to praise it.

Purdue had nowhere near the pharmaceutical industry's largest sales force. Other companies, some much larger than Purdue, were marketing opioids, too. Arizona-based Insys bribed doctors to prescribe its fentanyl-based Subsys painkiller, and hired a stripper named Sunrise Lee as a sales rep to help convince physicians with lap dances; she was eventually promoted to regional sales director. The government tried and convicted five Insys executives under the federal RICO statute—Racketeering Influenced and Corrupt Organizations— which is commonly used to target Mafia dons and gang leaders. Insys CEO John Kapoor was sentenced to five years.

Johnson & Johnson awarded high-selling reps of its painkiller Nucynta with Caribbean cruises and home theater systems. "You only have 1 responsibility," wrote a senior sales manager at Mallinckrodt, a drug distributor and one of the largest manufacturers of generic oxycodone, in an email in 2013. "SELL BABY SELL!"

That was the gung-ho motto of the Opioid Era in America and many companies jumped in. But Purdue embodied the era. The company's main product—virtually its only product—was an addictive narcotic, sold with outlandish claims about its risk-free nature, targeting overworked doctors and nurse practitioners with little training in pain management, by highly incentivized salespeople in a company run by a family-dominated board who saw its annual payouts connected to that product's sales and sought always to increase "cash flow" from the enterprise.

OxyContin tended to take patients up to towering daily levels of use. This was particularly true of the high-dose versions—40 mg, 80 mg—in the high quantities that Purdue reps prodded doctors to prescribe. Some doctors then cut off their patients; other patients lost their insurance. Either way, many of those patients migrated to the street market for prescription painkillers, where prices were a dollar per milligram. People habituated to 200 or 300 mg a day could not afford that. So they migrated again—to potent, cheaper heroin from Mexican traffickers, who had awakened to this new market. The first people I met who switched to heroin did so in the late 1990s, early in the life of OxyContin.

OxyContin, flogged by Purdue sales reps, did a lot to create our new wide market for heroin, which never existed when the opioids on the street were Vicodin, Percocet, and others. Those pills were mixed with acetaminophen as an abuse deterrent. Those who abused them did enormous damage to their internal organs, so their habits remained minor. They rarely grew desperate enough to make the leap to heroin. Indeed, for years there was no bridge from these prescription pain-killers to heroin—until OxyContin. As the trafficking underworld exploited the new heroin market the company's product did so much to create, it discovered fentanyl to be a more profitable option. Fentanyl's story on the streets of America is rooted in the demand for opioids created by the unprecedented supply of the pills that began with the release of OxyContin in 1996.

Amid this cataclysm, *Joss et Ses Amis* seemed just more evidence that the family possessed no feel for how poorly it came off. Stockholders might have seen the damage. They might have pushed the company to action, to diversify the company, rely on more than just revenue from an opioid, or related products. But the Sacklers did not. Perhaps OxyContin revenues had been too intoxicating for too long. Money will do that.

Just as the Sacklers socialized only with America's wealthiest, they occupied a similarly impervious bubble as Purdue's sole owners. New ideas had trouble filtering through. Bad news was not fodder for intro-spection. The family's attitude was that "the press has got it all wrong," said a former Purdue employee. "It was a PR problem—that was their view of the world."

The message of the late Howard Udell, the company's legal counsel, still resonated in Purdue corridors. Udell worked for Purdue for thirty years; he was one of three executives fined $34 million in the federal case the company pleaded guilty to in 2007. Udell had always urged a hard line: Purdue was assuaging people's pain, doing good; it had nothing to be ashamed of. The company shouldn't back down; it had to fight, Udell preached.

Thus Ms. Sackler's husband, David, laid an egg of his own in an interview with *Vanity Fair*. He reportedly heeded the advice of a New York PR expert who repeated the Udell philosophy that the family's error was that they hadn't been combative enough. David Sackler spent much of the interview complaining about news coverage of his family members, denying that they or Purdue had much of a role in the crisis. "To argue that OxyContin started this is not in keeping with history," he said. Only later in the interview did he mention the dead. "I'm sorry we didn't start with that," he told the reporter. "We feel absolutely terrible."

In 2018 Purdue disbanded its sales force and hired a woman to the unenviable job of director of corporate image—but it all felt cynical and late amid the avalanche of lawsuits. By mid-2019, the company had reduced its staff from 1,700 to 500.

A few months after *Joss et Ses Amis: Undeterred*, a hearing was held in a Suffolk County Superior Court in downtown Boston to decide whether the state of Massachusetts could actually sue the Sackler family members on Purdue's board. The room was packed with lawyers and families who'd lost loved ones to opioid overdose. The courthouse parking lot was full of more families, holding photographs of those who had died.

The hearing lasted all day. The lawyers Purdue and the Sacklers hired spent hours arguing that board members were protected from lawsuits. Weeks later, the judge denied their arguments and let the suit against the family proceed. The company promptly entered bankruptcy.

A year later, US attorney general William Barr announced an agreement with Purdue in which the company would pay penalties of $8 billion. Purdue would be transformed into a "public benefit company," proceeds from which would support drug treatment and rehabilitation. It also exposed the Sackler family to possible future criminal charges.

Purdue pleaded guilty to conspiracy to defraud the United States and violate anti-kickback laws, while the Sackler family remained liable for future criminal prosecution. In the plea, members of the Sackler family were to pay federal civil penalties of $225 million, though in a statement they insisted they had acted "ethically and lawfully."

A brief outlined all the behavior the company was admitting to, much of it described in the complaints written by state prosecutors in Massachusetts and Tennessee. Purdue admitted to conspiring to push doctors to prescribe medication "without a legitimate medical purpose and outside the usual course of professional practice."

"Purdue deeply regrets and accepts responsibility for the misconduct detailed by the Department of Justice in the agreed statement of facts," said Steve Miller, Purdue's new board chairman. "Purdue today is a very different company. We have made significant changes to our leadership, operations, governance, and oversight."

A Purdue bankruptcy plan proposed as I was finishing this book would settle lawsuits from cities, counties, tribes, and others against the company by funneling $4.25 billion in cash over nine years to those entities, and another $4 billion in naloxone and anti-addiction drugs.

The plan would end Sackler ownership of Purdue, which would at long last diversify into other drugs not associated with the opioid epidemic, though revenue from the new company would go to address the crisis.

Maura Healey led a group of states objecting to the plan. It didn't require the Sackler family to pay enough of what it earned from OxyContin sales, she said in a statement. "The Sacklers became billionaires by causing a national tragedy," she said. "They shouldn't be allowed to get away with it by paying a fraction of their investment returns over the next nine years and walking away richer than they are today."

A week before Christmas 2020, the US House of Representatives Oversight Committee held a Zoom hearing of testimony from David Sackler, his cousin Kathe Sackler, and Purdue CEO Craig Landau. No Sackler that day expressed any personal responsibility for what happened. Indeed, family members continue to vehemently deny that they had a role in the epidemic. Still, the hearing marked the first time I remember a Sackler speaking with seemingly sincere feeling.

"I want to start by speaking to the families who have lost loved ones to addiction and overdose," said Kathe Sackler, who said her brother Robert struggled with mental illness until his suicide at twenty-three. "Nothing is more tragic than the loss of a child. As a mother my heart breaks for those parents who have lost children. I'm so terribly sorry for your pain. It distresses and angers me greatly that the medication that was developed to help people and relieve severe pain has become associated with so much human suffering."

Yet the lawmakers showed little patience. "Evil," one representative called the Sacklers. "You and your family are addicted to money," said Raja Krishnamoorthi, a Democrat from Illinois. Another compared the family to Sinaloa drug lord Joaquín "El Chapo" Guzmán. Purdue's 2007 fine and settlement "was a signal to the family that . . . the efforts to maximize profits from OxyContin should be redoubled," said Maryland Democrat John Sarbanes. "You knew this cash cow was going to come to an end."

James Comer, a Kentucky Republican, said: "We don't agree on a lot on this committee in a bipartisan way . . . but our opinion of Purdue Pharma and the actions of your family, I think we all agree, are sickening. [Now] you file bankruptcy to avoid the majority of costs you've passed on to society. I share the outrage of just about every American. I'm sickened to see a family and company that's going to use the bankruptcy process to get out of this and to continue to be one of the richest families in America."

Richard Sackler is said to be living in no-income-tax Florida. And not long after *Joss et Ses Amis: Undeterred*, Joss and David Sackler put up for sale their four-bedroom, 3,300-square-foot apartment in Manhattan, asking $6.5 million. It was reported that they bought a $7 million home in Boca Raton, Florida. Boca Raton is located in Palm Beach County, which, coincidentally, is one of the hundreds of counties suing the Sacklers and Purdue Pharma.

ON THE FIRST Tuesday in June of 2019, Sandy Alexander and a colleague from the Massachusetts Attorney General's Office drove north in a government car again to the town of Beverly and the graduation ceremony at Northshore Recovery High School.

Each of the eleven graduating seniors spoke that day. They came from eastern Massachusetts, barely hanging on amid an underworld drug stream more deadly than ever in the country's history. Some had been thrown out of other schools. All were wizened veterans of relapse in the battle between the nucleus accumbens and the still-forming prefrontal cortex.

One girl, with daisies around her cap, said she had come to the school in 2016 a "broken soul" and was certain that, had she not, she'd be dead. Northshore offers yoga and meditation and a music studio, so students learn to calm their bodies without substances, said principal Michelle Lipinski. A physiology class delves into the neuroscience of addiction, the importance of balancing dopamine and serotonin, and of the effect of good nutrition and exercise on the brain. The ceremony's guest speaker, a Northshore alumnus who graduated from college in criminal justice, said that some don't believe this place to be a real school. "That's a lie," the *Salem News* quoted him as saying. "Mainstream education has not adapted to the drug crisis this country is experiencing. The future will look at this school as revolutionary."

Afterward there were tears, hugs, and smiles. Sandy Alexander chatted with the students. Alba Ward, a cheerleader, had a unicorn horn on her cap. In the front row, Alexander saw, were several girls—no older than six or seven—little cheerleaders wearing unicorn horns. All but two of the graduates that day would go on to college. A year later, they were studying social work, art therapy, emergency medicine, teaching. One fellow, six foot six, was studying preschool education and worked in a nursery school.

To Sandy Alexander, that day at Northshore again felt like oxygen, a welcome respite from the Purdue sales calls and Sackler board minutes. One day the case against Purdue and the Sacklers would end. He would cease reading the board's demands for ever more doctor visits and higher annual payouts. He would not study techniques to pressure beleaguered physicians to increase OxyContin prescriptions. But this other work—amid what the crisis bequeathed the country—that work would go on, among kids who walked in a world where the dope came fanged and pardoned no teenage mistake.

For that quiet work in schools like this one, and in neighborhoods and towns across America, as far as he could tell, there was no end in sight.

Clarksburg II

"A Meth Apocalypse"

In the spring of 2016 a thirty-year-old man from Montana stepped off the Greyhound in the former glass town of Clarksburg, West Virginia, on the run from a methamphetamine addiction that had hounded him since he was fourteen.

Norman Lowe was neither tall nor thin. He had worked construction and some other jobs, and despite years on the street and an abbreviated education, he was well-spoken. He also had three children by two women along the way. He had a sister who had lived in Clarksburg for many years, and she said the town had its troubles, but where meth was concerned, it was fine; she rarely saw it. So, wanting relief from the drug that had swallowed his life, Norman Lowe fled Butte and took a Greyhound to West Virginia.

About a year after he moved in with his sister in Clarksburg, all that changed. Large chunks of crystal meth, more potent than ever, flooded in from Mexico.

"It was like an epidemic overnight. Suddenly there was so much of it," Norman remembered. "It was crazy. Even the homeless guy on the corner had bags of dope in his pocket. The scene takes the cake in my almost twenty years of meth use. I'd never seen it that rampant, never seen so many people on it. They were zombies. They didn't care. It was a meth apocalypse."

A new supply spurred a new agony. Heroin/fentanyl addicts switched en masse to meth in Clarksburg. Meth was so cheap and permitted them to get high without the threat of overdose death. It didn't take long before they lost their jobs and their families, or their landlords threw them out. Soon they were babbling on the street, out of their minds.

"At first you could see them thinking they still had control of their lives because they still had their clothes, dragging around suitcases and backpacks," Norman told me. "Then you see them day by day. It goes from three backpacks and a suitcase to a suitcase and a backpack, then they don't have nothing, just a backpack—complaining about how their stuff got stolen."

By the fall of 2017 Norman was one of them, on the street, too. His day was one long trek in search of meth and a place to sleep that night.

THE HOSPITALS WERE among the first to see the effects of all this.

Kayla Toryak was a nurse in a psych ward. Toryak was the daughter of a woman whose addiction to heroin had grown from pills prescribed her by Lou Ortenzio, the former doctor turned pizza delivery guy. So Kayla assumed she had seen the worst. Then one day a thin young man was admitted to her ward. "He was seeing cheetahs," she remembered. "He was up against the wall, 'The cheetahs are going to get me.'" After that Kayla started seeing patients whose minds were mangled by this new meth. She had been doing this job for years and remembered when meth was made locally. It was addictive and gradually wore people out. But they posed no threat and were easy to control. They certainly weren't hallucinating. She didn't remember any who wound up in her ward. The new stuff, though, changed people quickly. It was winter, and this young man's mother had found him in a freezing creek. She was a housekeeper in the hospital. Kayla remembered the pain and weariness in the woman's eyes. "Her son had a good upbringing," she said. "Now he's seeing cheetahs."

The police also saw it arrive. Brian Purkey had been a cop since 1991, most of that in narcotics in Harrison County, when one day in 2017 he got a text on his undercover cell phone.

"I got ounces," it said.

The text made no sense, for it came from a young drug user whom Purkey had never known to have more than a pill or two on him.

Purkey had seen pain pills come, then go, replaced by heroin, then back to pills again as heroin faded after the bust of some prominent dealer. It all depended on who was selling and who was busted. For most of Purkey's career before that kid's text, the drugs on the street had changed like the weather. His undercover work focused on large-scale drug dealers. Purkey rarely bothered with low-level dealers, like this kid, who were addicts, thus notoriously unreliable and never trusted by their suppliers. In the past, when Purkey wanted to buy even just one pill from this kid who texted him, the young man had to run and get it to sell it to him.

When he received that text, Purkey texted back, Ounces of what? "I figured he'd stolen it, whatever it was," he told me. "Meth," came the answer.

An ounce of meth was a major bust in Harrison County; Purkey at the time couldn't have said how much a pound of meth cost because he'd literally never seen a pound of meth.

So Brian Purkey bought the ounce from the kid and arrested him. Later, he realized that street hustlers like this kid were like canaries in those now-shuttered West Virginia coal mines, warning what was coming. That someone had trusted that kid with ounces of methamphetamine was an ominous sign of a supply so vast that it changed the county's drug world. The drug stream no longer ebbed and flowed with different products every few months. Now it was just methamphetamine. Pounds of the stuff, everywhere. It just kept coming, and the price kept dropping. The consumers were not veteran meth users, for there were few of those in Clarksburg. Instead, opioid addicts were using it.

The quantities of meth from Mexico also withered the social misgivings that accompanied selling an illegal drug. As with fentanyl, the new meth and its easy money attracted people with no history in the drug game. These were ordinary folks who had no instinct for the trade. Lawyers. The owner of a pet grooming shop. A retired West Virginia state trooper. Oil-and-gas workers. A grocery-store manager.

In September 2018 Purkey and his team arrested a local named Phil Finley, whom they knew well. Finley had battled addiction for years, and had done prison time for possessing the small quantities that typified Clarksburg's drug world for so long. His first term in 1996 was for five ounces of cocaine; the next time, in 2005, for possession of enough Sudafed tablets to make slightly more than an ounce of methamphetamine. Released from prison in 2010 and convinced that he wasn't made for the drug business, Finley told me he spent the next years working on oil rigs, driving trucks for an oil company, and "trying to do the right thing. It was time to grow up."

But in late 2017, he was hurt on the job one night. With no one around to prove his injury was job-related, Finley told me, the company fired him. He had bills and needed two surgeries. Finley returned to drug dealing.

In the past, a limited meth supply had confined him to small-time deals. Now, Mexican crystal methamphetamine was everywhere. Finley didn't remember any homeless people two decades before. But this meth twisted people until they lost all control of their lives. "It went from a little bit to where they just started flooding us very quickly," Finley told me. "I had three different areas where I could pick up ten to twenty pounds any time I wanted." Soon he was selling a pound of meth a day. Finley noticed what he, too, had never seen in all his years in the drug world: users of opiates—heroin, fentanyl, Suboxone—were now switching to methamphetamine. By the end of 2017, as it was doing elsewhere, a massive and sustained meth supply had created demand for a drug few in Clarksburg seemed to care for the previous spring.

Finley once met a dealer and his Mexican connection in an apartment laundromat in a nearby town. He brought a suitcase holding $25,000 in cash; this is how much he was prepared to pay for five pounds, he told them. The Mexican fellow shook his head. Finley left; two hours later his connections called again, agreeing to his price.

Finley expanded quickly to become the kind of dealer he'd never been before—buying pounds and making $3,000 to $5,000 a day selling smaller amounts to an assortment of mid-level Clarksburg dealers. For the first time in his drug-dealing career, Finley told me, he actually fronted his product to customers who were users. A lot of them repaid him. But "at the price I got it," he told me, "it didn't matter if they screwed up and didn't pay."

Selling meth even became a dependable way for his customers to make the monthly rent, the weekly grocery bill, and pay for their dope habit, too. They got antsy when Finley was out of product. "They were on my ass saying, 'We need this. I gotta pay my truck payments.' Or, 'I totaled my car.' That's how they put food on their table. When I started, I thought I'd be struggling to make my bills, but I barely had time to do anything but sell drugs."

Finley lasted not quite a year. In 2018 five of his customers, arrested on small drug cases, opted to work them off by wearing wires for Brian Purkey's team. Finley said he was preparing to exit the drug trade and start driving trucks again for an oil company when he was busted with ten pounds of meth and $175,000 in his house. He was sentenced to prison for nineteen years.

BY THE SUMMER of 2018, downtown Clarksburg, once abandoned, teemed with homeless meth users. The P2P meth had them up for days, psychotic and hallucinating. They spoke in hurried, paranoid fragments that ended abruptly and made as much sense as their visions. P2P meth flogged users to gyrate and twist without reason, as if their bodies were the physical expression of their tormented minds. Or they "got stuck" and spent hours doing the same thing, repairing a bike, say, over and over. They were notoriously unwashed, with open sores, matted hair, and rotting teeth, in shoes that didn't fit and baggy coats and pants as stained and reeking as their bodies.

Hoodies became a uniform, the emblem of the Opioid Era, and they retreated within them. The hoodie is versatile apparel—cheap, warm, functional—and thus perfect for many healthy activities. But its versatility meant that as opioid, then meth, addiction spread across America, the hoodie became a hiding place for many, a refuge from a harsh world. "When we put up that hood," one recovering addict told me, "we're making the choice to separate ourselves from everyone else—instead of someone pushing us out. I think it's our way to hide from the world that doesn't accept us. The hood is the refuge. It's our safe place."

They constantly waxed themselves with deodorant, the men with Axe Body Wash, the women rubbing their faces with coatings of makeup to cover their meth sores. Fresh sanitary wipes offered a continuous shower through a muggy summer day. Women prized Summer's Eve feminine products. Constant misting of Summer's Eve spray "was how you kept clean," one woman told me. "I ran with a guy who would go into the mall and come out with ten packages of cologne and perfume; it was the expensive stuff. You only needed a couple sprays and you'd smell like a French whore."

They spilled out across downtown Clarksburg and into the road near the Pike Street McDonald's, which had Wi-Fi, or the Long John Silver's or China One restaurant.

This upset merchants in Clarksburg's empty downtown. Making a downtown shop profitable without foot traffic was only for the brave. Now they had foot traffic, but in a cruel betrayal, those walking the streets turned out to be drug-addled backpackers who terrified the few customers with money to spend. McDonald's put up nine laminated signs inside and out: "No backpacks allowed in this store!!!!!!!" Kroger had a similar sign.

It reminded Karen Alastanos of a scene from *The Walking Dead*. She had opened a women's clothing store a year before on Main Street and was transitioning to a beauty salon. When the health department opened a needle exchange nearby on Thursdays, Karen battled the clinic's loiterers until she finally just closed shop on Thursdays. The meth backpackers were that kind of nuisance—all week long. City leaders hoped a new theater would spark a downtown renaissance; the backpackers were an obstacle to that.

The churches of downtown Clarksburg had grown into maturity decades before as houses of worship for the town's middle class. Years of decline thinned their congregations; repair bills mounted. They locked their doors as downtown filled with wild-eyed, foul-smelling young people.

One of these churches was Central Christian. Built of venerable red brick and stained glass, erected in 1906 by members of the original congregation, Central Christian stands on Pike Street at the western edge of Clarksburg's downtown, just before the street slopes down to the strip of businesses where McDonald's and Kroger are located and where the backpackers hung out. Central Christian had a clearer view than most of the meth users, but that didn't mean its pastor, Jeff Hanlin, had any idea what to do about them. They looked sad, desperate, menacing, and there was no end to them.

Hanlin has a graying goatee and speaks with a slight southern accent. He was a member of the church when its longtime pastor retired. Hanlin was then fifty-four, and one of the youngest in the congregation, with a late-in-life interest in the gospel. The church board asked if he might take over pastoral duties. Hanlin had worked as a salesman, most recently selling cell phones, but he took the job, and when I met him he was taking Bible classes under the direction of another pastor. Decades earlier, Central Christian had a congregation of 350, and a choir of fifteen. Fifteen was now the size of Hanlin's entire flock. It survived largely on money left to it by members who'd died, money that would be gone in a couple of years. One of the congregation's preoccupations was how—or whether—the church could continue. As pastor at Central Christian, Hanlin had performed seven funerals and no baptisms. His pastoral work, he found, involved walking congregants through the last part of their lives.

"All these young people, half are high, homeless and hungry," he said. "You see them at the Gomart [gas station], leaning up against the wall, out of it. I'm used to ministering to elderly people. I have people with walkers and canes."

One of them was Brenda Smothers, now seventy, who used a walker and had retired on disability from her VA file clerk job. She had watched the backpackers multiply outside her church and felt for them, even as menacing as they sometimes looked. She still kept her doors unlocked, the inheritance of the Clarksburg era in which she was raised. "I grew up in the 1950s, 1960s—mom and dad and apple pie," she told me. "It wasn't an ideal life but everybody had a mom and a dad." She wanted to tell these kids that they didn't have to be that way, but she didn't know how she'd have fared growing up without a parent.

Brenda still served on the board of Central Christian, though it was hard to get around much. Hanlin would drive her to church and to doctor appointments. He saw some discarded syringes outside on her block. "Just be careful," he told her. Brenda began locking her doors after that.

Meetings of concerned business owners took place. Some owners theorized that the Mission, the town's homeless shelter, had bused them in from elsewhere. Soon, though, this group divided in two. One was interested in downtown beautification and upkeep. The other, smaller in number, wanted to know more about the backpackers. So one night in August, a half dozen of them strolled the streets and river trails where the backpackers hung out. They handed out flyers with phone numbers addicts could call to get help with treatment.

Among them was a woman named Katie Wolfe-Elbon, a Clarksburg native. "That first night, I probably talked to twenty people who were homeless," she said. "That was shocking to us." Many were from

Clarksburg and carried all they owned—clothes, water, needles, knives for protection—in those backpacks.

That first evening the walkers hiked down what in Clarksburg is known as Murder Trail—which starts near the downtown Wendy's but quickly shoots off into the woods by the West Fork River and ends by the VA hospital. The trail was usually empty. On this day, no sooner had they plunged down the trail when they came upon a group of people. The day was hot, and several of the men had no shirts. They looked scared and startled. Katie and the others offered them snacks and water.

Katie and other walkers began calling themselves the Change Initiative. They set up a Thursday feed in a parking lot, handing food to shell-shocked meth addicts who might have believed these people to be police or a pack of iguanas. Through their walks, they learned the stories of the street. That many of the backpackers had phones, but no cell service, and thus worked only off Messenger, connected through some businesses's Wi-Fi, which is why they hung out near McDonald's. Murder Trail went by the legendary Akro Agate marble plant, and backpackers often dug in the area for classic glass marbles they could sell.

The Change Initiative came with pepperoni rolls. Pepperoni rolls are the unofficial state food of West Virginia. The rolls—pepperoni sticks encased in bread and baked—were invented by Italian immigrants and became the favorite lunch item of West Virginia coal miners and other laborers. The rolls are cheap to make, contain protein and carbohydrates, sometimes cheese as well, are easy to pack, and don't need refrigeration. It's no exaggeration to say that for much of the twentieth century pepperoni rolls fueled the extraction of West Virginia coal and thus fueled the country. As it turned out, in these more desperate times, the Change Initiative found that the rolls were the perfect food to hand out to homeless drug addicts.

Toward the end of the summer of 2018, the Change Initiative was joined on these walks by Karen Alastanos, who, in her outrage, nevertheless wanted to know the story behind this backpacker plague. A half hour into her first walk, Karen encountered a man named Joe, homeless, doped up, with a dog. They took to talking, and later, with the fervency of the newly converted, Karen said, "That's when my life changed." Joe loved his dog and couldn't find housing that would allow the dog. He explained his years of drug use.

As weeks passed, Karen too became part of these walks, offering pepperoni rolls to backpackers.

One of these was now Norman Lowe. The refuge he hoped to find in Clarksburg had become a meth hell. After months on Clarksburg's streets, shooting up daily, Norman hit upon the idea of tattooing his face in strange rudimentary scrawls. When he was done, his face was lined like a road map. He had inked obscure biblical references and tattooed stitches from his left eye to the left edge of his mouth. That's how he became known—"Stitches." He cut his hair in a Mohawk and dyed it purple.

"It was my self-defense system," is how he explained his reasoning, once he was sober. He had a good heart, but couldn't show it on the street. "I would have got trampled. Instead of letting emotions turn me into a sour person and a person who hates everybody, I tatted my face and my pain was out there, and inside I kept my personality and sense of humor."

The hurricane of meth, meanwhile, added new momentum to house abandonment. Now, when older owners died, meth users squatted in their homes. In other cases, people were evicted as a result of their meth use. Without any place to move to, they left their lives behind. Squatters quickly stripped them of anything of value. First it was bedding, shoes, china, bicycles. Then it was bookshelves, faucets, and finally it was electrical wiring. Perfectly livable houses were rendered squalid.

Goods from those houses flowed like a river out into town. Clarksburg's street meth world became Bartertown. By 2018 a $20 bill was a rare sight. Household goods were traded for dope: classic Akro Agate marbles, silverware, shoes, jackets, hoodies, Bluetooth speakers.

Bicycles were a big item. Cell phones and chargers were bigger. Goods stolen from recently unoccupied houses were the currency of the downtown meth economy, which was based entirely on thieving. One cell phone might be stolen and traded for dope, and stolen again and traded again, over and over, until it ended up a week later back in the hands of the guy who originally stole it, who then traded it to the girl he stole it from.

"You fall asleep, your pockets will be cut out, your backpack will be stolen," Norman said. "I had twelve hundred dollars' worth of tattoo equipment stolen. I seen it passed around town. Everywhere you'd go, you'd see your stuff. Nobody had a concept of belongings anymore." Meth was so cheap that a user could get high with what he could barter for a stolen cell phone charger or bicycle.

Meanwhile, houses that once were home to a glassworker or a teacher, an accountant or a baker, fell to the meth users, who stripped them clean, slept in them until the housing department boarded them, then pried them open and stayed on, without water, without copper wire, as the toilet overflowed with feces and discarded pizza boxes pulsed with ants.

I walked into one such house, a two-bedroom foreclosure, then spoke to Theresa Washington, who runs a printing business next door. The bank, she said, paid a company to clean and board up the house. Then backpackers discovered it. "They tore the boards right off," she said. "Before the end of the year, there was no wiring." When I walked in months later, the house was a shell, littered and savaged. Two others nearby were in the same condition. Georgie, who still slept there, showed me around the wreckage as he explained his daily job: stripping unoccupied houses, then trading what he scavenged for dope. "People leave their whole lives behind," he told me.

The Change Initiative, meanwhile, kept at its Thursday walks, distributing pepperoni rolls, to the outrage of a good many Clarksburg citizens. Those pepperoni rolls gave addicts sustenance. They could keep using, stripping houses and avoiding the worst consequences of their behavior, while the town endured their destruction like a plague.

Amid this meth-induced civic turmoil came the winter of 2018–19 and news in January of a polar vortex marching down from the north. Single-digit temperatures, merciless winds. Katie Wolfe-Elbon didn't know what to do. Change Initiative walks were only four months old, but in that time she and the others had gotten to know the backpackers by name, knew their stories and their scars, had peered into their backpacks, and knew they would not survive without shelter. The churches in downtown Clarksburg had empty space.

She turned to the one person in Clarksburg she believed could help—and would want to.

Clarksburg III

Saving the Despised

Lou Ortenzio, Clarksburg's beloved Doc O, was now 66, a thin, soft-spoken and spectacled man with graying hair. He had spent the years since his fall from grace seeking atonement through his own recovery.

He volunteered at the county's drug court and at the probation department. After his stint as the town's pizza guy, he found work at the Mission homeless shelter in Clarksburg. There he saw people not much different from himself, and they illuminated what he deemed to be God's new path in life for him. In time he was made the Mission's executive director, occupying a windowless office furnished with a desk and a worn sofa. He dressed in a sweatshirt, blue jeans, and sneakers, drove an old Toyota Camry, and believed this is where he should have been all along.

The Mission had opened in 1969 in Glen Elk, Clarksburg's small red-light district, with gambling and bars. The shelter opened with five beds for alcoholics. A blue neon "Jesus Saves" sign outside remained illuminated all those years. The shelter expanded under the force of an epidemic of addiction to opioids and, now, methamphetamine that consumed of Clarksburg what economic decline had not.

Protestant Christianity was now Lou Ortenzio's daily companion, and this separated his life today from the one he led as a doctor trying to be the center of the Clarksburg universe. His Christianity mystified his children, who grew up agnostic and outside any church. Her father's frequent references to God and Jesus reminded Monica Ortenzio "of how different we are, and how we lived two totally different lives."

One day God told Lou to open a sober-living house downtown. Recovering addicts needed places where they could maintain sobriety, far from their drug-using friends. "We thought, 'This is going to be great. They'll throw a parade for us,'" said Ben Randolph, a businessman I talked to whom Ortenzio helped recover from pill addiction. Instead, the newspaper opposed it. The Catholic diocese feared it was too near a parochial school. Businessmen objected that the house might further harm the town's image. So did county officials.

A bank eventually funded the idea, and a six-bed home for men opened; another for women followed. But the episode showed where the town, and perhaps a lot of the country, was when it came to addiction: afflicted mightily while wanting it to go away and yearning for simpler times because no one knew what to do about it. "People are so beat up from the ugliness that comes with this crisis, fed up with the criminality, the death of it all," Randolph told me. They "are tired of it."

By the ominous winter of 2018–19, when the backpackers' numbers could no longer be ignored, it wasn't as if the town of Clarksburg felt sympathy for drug addicts. The city had more than a hundred houses slated for demolition. Many had been perfectly livable before meth.

Katie Wolf-Elbon knew all this when she called Lou Ortenzio as the winter bore down on Clarksburg. We're frantic, she said, to see what we can do for these folks. They'll die otherwise.

At Ortenzio's Mission, people were sleeping on the stairs. Many of the new meth addicts had been thrown out of the Mission for scandalous behavior.

Ortenzio called a few of the old and once-venerable downtown churches to urge them to help these people wandering stinking and lost in their midst. The churches needed a push, he had long thought.

Their connection to the community had withered. They had turned inward, focused only on their dwindling congregations and their leaky roofs. Like the meth addicts, these churches were in a condition that was potentially fatal. "As downtown Clarksburg changes," Ortenzio believed, "they have to either look outside their walls or die."

That was his message to them. At his urging, Christ Episcopal agreed to open its doors as a temporary shelter, if the Change Initiative would run it. With the polar vortex two days out, the volunteers raced to put a shelter together. Katie Wolfe-Elbon bought thirty air mattresses at Walmart. A Facebook alert went out asking for donations of bedding and clothes. Twenty-seven wanderers showed up at the church for refuge that night. "We had no real game plan," said Katie. Despite the walks, she said, "I've never been up close and personal with meth addicts."

She arrived late that evening to volunteer and found other workers leaving. She'd be running the shelter alone all night. Two back-packers stepped up to help. One fellow had a purple Mohawk and tattoos scrawled across his face like a road map. He unnerved her, but he was there to help when no one else was, so he and Katie and another guy spent that night inspecting the bathrooms and other parts of the church. The next morning, as volunteers pleaded with backpackers to help clean up, the only one who stayed was that fellow with the tattooed face. He swabbed the church floor. As Katie was about to leave that morning, he gave her a hug and thanked her. "His appearance was scary but he was sweet and soft and helpful," she remembered.

Some weeks before, lost on a path in some woods during a blizzard, sleep-deprived and wired, Norman Lowe had begun hallucinating. A demon in a wooden cocoon, then a flash of blue light. Just as he passed out in the snow, he looked at his phone. It was 9:30 p.m. He awoke, and his phone battery was at 2 percent. It was 4:30 a.m. He called 911. "Then my phone died. I leaned against the fence of the cell phone tower. I said this is where I'm going to die. Twenty minutes later, cops came and found me. They tracked my phone call. I was frozen almost all the way through."

Something new there began, he said. He'd etched tattoos on his face to keep people away. "Now, I opened myself up to everybody," he said later. "I started practicing humble. I accepted who everybody was, good or bad. Forgave them even before they trespassed against me. The light of God was shown to me down there. I hadn't been real religious my whole life until I moved to Clarksburg, and the stuff that I seen there after all that meth came to town."

THE MAKESHIFT SHELTER at Christ Episcopal Church saved Clarksburg's most repellent rabble from lethal cold and left the Change Initiative with new purpose.

The winter of 2019 was far from over. Temperatures plunged to below zero a week later. Now, though, the rest of downtown Clarksburg's churches came forward. So did the town, leaving behind its anger at the damage the meth users had caused. Perhaps many glimpsed family members, or neighbors, in the scabbed faces waiting to enter. Or they simply saw a way of moving beyond their own daily worries. Donations of food, bedding, and clothing poured in from across Clarksburg. The Farmers Market sent bread and fruit. Brenda Smothers brought toilet paper and paper towels. A church youth group visiting from Pennsylvania woke every morning to make breakfast for the backpackers.

Jeff Hanlin's Central Christian was the next to open its doors. After a phone called from Ortenzio, Hanlin went to his church board, which, to his surprise, voted unanimously to open the old church as a shelter. With temperatures painful even during daylight, Central Christian couldn't throw people into the street. Instead, a full week passed with the volunteers and backpackers cooped together. They played bingo. Some refugees babbled and saw visions they couldn't quite articulate. Karen and Anjelicca on 395 Scott organized karaoke sessions, and singers stood to perform "Amazing Grace," "Lean on Me," and Beyoncé's "Single Ladies." Others jumped up to sing Journey's "Don't Stop Believin'." They wandered among the air mattresses like Las Vegas lounge singers—pocked and thin, with mics in hand, eyes closed and coming alive as this spotlight broke them, however briefly, from their tormented haze. One backpacker sat at the church piano and played classical pieces for an hour.

It stunned Hanlin to see this happening in his church. One night a man walked by, his face covered in tattoos, with a Mohawk dyed purple. Hanlin wondered what could possibly drive someone to stain his face that way. That week at Central Christian, they showed action films, too. One night they ran the animated feature *Finding Dory* for a intellectually disabled boy of seventeen, whose father was a cashier but didn't earn enough to both raise his son and afford rent, so the pair lived in a storage shed.

In the end, four downtown churches opened as temporary shelters seven times before the blessed spring of 2019 arrived. Central Christian had such tender plumbing that forty meth addicts clogged it twice. The first time, a plumbing crew came out, free of charge. Two weeks later, with the shelter once again at Central Christian, the problem was too severe for immediate repair. At 1:30 a.m., a line of refugees trudged two blocks of snowy streets, carrying air mattresses and bedding and backpacks, to Clarksburg Baptist.

A week later Karen Alastanos called Hanlin. A backpacker wanted to speak to a pastor. Was he available? Hanlin was, and twenty minutes later he found himself sitting with the same purple-Mohawked man whose face was covered in tattoos. "What did I get myself into?" the pastor thought.

Norman Lowe, it turned out, was weary. He'd been three weeks without a shower, fighting to find a place to sleep each night. His tattoos had made him infamous. Humbling himself didn't keep his name from being mentioned in connection with various crimes that Norman insisted he had no part in. He avoided the abandoned houses, and he slept alone. The paranoia, the constant isolation, and the now almost twenty years of meth use wore him out.

Hanlin didn't know what to make of this man, skinny and not always lucid. They talked and it took a while, but staring into Norman's face, Hanlin got past his stench and disturbing facial tattoos and found, behind them, a soft-spoken man of surprising tenderness.

A few days later, when Norman headed into detox to rid his system of the meth, Hanlin went to visit. For an hour they sat and Norman spoke of all he'd lost—his jobs, his children. He remembered what it was like to play ball with his boy. Without the drugs in his system, Hanlin noted, Norman was clearheaded and had gained some weight. They made a jarring pair, this scarred street denizen and the pastor who didn't cuss.

From then on, Norman called Hanlin to talk. Hanlin visited him. Soon Hanlin was also talking to Norman's mother in Montana. He reported back to his congregation on Norman's progress. The congregation—retired teachers and secretaries—wrote cards of encouragement to Norman Lowe. One of them came from Brenda Smothers: "I'm praying for you as you enter this new life," she wrote.

A month later, in May of 2019, when Norman was ready to head home to Montana, Hanlin and Karen brought him bags packed with food for the sixty-hour bus trip. They had come up with the $179 to pay his Greyhound back to Butte, where his mother, who cleaned houses and worked as a beautician, was waiting. They hugged Norman Lowe. His smile stretched the etchings on his face as he hugged them back.

These were good stories, full of hope. The other truth, though, was that dozens of backpackers never made it to a place where they could even detoxify from the P2P meth gripping their minds. Their legal, doctor-prescribed pills led to trafficker-supplied heroin, then to illicit fentanyl; now it was meth made from sulfuric acid, lye, and whatever else. I tried to imagine the distorted brain chemistry of a person who'd gone through all that. Many of these folks, despite their escape from that lethal winter, continued to lurk in the streets, deranged, despoiling houses.

These days in Clarksburg, saving the meth users from the winter of 2019 is viewed as an epiphany for the old downtown churches that helped found the town. Opening their doors to the despised gave dying temples the blessing of rejuvenation. People they didn't know donated to them. Hanlin put up photos on the church's Facebook page of the shelters, of bedding, of folks donating food. The photos were shared thousands of times. Clarksburg seemed proud of these churches. At chance encounters around town, their members were praised, often together with references to Jesus feeding the hungry and sheltering the homeless.

Brenda Smothers donated paper towels, toilet paper, cereal, and Goldfish snacks. "They got a hot meal at night and a hot meal in the morning and for a few hours they were warm. They got to experience the love of God," she said. "I think we're all feeling our way through this problem. It's like walking into a dark room; you feel your way until you find a light. But once you know you're not mouthing words, that you're actually living them, it feels good, even if it's only for a night or two."

The downtown churches encountered a new energy and reconnection to their old town. The churches had discovered what recovering addicts also knew to be true: that helping others was the best remedy. Perhaps they had found a way toward a future, if they'd take it. Anyway, that's how Jeff Hanlin saw it. That winter "was the beginning of a ministry for us," he told me. "That's what we need—something to take us outside the four walls of the church. Jesus didn't have a building. He went about to people who were in the gutters—the sick and the hurting. He gathered them one by one."

Not long after Norman Lowe left for Montana, Hanlin enrolled in Lou Ortenzio's training to be a mentor for recovering addicts.

As for Lou, he went through a change of mind similar to that of the churches, but in a slightly different direction. It happened when the police began cracking down on the meth-addicted homeless in downtown Clarksburg, giving tickets for loitering, pushing people out of the area. "We were offended in the beginning," Lou said, "but then we saw it helped people. They needed to be away from each other. People don't respond to the light; they respond to the heat. There was a little heat on them."

The homeless addicts the police ticketed were placed in housing. That had been the model for years: get people housed, then treat their drug use. But P2P meth changed the model. These folks invited other users over, and together they tore up the apartments. Ortenzio watched this and realized that the new meth required places for users to detox, then spend time recovering—six weeks at least. Otherwise, "these people are unhousable," he told me. "They can't be managed. It's not sane to just put folks in housing when they're in this condition."

As COVID-19 hit, instead of continuing the Mission as a flophouse, Ortenzio opened a Resurrection Room, where addicts could spend ninety days quarantined in sobriety. Two users well-known to the Clarksburg street world—Melissa Carter and Jesse Clevenger, who stopped using when they were forced into drug court—found sobriety at the Mission and have become his recovery recruiters. Clevenger had been a major heroin dealer in town, selling to dozens of people a day while feeling, he said, "like you were a house-call doctor. Everybody you talked to all day were at their worst—sick, had no money, crying." Then Clevenger was forced into a drug court and treatment. It was either that or prison. "I wouldn't have got clean," he said, "if I didn't have that ultimatum." Now he was out among meth addicts and preaching recovery at the Mission.

Lou Ortenzio thought that was a better plan for the Mission than simply as a flophouse. "This is an adjustment for me," he said. "We want to stop enabling. We want to put some pressure on addicts to change, even if they don't like it. If you do love someone, you have to tolerate them hating you, at least for a bit."

So that's the story of Lou Ortenzio. Most mornings at six, he is up jogging through downtown Clarksburg. The connections he made as a doctor have come in handy, for the tone of his life doesn't differ much from his routine as a family physician—tending to one desperate person after another. But his medical career belongs now to the distant past. After all that's happened, it's something he doesn't much regret having lost.

Eric and Mundo II

Leave the Drug, Gain the World

O ut in Los Angeles, Eric Barrera's schizophrenia and paranoia vanished as he found his way out of methamphetamine.

Two years into sobriety, however, his depression remained, even as he worked in outreach to homeless vets. Depression kept him indoors at times, isolated, hiding from the world and contemplating suicide.

His therapists prescribed Adderall, which helped. But what really did it was something far simpler. It was Mundo.

Eric's girlfriend's sister spotted him running in and out of traffic in Pacoima: a homeless charcoal-gray pit bull. She opened the door, and he hopped in. She named him Mundo—Spanish for "world"—for he was wandering alone in the world. Turned out Mundo was a sweet-tempered pooch, just wanting to be loved. He played easily with her family's smaller dogs. They were about to give Mundo to the Humane Society when it occurred to Eric to adopt and train the stray as a service dog, which he did.

After the training, Eric began taking Mundo to work with him. Mundo's companionship, a small thing, was more helpful than any pill. At home, Mundo pestered Eric until he took the dog running. Soon the pair was running every day. Eric's endorphins began kicking in; his depression lifted. Mundo made Eric less likely to relapse. If he ended up in prison or jail or dead, who would care for his dog?

Eric began taking classes at a community college. Mundo helped him focus, and at school he brought Eric out of his shell. People stopped to pet Mundo and talk with Eric. He passed classes in statistics, psychology, political science, and history.

Through Mundo, Eric also joined the L.A. Skid Row Running Club. The club is made up of addicts, cops, public defenders, social workers, and judge Craig Mitchell, who founded the club in 2012. That year Mitchell began running through Skid Row. A few others joined him. Now, every Monday and Thursday, twenty to fifty people meet before dawn in front of a local shelter to run for an hour through the greatest concentration of homeless people in the United States.

To Mitchell, eight years after forming the running club, it was clear that in Los Angeles the most visible homelessness was due to the new crystal meth from Mexico. "There was a sea change with respect to meth being the main drug of choice beginning in about 2008," he said. "[Now] it's the number-one drug."

Eric heard about Mitchell's running club, but he didn't have the nerve to head there alone. That first run was easier when Mundo was the focus of attention. As weeks passed and he felt more comfortable in the club, he left Mundo at home. The dog was repelled by Skid Row's smell of urine, the screaming people, and the meth-tormented energy.

Remarkably, Eric noticed, meth rarely came up in city discussions on homelessness. Local newspaper articles about the issue never mentioned the cataclysmic supplies of crystal meth coming out of Mexico driving people mad in the last dozen years. Mitchell called it "the elephant in the room that nobody is willing to address. There's a desire not to stigmatize the homeless as drug users." Policymakers and advocates instead preferred to focus on L.A.'s cost of housing, which was very high, but hardly relevant to people rendered schizophrenic and unhousable by methamphetamine.

In 2014, as the flows of the new meth were just beginning, Californians passed Proposition 47. Rather than expanding the ways felony drug-possession arrests could be used as leverage by judges to push people into treatment and recovery, Prop. 47 made those charges misdemeanors. Cops stopped making those arrests. Those who were arrested tended to refuse treatment and judges had no leverage to force them into it. So they remained on the street and fewer addicts went to treatment, just as the street drugs they used became more prevalent, addictive, and brain-damaging than ever.

Eric's outreach work taught him that homelessness had many roots. Every story was complex. Some people were disabled, or just out of prison. Others lost jobs or health insurance and couldn't pay for both rent and the surgeries or medications they needed. They eked by until a landlord raised their rent. They kept their cars to sleep in. They still had welcoming families who offered couches or a bed in a garage. Eric thought of them as invisible, the hidden homeless, the shredded-safety-net homeless.

As an outreach worker, though, Eric walked among others—the visible homeless, the addicts living in encampments along freeways, taking up entire sidewalks. In L.A. County, this was well over half the unhoused population. Drugs turned their brains against them, had them abandon any survival instinct in the pursuit of dope. Their very visibility was an expression of their addiction, of what meth did to the prefrontal cortex and the locus coeruleus. So often this meth rendered them impossible to live with, incapable of simple life responsibilities. They rebelled against following rules and thus refused, were thrown out of shelters. They were utterly unwilling to seek treatment. Above all, he thought, it made them not care. He had felt this as well. On the new meth, "I remember wanting to care, but I couldn't," he said.

The encampments seemed to him to be enabling communities, places where meth addicts felt at home because there they could find camaraderie and dope together, they could feel the warm approval of others relenting to it as well—they could not care. There, he said, "nobody's going to look at you weird."

When asked how many of the people he met in those encampments had lost housing due to high rents or health insurance, Eric could not remember one. Meth was the reason they were there and couldn't leave. Of the hundred or so vets he had brought out of the encampments and into housing, all but three returned. Eric grew weary of wanting recovery for the people he met more than they wanted it for themselves. Such was the pull. Some were addicted to other things: crack or heroin, alcohol or gambling. Most of them used any drug available. But what Eric and Mundo most encountered by far was crystal methamphetamine.

Eric appreciated Mundo even more during these treks. He had spent years adrift as meth pestered his mind, wondering if he could ever let it alone. Without the drug, Eric found his problems were more simply resolved. In leaving dope he gained the world. The quietest kind of connection—a dog's companionship—meant the most. Now he and his stray had each other. Eric is husky, with short hair and a thick neck. That describes Mundo. Like Mundo, Eric told me, "I look like I'm this big tough mean guy, but really I was just this lost dude, didn't want to hurt nobody."

The last time I saw Eric Barrera, he was walking through lines of tents around the lake in Echo Park, west of downtown L.A., carrying bottles of water and Mundo trotting at his side.

"Hey, man," he said to one fellow after another, each alone in his tent, "can you use a water?"

The Least of Us

In August 2018 a drug I'd never heard of was discovered, having killed a person who overdosed near Cedar Rapids, Iowa. The drug was called isotonitazene—an opioid first synthesized in the 1950s that hits the same brain receptors as fentanyl. Iso—as it's now known on the streets—then was found in dozens of corpses in Chicago and Milwaukee, and from there it spread to Michigan, Indiana, Tennessee, killing at least 230 people in all. Researchers believe it may be marketed by Chinese chemical labs as a replacement for fentanyl, which the Chinese government banned in 2019.

In April 2020 isotonitazene seemed to fade, only to be replaced by another synthetic opioid, brorphine. Brorphine showed up in the corpses of 130 people in many of the same states. At least seventeen new synthetic drugs were identified in 2020 alone. The day I turned in my manuscript, another opioid was found on the rise, metonitazene.

"It's almost as though they're market testing," said Barry Logan, chief forensic scientist at NMS Labs, which does bodily fluid tests for coroners nationwide. Underground chemists seemed to be searching the chemistry literature for drugs that might be molecularly modified to be more potent. Then, like Paul Janssen did when he invented fentanyl, "they're experimenting," Logan said. "They're changing the molecule's [structure], which changes how rapidly it's taken up into the brain. Then they put it out there on the market."

The world Gary Henderson predicted when he coined the term "designer drugs" in 1988 is now with us. Counterfeit pills laced with fentanyl and made in Mexico now dominate the market and have replaced the sloppy Magic Bullet blender in a dealer's kitchen and the powder fentanyl coming from China. In Los Angeles, DEA agents seized 120,000 of these pills crossing the border in 2017, and 1.2 million of them in 2020.

In a time when drug traffickers act like corporations and corporations like drug traffickers, the forces looking to manipulate our brains for profit are frightening to behold. So many more synthetic blasts compete for our brain receptors—from chicken nuggets and soda to cell phones and social media apps, methamphetamine and fentanyl.

Yesteryear's myths about illegal drugs are coming true, largely due to their prohibition and lack of regulation. One hit of "heroin" *has* killed many people; so, too, has a line of coke. Meth does turn people mentally ill. Pot sends people to emergency rooms with psychotic episodes. There seems now no way to stop all the bizarre drugs devised by those whose own brain chemistry has been twisted by the profits of the underworld's free market.

Having lived in Mexico for ten years, I believe solutions will come only when Mexico and the United States work together.

This is crucial because walls don't stop dope. Not in an era of free trade. The price of meth hit historic lows by arriving via millions of trucks, cars, and people through our many official border crossings, some of the most heavily guarded places on earth. Same with heroin and fentanyl.

Drug demand is important in all this. But it must be said: these stories *begin* with supply. Our opioid addiction epidemic began with a mighty supply of pain pills prescribed every year, which created widespread addiction that continues to this day. Right about that time, traffickers were discovering that synthetic drugs were not just immensely profitable but could create or shift demand simply because they could be made in unprecedented quantities all year long. So they flocked to them.

The British Empire has rightly received history's condemnation for pushing its colonies' opium on China—waging the two Opium Wars to do so in the nineteenth century. Those supplies took what had been a minor problem in China and created a drug scourge that would afflict that country for a century.

Today in our hemisphere, Mexican traffickers' role in creating and spreading these drugs is just as undeniable and corrosive. Mexico's response has more than just failed. On the contrary, a new book by historian Benjamin Smith, *The Dope: The Real History of the Mexican Drug Trade*, shows that elements of the Mexican government have often controlled, guided, exploited, and aided those traffickers since the 1950s as they morphed from illiterate rancheros to criminal capitalists, even as these government officials went through the motions of battling the drug trade. The relentless quantities of meth flowing into American towns are a measurement of Mexico's inept criminal justice system. Mexico must stand up and deal with the corruption that cripples well-meaning people and the rule of law.

We have aided these traffickers in their work. They sell to our drug demand. What's more, they have armed themselves for decades with guns purchased easily in the United States and smuggled south.

The topic of US-bought weapons is beyond the scope of this book. Luckily, British journalist Ioan Grillo, based in Mexico, recently published *Blood Gun Money: How America Arms Gangs and Cartels*, which documents all the ways easily purchased guns in the United States are smuggled south to arm drug gangs of our Latin American neighbors. In 2018, according to Grillo, the Mexican military submitted records of sixteen thousand firearms it seized—70 percent were found to have been made or bought in the United States. Another study by the federal Bureau of Alcohol, Tobacco, Firearms and Explosives traced 150,000 guns seized in Mexico between 2007 and 2018 to US vendors and factories.

Whatever the exact numbers, it is indisputable that much of the violence and cartel impunity in Mexico is fueled by guns from the United States. We, all of us, pay for those guns. The price comes in the form of relentless supplies of meth, fentanyl, and other drugs on our streets that are produced with traffickers' brazen confidence that these US-bought weapons guarantee their operations. Those supplies torment people trying to get clean. The invoice for those guns is paid, too, by every American family whose loved one dies with a needle in her arm, or huddles in a sidewalk shanty that he shares with his hallucinations.

Business combines are now everywhere. We call them Big Pharma, Big Tech, and Big Oil. Now emerging is Big Dope—traffickers producing illegal synthetic drugs of abuse year-round with either their government's aid or its lack of antagonism, with easy access to world chemical markets to make their products, global banks to wash their money, and weapons to enforce their will. Big Dope fed on the US consumer market that formed when drug companies aggressively marketed narcotic painkillers to doctors as nonaddictive for all pain patients.

This ought to concern anyone who believes, as I do, that greatly expanded drug treatment is part of what America needs. No matter how many treatment options we provide, recovering addicts face scary odds as long as the drugs that torment them are widely available, potent, and almost free. The now-cliché is "We can't arrest our way out of this." We can't treat our way out of it, either, as long as supply is so potent and cheap.

Mexico's role in all this is clear. So is China's. So is our own. Each needs to step up. But focusing solely on one country also misses the point. It's accurate, but it's not the world we live in. Geography no longer matters. We've reached the end of the era when drugs can only be made in countries with the right mix of soil, weather, and corruption. A commodity that's profitable can be made anywhere in the world. Mexican meth traffickers have been discovered in Holland, Japan, Africa. Tomorrow's synthetic drugs may be from India or Chile, Outer Mongolia or Malaysia, the Czech Republic or a neighbor of yours.

I'm sympathetic to the idea of drug legalization as a response to this. We made a tragic mistake through the twentieth century in gradually criminalizing drugs that ought to have been dealt with—*were* being dealt with—medically. We created a profit center for mafias around the world. We stopped considering ways to reduce overdose deaths—studying, for example, how safe injection sites work elsewhere. Among other things, criminalization also prevented us from fully studying these drugs for their medicinal benefits and harms.

The problem is, I don't trust American capitalism to do drug legalization responsibly. The last fifty years are replete with examples of corporations turning addictive services and substances against us, fine-tuning their addictiveness, then marketing them aggressively. Remember when social media was going to be the great technological connective tissue, bringing people together, inaugurating a new era of understanding? Instead, it midwifed an era of virulent tribalism. The opioid epidemic began with *legal* drugs, irresponsibly marketed and prescribed. The Sacklers are only one example of a tendency that nestles into every corner of American capitalism when it is allowed to extract maximum profit from products and services that neuroscience shows our brains are vulnerable to. Meanwhile, alcohol and cigarettes kill more than any other drug by far, because they are legal and widely available. Alcohol also drives arrests and incarceration more than any other single drug. Our brains are no match for the consumer and marketing culture to emerge in the last few decades. They are certainly no match for the highly potent illegal street drugs now circulating.

Marijuana, up to now, gives me little reason to adjust that opinion. Pot can be responsibly legalized. Instead, we are choosing the route we took with opioids: a now-legal, potent drug is being made widely available and marketed with claims about its risk-free nature. Big Pot is only a matter of time. Altria, which owns Marlboro, is moving into legal marijuana. The final absurdity is that as we face climate change's existential threat, we make a weed that thrives under the sun legal to grow indoors, with a huge carbon footprint. Pot may well have medical benefits. Opioids certainly do. But supply matters. So does potency and marketing and distribution. The opioid-addiction crisis should have taught us that.

I'm sympathetic to the idea of decriminalizing drugs, as well. Yet I believe it misunderstands the nature of addiction and ignores the unforgiving drug stream every addict must face today. One reason overdose deaths during the coronavirus pandemic skyrocketed is that police in many areas stopped arresting people for the minor crimes and outstanding warrants that are symptoms of their addictions. Left on the street, many use until they die. Certainly the story of that death toll is as complex as those of the people whose deaths are counted in it. But I suspect we'll come to see the last ten months of 2020 and into 2021 at least in part as one long, unplanned experiment into what happens when the most devastating street drugs we've known are, in effect, decriminalized, and those addicted to them are allowed to remain on the street to use them.

Decriminalizing drugs also removes the one lever we have to push men and women toward sobriety. Waiting around for them to decide to opt for treatment is the opposite of compassion when the drugs on the street are as cheap, prevalent, and deadly as they are today.

We used to believe people needed to hit rock bottom before seeking treatment. That's another idea made obsolete by our addiction crisis and the current synthetic drug supply. It belongs to an era when drugs of choice were merciful. Nowadays people are living in tents, screaming at unseen demons, raped, pimped, beaten, unshowered, and unfed. That would seem to be rock bottom. Yet it's not enough to persuade people to get treatment. In Columbus, Ohio, Giti Mayton remembers a meth addict who was hospitalized with frostbitten, gangrenous hands, yet who left the hospital in midwinter to find more dope. San Francisco and Philadelphia, two cities with years of experience with heroin, are seeing users homeless and dying like never before. The dope is different now. Today, rock bottom is death.

We need to use arrests, but *not* as a reason to send someone to prison. Instead, criminal charges are leverage we can use to pry users from the dope that will consume them otherwise. Our era of synthetic street drugs requires this. "You can lead a horse to water, but you can't make him drink—however, you can make him thirsty," said Brandon Cox, a recovering addict in Lancaster, Ohio, who is now a paramedic. "You're not going to get better unless you're willing to get better. Finding that emerging willingness is critical. For me, it was the threat of doing years in prison." Some people find that willingness on the street. It happens. But many do not, cannot.

Happily, drug courts around America are doing this work—using the threat of prison terms to push addicts into treatment, where they can put some space between their brain and dope and slowly embrace sobriety. Life repair can then begin. It's happening across the country—as in Scott Barrett's Recovery Court in Kenton, Ohio. It's slow, hard work, with slip-ups and success. But this rethinking of courts and judging is harm reduction of the most elemental form. County drug courts are not a luxury. Synthetic drugs have made them a necessity. After all, people can't recover when they're dead, which is what decriminalizing today's fearsome synthetic drug stream risks.

In a time indeed when drug traffickers act like corporations and corporations like drug traffickers, our best defense, perhaps our only defense, lies in bolstering community. America is strongest when we understand that we cannot succeed alone, and weakest when it's every man for himself. The opioid epidemic was in full swing in Appalachia by the late 1990s. We should have stood shoulder to shoulder with Appalachia back then. We didn't. We lacked that collective spirit; it wasn't our problem—the reigning attitude of the Opioid Era in America. The scourge spread from Appalachia because, as the pandemic is showing us years later, you cannot escape it. That's why the lesson we must learn is that we're only as strong as the most vulnerable, as people who are in pain. Black Lives Matter is about that as well—that we cannot move forward without recognizing pain long ignored and a population with talents and energies stifled.

The greatest foreign policy initiative in modern history was the Marshall Plan after World War II. Mostly through loans and grants, America helped resurrect ruined countries, among them Germany, which we'd only recently despised. I see no unintended consequences from the Marshall Plan. It grew from the idea that our self-interest lies in helping the ruined, the once-hated, those who are flat on their backs.

Today, much of our culture grows from the opposite of what motivated the Marshall Plan. It grows from the self-centered nucleus accumbens. That urge to always think *we* don't have enough. Dopamine convinces us that happiness lies around the corner, just a little bit more, and this prevents us from enjoying serotonin's contentment with what we already possess.

I see connections to our national drug-addiction epidemic in the fact that every year dozens of Fortune 500 corporations pay no federal income taxes, while many American families worry about rent and food. I see the epidemic connected to the massive amount of US wealth diverted from the bottom and the middle to the top in the last forty years. Jobs that went overseas were just the free market at work—nothing to be done.

I don't think we should wonder why so many of our towns and neighborhoods are threadbare and drug addiction so widespread. There's a ravaging of communities that's gone on.

In nature, species at the top of the food chain and habitat help maintain their environment. We've done the opposite. We have corroded the sense of community in places where we live—in poor neighborhoods and wealthy ones. Our streets and parks are vacant. We hardly know each other. We've destroyed the places where we came together. We survived as a species through always wanting more—much as classical economists would imagine us. Nowadays, though, seems to me we need the bounty of less.

We need to again make policy of the belief that we can't go it alone. The spirit of community needs to be built out, collectively, not just in a shift of heart, which is necessary, but in taxation, in health care, in improved infrastructure—in other words, a shift in where the resources go.

Our drug-addiction crisis, the coronavirus, Black Lives Matter demonstrations—they are all exposing our weakness as a country and calling on us to mount a Marshall Plan of American recovery, a plan that takes into account our neighbors who can't fully breathe amid our prosperity.

I find comfort that much of what neuroscience has learned about our brain confirms religion's truths: humans need love, purpose, compassion, patience, forgiveness, and engagement with others. We're built for simple things—for empathy and community. *That* is our defense.

Neuroscience also endorses the tool-and-die approach to life: fulfillment comes when we find a passion, and we work every day toward getting better at it, with others, undaunted by failure. Another defense, it seems to me.

I'm enormously hopeful, which might be strange to hear after all you have read. But all that besets us grows, I believe, from turning away from what has made America great.

The addiction crisis has been telling us that to defend ourselves we'd be wise to reexamine how we live. To rethink what we eat and drink. To limit or block social media and disconnect twenty-four-hour cable news, reducing the firehose of narcotic outrage and changing our "junk-food media diet," per Nebraska senator Ben Sasse. "Many people who yell at strangers on Twitter," he wrote in the *Atlantic*, "don't know their own local officials or even their neighbors across the street." Cable news has learned to alarm us, anger and outrage us, and tell us how those of us who think one way have been right all along, and those who don't are moral degenerates. But cable news is no longer journalism; the job of a journalist is not to relentlessly tell us how right we are, and thus how virtuous.

The crisis is teaching us that we'd be wise to get our news by reading it, and demand more of ourselves as we develop opinions instead of swiping them from memes and ranters. That we'd be equally wise to shed inquisitorial political correctness, cancel culture, and bizarre QAnon conspiracies, and instead fight hard for what brings us together. It's telling us that we'd be wisest to get outside, be among other Americans. Then we see that we are every man who can't breathe. We are every masked nurse on a packed ward, every addict eating from the trash, every kid hoping for more than his crack-ridden street. We are every cop carrying someone's child from a meth house.

The pandemic is schooling us in our need for each other, in how we need to be touched. In its aftermath, as workers commute less, we may see a renewal of life on streets that have been barren for years. That's my hope.

Community reconstruction doesn't have to always be complex. It comes down to the unnoticed "constant habit of kindness" that French observer Alexis de Tocqueville in the mid-1800s saw strengthened us locally and kept Americans from destructive isolation and the worst of individualism. Often, I think, it's about doing the low-tech, small stuff to pull neighbors out of their houses. It's cookouts and block parties. On my street, we started Street of Heads a week before Halloween, in which kids and families from all around decorate wig heads and paint faces on canvas, then stick them on stakes along the sidewalk in a (now seventh) annual open-air art gallery. I believe Street of Heads has helped the block come together. Filling those empty streets—that's our defense—little by little, as they're attempting to do on the south side of Muncie, Indiana.

Like the pandemic, fentanyl and methamphetamine present us with a huge opportunity for change. They are calling on us to embrace the ignored, the forgotten, and the despised around us, allow them space so they might unlock their energies and abilities. When they do, like a natural resource, they will push us all forward.

I'm not a Christian, but as I was writing this book, I read the Gospel of Matthew. The words of Matthew's Jesus to his disciples, encouraging them as they help the poor, struck me: "Inasmuch as ye have done it unto one of the least of these my brethren, ye have done it unto me." Matthew's Jesus urges us to attend to the unnoticed stuff, which will never appear on Instagram or the local news.

That is our defense, too, and the kind of story I was looking to tell here. It's raising an infant and caring for her bedridden mother. It's the joy that comes from removing a prostitute's pimp tattoo. It's running a community center in a crumbling neighborhood and saving a town's most reviled from lethal winter weather. Adopting a pit bull and hiring an addict in recovery.

After years of interviews, research, and writing, finally, that's what this national saga has left me with. That the lessons of neuroscience, the epidemic, and the pandemic are really the same: that we are strongest in community, as weak as our most vulnerable, and the least of us lie within us all.

Angie and Starla VI

Starla Hoss died on the afternoon of Thursday, November 14, 2019, in the nursing home in Elizabethton, Tennessee, where she had lain for most of the seven years since she arrived, her feet filthy and worn, from Sacred Heart Hospital in Pensacola. She was thirty-three.

Her decline came quickly as her body began to fail. Angie called Maude Buchanan to ask if there was anyone from the family who might want to come visit Starla one last time. No, Maude said, there wasn't.

Angie thought back to her few encounters with Starla before her overdose—the first meeting in a group home, then Starla's jailhouse wedding. Angie remembered the promise she made to this lost young woman, casually at the time, and how that had changed her own life as well. She remembered laying the infant against Starla's cheek.

Angie feared Bella would resent Starla, who had bequeathed her a life of medical problems. The little girl might live with the anger that Angie felt as a young woman before that night tied to the back of the USS *Cape Cod*. Angie had to cross the Pacific Ocean to leave bitterness for love. She hoped Bella could learn it sooner. To Angie, that was part of protecting the girl through to adulthood—that she should be the first in her blood family unscarred by drugs and all that came with them.

It sometimes overwhelmed Angie to see Bella's desire to love the mother who could neither hug her nor speak. One morning they rolled Starla outside the nursing home to a garden. Bella picked a flower and placed it on Starla's arm over the scars where Starla had cut herself so often as a teenager.

A few years passed before Bella grew old enough to realize that Starla couldn't see or talk. Starla's son, Ezra, visited. Bella asked him how Starla sounded when she spoke. "She didn't have a loud voice," Ezra told her. "She laughed a lot. She jumped in the leaves with me."

When Bella turned six, she asked Angie how Starla came to be this way. Starla used drugs, Angie said, and was around people who weren't nice. Angie told an abbreviated version of Starla's story. This harmed you as well, she said, because you were in her tummy. It took a while for all this information to settle on the little girl. What could have happened, Bella wondered, that made her mother use drugs, which everyone knew to be bad? Wouldn't Starla know this as well?

The day Starla passed, Angie sat with the body, brushed her hair, washed her, and changed her clothes—the things she had always done, one last time. It was sad that none of Starla's blood relatives were there, but by now Angie and Bella were her family. That night, at home, Angie told Bella that Starla had died. "She's not sick anymore," the child said. "She's happy."

The next day, Angie and Bella visited the funeral home to make arrangements for the service. When they were leaving, Bella asked, "Mom, where's the cake, chips, and piñata? It's a celebration, there has to be cake." From the parking lot, Angie called a baker. Bella took the phone from her mother. She needed, she said, a pink cake with strawberries around the side. She told the baker, too, that the cake had to have words on it, and she told the baker what those words should be.

Four dozen mourners attended the memorial that Sunday at the funeral home in Elizabethton. Maude Buchanan and a few others from Starla's family showed up and stayed as long as the service. It was almost seven years since Maude had appeared at Angie's TLC Clinic with that infant in the car seat. Now the girl was growing up, cheerful and healthy. Bella greeted friends and admired their flowers. Starla had gone to the angels, she said, so it was not a time for sadness. Angie stood and spoke, remembering Starla's smile, her desire to be accepted.

Then they went downstairs, where balloons and chips were set out on folding tables. A large, flat pink cake, dotted with strawberries, lay on one table. On it were the words, in red icing, that Bella had asked the baker to print. Those words, which Angie later put on Starla's gravestone, were these:

"I Love You no matter what happened."

Epilogue

Return to Dreamland

In December of 2019 a temporary ice-skating rink went up on a lot in downtown Portsmouth, Ohio, a small town on the Ohio River.

Once upon a time, in the 1990s, Portsmouth led the country into the epidemic of opioid addiction. The town was the nation's capital of the scandalous pain clinics—pill mills—where doctors prescribed opioids by the millions, for cash.

I'd been to Portsmouth many times to write that story. This time was different. I'd come to see Winterfest, an outdoor celebration of Christmas organized by folks who were the guerrilla fighters in a counterinsurgency against dope.

Winterfest was simple—it was the skating rink, bounded by stands of vendors selling popcorn, smoked pulled pork, and deep-fried Oreos. Second Street ran alongside it, and the street was now bathed in the glow of the Christmas lights wrapped around trees and in store windows.

On the Saturday night before Christmas, the cold was bitter but the crowd was large. Children wobbled by on skates, chirping and yelping as they held desperately to the rail before falling on their butts, laughing. "It's Beginning to Look a Lot like Christmas" played over the loudspeaker. Mothers held out their arms to their daughters inching forward. A few skaters confidently curved around the rink.

Standing at the railing and quietly watching them pass stood a fellow who was not from Portsmouth. Josh Wood had come down from northern Ohio. He was from the rural hamlet of Crooksville, pop. 2,500, east of Columbus. He was thirty-two. He had spent years addicted to heroin and methamphetamine. He knew some carpentry and landscaping, but most of what he'd done with his life involved those drugs. He'd sold his car for meth. After that he walked a lot, fed himself on what he could buy at Crooksville's Dollar General, and spent most of his time looking for dope.

Then he was arrested. He detoxed in jail and began to think more clearly. Hearing that the town of Portsmouth offered job training to recovering addicts, he asked to be sent there. He arrived in January 2019, a felon with a shaved head, handsome but gaunt from the dope, and ashamed of what he'd made of his life. He lacked confidence in his future.

Josh Wood had that in common with the town. Portsmouth had once been named an All-America City, with a steel mill, shoe factories, a bustling Main Street, and an enduring optimism. Then the mill left; so did the shoe factories and the optimism. Half the town's people fled in the 1980s. With them went skilled tradesmen and an invigorating, seat-of-the-pants entrepreneurism. Chillicothe Street downtown emptied. Buildings and houses stood vacant. Town governance disintegrated into back-biting and recalls. Dreamland, the town's enormous pool, its soul and central meeting place, was dug up in 1993 and replaced by a parking lot and a strip mall. A couple of years later, prescription narcotic pain pills blew in like locusts.

In Ohio, pain-pill addiction and its consequences got bad first in Portsmouth. After that, the state's public health maps each year showed the red stain spreading north, as if dope had captured an outpost and from there it conquered more of Ohio every year. Meanwhile, Ohioans, if they thought about Portsmouth at all, gave up on the town. Many in town did the same. On paper, Portsmouth was the last place anyone like Josh Wood would turn to for sobriety.

His first night in the town, though, he attended a meeting of Alcoholics Anonymous at the All Saints Episcopal Church. It was packed. Close to two hundred people. Wood had been to many AA meetings, but never one like this. Folks were standing or sitting along the walls. The largest AA meeting he'd been to had fifteen people. Wood was startled to see so many people, and he left that night with some hope for himself as well.

Now, a year later, Wood had filled out. He smiled more. Spoke confidently. He met Tiffany Robinson, who was from up north and, like Wood, requested to be sent to Portsmouth for treatment. Together they formed the kind of relationship that neither had experienced in addiction; one in which life was not grim, but fun in each other's company. That's how it seemed, anyway, from the videos of duets they sang in the car that they put up on Facebook.

Wood now supervised a small construction crew rehabbing abandoned brick buildings downtown, and lived in a remodeled apartment in one of them. He felt part of something creative and affirming, and this allowed him joy of the kind he hadn't felt in years. He was, furthermore, one of the guys who had installed the ice-skating rink that brought out these kids and their families on this cold Saturday night before Christmas. Winterfest and the skating rink seemed simple ideas. But they amounted to something powerful, almost radical: they formed the first large public place since Dreamland pool closed where people in Portsmouth could actually be outside together.

"It's good memories for them—the world is about creating good memories for your kids," he told me. "I didn't forget my first time ice skating."

I FIRST CAME to Portsmouth in 2013. I was working on my book about the plague of opioid addiction stretching coast to coast. I saw only the town's dope story: a generation of addicts who stole the manhole covers and copper wire and pawned their children's Christmas presents. But

I returned several times, and as I did, as I was finishing the book that I named for the town's vanished pool, it struck me that another story was taking shape. It was a tentative thing, of addicts in sobriety and struggling to keep it while adding energy and optimism to the town. Twelve-step meetings took place every day. I saw tiny businesses forming, lonely outposts in a vacant downtown, creating the slightest quiver of economic activity. There was a café, then another, a couple of gyms, a yogurt shop, a vendor of comic books and graphic novels.

Residents and business owners who wanted to push this optimism formed Friends of Portsmouth. They organized public events to promote community pride. In August of 2018 hundreds came out to paint downtown curbs and light poles, replace streetlights, and plant trees—none of which had been done in years. At the first Winterfest a few months later, the town set the Guinness World Record for most people outside singing Christmas carols at one time. They did this in the pouring rain.

The town's dire drug situation did not let up. On the contrary, as Ohio's overdose deaths fell, they rose in Portsmouth. In 2019 they would triple, mostly now because fentanyl and its analogues that Paul Janssen had identified decades before had followed the pills. Then came that flood of P2P crystal meth, and the opiate users switched to this new option. The visitors to the town's Friday needle exchange grew.

In fact, when I returned that year, it seemed that a war was underway for Portsmouth's soul. It pitted the fiercest synthetic drugs the global underworld could muster against the town's new micro-capitalists and recovering addicts.

All that, though, made another remarkable story easy to miss, and that story was this: addicts attempting recovery from all over Ohio were now *asking* to be sent to Portsmouth. The town was becoming a center of addiction recovery.

Having once led the country into the opioid addiction epidemic, Portsmouth seemed to be quietly leading it out. Those among the new arrivals who did well were staying, repopulating the town. Some relapsed. Others, though, were finding their footing in Portsmouth. Slowly they were filling the gaps left by factory workers who'd departed thirty years before, bringing gratitude, energy, and some of the optimism that the town hadn't felt in a while.

Many came for a nonprofit known as the Counseling Center. TCC began years ago as a small house. As the opioid epidemic cut through Portsmouth, the center grew and was now one of the largest employers in Scioto County—with 375 people on staff, many of them once deemed unemployable due to years of street addiction. Beyond the refuge it offered addicts, TCC had assembled a set of treatment, job, and housing services that was unique across Ohio.

Eleven treatment centers now operated in Portsmouth, with many more located within a twenty-five-mile radius. Salaries for licensed social workers and drug counselors leaped as those centers competed for their labor.

A few things made all this possible. For one, the most visible sign of Portsmouth's long decline: abandoned buildings. The Counseling Center alone had refurbished and expanded into forty-eight of them, and this gave it space to accommodate the addicts who began to flow into Portsmouth. Other treatment centers did the same. Abandoned houses were renovated and seeing new life as sober-living homes. This included majestic three-story mansions that dated to the early 1900s in the town's now-withered East End.

Portsmouth's rejuvenation was due to the expansion of Medicaid under Obamacare, which Ohio governor John Kasich, a Republican, had accepted over the objections of his own party's legislators. By expanding Medicaid, Obamacare covered addiction treatment for hundreds of thousands of Ohioans. This included virtually all the clients coming south to the Portsmouth treatment centers. Kasich "saved many lives single-handedly in doing that," said Jay Hash, director of HopeSource, one of the new treatment centers in Portsmouth, who had worked at the Counseling Center. Because of Medicaid expansion,

Hash told me, "people are also now earning a wage treating a crisis. The substance-abuse professional has grown in esteem."

The Counseling Center plowed the money it made from residential treatment into services that were unprofitable but necessary to recovery: sober housing, child care, job training, daily meals for addicts in treatment, and exercise through it all. The promise of these services attracted the addicts coming down to Portsmouth.

I met a guy named Brandon Elkins, whom I found to be fairly eloquent on the topic of what Portsmouth meant to recovering addicts. Elkins spent years hooked on heroin in his small town of Washington Courthouse, Ohio, before asking a probation officer to send him down to TCC. There he relapsed twice, but he stayed, and now seemed to be doing well. "As a recovering addict, this is the mecca," Elkins told me. "If you want a solution, a new way to live, you can find it here in Portsmouth now. There's also tons of dope. I hear shopping carts going down my alley every single night; they're digging through my trash.

"It's whether you have the willingness to change who you are, or you don't. You can get behind the idea that it's not my fault and it's a disease. But it's like a diabetic continuing to eat the same sugary crap that's going to put him in a coma. You got to take responsibility for your drug use."

WHAT WAS GOING on in Portsmouth involved more than just folks like Brandon Elkins and Josh Wood, coming from across Ohio seeking recovery.

There was also the homegrown energy of small entrepreneurs who'd somehow found each other when the town seemed a depot of drug users.

One of them was Dale King. King had left the region to join the army and, in 2005, was sent to Iraq. He arrived at the beginning of the worst of the Sunni counterinsurgency against the American invasion. King's job was training Iraqis as special forces. The idea was to train alongside them, build them up. "The biggest way to teach people to overcome things is you have to provide physical challenges for them to do," he said. "You have to get them to believe in themselves. Common suffering creates common bonds. That was the model in Iraq. Take people off the street who know nothing of warfare. In Iraq within six months we had guys going on missions and taking back their country."

King returned from Iraq in 2007 to find Portsmouth embroiled in what he called "an opioid insurgency"—dilapidated buildings, pill mills, drug addiction everywhere. He spent three years angry at the town and doing a job he hated. Finally, he quit the job, bought an abandoned downtown car dealership, and opened a CrossFit gym. The gym was among the first new businesses in downtown in years. Its customers were people like him, upset at Portsmouth's condition and folks in it. King took energy from the venture, daunting though it was. "It gave me a new unit to belong to," he said.

The psychology of exercise fascinated King, and he wondered why addiction treatment rarely included it. "You can only sit and talk your way through it so much in group sessions. They're great. But they're missing the physical component. You have to sweat. Let those demons out; beat them into submission." He called the gym's Saturday-morning workouts "pain clinics"—a middle finger to the pain clinics/pill mills that were at the time dispensing narcotics all over town. On the wall he painted a quote from punk-rock singer/philosopher Henry Rollins: "Pain is not my enemy. It is my call to greatness."

What was germinating in Portsmouth, in fact, had a good bit to do with a kind of punk rock, do-it-yourself attitude. King added another motto to his gym: "Nobody's coming." Folks had to depend on each other to emerge from dope and decay. Meanwhile, drug users walked by his gym all day long, and never once did he talk to them or ask their names. He saw them as slothful and part of the problem. Dale King spent the next several years hunkered down in this outpost in a lonesome grapple with Portmouth's collapse.

Then one of his CrossFit clients, Bill Dever, a lawyer for the Counseling Center, pushed TCC to incorporate King's training into treatment for its clients. TCC began paying for workout sessions. With that, many of the people King recognized as downtown drug users began to show up in his gym, running, squatting, pumping, pulling themselves up. Finally he had to learn their names.

Among his clients, beginning in January 2019, was Josh Wood, just in from up north. He became a CrossFit regular. Working out with others showed him in little ways what he was capable of after years of dope convincing him of all he couldn't do. It released his brain's endorphins. He felt in control again.

A node of economic energy began to form in a zone of Portsmouth that hadn't seen it in a generation. King went on to open an apparel line, 3rd & Court, for the corner he occupied, and an all-natural skin care line, Doc Spartan. He watched the clients from the Counseling Center work out, and he hired the most committed. When I visited him, he employed eighteen people in his three companies. Decades before, the town's prosperity had grown from a few large factories, each employing hundreds. Those days were over, King believed. Now Portsmouth needed many small businesses, each employing a few people. That's how the beachhead would form.

A few blocks away, Tim Wolfe was another who applied military experience to rebuilding the town. He'd served on a team of engineers in the Ohio National Guard that went to Iraq when the United States invaded in 2003. Over the next two years, the team rebuilt high schools and hospitals. Back in Portsmouth several years later, Wolfe migrated into construction. Portsmouth's downtown was full of beautiful, empty brick buildings, some of them a century old, which the town had the good sense not to knock down. In 2014 Wolfe and a partner bought one of them for $2,000 and set about remodeling it into apartments. He was new to the business of rebuilding a town, but it didn't feel too daunting. "I done that in Iraq while I was being shot at," he said, "so I thought surely I can figure out how to tuck-point a brick building in Portsmouth, Ohio."

Wolfe's problem was finding workers. They were scarce. Addicts, though, were everywhere. When Wolfe dug into their backgrounds, he found they were truck drivers, carpenters, ironworkers, architects. Unions were as avid for workers as he was. Two things stood between addicts and a decent job: a clean drug test and a valid driver's license. The first of these was easy, the second a torment. Many had lost their driver's licenses, had fines they couldn't pay, warrants for driving without a license. Wolfe discovered that this forced many of them to live like survivalists. They walked everywhere. Without reliable transportation, they couldn't find or keep a job. They also avoided bank accounts, which could be garnished to pay those same fines. They worked for cash only. This one predicament—the lost driver's license—stunted their lives and kept them in addiction.

Wolfe hired a couple of them just in sobriety and helped them pay off their fines. He teamed with the Counseling Center to form a job-training program in the trades he needed. As part of that, TCC expanded its continuum of medical care to include helping recovering addicts pay fines and regain those licenses. By the time I visited in 2019, the center was opening a line of credit at a local bank to pay off the fines of clients who completed its job-training program.

Among the first to go through this was Josh Wood. He owed $600 in court fines he couldn't pay. When he completed the center's job training program, Wolfe hired him, paid his fines, and took $20 out of his weekly paycheck. With that, Wood recovered his driver's license and could drive the center's van.

Wolfe, meanwhile, employed Wood and others trained at TCC in the details of caring for those century-old brick buildings. In one building he put a restaurant, Patties and Pints. The restaurant attracted people downtown for the first time in many years. Above it he remodeled spaces for apartments, some of which he rented to his workers.

Wolfe joined TCC's board. He urged it to buy a hulking building on Portsmouth's East Side. Known as the Mitchellace building, it was where a shoelace factory, the last of the town's once-thriving and innovative shoe industry, was housed. A lot of the town's history was wrapped up in it. The original owners had invented a machine to weave shoelaces back in the early 1900s. In its prime Mitchellace had provided work for a thousand people and created shoelaces by the millions every year. It was owned for years by the extended Williams family, one of whose members owned Dreamland pool. The company, after changes of ownership, continued to pump out shoelaces, though it was now a smaller operation, one that could be housed elsewhere. But the building's size echoed its past. It comprised seven floors, each seemingly the size of a football field. Wolfe thought it could be part of the town's future. The building, Wolfe believed, could consolidate the Counseling Center's operations, which were then flung across those forty-eight once-abandoned buildings. In the Mitchellace building, TCC would provide a clinic for addicts coming in off the street.

"The idea that somebody could walk in, in crisis, and be diagnosed and treated—what a novel idea!" said Ed Hughes. "At a hospital, I think they call it an emergency room."

Hughes was TCC's director while I was writing *Dreamland*, and we spoke often. He had started at the center, a recovering alcoholic, when it was one small house. Then in the mid-1990s the epidemic gathered force, and the center had to expand. That expansion hadn't stopped. Now retired, Hughes saw TCC evolving as hospitals had. Hospitals created areas of care, all in one health network. The profitable parts of those health systems—surgery, say—supported the others. Americans took for granted this continuum of health care, yet it did not exist for addiction. "If I had appendicitis and called up and there's refusal of care, long waiting lists—we wouldn't tolerate that," he said. "Things you would never tolerate in health care still happen in the addiction industry."

The Counseling Center, he said, was building that continuum of care for addicts, plowing money from residential treatment into the other services that weren't profitable. For if the epidemic showed anything, it was that three or six months of residential treatment was not enough.

Hughes's wife was a dietician for years in a dialysis clinic. Half the patients had Type 2 diabetes and were addicted to sugary food; they could not stop consuming the food industry's processed carbohydrates. Doctors kept upping their insulin, even as the patients lost limbs and eyesight. There wasn't much attention paid to the roots of their food addiction. "Nobody's helping them. People just say, 'Why are you still eating that?'" Hughes said. "The docs don't know what to do about the addiction part of it. They just know to say 'Quit eating doughnuts.'"

Life repair was the key, Hughes was convinced, and it turned out that that was done most successfully in community with others. The numbers of recovering addicts were growing and forming a market for that idea in Portsmouth.

Across town was a full-service gym, housed in a cavernous building that had once been the racquetball club attached to the Dreamland pool. The gym now had six hundred members. Within it, a CrossFit started with a hundred or so people, taking the name CrossFit Dreamland.

Michael Longmire runs CrossFit Dreamland's sessions for recovering addicts. A bearded redhead and a former high school basketball player, Longmire got addicted to meth and cocaine in the early 1990s, then quit. "Food was the next thing that was making me feel good," he said. He ballooned to three hundred pounds. "I couldn't just eat a slice; I'd eat a whole eighteen-inch pizza. The processed food was the stuff that was killing me," he said. "Sugar is just as powerful a drug as anything else. It'll kill you the way meth or heroin will. Around here, people are starting to notice that."

Longmire discovered CrossFit seven years ago. He dove into it with the zeal he'd once reserved for cocaine or processed food. He obtained his CrossFit instructor's license. He fell in love, married, and had two children. Now, in his forties, Longmire weighs two hundred pounds. CrossFit was the opposite of addiction, Longmire believed. "CrossFit gives you this feeling that I achieved this. In your daily routine, that confidence goes with you," Longmire said. "That's why once students get a taste of hope, see change happening, they become evangelists for it."

I spoke to Nelson Klaiber, a firefighter, pastor, and CrossFit Dreamland member who runs Iron Body Community Church out of the gym, and whose wife, Amanda, is a trainer.

"For some reason, people are sitting around waiting for the next big business, or the government, to save them," Klaiber said one day when we met at the gym, speaking over the noise of clanging barbells. "It's community that's going to change this. People won't go next door and borrow a cup of sugar from their neighbors anymore. They don't know their neighbors. They don't have relationships. We should be the most connected people of all time, and we're the most disconnected. Christ took twelve men and changed everything. He did it with relationships. The entire model of Christianity is relationship based. That's what you see at this CrossFit."

SEEING THIS NEW energy, Shawnee State University opened a center for entrepreneurial training in a downtown building that had once been a beauty school and, before that, a furniture store. Through grants, the Kricker Innovation Hub was, among other things, designing training for recovering addicts in starting a business.

David Kilroy, the Hub's director, had studied city planning at Ohio State University and knew little about addiction when he took the job, but he had learned. Recovering addicts, he saw, were one of only two groups in town whose populations were growing—the other being students at Shawnee State.

Social outcasts had been one of the keys to urban revival in America. Activating the energies of the newly arriving population of outcasts—recovering addicts—was among Kilroy's many unexpected jobs at the center. He was surprised to see that many of them feared starting a business—believing it wasn't for them. That was strange, he thought, for their resourcefulness was undeniable. They were natural entrepreneurs. No one displays more ingenuity and focus than an addict in finding drugs each day.

As it happened, Kilroy got to know his new town, in part, by going often to the Lofts Coffee Company, one of two independent cafés that had opened downtown. These cafés marked a return to the kind of communal life that had been a part of Portsmouth when Dreamland pool existed. The cafés also offered a nonalcoholic place to meet with others.

I saw them as barometers. I'd concluded while traveling the country that you could gauge a town's economic effervescence by how many cafés it had. Wi-Fi, laptops, and cellphones had transformed the café into the new office. "People go to a coffee shop to talk about what they're working on," Kilroy said. "That's how businesses start. Those third places—not home and not the office—are so important." A Starbucks along the interstate didn't boost a town's public life. "There's something different about an independent coffee shop," he told me. "It's socially driven, and not following a corporate strategy."

A Tuesday-morning leadership group had been meeting there since the place opened in 2016. It was at that leadership group, one Tuesday morning, that Kilroy met Brandon Elkins. They struck up a conversation about books they'd read. Elkins was reading Jack Kerouac's *On the Road*. A friendship developed, and Kilroy hired Brandon at the Kricker to help plan a speaker series.

By now, Brandon Elkins had lived in Portsmouth for three years, and virtually everyone he knew in town was in recovery. Their presence angered some local folks; recovering addicts, they felt, added to Portsmouth's crime-and-drug image. But Elkins thought this was unlikely. Those he knew who relapsed—they left town. They didn't stay. They went back home, where they knew the dealers. Those who stayed, like Elkins himself, usually did so because they were in recovery and *afraid* to go home.

Portsmouth was taking in the state's lost and hollow-eyed junkies. The town offered a bubble of protection to keep the dope at bay. Now patients could restore luster to their skin, rediscover gratitude and a fresh energy for life's possibilities. From across Ohio they had come riding into Portsmouth—a cavalry of skinny, pocked folks, terrified of the street dope they were compelled to use and armed only with the "gift of desperation." As word of Portsmouth spread across the state, they saw in this Appalachian outcast a last chance.

And, in turn, they were like a shot of naloxone, jolting Portsmouth alive again. Beaten and bruised, each—the town and the addicts—leaned on the other. An addiction-recovery scene was forming. There were rivalries, frictions, competition. Some of what was tried worked, some of it didn't. Elkins could be critical of the Counseling Center, which was the reason he had come to Portsmouth. Now, he believed, it had grown too big, had strayed from the twelve-step approach to addiction recovery that he believed had saved his life. But he knew there were many paths to addiction recovery.

So Brandon Elkins preferred to see the energy in all this. This part of the Ohio River Valley was forming into something like a Silicon Valley of addiction recovery for Ohio. Maybe one day for the country. Either way, the business of addiction treatment was now everywhere. Why don't people here embrace it? Elkins thought. The steel mills sure aren't coming back.

THE SATURDAY BEFORE Christmas in 2019, I stood with Josh Wood and Tiffany Robinson in front of the Winterfest skating rink. During winter freezes decades ago, the town had sprayed water on parkland; that ice is where kids learned to skate. No one sprayed that water anymore, so knowledge of ice-skating had skipped a generation. Now, at Winterfest, kids lurched around the rink, learning again.

"It puts a smile on my face every time," Wood said.

Josh Wood was planning on staying in Portsmouth. He was surrounded by a family of recovering addicts and twelve-step meetings of all sizes. He was still reluctant to take a higher-paying union job. Some of the workers on those jobs would be using, and he didn't think he was ready for that. So he was remaining in Portsmouth's protective cocoon of recovery. "I've never been this positive, this happy," he told me. "The better I do, the more I want to become."

The year of 2020, in fact, would turn into one of his best. He and Tiffany married. Josh started his own business, Woody's Remodeling, rehabbing houses. Tiffany did as well, starting a cleaning service called Get It Done. "We've been blessed getting the opportunities we've had down here," Josh said. No one had spoken of Portsmouth as a town of opportunity for a long time. In 2020, the town would again be named an All-America City, citing its response to the opioid epidemic.

Josh and Tiffany were part of a collective rewiring of the brain's reward pathways in Portsmouth, toward enjoying again the dopamine released by what our brains had evolved to prize: exercise, moving forward, and being with others in public, the way townspeople did at Dreamland pool years before. Downtown restaurants, the cafés, the remodeled old brick buildings, the CrossFits—to people here these were more than just new businesses. They were beachheads, thin bulwarks of community defense against dope, fatalism, processed food, obesity, blight, and the reliance on pills for health.

Portsmouth was slowly emerging into the kind of recovery-ready community that Jason Merrick envisioned for Kenton County, Kentucky. Maybe it wasn't too far-fetched to imagine those Ohio public-health maps one day showing the blue of health and revival spreading north out of Portsmouth the way the red of addiction did for years. A long shot—but who knows?

Folks once among the walking dead were emerging as a precious new natural resource, indeed, like fossil fuel, energy rising from decay.

More addicts sought refuge here. Portsmouth seemed to show that a community could grow strong again by aiding the despised.

Josh Wood clung to all this as he made this last chance his home. We stood beside the skating rink in that crisp, cold Saturday night before Christmas. He was just proud, he said, to have helped build something that brought people outdoors together, where kids chirped and squealed as they wobbled along.

"They got so much more plans for what all this is going to be. I'm so excited to be part of it, to actually help it become what it's going to become.

"That," he said, "is going to be a great story."

ACKNOWLEDGMENTS

I'm grateful to all the people I've interviewed for this book—those I mentioned above and those I cannot. I am also thankful to all who invited me to come speak to their towns, their associations, their professional conferences, their classes, and book groups. They provided me a way of seeing the country that I had not expected but which allowed me a new view of all that was going on.

Wall Street Journal editor Sam Enriquez, who hired me at the *Los Angeles Times* years ago and remains the best editor I've ever had, read the manuscript and, as usual, provided essential edits and comments.

I don't drink coffee, but I wrote a lot of this book at independent cafés, which were my offices before the pandemic: Kaldi's Coffee, Jones Coffee, Charlie's Coffee, Jitterz (Kenton, Ohio), Lofts Coffee Company (Portsmouth, Ohio), Stonewall Coffee (Clarksburg, West Virginia). Independent cafés add so much to a town. Thanks also to Freedom.to, the software that allows me to shut down social-media apps and as much of the internet as I need to and focus.

My thanks are to Anton Mueller, my editor at Bloomsbury Publishing, for pushing me to do this book when I didn't know what I would write, to Stephany Evans, my agent, for arranging it to happen, and to Miranda Ottewell for her assiduous copy editing.

Finally, I give my thanks and love to my wife and daughter, who lived cheerfully and with support and patience with another long journalistic trek through this national saga.

VOCABULARY

This book of journalism tries to distill and explain issues connected to drug trafficking, addiction, and neuroscience. These topics are now of top importance to daily life in America, to policy formulation, how budgets are allocated, and more. Thus my intention throughout has been to make them understandable to laypeople with no background in science or in the manufacturing of illegal drugs.

But there are some terms that are helpful to know.

Opiate/Opioid: I use the words *opiate* and *opioid* interchangeably for the most part. Technically, though, opioids are all drugs that attach to the brain's opioid receptors. Opiates are those opioids made from the opium poppy. However, in the United States in the last few years they have become synonymous in popular speech—hence my usage.

Naloxone/Narcan: Naloxone is the antidote to opiate overdose. It reverses the overdose, typically sending the user into withdrawals; Narcan is its brand name and has become a verb—*to Narcan* someone.

Suboxone: The brand name of a combination of buprenorphine and naloxone. Buprenorphine is an opioid that partially attaches to the brain's opioid receptors. It generally keeps users from overdosing and lessens withdrawals. Like all opioids, it is addictive. But it is also one of three drugs used for what is known as medically assisted treatment of addiction, the others being methadone and naltrexone (brand name Vivitrol).

Dopamine: The brain chemical—neurotransmitter—that is produced when we engage in activities the brain has learned are rewarding.

Nucleus accumbens: The part of the brain at its base that receives dopamine and urges us on to immediate pleasure and reward.

Prefrontal cortex: The part of the brain, located behind the forehead, that considers the consequences of our actions, often a balance to the nucleus accumbens.

Ephedrine: A precursor in a method of manufacturing methamphetamine that is usually deemed the easiest and most efficient, as ephedrine needs only minor molecular tweaks to be transformed into meth. Ephedrine and its cousin, pseudoephedrine, are similar in molecular makeup and both can be used to make methamphetamine. Both are derived from the ephedra plant, which has been used throughout human history as an antihistamine. Pseudoephedrine is used in modern over-the-counter decongestants, such as Sudafed.

Phenyl-2-propanone (P2P): A precursor in a more complicated method of manufacturing methamphetamine. Unlike with ephedrine, there are many chemical recipes to make P2P, using a wide variety of industrial chemicals.

NOTES

This is a book of journalism. The great majority of it draws from interviews I did, either in person or over the phone. In some cases, entire chapters relied on interviews. These include Angie Odom's story, as well as those from Hardin County, Ohio; Muncie, Indiana; and Portsmouth, Ohio.

The chapters on neuroscience owe much to Nicole Avena, her willingness to talk to a layman like me, and the studies she and her colleagues performed at the Hoebel neuroscience lab at Princeton in the early 2000s. Ashley Gearhardt was also very generous in taking time to explain the work she's done at her food lab at the University of Michigan. David Linden took time out from his work at his lab at Johns Hopkins University in Baltimore to help me understand the fundamentals of the brain's reward pathways. Each reviewed small portions of the early manuscript and helped point out what I'd missed. I'm grateful, too, that Tom Gould at Penn State University and Bruce Armitage at Carnegie Mellon University were willing to offer their perspectives on neuroscience, addiction, memory, and other fascinating topics.

Gary Henderson, now retired from UC Davis, gave me his recollections on the early days of fentanyl, his visits to the Janssen lab in Beerse, Belgium, and his months testing blood samples for fentanyl. Carlos Valdez at Lawrence Livermore National Laboratory spent several telephone calls explaining the details of what makes fentanyl, heroin, and morphine effective painkillers. Carl Anderson at Duquesne University's School of Pharmacy was nice enough to explain to me the intricacies of pharmaceutical mixing. Martin Paulus, director for the Laureate Institute for Brain Research at the University of Tulsa, helped me better understand meth's effect on the brain. Barry Logan at NMS Labs spent time giving me his perspectives on emerging trends in synthetic drugs.

I went to visit Angie Odom at the urging of Sullivan County district attorney Barry Staubus while I was giving speeches in Bristol and Johnson City, Tennessee, in November of 2018. It was only toward the end of a two-hour chat that Angie told me the story I never forgot, of her nighttime watch tied to the back of the USS *Cape Cod*. I was mesmerized. It seemed connected to the other remarkable tale of Starla Hoss, and how Angie came to adopt her daughter. These seemed the kind of stories I needed to tell in this book. In Florida, Dr. Jim Thorp, Chaplain Ellen Blaise, and retired nurse Ellen Stanley told me of caring for Starla in a vegetative state until her child was born. Maude Buchanan spent time with me, telling me the story of her daughter and Maude's visits to Florida. I want to also thank Earl and Bella Odom for all their kind help.

I came to Kenton County in the fall of 2015 as Unit 104 was about to open because by then I was convinced that changing how jail was done had to be part of our response to the addiction epidemic, and I wanted to see how that might happen. Over the years, I visited another four or five times. There I met Jason Merrick, who was trying to figure it out. Jason's perspective was always thoughtful and provided me with new directions I might investigate. I also met Will Pfefferman, whose story of fall and rise was especially fascinating. Never had a boring conversation with Will, that's for sure. I want to thank the top officials in that county, Terry Carl and Kris Knochelmann, for their openness and willingness to talk. Steve Fariello met with me twice at length, and spoke to me over the phone at length as well, to tell me about his trek from prison to recovery. Jo Martin met with me in her Tattoo Removal Ink studio to show me how tattoos were removed and tell me her story. Charlotte Wethington met with me, as well as spoke to me by phone, to tell her son's story and the story of the law that bears his name. I met Alecia Webb-Edgington at the Life Learning Center, where she explained to me how the LLC came to expand its role in the community. Many others, too numerous to name, helped me understand the changes in Kenton County. I want to say, too, that I interviewed numerous men and women in Kenton County Detention Center's Unit 104 over several visits, all of whose input was invaluable.

I first interviewed Lou Ortenzio over the phone in the summer of 2018. Months later, I met him when I went to Clarksburg to write his story of redemption, which first appeared in the *Atlantic* magazine. As I continued to visit Clarksburg, I saw the damage inflicted by P2P meth and the home-lessness it provoked. I also heard the astonishing story of the winter of 2019 from Lou, Karen Alastanos, Katie Wolfe-Elbon, Anjellica Scott, Jeff Hanlin, Norman Lowe, and others. That tale, like others in this book that I learned on the road, seemed to me to be something worth telling. I also thank Kayla Toryak, Ben Randolph, Brenda Smothers, Phyllis Mills, Tom Dyer, Jim Harris, Gary Hamrick, Jesse Clevenger, Melissa Carter, Joe Shaffer, Dr. Denzil Hawkenberry II, and the cozy Stonewall Coffee, near the courthouse in Clarksburg, where I wrote some of this book.

I went to Muncie, Indiana, after meeting Jud Fisher at a medical confer-ence where I spoke, and hearing his approach to development: building base-ball diamonds first as a south-side beachhead and a way of energizing a small neighborhood. That seemed right in line with the kind of story I was looking to tell. When I got there, I began to see the importance of the tool-and-die shop to the town and the country. Along the way, I heard the remarkable story of Mike "Bird" Kissick. Many people more than I can mention here helped me understand the town and tool-and-die shops. But among them I'd like to thank Jackie Cooper, Shannon McCormick, Jackie Hanoman, Lindsey Arthur, Wes Russell, Craig Graybeal, Jeremi Dobbs, and Gordon Cox.

I met Hardin County sheriff Keith Everhart at a speech I gave at Ohio Northern University. He told me a little about Rob Burd, who was working then as a sheriff's dispatcher after years of addiction. That seemed the kind of quiet but remarkable story I wanted to tell. I visited Hardin several times. Rob Burd was always forthcoming, happy to talk, as were Keith Everhart and members of his department. Judge Scott Barrett spoke with me about his life and the beginnings of his Recovery Court, and allowed me to sit in on the court and his planning sessions. At the court, I met Aaron McPherson and Mimi Zarzar, both of whom were illuminating about their jobs, and the addic-tion and recovery of their court clients. Thanks also to Scott Holbrook, Terry Sneary, Laurel Rogers, Cheryl Brooks, Becky Rish, Danielle Snyder, Josh Van Atta, Jawna Ferrell, Sherry Magann and Ray Legge, the wonderful Tracy Morrison (once again), and the folks at the warm and welcoming Jitterz in Kenton, where I did interviews and wrote a lot.

I returned to Portsmouth, Ohio, three times for this book because I wanted to see whether the glimmer of recovery I saw writing *Dreamland* had grown.

It had. Not that the town doesn't have many problems, but I found an energy, optimism, and progress that was undeniable. Bill Dever spoke to me several times by phone to talk about what he saw as the exciting elements taking shape in Portsmouth. Dale King and Tim Wolfe took time to meet with me and talk about their entrepreneurial projects downtown. I met Brandon Elkins and David Kilroy at the Kricker Innovation Hub in downtown Portsmouth. Both of them spent time explaining their lives and perspectives on what was going on in Portsmouth. Josh Wood and Tiffany Robinson Wood also explained their struggles with addiction, and why Portsmouth meant a new beginning for both of them. As always, the magnificent Lisa Roberts helped me with background to the city and its drug issues, which she sees firsthand at the health department. At CrossFit Dreamland, Nelson and Amanda Klaiber and Michael Longmire were among the many who helped me understand the importance of CrossFit to what was happening in Portsmouth. Andy Albrecht, Jay Hash, and Ed Hughes (the Man). Lofts Coffee Company in downtown Portsmouth is an invaluable addition to the new downtown Portsmouth, and it's where I wrote a portion or two of this book.

The entire family of Tommy Rauh in Akron very kindly invited me to their home to talk about the life of their son and brother. I especially want to thank Jim and Valorie Rauh, and their daughter, Ursula Messina—each of whom I also spoke to over the phone. Akron police detectives Mike Schmidt and Tim Harvey met to speak with me about their fascinating investigation into the deaths of Tommy Rauh and Bryan Stalnaker, and how they connected these deaths to Gordon Jin in China. DEA agent Matt Fitzpatrick and federal prosecutor Matt Cronin spent time over the phone and in person describing the investigation into Gordin Jin. Thanks also to Gary Guenther at the Summit County Medical Examiner's Office, and to Cleveland's US attorney Justin Herdman.

Meia Christian and Megan Pitts were nice enough to meet with me (via Zoom) to talk about their brother, Michael Tanner Jr. Thanks also to Jessica Sundell, to Marisa Darden, and to Tom Gilson, Cuyahoga County medical examiner.

I spent a lot of time interviewing people about the mental effects of P2P meth. This process went on for weeks, as I was concerned—because this aspect of the drug had not been reported in the news, nor had it been studied scientifically—about whether I was on the right track. As those weeks passed, these included recovering addicts, drug counselors, police officers, drug-court administrators, and psychologists, all of whom had firsthand experience with this new form of methamphetamine.

What I heard were similar stories from every part of the country. Eric Barrera first alerted me to the psychological damage of P2P meth. From there, I spoke to, and want to thank, L.A. County judge Craig Mitchell; John Gray, Juan Navarro, and Bill Tarkanian at L.A. CADA in Los Angeles; Matt Scharf at the Mission in Los Angeles; L.A. police officer Deon Joseph; Dr. Susan Partovi; Talie Wenick, Dr. Rachel Solotaroff, and Ed Blackburn in Oregon; Sarah Skoterro in Albuquerque; Lt. Matt Dietzel at Albuquerque Police Department and attorney Michael Cox; Jim Mahoney at West Virginia University; Jeri Thomas in Nashville, Dr. Jennie Jobe in Morgan County, and Chad Duncan, Lisa Tipton, Monica Tucker, and Kelsey Nicalek-Nelson in Johnson City, Tennessee; Cortney Baudendistel, Courtney Pence, Megan Hart, Melissa Miller, Linda Grove-Paul, and Judge Mary Ellen Diekhoff in southern Indiana; Eric Greene in Virginia; Zippy Dirkes and Kreg Gomez in Phoenix; and Giti Mayton and Dr. Megan Schabbing in Columbus, Ohio. Again, others spoke to me on the condition that they would not be identified. Their contributions to my understanding were priceless.

In writing about Purdue Pharma and the Sacklers, I relied heavily on legal complaints brought against them by attorneys general's offices around the country. I want to acknowledge the great help I received from staff of two offices in particular: Tennessee and Massachusetts. In Nashville, at the office of Attorney General Herbert Slatery, prosecutors Maggie Rowland and Brant Harrell spent time with me twice, explaining their investigation, digging into the subpoenaed company records. Thanks also to Samantha Fisher. In Boston, Attorney General Maura Healey was kind enough to talk to me (via Zoom). I picked the brains of prosecutors Sandy Alexander and Gillian Feiner, who explained their investigation and how they came to sue the Sackler family by name. I thank also their media officer, Jillian Fennimore.

Throughout my career, I've often reached out to those in custody to hear their stories. I've rarely had a bad interview with someone in custody on a story I'm working on. This project was no exception. I'd like to thank Rashad Martin, Phil Finley, Wyatt Pasek, and April Kelly, and some others I can't name. They were each of them kind enough to discuss their own criminal activities, while they strictly avoided talking about anyone else. I interviewed many others in custody as well who asked that I not mention them, nor use their stories, or whose stories didn't quite fit into what the book became. What they told me was nonetheless so important in shaping this book.

The Drug Enforcement Administration made available a number of agents whose perspectives, case details, and thoughts on the evolution of drug trafficking were invaluable. Several DEA agents I spoke with cannot be named due to the nature of their work. But they were nonetheless essential in helping me understand Mexican drug-trafficking organizations, the evolution of the trafficking trade, and the key figures involved.

However, I'm pleased that I can offer my gratitude publicly to Matt Donahue, who helped make these interviews possible. Eduardo Chavez and Ryan Rapaszky both spent a lot of time telling me their stories, as they related to the first Mexican fentanyl lab in Toluca, Mexico, and, in Chavez's case, how he saw methamphetamine unfold from the vantage point of his various DEA postings. Harvard professor of psychobiology Bertha Madras helped me understand the breadth of that Toluca case.

Tim Fritz explained to me the story of how large quantities of methamphetamine began coming into Louisville and changed that market. Todd Scott told me how he saw counterfeit pills, laced with fentanyl, emerge as the Mexican trafficking world's next product. Jon DeLena explained to me how the arrival of fentanyl had changed the drug-trafficking world in New England, and how the Magic Bullet blenders factored into all this. DEA chemists Joe Bozenko, Dean Kirby, and Steve Toske were huge in helping me understand trends in fentanyl and methamphetamine and their experiences investigating clandestine labs. Thanks to press officers Kevin McWilliams, Brian McNeal, Kameron Korte, Chuvalo Truesdell, Kevin O'Brien, and Mary Brandenberger for helping arrange these interviews.

Several retired agents provided history that was crucial to helping me understand how we got to where we are. Among them were Abe Perez, Milt Galanos (in Louisville), Mike Vigil, and Mike Cashman, who first explained to me about Magic Bullet blenders and their connection to clusters of fentanyl overdoses.

I spent several interviews, in person and over the phone, with now-retired federal prosecutor in San Diego Sherri Walker Hobson, talking about the emergency of fentanyl crossing the border from Mexico. I spoke also with Judge Larry Cho and attorney Luis Li, who helped me understand the 1990s, when they were both federal prosecutors and the Mexican meth industry and the Amezcua brothers were partly based in California. So, too, did Bob Pennal and Craig Hammer, both retired from California's now-disbanded Bureau of Narcotic Enforcement.

Of course, a journalist consults many published materials as well, and in my case, they were essential in shaping this book.

NEUROSCIENCE

For the neuroscience chapters, I consulted early studies on sugar-dependent rats done at Bart Hoebel's Princeton laboratory. These included:

Carlo Colantuoni, Pedro Rada, Joseph McCarthy, Caroline Patten, Nicole M. Avena, Andrew Chadeayne, and Bartley G. Hoebel, "Evidence That Intermittent, Excessive Sugar Intake Causes Endogenous Opioid Dependence," *Obesity Research* 10 (2002): 478–88.

Nicole M. Avena and Bartley G. Hoebel, "Amphetamine-sensitized Rats Show Sugar-Induced Hyperactivity (Cross-Sensitization) and Sugar Hyperphagia," *Pharmacology Biochemistry and Behavior* 74 (2003): 635–39.

N. M. Avena and B. G. Hoebel, "A Diet Promoting Sugar Dependency Causes Behavioral Cross-sensitization to a Low Dose of Amphetamine," *Neuroscience* 122 (2003): 17–20.

Nicole M. Avena, Carmen A. Carrillo, Lance Needham, Sarah F. Leibowitz, and Bartley G. Hoebel, "Sugar-Dependent Rats Show Enhanced Intake of Unsweetened Ethanol," *Alcohol* 34 (2004): 203–9.

P. Rada, N. M. Avena, and B. G. Hoebel, "Daily Bingeing on Sugar Repeatedly Releases Dopamine in the Accumbens Shell," *Neuroscience* 134 (2005): 737–44.

Erica M. Schulte, Nicole M. Avena, and Ashley N. Gearhardt, "Which Foods May Be Addictive? The Roles of Processing, Fat Content, and Glycemic Load," *PLOS One* 10 (2015): e0117959.

David A. Wiss, Nicole Avena, and Pedro Rada, "Sugar Addiction: From Evolution to Revolution," *Frontiers in Psychiatry* 9 (2018): 545.

On plant pesticides as human drugs of abuse, I consulted:
Edward H. Hagen, Casey J. Roulette, and Roger J. Sullivan, "Explaining Human Recreational Use of 'Pesticides': The Neurotoxin Regulation Model of Substance Use vs. the Hijack Model and Implications for Age and Sex Differences in Drug Consumption," *Frontiers in Psychiatry* 4 (2013): 142.
William Herkewitz, "Addictive Drugs That Are Actually Pesticides," www .mentalfloss.com, March 5, 2014.

A lot has been written on the locus coeruleus. I consulted:
N. Mehranfard and M. Navidhamidi, "Locus Coeruleus and Opioid Dependency," *Austin Addiction Sciences* 1 (2016): 1002.

"The Pleasure Centres Affected by Drugs," *The Brain: Bottom to Top* (blog), https://thebrain.mcgill.ca/flash/i/i_03/i_03_cr/i_03_cr_par/i_03_cr _par.html.
E. J. Van Bockstaele, B. A. S. Reyes, and R. J. Valentino, "The Locus Coeruleus: A Key Nucleus Where Stress and Opioids Intersect to Mediate Vulnerability to Opiate Abuse," *Brain Research* 1314 (2010): 162–74.

Much also has been written about Henry Molaison, neuroscience's most famous patient. The sources I used were:
Larry Squire, "The Legacy of Patient H.M. for Neuroscience," *Neuron* 61 (2009): 6–9.
Jenni Ogden, "HM, the Man with No Memory," *Psychology Today*, January 16, 2012. Dr. Ogden also published a wonderful book, *Trouble in Mind: Stories from a Neuropsychologist's Casebook* (New York: Oxford University Press, 2012), that includes a chapter on Mr. Molaison.

To help understand the evolution of the brain, I consulted Leda Cosmides and John Tooby, "Evolutionary Psychology: A Primer" (Center for Evolutionary Psychology, University of California, Santa Barbara, 1997).

I listened to many podcasts on neuroscience, but NPR's *Hidden Brain* proved especially helpful. Of the many episodes I listened to, those with Dr. Wendy Wood on breaking habits ("Creatures of Habit") and Dr. Molly

Crockett on outrage ("Screaming into the Void") were especially illuminating.

Several books were important in my understanding of the brain's reward pathways, including:

David Linden, *The Compass of Pleasure: How Our Brains Make Fatty Foods, Orgasm, Exercise, Marijuana, Generosity, Vodka, Learning, and Gambling Feel So Good* (New York: Viking, 2011).

Wendy Wood, *Good Habits, Bad Habits: The Science of Making Positive Changes That Stick* (New York: Farrar, Straus and Giroux, 2019).

Robert H. Lustig, *The Hacking of the American Mind*: The Science Behind the Corporate Takeover of Our Bodies and Brains (New York: Avery, 2017). Several videos of Dr. Lustig's speeches on YouTube were quite helpful. Among the best is this speech to the Silicon Valley Health Institute: https://youtu.be/bhh19cQukfg.

SACKLERS

I quote often from the attorneys general complaints from Tennessee and Massachusetts, which formed the foundation of the chapters on Purdue Pharma and the Sackler family. Both are available online.

TENNESSEE

https://www.tn.gov/content/dam/tn/attorneygeneral/documents/foi/purdue/purduecomplaint-5-15-2018.pdf.

MASSACHUSETTS

https://www.mass.gov/files/documents/2019/07/11/43_01%20First%20Amended%20Complaint%20filed%2001-31-2019_0.pdf.

In addition, Massachusetts compiled files on McKinsey's work for Purdue. Their files of documents were made available to the public on July 3, 2019, and remain available at the attorney general's website, https://www.mass.gov/orgs/office-of-attorney-general-maura-healey.

I also read the Tufts University investigation into Sackler family influence: https://president.tufts.edu/wp-content/uploads/Final-Report-Tufts-Sackler-and-Purdue-Pharma-December-2019.pdf.

I used two articles that helped in the latter chapters on the family:

Hamish Bowles, "Wild at Heart," *Vogue*, October 2013, https://archive.vogue.com/article/2013/10/01/wild-at-heart.

Norman Vanamee, "How Sackler Became the Most Toxic Name in Philanthropy," *Town & Country*, May 16, 2019.

On Northshore Recovery High School's graduation: Paul Leighton, "Recovery School Graduates Beat the Odds," *Salem News*, June 5, 2019.

DRUG TRAFFICKING

I made frequent use of the Drug Enforcement Administration's annual *National Drug Threat Assessment*, going back to 2008.

Ioan Grillo, *Blood Gun Money: How America Arms Gangs and Cartels* (New York: Bloomsbury, 2021).

Michael Pollan, *The Botany of Desire: A Plant's-Eye View of the World* (New York: Random House, 2001).

Philadelphia: "Unintentional Overdose Deaths," Substance Use Philadelphia, 2020.

San Francisco: Dr. Phillip Coffin, "Opioid and Stimulant Overdose Mortality in San Francisco: 2020 Update," San Francisco Department of Public Health.

Cuyahoga County: Cuyahoga County Medical Examiner, "Preliminary Drug Deaths Report," June 1, 2018.

FENTANYL

For the story of Paul Janssen, as well as the history of fentanyl, I relied on:

Harry Schwartz, *Breakthrough: The Discovery of Modern Medicines at Janssen* (Bartonville, IL: Skyline, 1989).

Theodore H. Stanley, "The Story of Fentanyl," *The Journal of Pain* 15 (2014): 1215–26.

Paul Janssen and Cyriel A. M. Van der Eycken, "The Chemical Anatomy of Potent Morphine-Like Analgesics," in *Drugs Affecting the Central Nervous System*, vol. 2, edited by Alfred Burger (London: Edward Arnold, 1968), 25–60.

Gary Henderson's article "Designer Drugs: Past History and Future Prospects" (*Journal of Forensic Sciences* 33 [1988]: 569–75) was essential. So, too, was an autobiographical monograph that Professor Henderson provided to me, "Fentanyl and Me."

Information for the story on the fentanyl laboratory in Toluca, Mexico, run by Ricardo Valdez-Torres in 2006 came primarily from Ryan Rapaszky and Eduardo Chavez, and from Dr. Bertha Madras at Harvard University.

The Zhengs' alleged drug-trafficking organization is described in a US Department of Justice press release at https://home.treasury.gov/news/press -releases/sm1063, and in a US Department of Justice diagram at https://home .treasury.gov/system/files/126/zheng_kpa_07172020.pdf. The federal indictment against the Zhengs can be found online at https://www.justice.gov/opa /press-release/file/1089101/download.

The effects of fentanyl on Mexican opium poppy farmers are detailed in Romain Le Cour Grandmaison, Nathaniel Morris, and Benjamin T. Smith, "No More Opium for the Masses," Noria Research, February 10, 2019.

METHAMPHETAMINE

Sam Dillon's "Mexican Drug Dealer Pushes Speed, Helping Set Off an Epidemic in U.S." (*New York Times*, December 27, 1995) gave information on Jesus Amezcua, as did Frank Owen, *No Speed Limit: The Highs and Lows of Meth* (New York: St. Martin's Press, 2007). Norman Ohler's *Blitzed: Drugs in the Third Reich* (New York: Mariner, 2018) tells the story of the Japanese invention of ephedrine-based methamphetamine and its use in Japan and Nazi Germany.

The many ways to synthesize P2P (phenyl-2-propanone) are catalogued at https://erowid.org/archive/rhodium/chemistry/phenylacetone.html. Uncle Fester, *Secrets of Methamphetamine Manufacture* (Port Townsend, WA: Loompanics Unlimited, 2002).

Virtually all of the information in the chapters on Clarksburg, West Virginia, came from interviews with people in town, identified in the chapters, over several visits. However, Ken Fones-Wolf's *Glass Towns: Industry, Labor and Political Economy in Appalachia, 1890–1930s* (Urbana: University of Illinois, 2007) was helpful in providing the history of the glass industry. So, too, was "Walls Become Windows" in *The Americans* by Daniel Boorstin (New York: Random House, 1973).

A NOTE ON THE AUTHOR

Sam Quinones is a journalist, storyteller, former *Los Angeles Times* reporter, and author of three acclaimed books of narrative nonfiction, including *New York Times* bestseller and National Book Critics Circle Award winner *Dreamland: The True Tale of America's Opiate Epidemic.* "The most original writer on Mexico and the border" (*San Francisco Chronicle*), he lives with his family in Southern California.

A NOTE ON THE TYPE

Janson is the name given to a set of old-style serif typefaces cut by Hungarian punchcutter Miklós Kis in the Netherlands in 1685. This crisp, upright, and compact face represented the height of the Dutch Baroque typographic style and was incorrectly attributed to the Leipzig-based printer Anton Janson until the 1950s. The revival printed in this book was designed for hot metal casting by Hermann Zapf for Monotype in 1954 and digitized for Linotype under the supervision of Adrian Frutiger in 1985.